INTRODUCTORY Readings In CANADIAN GOVERNMENT & POLITICS

ROBERT M. KRAUSE

R.H. WAGENBERG

University of Windsor

Copp Clark Pitman Ltd.
A Longman Company
Toronto

ISBN 0–7730–5130–9

Executive Editor: Brian Henderson
Editor: Brenda Clews
Index: Susan Quirk
Cover and Interior Design: Steve MacEachern
Typesetting: ECW Type & Art
Printing and Binding: Webcom Ltd.

Canadian Cataloguing in Publication Data

Main entry under title:
    Introductory readings in Canadian government and politics

Includes bibliographic references and index.
ISBN 0-7730-5130-9

1. Canada – Politics and government. I. Krause, Robert M.
II. Wagenberg, R.H., 1939-

JL65 1991.I68 1991 320.971 C90-095569-4

73884

Copp Clark Pitman
2775 Matheson Blvd. East
Mississauga, Ontario
L4W 4P7

Associated Companies:
    Longman Group Ltd., London
    Longman Inc., New York
    Longman Cheshire Pty., Melbourne
    Longman Paul Pty., Auckland

Printed and bound in Canada

1 2 3 4 5   5130-9   95 94 93 92 91

OTABIND

Publisher's Note
Otabind (Ota-bind). This book has been bound using the patented Otabind process. You can open this book at any page, gently run your finger down the spine, and the pages will lie flat.

Bound to stay open

| PREFACE |

The gathering of these introductory essays on Canadian government and politics was occasioned by our feeling that we didn't have just the right book of readings for our first year courses in Canadian government. Several of the existing readers appeared not to be written for introductory students but rather were aimed at more advanced students. Additionally, the writing style found in many of the essays was designed more for an audience of professional academics than for students. Also, essays tended to vacillate between two extremes: either too historical, descriptive, factual or too theoretical. Finally the choice of topics covered in some of the readers was debatable to say the least.

  To alleviate these perceived shortcomings in the field our reader was designed, at the outset, explicitly for first year students of political science. Second, it was to be composed of original essays written in clear precise prose suitable for its intended audience. Further, to more adequately supplement and complement basic introductory textbooks the selection of essay topics chosen for inclusion in the reader were those which are most frequently covered in first year Canadian government and politics textbooks. Authors, however, were instructed not to merely duplicate or repackage material found in those texts, but rather to design their essay around questions which would stimulate thought, interest, and discussion from student readers. Lastly, essays were commissioned in areas of Canadian government that often times were either excluded

iii

from introductory texts or were topics which often received only passing attention (Municipal Government, Foreign Policy, Administration of Justice).

We have been fortunate in being able to interest several of our colleagues at the University of Windsor as well as contributors from many universities across Canada. In doing so we hope to be giving readers a good cross-section of scholarship and opinion on Canadian politics and government. No particular approach to the discipline is represented by the essays. The authors have been encouraged to introduce their subjects to the student in a context they think appropriate to provide basic background information and to stimulate thought. Each author was also asked to provide a short annotated bibliography for their chapter which students could utilize to probe further the topic under discussion in their chapter.

The order in which the essays appear is meant to approximate as much as possible the way in which topics are introduced in introductory courses. Of course, since there is no rigid uniformity in the teaching of those courses or the texts which are used in them students may not necessarily be asked to read these essays from one to nineteen in order. That should not be any problem since each of the contributions stands on its own.

Our thanks in preparing this book go first, of course, to our co-essayists. They were remarkably easy to work with and produced what we consider to be first rate work in a timely fashion. Brian Henderson of the Copp Clark team made the sometimes trying process of getting a book to its readers a surprisingly stress free enterprise. We would like to thank Stephen MacEachern for a fine design and Brenda Clews for her perceptive editing.

Lea Wilkinson and Barbara Faria of the Department of Political Science at the University of Windsor provided superb secretarial assistance in preparing our own essays. The staff of the Word Processing Centre at the University of Windsor under the supervision of Mrs. Lucia Brown made it possible for us to deliver our manuscript to the publisher on time, and in good shape. After all of this help any imperfections left in the presentation of these essays must be on our editorial heads, the merits, however, reside in the contributions of each of our essayists.

.

Robert Krause - R. H. Wagenberg
University of Windsor

iv

TABLE OF CONTENTS

DETAILED CONTENTS

ix

CHAPTER 3

ORGANIZED INTERESTS.. 248

CHAPTER 14

MASS MEDIA IN CANADIAN POLITICS: A SURVEY OF CONTEMPORARY ISSUES 268

CHAPTER 5

CANADIAN POLITICAL PARTIES......................... 288

CHAPTER 16

THE CANADIAN VOTER 303

CHAPTER 17

THE ADMINISTRATION OF JUSTICE.................. 322

ISSUES IN MUNICIPAL GOVERNMENT............ 347

CANADA AND THE WORLD................. 371

AUTHORS' AFFILIATIONS

Agar Adamson	Acadia University
Joan Price Boase	University of Windsor
Stephen Brooks	University of Windsor
Stan Drabek	University of Calgary
Joy Esberey	University of Toronto
Ian Greene	York University
T.A. Keenleyside	University of Windsor
Robert M. Krause	University of Windsor
Lawrence LeDuc	University of Toronto
Richard A. Loreto	Loreto Consulting Ltd.
Maureen Mancuso	University of Windsor
Mary Beth Montcalm	University of Manitoba
F. L. Morton	University of Calgary
Ralph Nelson	University of Windsor
Neil Nevitte	University of Calgary
Richard G. Price	University of Windsor
Grace Skogstad	University of Toronto
David E. Smith	University of Saskatchewan
Walter C. Soderlund	University of Windsor
R.H. Wagenberg	University of Windsor

| CHAPTER 1 |

THE DYNAMICS OF CANADIAN
POLITICAL CULTURE(S)

NEIL NEVITTE

Our goal in this chapter is to explore some of the central characteristics of the Canadian political culture. The discussion will consider four broad topics. In the first section we will outline what factors were critical in the making of Canadian political culture during the formation of the Canadian state. The next section will provide an overview of the major interpretations of why Canadian political culture turned out the way it did. In the third part we examine the dynamics of Canadian political culture and in the conclusion we will suggest what kinds of challenges will likely face Canadian political culture in the future. Before we turn to those specific tasks, however, we need to step back from the particulars of the Canadian experience and to set the stage by making some general observations about the nature of political culture itself.

The first point to note is that there is a vast literature dealing with the subject of political culture; definitions of the concept abound. Some scholars view political culture as "as system of beliefs about patterns of interaction and political institutions."[1] Others suggest that political culture includes "all politically relevant orientations of a cognitive, evaluative and expressive sort."[2] While yet others take political culture to include attitudes, beliefs and sentiments that give order and meaning to the political process and

| 1 |

provide the underlying assumptions and rules that govern behavior."[3] The sheer number of definitions, twenty five by one count, creates the impression that there is a great deal of confusion about what political culture means. But for the most part the differences between those definitions are a matter of emphasis and if we compared them all side by side we would find substantial agreement about the core meaning of the concept. In a nutshell, political culture refers to *how citizens are oriented towards their political community.*

Precisely because political culture is such a broad-gauged concept, formal definitions of political culture, typically, are fairly abstract. But we can get a more concrete sense of the central ideas at stake by considering what kinds of questions students of political culture usually explore. For the purposes of convenience we can list those questions under four broad headings:

ATTITUDES TOWARDS POLITICAL SYMBOLS AND INSTITUTIONS

How strongly do citizens feel about such political symbols such as the flag and the national anthem? Do citizens believe their government institutions — parliament, the courts, the bureaucracy — are effective? Can government, the Prime Minister, elected and appointed officials, be trusted to do the right thing? What kinds of duties and obligations are implied by the idea "citizenship"? Is the constitution fair?

ATTITUDES TOWARDS OTHERS IN THE POLITICAL SYSTEM

Do citizens have strong loyalties to particular groups or regions? With what and with whom do citizens identify? How tolerant should majorities be of minority groups? Should citizens be tolerant of those who are critical of the political status quo? What types of protest behaviour are appropriate? How important is freedom of speech?

POLITICAL KNOWLEDGE, VALUES AND EVALUATIONS

How much do citizens know about politics, about the workings of institutions, policy-making and political leaders? What kinds of beliefs, values and sentiments do citizens have? How widely are they shared? What is the proper role of government in society and the economy? How should resources be distributed? How much support should be given to such disadvantaged groups as the old, the poor, the handicapped and minorities?

Where do beliefs and expectations about political life come from? How are they learned? How effectively are they transmitted from one generation to the next? Are citizens' beliefs becoming more coherent, more ideological? Or, are citizens becoming more "issue driven"?

Clearly, this list illustrates that an enormously broad range of topics fall under the general umbrella of political culture. Before we turn to consider the specifics of the Canadian setting two other general observations are worth noting. First, political cultures are dynamic; they are not set down once and for all, they are subject to change. The broad configurations of the Canadian political culture may well have been set in motion in the distant past. But then conditions change, populations are replaced and the remote historical episodes can easily fade from collective memory. The second point is that although political culture places emphasis on the subjective aspects of political life, it is nonetheless relevant to political behaviour. Thus political culture plays an important role in our understanding of how citizens vote, the ways political parties work, the effectiveness of political institutions, the formation of foreign and domestic policies, interest group behaviour and the workings of the constitution. Many of these topics are considered in detail in other parts of this book and a reading of those chapters will provide a much fuller appreciation of the concrete ways in which Canadian political culture is played out. In this chapter we shall paint in very broad strokes to highlight general themes.

I The Making of Canadian Political I Culture: An Overview

Some distinctive aspects of Canadian political culture are very easy to recognize. The Canadian flag and the national anthem, for example, provide Canadians with unique political symbols which function as common points of reference, foci for communal loyalties. As such, they evoke a variety of feelings. For some, they signify pride in the past; they symbolize a history of collective achievements. For others they represent a set of common aspirations for the future. The mix of feelings may well differ but, as symbols, they are nonetheless unique and unambiguous.

I 3 I

Isolating the precise ways in which Canadian *orientations* towards collective political life are unique is a much more difficult task. Clearly, as Van Loon and Whittington suggest, Canada stands as one of the world's oldest continuing democracies and the essential components of Canadian political culture are much the same as those of other longstanding democracies. Canadian political values are rooted in the Western tradition and like other states the essential liberal elements within that tradition have been similarly modified by democratic practices that have evolved since the eighteenth century.[4] Consequently, Canadian political culture embraces such values as equality before the law, the right to hold private property, the right of free speech and assembly, the right to vote and to run for office. Unquestionably, these values are widely shared and occupy a central place in Canadian orientations towards collective political life. But they do not set Canadian political culture apart from the political cultures of many other advanced industrial liberal democratic states. In other words, it is useful to recognize that Canadian political culture can be placed within the broader framework of other advanced industrial states. By the same token, to see what makes Canadian political culture distinctive we must make finer distinctions.

To come to grips with the unique elements of Canadian political culture we have to consider how geographic, economic, cultural and political factors historically combined to shape the formative experiences of the country. First, the sheer geographic size of Canada has had an enormous impact on the structure of political life. After the Soviet Union, Canada ranks as the second largest country in the world: it occupies some 9.2 million square kilometres; it spans six time zones; it sprawls across an entire continent.

Second, relative to land size, the Canadian population is small. Furthermore, that population is unevenly distributed. About 80% of all Canadians live within about 320 kilometres of the American border; 60% reside in Ontario and Quebec. The cultural distribution of the population is also uneven. Eighty percent of all francophones live in Quebec and Canada's Native peoples form majorities in the largely uninhabited Yukon and Northwest Territories.[5]

The physical expanse of the country, the harsh climate, the size, make-up and distribution of the population, posed unique problems of communication and governance particularly during Canada's early years. The decision to adopt a federal political framework, which is a division of powers among regional and central governments, can be seen as an institutional response to those problems; federalism aimed to make government less remote to a far flung and diverse population.

Third, the presence of a substantial linguistic minority, francophones,

|4|

concentrated in one part of the country also set the Canadian political culture apart from that of other Anglo-American democracies with which it is most frequently compared. The rifts between anglophones and francophones had a profound impact upon Canadian political life from the start and it continues to influence Canadian culture, politics and economics in fundamental ways. The origins of contemporary conflicts can be traced to the British conquest of Quebec in 1759. Early attempts on the part of the British to assimilate the vanquished francophone Catholics failed although the memory of those efforts lives on. *The Quebec Act* of 1774 reflected a shift in policy, a shift inspired partly by American attempts to recruit Quebec's population in a joint effort to rid North America of the British. The British colonial authorities gave the francophones of New France guaranteed rights to language and religion in exchange for their loyalty to the British Crown. Those rights have remained intact; they lie at the root of Canada's linguistic duality and they have also worked as the chief instruments of the survival of Canada's francophone community. It might also be argued that those rights, in conjunction with the expanding shield of provincial government, have formed the historical basis of Quebec's political self-definition as a "nation" and, by extension, the moral claim to national self-determination.[6]

A fourth factor that has significantly influenced the evolution of Canadian political culture is proximity to the United States. Indeed, it would be more remarkable if Canada had not been affected by sharing its borders with one of the world's great powers. In some senses, the relationship between Canada and the United States is a curious one. As Lipset observes, "these two peoples probably resemble each other more than any other two nations on earth."[7] That fact, coupled with geographic proximity, has consistently represented a challenge to Canadian national identity. The United States simultaneously represents both a benchmark *and* a lightning rod for Canadian political culture. As Malcolm notes, "Canadians agree on very few things but they can agree on what they are not—Americans."[8]

To understand the reasons why the United States has preoccupied Canadians concerned about national identity, and the ability of the culture to develop and maintain a distinct political culture, requires some historical background. The American revolution was a decisive political event in the early formation of both countries; it launched both countries into very different political trajectories. Along with the rejection of British colonial rule, the American revolutionaries also rejected a taste for strong central government; they embraced individualism and republicanism. Many of those on the losing side in the revolution, the United Empire Loyalists, left the United States and resettled in Canada. In effect, they were political refugees

| 5 |

CANADIAN GOVERNMENT AND POLITICS

who were by-products of the revolution, but they became influential shapers of Canada's early political culture. The Loyalists brought to Canada "counter-revolutionary values" which by most accounts included a concern for maintaining ties with Britain, a willingness to accept bureaucratic and political leadership, a distaste for disorder, and a preference for a collectivist style of conservatism.

Sustained hostility between Britain and the United States in North America and the ideological differences between the revolutionaries in the United States and the counter-revolutionaries go some distance towards explaining why the two countries adopted different political institutions. Canadians grafted the logic of British parliamentary practice — responsible cabinet government and the fusion of legislative (i.e. law ratifying) and executive (i.e. law formulating) powers — onto a federal framework while keeping a constitutional monarch. In other words, early Canadians' political instincts directed them to employ tradition and convention as a guide. Americans did not; they learned different lessons from British colonial experience. It has also been suggested that the ideological differences between the revolutionaries and counter-revolutionaries continue to influence the political belief systems, and values of the two societies.

I Interpretations of Canadian I Political Culture

There is widespread agreement that geographic size, population distribution, the presence of two founding cultures — English and French, and proximity to the United Sates, all contributed to the early formation of the Canadian polity. But how? It is easy to see that when all of these factors are considered together, they must have presented significant obstacles to the development of a single, clearly focused political culture. Nonetheless, several different interpretations have been offered to explain how these factors combined to give Canadian political culture its unique hue.

One interpretation outlined by the American historian Louis Hartz, in *The Founding of New Societies*,[9] has been particularly influential. Hartz argues that "new societies," such as Canada, Australia and the United States, are profoundly shaped by the values carried to those societies by early settlers and immigrants. The explanations for variations in the prevailing ideologies of new societies, according to Hartz, depends upon what kinds of answers history gives to three questions: First, what was the nature of the "founding fragment?" Or more specifically, from what specific segment of the origi-

I 6 I

nating cultures did the founding fragments come? Second, what was the point of departure? Or, at what moment in the ideological evolution of the originating culture did the founding fragment leave? And third, what was the point of congealment? When did the values of the new society take on a distinctive and self-sustaining character?

From the Hartzian perspective, the prevailing radical working class ideology of Australians is explained, for example, by the fact that Australia was peopled predominantly by segments of the English working class who left Britain relatively late — after the industrial revolution had taken hold and after they had been exposed to English-style Fabian socialism. By contrast, Canada and the United States were settled earlier and by English middle classes; both countries therefore took on values reflecting the middle class values of liberalism and conservatism. Similarly, settlers to New France were pre–French Revolution rural Catholics and the prevailing values of New France reflected collectivist and anti-materialist beliefs.

The fine points of the Hartzian hypothesis have been vigorously debated and they have been extended in a variety of intriguing directions. Gad Horowitz, for example, argues that in its original application, the Hartzian approach tended to understate the differences between Canadian and American political cultures.[10] Unlike the United States, Horowitz contends, Canada developed a significant British and non-Marxist strand of socialism because of early British working class immigration and because of the collectivist nature of its conservatism. It is these elements which help to explain not only an historic attachment to the British crown and a deference to elites but also Canada's greater acceptance of a larger role for government in society and the economy.

A second and complementary interpretation of Canadian political culture has been advanced by Seymour Martin Lipset.[11] Lipset emphasizes the importance of formative events by drawing attention not only to the British conquest of Quebec, the American Revolution and the role of the Loyalists, but also to the impact of the Rebellions of 1837, 1838 and the Riel Uprisings of 1870 and 1885. Canadians, Lipset argues, are more accepting of authority than Americans, because of these formative events. They are more likely to give governments a larger role in society and the economy and they are more risk averse than their American counterparts. After sifting through a great deal of comparative evidence, Lipset concludes that Canadian society is less open, there are fewer opportunities for upward social mobility. At the same time, the Canadian version of the welfare state is more fully developed; there is universal access to health care and a variety of social supports that are considerably more expansive.

| 7 |

CANADIAN GOVERNMENT AND POLITICS

A third line of interpretation focuses upon the central role that elites play in Canadian society. John Porter's path-breaking book, *The Vertical Mosaic*[12] is a study of how power is organized and exercised in Canadian society; it provides a provocative analysis of the ways in which Canadian elites, both anglophone and francophone, exercise far more influence over Canadian society than is typical of elites in other similar advanced industrial states. These elites, he contends, are crucial gatekeepers who exercise control over the economy, the bureaucracy, elected officials, the media and intellectual and religious life. All societies have elites but Porter argues that Canadian elites are particularly powerful because they are small, closed groups and their influence is overlapping. Moreover, because such small groups exercise influence over all of these domains, they have been able to deflect attention away from class divisions in Canadian society and attention is drawn instead to ethnic, religious and regional divisions.

Porter's analysis inspired a spate of other studies which essentially extended and elaborated his central findings in greater detail. Some focused on corporate elites, others on political and bureaucratic elite. But most concluded, along with Porter, that the ability of these elites to act as power brokers relatively freely has been greatly facilitated by the widely held political cultural values that have already been described — the preparedness of Canadian public to defer to figures of authority.

No review of interpretations of Canadian political culture can fail to consider the perspective provided by the influential political economist Harold Innis.[13] Innis explains that a full appreciation of the forces that shaped Canadian political culture requires an understanding of the broad importance of economic factors, particularly the historic significance of such primary resources as fish, fur, minerals and wheat. These primary resources formed the very core of the Canadian export economy from the outset and that economy, historically, has been directed towards the markets of other advanced industrial states.

To a substantial degree, one's self-understanding, one's place in society, is determined by the workplace and the kinds of rewards that the workplace brings. Consequently, Innis suggests, Canada's collective psyche, its culture, can be understood as having been conditioned by a preoccupation with the export of staples into world markets. The significant point is that Canada does not and cannot control the global economic factors that create the demand for Canadian staples; the markets are subject to large fluctuations in demand and supply. As a result, the economic benefits of exporting staples have frequently been only marginal. Thus Canadians, Innis contends, have developed conservative, cautious and even pessimistic or fatalistic attitudes

| 8 |

largely because they are not able to control their own economic destiny. This cautiousness though, is not just limited to economic matters, it also filters through to the way Canadians think about their society and about political life and from Innis' point of view, it helps to explain why Canadians hold cautious views about social and political change.

A careful consideration of these four broad interpretations of Canadian political culture suggests that they do not reach fundamentally different conclusions about Canadian political culture. In fact, the conclusions complement each other. The difference between the interpretations, is a matter of emphasis: where Hartz emphasizes founding peoples, Lipset's focuses on founding events. Porter's analysis of elites is narrower in scope and his findings might well be interpreted as a result of cultural, social and economic forces that Hartz, Lipset and Innis place in a more sweeping historical context.

I The Dynamics of Canadian I Political Culture

In exploring the making of Canadian political culture we have stressed how a variety of background factors worked to influence the early development of the Canadian polity. When we turn our attention to more recent developments, however, it would appear that the task of forging a single harmonious national culture is far from complete. Divisive contemporary debates about constitutional change, senate reform, Native rights, language rights and multiculturalism point to deep fractures within Canada. In fact, these divisions might well be interpreted in terms of conflicts between different political cultures and from that standpoint it might be argued that cultural differences in Canada are getting stronger, not weaker.

Why has Canadian political culture become so fragmented? To provide a complete answer to that provocative question would require a separate study but we can briefly point to three dynamics that appear to be crucial to these developments — transformations within Quebec, the new vitality of regionalism, and the pull of continentalism.

THE QUEBEC DYNAMIC

The fundamental question facing New France after British conquest was: How to sustain a viable francophone culture under British rule? As we have already indicated, the early solution to that problem emerged from a deal

I 9 I

struck between the political elites of New France and the British Colonial administration; francophones exchanged loyalty to the British administration in return for guaranteed language and religious rights. Francophone concerns for "nationhood" clearly have very deep historical roots; they have been an enduring feature of Quebec's political landscape. But the ways in which those concerns have been expressed have changed in quite dramatic ways and those changes, in turn, can be traced to profound social transformations within Quebec itself.

Prior to the 1960's, Quebec's traditional form of nationalism revolved around the idea of *survivance*. *Survivance* was an anti-liberal ideology; it idealized an organic, rural and largely anti-materialist set of values, values which were organizationally reinforced by three institutions — the parish, the school and the family. The fact that these traditional values and institutions held sway well into the middle of the twentieth century is remarkable given the vitality and individualism of the North American continent. It might be partly explained by the barrier of language, the enormous power of the Roman Catholic Church in Quebec and, perhaps, by anglophone and francophone elite preoccupations with the importance of stability. But the long run consequence of *survivance* resulted in the progressive cultural isolation of Quebec. Concerns about the Quebec nation were inward looking and consequently traditional forms of Quebec nationalism took on a "culture under siege" quality. French-Canadians were under-represented in Canada's powerful federal institutions; the Quebec economy became increasingly dominated by anglophone interests; and demographic trends, by the 1950's were pointing to the eventual disappearance of a francophone society. The future looked bleak.

By the 1960's the tide turned. The death of Maurice Duplessis in 1959 and the electoral defeat of Quebec's last traditional nationalist party, the Union Nationale, marked the political turning point. The social turning point was captured by the phrase "the Quiet Revolution." The Quiet Revolution symbolized a reorientation of Quebec society in two related respects: first, it represented a willingness of Québecois to participate more fully in a modern industrial society; and secondly, it entailed a new confidence in the vitality of Quebec's francophone culture and a search for new strategies to promote that culture. In short, the Quiet Revolution signified a transition from an old Quebec to a new Quebec and that transition was accompanied by the development of new political strategies aimed at maintaining and advancing the Quebec nation.

The 1960's was a period of considerable political turmoil. New nationalist parties emerged, parties of both the left (i.e. advocating social change) and

| 10 |

the right (i.e. advocating the status quo). These parties held in common the view that the Canadian system of federalism was an obstacle to the flowering of Quebec's aspirations. They also believed that political independence from Canada was Quebec's best solution to the problem. But their views of Quebec's future were quite different in other respects. The Alliance Laurentienne, for example, wanted a new state that would promote such values as French humanism and Catholic fundamentalism. By contrast, the parties of the left saw economics at the root of Quebec's problems. They denounced anglophone Canadians as "colonialist ogres" and called for the "proletarian national liberation of French Canadians" to end "the exploitation of Quebec."[14] The political origins of modern Quebec nationalism can be traced to the policies of the Rassemblement pour l'indépendence nationale (R.I.N.). The R.I.N. foundered on the rocks of internal party disputes and the Parti Québecois (P.Q.), led by René Lévesque, inherited the modern mantle of Quebec nationalism, a nationalism that has changed the course of both Quebec and Canadian politics since the 1970's.

The dramatic victory of the P.Q. in the provincial election of November 1976 marked a critical turning point in the political dynamics of Quebec. In what ways? First, the victory indicated that a fundamental political realignment had taken place. Like many other parties which had emerged in the 1960's, the P.Q. started life by attracting a hodgepodge of supporters — young Québecois, intellectuals, artists, and those of the disaffected left. Unlike the other parties, the P.Q.'s bases of political support broadened and deepened. It attracted the new middle classes, respectable professionals, francophone business interests and organized labour. In many ways, the victory of the P.Q. was the culmination of the social forces unleashed during the Quiet Revolution.

Secondly, the P.Q. came to power with a mandate to accomplish social change. At the heart of that program for social change was the idea of economic reorganization. It was argued by the P.Q. that through new political leadership, Quebec's economic dependence could be reduced through a greater participation by francophones in the direction and management of the economy. The P.Q. saw the Quebec government as the political instrument for advancing the economic and social interest of Québecois: they saw the Quebec government as a "state in waiting."

Thirdly, the P.Q. carried a platform for "independence" and it developed blueprints for a social democratic "progressive" state. The strategy for independence was a gradual one; the P.Q. believed that "independence" could be achieved in gradual stages — *étapisme*. The viability of a politically independent Quebec and the precise forms that it might take were and are

| 11 |

hotly debated. The significant point is that the P.Q., between 1976 and 1985, established itself as a credible political party which could effectively govern by harnessing the substantial nationalist aspirations of broad segments of Quebec society.

In retrospect, it might be argued that Lévesque's P.Q. ultimately failed. They were defeated in the 1980 referendum, a referendum which would have given Lévesque the opportunity to seek sovereignty-association, and they were defeated by Robert Bourassa's Liberals in 1985. That view, however, is a short sighted one and it fails to take into account the very significant role that the P.Q. played in transforming Quebec politics in the last two decades. The P.Q. was the vehicle for the political modernization of Quebec nationalism. State intervention was the instrument of that transformation and through the efforts of a P.Q. government francophones moved decisively to recuperate their position in Quebec society and the economy. Furthermore, the credibility of the P.Q. as a political alternative to the Liberals is well-entrenched and the consistently strong level of support for the P.Q. has had a significant impact upon constitutional discussions aimed at reshaping Canadian federalism even when the P.Q. has not held office.[15]

THE REGIONAL DYNAMIC

Describing Canada as two nations within a single state focuses attention upon the historic role that anglophone–francophone conflicts have played in the evolution of the Canadian polity. Quebec, of course, counts as a region precisely because 80% of Canada's francophones live in the province. Language, however, is only one aspect of political culture and in the past twenty years or so it has become increasingly clear that other relevant regional divisions also shape the collective lives of Canadians in very significant ways. Indeed some observers have gone so far as to suggest that Canadian politics *is* the politics of regions.[16]

Evidence of the political importance of regions takes many forms. There is a longstanding tradition of taking into account regional considerations in the recruitment of ministers to the federal cabinet. The conflicts between regional and national interest are routinely displayed at federal-provincial conferences. Debates about the distribution of economic resources and social services typically take on a regional hue and regional considerations shape the ways in which political parties are organized. In one sense, those regional differences are hardly surprising. After all, Canada is a federal state and federalism, as a principle, acknowledges that there are differences

| 12 |

between parts of a country; it aims to accommodate those differences. Two background factors contribute to Canadian regionalism — population and economics. Canada, more than most countries in the world, has relied upon immigration as a population source and the patterns of immigrant settlement, historically, have resulted in an uneven cultural distribution of the population. The Atlantic provinces, Quebec and Ontario, were settled early and they were peopled, mostly, by immigrants from Britain and France. The Prairie provinces were settled much later and they were peopled disproportionately by German, Dutch, Scandinavian, Polish, Ukrainian and American settlers. In 1931 roughly half of the prairie populations were of British or French origin compared to an average of more than 80% for Canada as a whole. That ethnic, linguistic and religious diversity gives the Prairies a distinctly multicultural quality which, in turn, helps to explain, according to one observer, why western Canadians tend to view French Canadians as simply another minority.[17]

Economic historians, following Harold Innis, have argued that regional differences in economic development and in the modes of economic production contributed to the development of regional political cultures.[18] In the industrialized regions of Ontario and Quebec, the occupational mix of working populations is quite different from that of populations in the Atlantic provinces, the Prairie provinces or British Columbia, regions which rely heavily on extractive and resource-based enterprises. Increasingly, all economies are exposed to the rigors of world markets. But the economic fortunes of regional economies fluctuate more or less and they do so at different rates and times depending upon the particular economic base of the region. Thus while some regions enjoy prosperity, others falter and the uneven performance of different segments of the Canadian economy aggravates regional political differences.

The cultural and economic features of different parts of the country certainly make Canada's five regions look very different. But are these *regional political cultures?* Or, to put the matter more precisely, do regional populations have different basic orientations towards political life *after* these other differences have been taken into account? There is a substantial body of evidence which suggest that they do. Simeon and Elkins,[19] in a now classic study, demonstrate significant differences across the provinces with respect to two sets of orientations that are central to political culture — in *political trust,* that is, the extent to which individuals feel they can trust governments, and in *political efficacy,* that is, in the extent to which individuals feel that they count politically. Analyzing data from the 1965 and 1968 national election studies, Simeon and Elkins show that British Columbians, Mani-

CANADIAN GOVERNMENT AND POLITICS

tobans, Ontarians and English Quebeckers tend to have high levels of political trust and efficacy. By contrast, Newfoundlanders, New Brunswickers and Nova Scotians tend to have much lower levels of trust and efficacy.

Scholars have demonstrated regional differences in other aspects of political culture as well. Roger Gibbins, for example, demonstrated significant provincial differences in the communal identifications of Canadians. In 1983, he asked a national sample of Canadians whether they identified first with their country or with their province. These data show, not surprisingly, that most respondents (73%) thought of themselves as Canadians. But the evidence also points to remarkable regional variations in provincial identifications. The proportion of respondents identifying with their province first was high in Newfoundland (47%), Prince Edward Island (38%), Quebec (34%) and Nova Scotia (30%).[20] By contrast only 5% of Ontarians identified with their province first, a finding that supports the contention that Ontarians tend to equate the interest of their province with the interests of the country.[21]

If, as we have indicated, there are strong regional differences in economic interest and political cultures, how does the "regional dynamic" play in contemporary Canadian political culture? A strong case can be make to suggest that the regional dynamic frustrates the development of a national political community in a variety of ways. First, there is the rugged political arithmetic of the electoral system. The simple fact that about 60% of Canada's population resides in two provinces, Ontario and Quebec, means that votes in these two provinces carry enormous electoral weight; they can make or break nationally elected governments. Voters in regions outside of Ontario and Quebec, and who have economic interests that are different from those of the industrial heartland, have fewer reasons to be confident that their concerns will occupy a central place in the national agenda. If the simple homily "he who pays the piper calls the tune" has any political application, then the incentives of national governments to listen to the concerns of Ontario and Quebec are strong.

Secondly, it has been argued that Canada's particular style of federal parliamentary institutions tends to aggravate rather than moderate regional divisions. All federal political systems have upper and lower houses; and, typically, lower houses are based on representation by population while upper houses represent regional concerns. But does the Canadian Senate do a good job of representing regional concerns? Probably not. If population size is the benchmark, it is clear that some provinces, most of the small ones, are indeed overrepresented in the Senate. But then others, such as Alberta

‖ 14 ‖

and British Columbia are underrepresented. But the more significant point stems from the fact that the Senate is an appointed, not an elected, body. The appointment process is often highly politicized as when Mulroney appointed senators to break the G.S.T. blockade; some appointees are placed in the Senate as a reward for service to the party. The perception is that the Senate lacks broad legitimacy and the reality is that it has little power to challenge the House of Commons, although it has begun to do so, first over the Free Trade deal and then over the Goods and Services Tax (G.S.T.). Compared to Upper Chambers in other federal states, however, the Canadian Senate appears to be much weaker. Those promoting stronger regional representation argue that the Senate must be reformed, but then political power is a zero sum game where, in order for someone to win, someone else must lose, and persuading others to give up powers is a difficult business.

Party discipline is a third institutional practice that frustrates balanced regional representation and hence the development of a national political community. In the parliamentary tradition, party discipline is central to the workings of responsible government. MP's may lobby for regional concerns in caucus, they may press regional issues in private, but MP's have few opportunities to place the interest of their region over those of the party. The same applies to cabinet ministers. Despite the fact that there is a long-standing tradition of regional representation within federal cabinets, cabinet conventions of secrecy and collective responsibility tend to obscure evidence of regional representation from public view.

The majoritarianism in the electoral system, the weakness of Senate and workings of party discipline might be argued, all combine to frustrate a national representation of regional concerns. But, the other side of the regional dynamic has been the emergence of provincial premiers as the front line champions of regional interests in national political life.

THE CONTINENTAL DYNAMIC

Linguistic duality and regionalism are both dynamics that appear to undermine the development of a clear, single political culture. These domestic sources of fragmentation, however, combine with a contextual dynamic, Canada's continental location, to further obscure the evolution of a powerful and easily identifiable political culture. John Redekop assesses the impact of Canada's continental position. "The overall American impact on Canada," he says, "is the most important single fact for Canada and the main key to understanding Canada's emergence, development and current situation."[22] Redekop is referring, of course, to the multiplicity of ways in which the

| 15 |

United States dominates the North American continent — by its sheer population size, the power of its economy, and the vitality of its cultural institutions.

The extent to which Canada's economic fortunes are tied to those of the United States are well documented elsewhere[23] and they require no detailed elaboration here. Canada and the United States have the largest single trading relationship in the entire world. Since the Second World War, American direct and indirect investment in Canada has grown to account for more than 75% of all foreign investment in the country. Furthermore, American control of a variety of key industrial sectors — fossil fuels, chemicals, rubber, transportation — to name but a few, are remarkably high. According to one estimate, American enterprises account for about 60% of Canada's manufacturing sector.[24]

The American penetration of the Canadian economy is a mixed blessing. There is little doubt that Canadians enjoy a high standard of living in large part because of high levels of U.S. investment. By the same token, the level and type of U.S. interest in Canada has limited the abilities of Canadian government to exercise complete control over domestic economic policy-making. It has been argued that with the progressive integration of Canada into the continental economy, Canada has become little more than a branch plant of the United States. Left to the mercy of an "open" marketplace dominated by U.S. policy, the Canadian economy will remain "in service" to its American parent. The recently signed Canada-U.S. Free Trade Agreement provides according to this view an institutional framework which authorizes the continuation of that process. Furthermore, the continentalization of the economy both undermines Canadian political sovereignty and erodes the distinctiveness of Canada's social and cultural fabric.

Economics, undoubtedly does have important political, social and cultural consequences although the extent to which it does so is not very well understood. Nor is it possible to precisely measure the extent to which Canadians have absorbed American values. But certainly, proximity, population distribution and the fact that a large majority of Canadians and Americans speak the same language means that American cultural industries have easy access to Canadian households through the print and electronic media. Again, data[25] show that the Canadian consumption of American T.V., film and printed media is very high indeed. From time to time Canadian governments have attempted to stem that flow and to encourage domestic Canadian cultural industries as a way of protecting Canadians from Americanization and as a way of fostering a distinct Canadian identity.

In some respects, the record of government involvement in domestic

| 16 |

cultural industries is a rather remarkable one. Clearly, the *opportunities* available to the American cultural industries for penetrating Canada are unique. The *motive* is also clear — Canada provides those industries with an additional marketplace. But if a crime has been committed — the Americanization of Canada's culture — then Canadians must be counted as accomplices. Available evidence consistently shows that anglophone Canadians consistently prefer American to Canadian T.V. programming. In 1976, the Canadian Radio-Televison and Telecommunications Commission (CRTC) ordered Canadian FM cable stations to drop American stations in favour of Canadian ones. The angry public response forced the CRTC to cancel its Canadianization policy barely three months later.[26] The economic reality is that Canada is a small market and that reality presents serious obstacles to the development of strong domestic publishing industries and such electronic cultural industries as radio, television and film. For these reasons cultural nationalists remain alarmed at the long run implications of sustained exposure to American cultural media and the values these media impart.

Remarkably, little systematic research has been undertaken to explore the impact of American values upon the patterns of political socialization in Canada. And the sketchy evidence that does exist indicates rather mixed results. One study, which examined the impact of exposure to American television on Canadian children's recognition of American and Canadian authority roles, found that Canadian children could correctly identify the American flag more often than they could correctly identify the Canadian flag. Furthermore, many children confused authority roles, a significant proportion of younger children identified the American president as the Prime Minister of Canada.[27] These data, while intriguing, do not provide us with sufficient grounds for drawing firm and focused conclusions about the long run impact of American values on Canadian political culture. Regardless of the quality of systematic evidence, however, observers of Canadian–United States relations are united on one point: the impact of the United States upon Canadian political cultural life has been enormous.

I The Challenges Facing Canadian I Political Culture

The major themes that we have addressed in this chapter all broadly point to the conclusion that Canadian nation builders, from the very outset, confronted significant obstacles in pursuing the task of developing a single coherent political culture. The challenges are still formidable for it would

I 17 I

seem that, unlike the United States, Canadian political culture does not project a single powerful image. Canada has no equivalent to "the American way." Instead the prevailing image of Canada is one of a "community of communities." Diversity has produced diversity and Canadian political institutions and leaders expend a great deal of energy simply managing that diversity. In that sense, it appears to be more accurate to speak of Canada's political cultures.

But are there any particular characteristics which set Canadian political culture apart from those of other advanced industrial states? There are a combination of characteristics about which most analysts would agree. First, most social scientists have come to expect social class to play a significant role in shaping such political behaviours as voting.

A long-standing puzzle of Canadian politics has been the apparent absence of a strong or consistent relationship between class and vote. Pammett's exhaustive analysis of 1974-79 national election data found only 4% of the Canadians sampled thought of themselves in class terms—and most of those thought of themselves as middle class.[28] A second significant non-finding that sets Canadian political belief systems apart from others is the apparent weakness of left-right orientations within the population. John Meisel's analysis of 1965 and 1968 evidence indicates that Canadians saw almost no class or ideological differences between the two major political parties — the Progressive Conservatives and the Liberals. And the differences between those two parties and the New Democrats were very slight.[29] Moreover, unlike publics in other industrial states, a very high proportion of the Canadian public do not think of themselves or political parties in terms of "left" or "right." Other studies have also noted the comparative weakness of ideology in Canadian political life.[30]

To these findings we can add other evidence that is central to the analysis of political culture. Canadians exhibit levels of political trust that are similar to those found in the United States and Western European democracies. More than half of all Canadians believe that people can be trusted although the level of social trust among Quebec francophones is substantially lower. When it comes to political trust, Canadians have a high regard for those who govern, at least they did in 1979, 1983 and 1984. At the same time it has been observed that Canadians are more likely than Americans and publics in other industrial states to defer to the political authority of leaders. In fact, studies conducted in 1983 and 1984 indicated that the Canadian public is much more likely to comply with what government does or asks of them. This, however, may be rapidly changing. Further, it seems Canadians are more interested in politics than are people in Western Europe, and on this

DYNAMICS OF CANADIAN POLITICAL CULTURE(S)

score there is little difference between Canadians and Americans. Canadians, however, are quite different from Americans when it comes to preferences about the role of government in society and the economy. Canadians have a much more positive view of the state. Unlike Americans they want the state to "do more."[31]

What these findings collectively suggest is that, despite the difficulties of linguistic and regional differences, despite the substantial obstacles to the development of a potent and easily identifiable national political identity, and despite the powerful pull of continental forces, a distinctive *combination* of political values *are* discernible. Whether those values which make up Canadian political culture will remain distinctive depends, of course, on a variety of factors. Two are of particular note and both have very large implications for the future character of Canadian political identity — population replacement and value change.

At the outset and in various parts of this chapter, we have emphasized the point that political cultures are dynamic. Part of the dynamics relate to population replacement and the nature of political socialization. In the past twenty-five years, Canada has experienced two trends that indicate marked departures from the traditional patterns of population replacement. First, fertility levels have fallen to the point that the Canadian population cannot replace itself by natural population increase alone. The burden of population increase, in other words, has shifted almost entirely to immigration. Between 1956 and 1960 Canadian immigrants coming from traditional sources outnumbered those coming from non-traditional sources (non-European) by a ratio of 15:1. By 1980, that trend reversed; immigrants from non-traditional sources outnumbered those from tradition sources by a ratio of 2:1. The long run implications of that continued trend are enormous. Canada is far more culturally diverse than ever before; it is less "European." How will new immigrants be politically socialized to Canadian life? Will Canada's "founding experiences," largely European ones, be meaningful to them? Answering those questions will undoubtedly be a major challenge and how they are answered will have a substantial impact upon Canada's future political culture.

The second challenge has to do with the value changes that have swept across all advanced industrial states in the course of the past two decades. A substantial body of evidence indicates a new fluidity in the ideological environments of most advanced economies. Those changes include the rise of new movements concerned with such issues as environmental protection, the status of women, the treatment of minorities and the quality of life. The importance of class is declining and new belief systems are replacing old ones.

| 19 |

Some scholars have provided comprehensive accounts for why these shifts are taking place and some predict the emergence of an entirely different style of politics as publics become better educated and informed about politics. The prediction is that publics will become more outspoken, more likely to engage in direct political action rather than making their political demands through traditional political parties.[32] There is some evidence that this "new politics" is also under way in Canada.[33] One implication is that political cultures in all of the advanced industrial democracies are changing *in the same direction*. The implications for the future of Canadian politics are far-reaching for the thesis suggests that Canadian political culture is shaped not just by the proximity of the United States or the particular cluster of domestic forces, but by larger forces that are sweeping across the entire post-industrial world. How Canada answers that challenge will not likely have much to do with domestic policy making; it stems from exposure to global change.

NOTES

[1] Gabriel Almond and G. Bingham Powell, *Comparative Politics: A Developmental Approach* (Boston: Little, Brown, 1966) p. 50.

[2] Sidney Verba, "Comparative Political Culture," in Lucian W. Pye and Sidney Verba, *Political Culture and Political Development* (Princeton: Princeton University Press, 1966) p. 518.

3 Lucian W. Pye, *Aspects of Political Development* (Boston: Little, Brown, 1966) p. 1045.

[4] Richard Van Loon and Michael Whittington, *The Canadian Political System* (Toronto: McGraw-Hill Ryerson, 1981) Chapter 2.

[5] Allan Kornberg, *Politics and Culture in Canada* (Ann Arbor: Center for Political Studies, Michigan, 1988) p. 4.

[6] François-Pierre Gingras and Neil Nevitte, "The Evolution of Quebec Nationalism" in Alain G. Gagnon (ed.), *Quebec: State and Society* (Toronto: Methuen, 1984) pp. 2-14.

[7] Seymour Martin Lipset, "Canada and the United States: The Cultural Dimension," in Charles F. Doran and John H. Sigler (eds.), *Canada and the United States: Enduring Friendship, Persistent Stress* (Englewood Cliffs, N.J.: Prentice-Hall, Inc., 1985) p. 109.

[8] Andrew Malcolm, *The Canadians* (New York: Times Books, 1985) p. 69.

[9] See Louis Hartz, *The Founding of New Societies* (New York: Harcourt Brace, 1964).

[10] Gad Horowitz, "Conservatism, Liberalism and Socialism in Canada," in Orest M. Kruhlak et al. (eds.), *The Canadian Political Process* (Toronto: University of Toronto Press, 1965).

[11] Seymour Martin Lipset, *op. cit.* pp. 110-118.

[12] John Porter, *The Vertical Mosaic: An Analysis of Social Class and Power in Canada* (Toronto: University of Toronto Press, 1965).

[13] Harold A. Innis, *Essays in Canadian Economic History* (Toronto: University of Toronto Press, 1956).

[14] Gingras and Nevitte, *op. cit.* pp. 4-10.

[15] For an account of these changes, see Kenneth McRoberts, *Quebec: Social Change and Political Crisis*, 3rd ed. (Toronto: McClelland and Stewart) chapters 5-8.

[16] See, Richard Simeon and David J. Elkins, "Regional Political Cultures in Canada." in Richard Schultz, Orest M. Kruhlak and John Terry (eds.), *The Canadian Political Process* (Toronto: Holt, Rinehart and Winston, 1979) p. 15.

[17] Roger Gibbins, *Conflict and Unity*, 2nd ed. (Scarborough: Nelson Canada, 1990) pp. 118-20.

[18] See for example, David J. Bercuson, *Canada and The Burden of Unity* (Toronto: Macmillan, 1977); Larry Pratt and John Richards, *Prairie Capitalism: Power and Influence in the New West* (Toronto: McClelland and Stewart, 1979).

[19] Richard Simeon and David I. Elkins, "Regional Political Cultures in Canada,"

CANADIAN GOVERNMENT AND POLITICS

Canadian Journal of Political Science VII:3, 1974, pp. 397-437.

[20] Roger Gibbins, *op. cit.* p. 139.

[21] François-Pierre Gingras, "Ontario," in David J. Bellamy, Jon H. Pammett and Donald C. Rowat (eds.), *The Provincial Political System* (Toronto: Methuen, 1976).

[22] John H. Redekop, "Continentalism: The Key to Canadian Politics," in John H. Redekop (ed.), *Approaches to Canadian Politics* (Scarborough: Prentice-Hall, 1978).

[23] For example, see Kari Levitt, *Silent Surrender: The Multinational Corporation in Canada* (Toronto: Macmillan, 1970).

[24] John H. Redekop, *op. cit.*

[25] See, *Report of the Task Force on Broadcasting Policy* (Ottawa: Ministry of Supply and Services, 1986), pp. 17-18.

[26] John H. Redekop, *op. cit.*

[27] Donald Higgins, "The Political Americanization of Canadian Children," in Jon H. Pammett and Michael S. Whittington, *Foundations of Political Culture: Political Socialization in Canada* (Toronto: Macmillan, 1976) pp. 251-264.

[28] Jon Pammett, "Class Voting and Class Consciousness in Canada," *Canadian Review of Sociology and Anthropology* 1969, 24: 269-89.

[29] John Meisel, *Working Papers on Canadian Politics* (Montreal: McGill/Queen's University Press, 1973).

[30] Neil Nevitte and Roger Gibbins, *New Elites in Old States: Ideologies in the Anglo-American Democracies* (Toronto: Oxford University Press, 1990).

[31] Allan Kornberg, *op. cit.* pp. 20-24.

[32] For example, Claus Offe, *Contradictions of the Welfare State* (Cambridge, Mass.: M.I.T. Press, 1984) and Ronald Inglehart, *Culture Shift in Advanced Industrial Society* (Princeton: Princeton University Press, 1990).

[33] Herman Bakvis and Neil Nevitte, "In Pursuit of Postbourgeois Man: Postmaterialism and Intergenerational Change in Canada," *Comparative Political Studies* 20, 1987, 357-89 and Neil Nevitte, Herman Bakvis, and Roger Gibbins, "The Ideological Contours of 'New Politics' in Canada: Policy, Mobilization and Partisan Support," *Canadian Journal of Political Science* XXII:3, 1989, 475-503.

ANNOTATED READINGS

Almond, Gabriel and Sidney Verba. *The Civic Culture.* Princeton, N.J.: Princeton University Press, 1963. The pioneering cross-national study of political culture.

Doran, Charles, and John Sigler, eds. *Canada and the United States.* Englewood Cliffs, N.J.: Prentice-Hall, 1985. A collection of essays that provide an overview of the economic, political, social and cultural dynamics between the two countries.

Dumont, Fernard. *The Vigil of Quebec.* Toronto and Buffalo: University of Toronto Press, 1974. An accessible and sensitive account of Quebec's transformations and its hopes.

Gibbins, Roger. *Conflict and Unity,* Second edition. Scarborough: Nelson Canada, 1990. A perceptive analysis of how the interactions between cultural, regional, institutional and continental factors have shaped domestic politics.

Hartz, Louis. *The Founding of New Societies.* New York: Harcourt Brace, 1964. Sets out the logic of how founding fragments are crucial to the shape of political culture in new societies.

Levitt, Kari. *Silent Surrender: The Multinational Corporation in Canada.* Toronto: Macmillan, 1970. A new classic analysis of the economics and politics of dependence and the roles of multinational corporations.

Porter, John. *The Vertical Mosaic.* Toronto: University of Toronto Press, 1965. A definitive study of class, status and power in Canada.

Simeon, Richard and David Elkins. "Regional Political Cultures in Canada" in *Canadian Journal of Political Science.* September 1974. Provides detailed empirical evidence of regional political cultures in Canada.

| CHAPTER 2 |

IDEOLOGIES

RALPH NELSON

Most treatments of ideology usually begin with a definition by which the author attempts to show that an ideology is a set of ideas which is neither science nor philosophy, although it has a cognitive[1] content to it. Sometimes a total ideology, or worldview, is distinguished from a partial ideology, such as a political ideology. For instance, Christianity is sometimes referred to as a total or general ideology. We shall confine our attention to political ideology.

It is important to distinguish between the nature of an ideology and its functions. Among the terms used to denote the nature of ideology are: the science of ideas (the original meaning), false consciousness, that is, where class position distorts political awareness (the Marxist meaning), perspective, or simply myth. The approach in this treatment is to avoid any attempt to stipulate a very precise definition of the nature of ideology, staking out a particular position at the outset, but to adopt a meaning which is widely used in political discourse. Political ideology is a political doctrine which does not just express the "truth" about politics, but is action-orientated as well.

Starting with this general concept, we note that it entails beliefs, attitudes, and orientations. From here on the emphasis will be on the functions of ideology: representation, justification, and recommendation. Some might want to say that in addition to representing, justifying, and directing, an ideology also conceals. For instance, it is common for Marxists to say that liberals tend to hide the power and exploitation underlying economic relationships by dint of emphasizing the existence of freedom of contract. But we leave aside for the moment a full discussion of the degree to which any political ideology either intentionally or not conceals significant aspects of political reality.

Now a mainly cognitive approach to ideology stresses it as a perspective, vision, or representation. It is a way of looking at the political world. Such a presentation may be a more or less adequate picture of reality, depending on the extent to which it reveals or conceals certain aspects of social and political situations. A mainly ethical approach to ideology, that is an action-orientated approach to it, stresses ideology as providing grounds for accepting laws and policies, thus giving direction to decision-making and offering arguments for particular positions and policies. Both approaches are necessary since ideology is about knowledge *and* action.

First, what is called representation in a political doctrine involves a view of the social and political world; let us say a view of the social configuration and its political consequences. Clashes between and among ideologies are rooted in differing perspectives. (We leave aside the question whether the representation is the expression of an interest or not.)

Secondly, an ideology involves a justification for doing or not doing something, for maintaining a state of affairs or trying to change it. When an attempt is made to persuade others of a particular course of action, arguments will be employed. Appeals will be made to the values people hold, the interests that motivate them, the goals that they share. While a philosophical argument is primarily an appeal to reason, a rhetorical argument, the kind that predominates in the public forum, is more than an appeal to reason. It is an appeal to passions and interests as well.

Thirdly, a political ideology emits recommendations and directives. It has an orientation, be it toward change or toward conservation, toward revolution or toward reform, toward social reconstruction or toward adjustments to preserve an established order.

We shall concentrate on three political ideologies which we think are particularly relevant to Canadian politics in the late twentieth century: liberalism, neoconservatism and socialism. We shall explain why this treatment of ideology downplays two other possible candidates for inclusion: populism and nationalism.

| 25 |

I Liberalism I

In the nineteenth century, Canada developed in a manner which was similar in many ways to other liberal societies. In the first half of the nineteenth century, there was the opposition to the oligarchies of privilege, the Canadian counterpart of an aristocracy which owed its predominance not to achievement in a competitive framework, but to the efforts of non-elected groups to maintain their power and prestige. These groups were the Chateau Clique and the Family Compact. Not as dramatic as the revolutions which brought down the old nobility, the struggle against these groups nevertheless had certain analogies with the revolutionary struggle. Then Canada went through a protracted revolt aimed at establishing responsible government, embodying the liberal ideas that the legislature must be supreme and the executive subordinated to it. Liberals had consistently fought for the division of power, even though they condoned cabinet government, which combines legislative and executive power, because those who exercised power in it had been elected. Then an evolution took place from a liberal regime to a liberal democratic one. During the Confederation Debates, there were a number of manifestations of anti-democratic sentiment, but a generation later, Canada, like Great Britain, and the United States earlier, became a liberal democracy, although it is true that democracy was only fully realized when both adult men and women were included in the suffrage in the 1920s. Finally, Canada like other liberal societies passed through a period of national self-assertion in the nineteenth century, even though it was somewhat diluted, for while control over domestic affairs was in Canadian hands, the exercise of external affairs was conditioned by the imperial connection. If one wants to speak of full-blown political independence, it was only achieved in the twentieth century.

Liberal ideology, then, has been the predominant ideology in Canada. Perhaps in the nineteenth century, the liberalism of the philosophic radicals[2] (Lord Durham being of their number) was more influential than the natural rights philosophy articulated in the American Constitution and the French Declaration of the Rights of Man and the Citizen. However, in the twentieth century, Canadian liberalism has been preoccupied with the political protection of rights, first in a federal Bill of Rights, then in the Charter of Rights and Freedoms. It is customary to distinguish between civil rights and liberties and political rights and liberties. The former concern such freedoms as freedom of religion, of association, of assembly, of speech, and of the press.

I 26 I

Political liberties bear directly on political participation, that is, the right to vote and to hold office.

Liberalism has been identified with constitutionalism and the rule of law. An important part of this is the attribution of the power to the judiciary to review the laws passed by parliament. While the power of the Canadian Supreme Court once seemed confined to the task of ascertaining whether or not a particular piece of legislation was properly in federal or provincial jurisdiction, the Charter of Rights and Freedoms extends considerably judicial purview. This is often expressed by saying that the Canadian political system now seems to be closer to the American political system, in the limitations it places on legislative, that is parliamentary, supremacy. Liberals are sometimes criticized for a non-democratic reliance on judicial decision-making, presumably relying on the wisdom of judges in contrast to the sporadic folly of elected assemblies. However, liberals have endorsed both parliamentary supremacy and extensive judicial review and if the two come into conflict, that is basically a dilemma within liberal ideology. It is not the only one.

Clearly, there is a strong legal cast to liberal ideology. Its emphasis on constitutional law, government under law, civil and political rights, in short, human rights, and on rules of procedure — what lawyers call natural justice — give it a strong legal character. To make the point, let us contrast liberal ideology with a politics of power, a political doctrine concerned solely with how one acquires power, how one maintains power, how one increases power, and how one exercises power in terms of success or failure. The name of Machiavelli, generally considered a bad influence in English-speaking countries, is often associated with this kind of politics. Now the proto-liberals of the seventeenth century, notable writers like Thomas Hobbes and John Locke in England, were indeed concerned with power, but they were mainly concerned with the process by which power became legitimized, that is, not with technical prescriptions about seizing power, but principles that rendered the possession and exercise of power rightful. This meant that power had to be limited in practice. Consent theories of government, in which governments are legitimately constituted by the consent of the governed, were developed to explain why the possession of power by certain people was justifiable, but also set down guidelines for the use of that power. It may well be the case that the original concern with power has somewhat faded in liberal ideology with the success of its basic principles of government. In any case the liberal theory of politics is clearly different from a pure theory of power.

Liberal ideology not only has a strong legal cast to it, but it has developed

| 27 |

certain conceptions about justice as well. Since questions of justice concern equality and inequality, we can get a grasp on the liberal conception of justice by examining the forms of equality which it endorses and the kind it disdains. In so far as the context is one of competition, the liberal stresses equality of opportunity or equality of access. As in a race in which all begin at the same mark, the unequal results will be justified by the fact that the starting line is the same for all. Thus liberalism is associated with equal opportunity, but not equal results or outcomes. In so far as the issue of justice concerns procedures, the liberal advocates equal treatment and abhors special treatment by which privilege re-enters the picture. The liberal supports equality before the bar, that is, the law. Now, in fact, it may be difficult to achieve either equality of opportunity or equal treatment, but they remain norms of justice for the liberal. If we examine justice from a distributive point of view, the liberal usually supports both desert and need as criteria. For instance, desert or merit is an appropriate basis for constituting a civil service; while need is appropriate in assuring subsistence. Here a split is possible; for some liberals give desert priority over need, and some give need priority over desert (and may even completely reject the notion of desert as a criterion). This is one of those tensions within liberalism that will be discussed later.

If a liberal is a person who gives primacy to freedom as the leading value, it is understandable that some liberals may want to speak of justice as equal liberty. However, it is not evident that all questions of justice can be translated into issues of freedom. Hence conflict between freedom and justice is possible. Does this mean that the liberal will prefer freedom in such a contest? That might be a reasonable assumption.

Among the basic freedoms of the liberal creed is freedom of association. The presence of this freedom has led to a proliferation of groups of various kinds and, indeed, the social perspective of the liberal is pluralistic. In contrast to the socialist, for instance, who maintains that society, the social whole, should or must be understood as an arena of class conflict if one is not to mystify people, the liberal does not give priority to socio-economic groups in his or her social vision. Of course, such groups are among the multiplicity of intermediary bodies between the individual and the government, but they are not necessarily front and centre. In some instances, ethnic groups may be given special attention, in other instances religious groups, in still other instances professional groups. Of course, in some instances, the conflicts between labour and management, workers and employers, may be paramount. The widely held view that we live in a broadly middle class society may account for the depreciation of class concerns. Of course, there are the rich and the poor at the opposite ends of the social spectrum, but

IDEOLOGIES

that broad middle rank is the significant feature of society.

These intermediary bodies or interest groups are an important feature in the process of government. Many of them exercise pressure on parties and on government at various levels to achieve their aims (thus an interest group becomes a pressure group.) Some of them — one thinks of the medical profession — have authority delegated by the government. The process by which particular interests attempt to influence policy is considered legitimate in Canada, assuming that it does not involve the corruption of public officials. Realistically one has to face the fact that conflict of interest is a constant problem for democratic government in Canada and, indeed, in all political societies.

Liberal societies pride themselves on being pluralistic not just concerning freedom of association, but in regard to the different values people adopt. For instance, the liberal is considered to be more permissive than a conservative about what one reads and what one sees (e.g. films and television), and thus is opposed to censorship. The liberal takes a permissive view on abortion, being pro-choice. The standard liberal form of secularism views religion as a private matter and that means resentment over the "intrusion" of religious groups in politics, such as the recent fundamentalist involvement. However, interest group liberalism, far from negating this "intrusion," sanctions it.

Earlier several tensions within liberal ideology were identified: parliamentary supremacy and extensive judicial review, the criterion of desert and that of need in distributive justice. This section will end with other tensions or dilemmas within liberalism. The first concerns affirmative action; the second concerns the management of the economy.

Liberal ideology has advocated equality of opportunity or access to various positions in society (e.g. competitive examinations for the civil service and equal access to education). A tension has developed in liberal theory which had supported a meritocratic approach, that selection of individuals for limited positions should be based on relevant differences (merit) in a situation of equal opportunity. To eliminate irrelevant and unfair criteria being employed, liberals pushed for prohibitions against discrimination on the basis of factors like age, race, gender, national origin or similar factors. However, recently there has been a conception that has received liberal endorsement that appears to run counter to the first approach. It is called affirmative action, reverse discrimination, or simply preference. If racial criteria are irrelevant, they must be excluded. You cannot be both colour-conscious and colour-blind. You cannot be both gender-conscious and gender-blind. You cannot maintain equality in competition and then give

| 29 |

preferential treatment, and say this is fair, no matter how expedient it seems to be. It is not easy to see how this tension or dilemma can be overcome. Either it is wrong to use such factors or it is not. In the former case, non-discrimination seems to predominate, although to be gender-blind, for instance, perpetuates discrimination. In the latter cases, a kind of discrimination is employed to fight other kinds.

Another source of division within liberal ideology that has produced a schism concerns the management of the economy. It is worthwhile employing the distinction between egalitarian liberalism and liberterian liberalism to make the point.[3] The former kind of liberalism may mean staunch support for the welfare state, the use of taxation and allocations to achieve greater equalization in the economic system. It favours a selective kind of state intervention in the marketplace. The latter kind would object to any attempt by government to achieve some pattern of social equality, though it might accept the idea of a social minimum. The government should leave the marketplace alone. Egalitarian liberals have accepted the mixed economy; liberterian liberals are opposed to it. Egalitarian liberals may support wage and price controls; liberterian liberals would not. Another way of referring to liberterian liberalism is to use the term neoconservatism.

I Neoconservatism I

During the great depression of the 1930s, the government adopted a policy of intervention in the economy influenced by the economic theories of John Maynard Keynes. One of the most important of these policies was that of pump-priming, that is, the government stimulates demand by pouring money into the economy through deficit spending, so that buyers will have the funds to purchase goods and services. It was assumed that the absence of effective demand, meaning demand with resources, was a contributing cause of the economic crisis.

The government's intervention in the economy increased during the Second World War and continued thereafter with the extension of welfare state provisions. However, a challenge to Keynesian policies came about because of the failure of government to control inflation. In fact, contrary to expectation, inflation and economic stagnation occurred simultaneously producing what was known as "stagflation."

In the 1970s in Canada, the aim of controlling inflation led to the imposition of wage and price controls, both at the federal level and, later, in

IDEOLOGIES

the province of Ontario. It might be argued that in addition to the use of fiscal policy (that is, taxation) to manage the economy, the imposition of controls over wages and prices seemed to be a "liberal" approach. If so, it was short lived.

The growth of the interventionist state, the cost of its operation, the increasing deficits generated by its policies, and a perception that aspects of the welfare state had failed, gave rise to a reaction against the prevailing policies and this reaction which occurred in the United Kingdom, then in the United States, and about the same time in Canada, has become known as neoconservatism.

Now even when Keynesianism had been in vogue, there had been a dissenting view, expressed notably by Friedrich Hayek which became known for the thesis that the development of the interventionist welfare state was leading down the road to serfdom.[4] But where Hayek had once been considered to be a marginal defender of laissez-faire (letting the economy alone), his ideas, and those of his disciples, were now at centre stage.

This school of thought is described by economists as liberterian. Among political scientists, it is more customary to refer to it as neoconservatism.

As should be evident by now, the focal point of neoconservatism is the relationship of the state to the economy.

The main tenets of the ideology have been formulated by economists who take a rather narrow focus on politics. If the drift must be away from the interventionist state to a greater reliance on a relatively free market economy, then it makes sense to de-regulate that economy. If the government is considered to be involved in areas which properly belong in the private sector, then it makes sense to privatize crown corporations. Indeed, the initial attempt, rescinded and then later renewed, to privatize Petro-Canada seemed to be the opening gun in the privatization battle, and subsequently such public entities as Air Canada, De Haviland, Polysar, and Teleglobe Canada have been placed on the auction block by the federal government. In Saskatchewan, there has been an ideological dispute concerning the provincial government's proposal to privatize the crown-owned natural gas monopoly. The potash corporation had already been privatized in that province.

Of course one of the leading neoconservative assumptions is that governments cannot operate enterprises as well as private industry can. However, there has not as yet been any serious attempt to privatize the Canadian medicare system. Nor has the government proposed the encouragement of a privately-run system of post-secondary education, although it expects a certain portion of the budgetary needs of such institutions to come from the contributions of private individuals and groups. There have been some

| 31 |

CANADIAN GOVERNMENT AND POLITICS

proposals for private universities, but the initiatives have not been governmental.

Another component of the neoconservative approach is to aim at a balanced budget or, at least, to sharply reduce the public debt. In the United States, there have been legislative requirements to balance budgets; in Canada, there has been a set of governmental proposals to do so. These include raising new revenues to increase assets and reducing government programs in order to decrease the debt. Contradictions are apparent here, however, since these actions are themselves interventions in the economy.

Unlike the United Kingdom and the United States, the neoconservative trend in Canada has not adopted some of the monetarist policies usually associated with neoconservatism; that is, it has not depended primarily on manipulation of the money supply to achieve its goals, although the maintenance of high interest rates by the Bank of Canada recently fits the pattern. Obviously any government in Canada must be attentive to the value of the Canadian dollar on the world market and to the prime interest rate, since these factors have so much importance in foreign trade, most of which takes place with the United States. When the interest rate is maintained at a certain level for other purposes, that suggests a neoconservative strategy.

In this context, something should be said about the ideological significance of free trade. It is the contention here that the advocacy of free trade, aside from purely pragmatic considerations of relative economic advantage in tariff reduction, is basically a nineteenth century liberal conception. The most notable instance of this in earlier Canadian history was Wilfrid Laurier's endorsement of what was then called the reciprocity treaty. Free trade was a central feature of liberal internationalism in the nineteenth century and a corollary of a generally pacific view of international relations. For some today, the development of trading blocs, particularly the European Community, have made free trade a necessity rather than an ideological preference. Nevertheless, it was originally a liberal idea.

Now the impression has no doubt been given that neoconservatism is a narrow kind of ideology. With de-regulation, privatization, and balanced budget proposals, the emphasis has been on economics alone. If the welfare state is not dismantled, but reduced by neoconservative governments, this is because the neoconservatives adopt the minimalist notion of the state as providing a safety net. The metaphor used implies that life is a kind of high wire act and the state will ensure that if you are among those who fall (the unemployed, the sick, the dependent, the destitute), you will be minimally provided for. Provision, however, should not encourage laziness. There would be incentives for people to work or disincentives for those who do not. The "safety net" is a metaphor, however, that takes no account of unequal access to resources.

What of law and justice? Neoconservatism in its more developed forms — and again Hayek is a useful source — has a theory of law rather than a theory of justice. If there is a defence of equality, it is equality under the law, and the neoconservative is critical of any kind of preference given to special interests. While liberal ideology legitimizes interest group activity, the neoconservatives, though not wishing to impose restrictions on freedom of association, tend to view interest groups negatively and castigate special interests that look for public support for their interests, such as labour unions seeking legislation against strike-breakers, businesses seeking guaranteed loans, farmers demanding subsidies — although business, as construed as the engine of society, often ends up with many kinds of special support under real neoconservative regimes. The neoconservative may also be wary of ethnic, racial, or gender interest groups. So what liberal ideology views as normal and legitimizes, neoconservative ideology views as abnormal and tries to counter.

Now appeals to a public interest over special interests may indeed conceal support for some interests over others. Still when the government becomes involved not only in supporting the demands of special interests, but in giving grants to interest group organizations, as in the case of the National Action Committee on the Status of Women (NAC), consumer advocacy groups, industry associations and labour councils, the legitimization process seems to go too far for neoconservatives. So there is a marked contrast between the liberal view of interest groups and their political activities and the neoconservative views.

The notion of justice in neoconservative ideology is more problematic. Patterns of distribution produced by the operation of an ideal free market are not considered just, nor unjust for that matter. They are like the rain that falls on the good and the wicked alike. No doubt the neoconservative thinks that the results of voluntary contracts should be considered fair, no matter which party begins with more capital or more resources. That means that fairness is reckoned in terms of the satisfaction of certain conditions of exchange and not in terms of the results of the transaction. It strongly opposes efforts by government to establish certain distributive patterns by the redistribution of income and transfer payments. The goods acquired by individuals and organizations under minimal market laws should be respected, and force and fraud in the marketplace condemned. Need is addressed by ensuring a basic minimum, the safety net referred to earlier. To sum up, neoconservatives seem to be more noticeable for their attacks on

| 33 |

the concept of social or distributive justice than for any original or distinctive theory of justice of their own.

It would not make sense to refer to neoconservatives as libertarian liberals unless they accepted the idea that the basic political value is freedom. Liberals are criticized, however, because they are concerned with civil and political freedoms, while restricting economic freedom. The neoconservative on the other hand is often preoccupied with the issue of economic freedom. It is not freedom of choice in regard to art, literature, and entertainment, or with regard to abortion or pornography, but freedom of choice in the economic sphere that holds the neoconservative's attention, although the attention neoconservatives pay to issues of the traditional family and attempts to solidify it are often not merely passing. We should recognize that everyone is interested in particular kinds of freedom. Journalists are primarily interested in freedom of the press, artists and writers in freedom of expression, dissidents, perhaps, are largely concerned with freedom of association, university teachers with academic freedom, and certain religious minorities with religious freedom when their beliefs collide with the law. The freedoms we enjoy do not have the same kind of importance for us as do the freedoms we are denied.

The neoconservative conception of freedom is the absence of coercion. When this is examined, it is clear that the freedom at stake is the freedom of the entrepreneur, on one hand, and the freedom of the consumer, on the other. This appeal to economic freedom has a popular flavour since even if few of us are or will ever be entrepreneurs, we are all consumers. The economic freedom of the employee or worker does not enter in. Neoconservative ideologists have been anti-union, frequently arguing against unionism as a form of labour monopoly. The employee or worker is presumably free to choose where to work, though this may require the person to move elsewhere to find employment. The ideology must include all economic categories in the exercise of economic freedom. Suffice it to say that such people have not been the usual clientele of neoconservatism. The neoconservative rejects the identification of freedom and power; freedom is one thing and power is another. The employee or worker will be more concerned with relative power in the marketplace than with a frequently elusive freedom to choose a place of employment.

The real enemy of neoconservatism is not so much interventionist liberalism, but socialism, which attempts an equitable redistribution of wealth rather than an accumulation of it. Socialism is distinct from liberalism in that it would like to see an equality of results rather than simply one of opportunity.

I Socialism I

Two conceptions of socialism have been influential in the formation of socialist ideology in Canada: democratic socialism and Marxism. To the extent that society is viewed in terms of the class conflict between the proletariat (industrial working class) and the bourgeoisie (those who own the means of production, distribution, and exchange), the two conceptions share the same general perspective. However, if the perspective is that class conflict will only be resolved by the political and social dominance of the working class, initiating a process to replace capitalism by socialism, primarily by public ownership of the means of production, distribution, and exchange, to the end of creating a classless society, it is the Marxist vision that is paramount.

On the other hand, if socialism is presumed to come about through peaceful electoral means, and the emphasis is placed on public control of the economy rather than complete public ownership, the vision is that of democratic socialism. Observers have argued that democratic socialism, in Sweden for instance, has made its peace with capitalism since the control over the economy does not entail a significant amount of public ownership. However, the goal of social equality is given priority. Perhaps a useful way of differentiating this kind of democratic socialism from Marxism in economic terms is to say that the former is a socialism of distribution and the latter is a socialism of production.

It is not that democratic socialists are not concerned with freedom; they are. But the socialist value system accords priority to equality over freedom, more specifically social equality is accorded priority over economic freedom. It sees the social configuration in terms of classes and conflicts between them. It respects civil and political freedoms, as the liberals do. Still the aim of a more just, that is, more equal society requires redistribution, effected through tax policies and social welfare programs to ensure social justice, another name for distributive justice. The main criterion of distributive justice is need. If basic needs are the same, the outcome of distribution according to need should be a more egalitarian society.

While it appears that the main emphasis in democratic socialism is on distribution rather than production, on government policies to achieve social equality rather than on public ownership, the socialist may be in favour of strategic nationalization, that is, public ownership of key aspects of the economy, such as investment banking. So by and large this kind of socialism combines a general acceptance of private ownership along with government intervention to ensure greater equality through tax policy, welfare policy, and transfer payments.

Historically, Canadian democratic socialism began with an emphasis on nationalization, state ownership, in the famous *Regina Manifesto* of 1933. After an introductory recital of the evils of the capitalist system, it states: "We believe that these evils can be removed only in a planned and socialized economy in which our natural resources and the principal means of production and distribution are owned, controlled and operated by the people."[5] However, democratic socialism has moved from this emphasis on public ownership and, since let us say 1970, has limited itself to distributive concerns, that is, to achieving greater equalization within Canadian society. To that extent it, like Swedish socialism, has come to terms with capitalism; it offers to its adherents a form of socialist capitalism.

Along with the call for a planned economy and the notion of a co-operative commonwealth, Canadian socialism has expressed the ideal of an industrial democracy. The term is vague unless it refers to the movement for greater worker self-management in the work place, as opposed to the perpetuation of the adversarial relations of management and labour. More often the term is used more indiscriminately to indicate that socialism means better housing, better health care, provision for the elderly, greater access to higher education, and a reformed system of taxation which will force the rich to pay their fair share (certainly more than they do now). In other words to realize in the socio-economic sphere the kind of equality presupposed in the democratic principle of the universal suffrage.

To accomplish these goals a strong central state is required with an extensive bureaucracy. Thus bureaucratic socialism is not an accident or a distortion of the socialist ideology, as Marxists might want to say, but the inevitable outcome of the social service state. Of course, the bureaucracy even in the liberal welfare state is already quite extensive. You simply cannot offer public provision and attempt to bring about redistribution of income without such public agencies.

Whatever may have been its former radicalism — during the great depression — democratic socialism in Canada now appears to pursue a prudent policy of reform, more radical no doubt than the liberals, yet scarcely close to western Marxism. It has little of the internationalism of European democratic socialism and, in fact, is strongly nationalistic, concerned about the American penetration of the Canadian economy, seen as growing particularly with the Free Trade Agreement.

IDEOLOGIES

I Nationalism I

Now nationalism has not been, and will not be, treated as a separate ideology for there are various conceptions of Canadian nationalism which are conditioned by the particular ideology one endorses. There is the nationalism of Conservatives like John Diefenbaker, of Liberals like Walter Gordon, and of New Democrats like Ed Broadbent. For some nationalists the focus is political, the pursuit of an independent foreign policy, for others it is primarily economic, for others it is primarily cultural, or several of these are combined. For some it may entail a national vision, such as Canadian unity or a planned economy; for others it is mainly negative, expressed in anti-Americanism. And we can hardly ignore Quebec nationalism.

An observer of the federal elections in Canada and the United States in 1988 would have concluded that nationalism was on the left in Canada (meaning the NDP and the Liberals) and on the right in the United States (meaning the Republican Party). As noted nationalism in Canada has three dimensions: political, economic, and cultural and to some extent all three of these dimensions were at stake in the free trade debate.

I Populism I

Finally something should be said about populism. Populism once flourished in Canada but has gradually disappeared as a significant ideological movement. Populist ideology originated in the Prairie provinces and had links with the American populist movement, mainly because of the large number of farmers who immigrated from the United States. The ideology appealed to the undifferentiated people against the elites, and defended western interests against the alleged oppression of eastern interests, particularly financial ones. It advocated an egalitarian democracy and the capitalism of small producers.[6] Indeed there are still populist attitudes, and populist measures, like the privatization of the British Columbia Resources Investment Corporation through its sale to the people of the province.[7] However, such occasional manifestations and the durability of populist appeals to a democratic electorate do not constitute the kind of pattern discernible in liberalism, neoconservatism, and socialism. Still the campaign of the Reform Party in Alberta for an elected Senate may indicate a resurgence of populism, for it too began as a western protest against dominant eastern interests.

I 37 I

I Conclusion I

We conclude, then, by noting that ideologies vary in their durability. Liberalism is surely the most durable ideology in Canada, principally because it has evolved, has been transformed, has been modified to suit the times. Populism, on the other hand, waxed and waned. The current prominence of neoconservative ideology may be short lived. In Eastern Europe, it may have a future denied to it in North America. One thing we do know is that ideologies once thought dead and buried have had a second life, while communism one of the most powerful ideological influences in Western history, is currently in a state of rapid decline. Perhaps the surprising aspect of the ideological phenomenon in the modern period is not that ideologies too are mortal, but that certain ideologies have survived repeated announcements of their demise.

NOTES

[1] This means that it involves a kind of knowledge.

[2] These were British intellectuals, like Jeremy Bentham and John Stuart Mill, concerned with economic, political and legal reforms.

[3] Michael Sandel (ed.), *Liberalism and Its Critics* (New York: New York University Press, 1984) p. 4. W. Christian and C. Campbell speak of the distinction between negative (business) liberalism and positive (welfare) liberalism. *Political Parties and Ideologies in Canada* (Toronto: McGraw-Hill Ryerson, 1983) p. 58.

[4] F.A. Hayek, *The Road to Serfdom* (London: Routledge and Kegan Paul, 1944).

[5] H.D. Forbes (ed.), *Canadian Political Thought* (Toronto: Oxford University Press, 1985) p. 241.

[6] W.L. White, R.H. Wagenberg, R.C. Nelson, *Introduction to Canadian Government and Politics* (Toronto: Holt, Rinehart and Winston of Canada, 5th Edition, 1990) pp. 77-81.

[7] See Michael Bliss, *Northern Enterprise: Five Centuries of Canadian Business* (Toronto: McClelland and Stewart, 1987) p. 574n.

ANNOTATED READINGS

Brooks, Stephen J., ed. *Political Thought in Canada: Contemporary Perspectives.* Toronto: Irwin, 1984. In this wide-ranging collection of essays, such issues as religion and politics, social and political democracy, French Canada, liberalism and federalism are examined.

Christian, William and Colin Campbell, *Political Parties and Ideologies in Canada*, Third edition. Toronto: McGraw-Hill Ryerson, 1990. What has been and is now the influence of different ideas or ideologies on Canadian party politics? The authors identify four ideologies, liberalism, conservatism, socialism, and nationalism. It is argued that the three major parties combine ideological elements and that recent Canadian politics has seen an ideological shift to the right.

Horn, Michiel, *The League for Social Reconstruction: Intellectual Origins of the Democratic Left in Canada 1930-1942.* Toronto: University of Toronto Press, 1980. This valuable historical study tells us about the left leaving intellectuals of the League, their ideas and their influence on social reform in Canada.

Marchak, M. Patricia. *Ideological Perspectives on Canada*, Second edition. Toronto: McGraw-Hill Ryerson, 1981. The study examines various aspects of Canadian society in view of the confrontation between the dominant ideology (liberalism) and the counter ideology (Marxism). Shortcomings are discerned in both of these ideologies.

Qualter, Terence H. *Conflicting Political Ideas in Liberal Democracies.* Toronto: Metheun, 1986. There are three major ideologies in Canada: the Liberal Mind, the Tory Tradition, and the Socialist Faith. Democratic ideology is also discussed in an analysis that indicates the influence of the late C. B. Macpherson, an eminent Canadian political theorist.

CHAPTER 3

THE LIVING CONSTITUTION

F.L. MORTON

Questions of constitutional reform and amendment play a major role in contemporary Canadian politics. Canada is unique in this respect. While other Western democracies debate such issues as taxes and social services, Canada's political agenda has been frequently preempted by the more fundamental challenges of national unity and major structural and institutional reforms. Quebec separatism, the Charter of Rights, the Meech Lake Accord, western alienation and Senate reform — these are the issues that have engaged the energy and skills of Canadian leaders for the past twenty years.

Constitutional issues such as these cut to the core of Canadian politics. They address not the question of "what" laws to make, but the prior and more fundamental question of "who" shall make the laws and "how." While there is unanimous agreement that "the people" shall govern, there is no agreement on who constitute "the people." Is Canada a single nation state, or a "community of communities" encompassing two (or more) distinct societies? Which level of government — federal or provincial — should be more powerful? Should Quebec enjoy special status different from the other provinces? Should Canada's two founding races — the French and the English — enjoy a higher constitutional status than the many other ethnic groups that make up the Canadian mosaic? Are individual rights more

CANADIAN GOVERNMENT AND POLITICS

important than provincial rights? Should the Supreme Court be allowed to overrule legislatures in the name of rights? Or should legislatures be able to overrule the Supreme Court in the name democracy?

Answers to these questions shape the structure, the powers and the institutions of Canadian political life. Currently there is no consensus on these fundamental constitutional issues. Yet how they are answered will determine Canada's future, perhaps even its existence. This chapter introduces some of the important constitutional issues as Canada enters the 1990s.

I The Constitution: I
Law and Convention

THE LIVING CONSTITUTION

We must first clarify what we mean by the constitution. The constitution defines the structure of the state, its major institutions, their composition and powers, and their relationships to one another and to the citizens and groups who make up society. It is tempting to say that Canada's constitution consists of the **British North America Act, 1867** (now known as the **Constitution Act, 1867**) and the **Constitution Act, 1982** (which includes the **Charter of Rights and Freedoms**). These are indeed the two most important documents in Canada's written constitution,[1] but to stop here would reduce the constitution to a formal set of documents, to be dickered over by lawyers and judges. The written constitution is complemented and brought to life by a rich and complex set of constitutional conventions and traditions, which constitute the unwritten (or informal) constitution. The unwritten constitution operates independently of the courts and judges, and ultimately shapes and limits the practical meaning of the written constitution and judicial decisions. The unwritten constitution has been formed and maintained by successive generations of Canadian leaders, and ultimately by the loyalties, beliefs and practices of the Canadian people.

We will discuss below the important elements of both the written (formal) and unwritten (informal) constitution, but it is important at the start to be clear that Canada's constitution consists of both. This allows us to understand that the constitution is not some century old document, a static nineteenth century code, but rather, as Allan Cairns has written,[2] a living institution:

I 42 I

To view the constitution in terms of what the Fathers [of Confederation] intended and immediately achieved fails to see that the constitution is in continuous creation. It contributes too much deference to the constitution as it existed in 1867, and too little attention to the contribution of subsequent generations to its evolution.

This "living constitution" is very much rooted in the BNA Act. But many provisions of the founding pact are now "dead letter" and without effect, just as there is much of the "living constitution" that is new and cannot be traced to 1867. Thus "in a practical sense, the constitution is always contemporary."[3] It is a process of continuous renewal, rejection and addition, on which each generation leaves its mark. By understanding the constitution as a "living constitution," we can better understand both the historical origins of the constitutional challenges that face Canada today, and our own generation's responsibility for meeting these challenges.

CONSTITUTIONAL LAW

The BNA Act was the act of union that created Canada out of the then British colonies of Lower and Upper Canada (Quebec and Ontario), New Brunswick and Nova Scotia. While drawn up by Canadian leaders, the Act was enacted by the British Parliament in Westminster. Its preamble declares the intention to create a constitution "similar in principle to that of the United Kingdom," that is, a system of parliamentary democracy. The BNA Act created the office of the Governor General, the House of Commons and the Senate, and specified the composition and powers of each.

The BNA Act also established a federal structure for the new Canadian state. Federalism denotes a state in which the legislative (law-making) powers are divided between the new national government in Ottawa and the provincial governments. This was a deviation from the British model, made necessary by the distinctive and independent character of the four founding provinces. Each of the provinces — especially French-speaking Quebec — did not want to lose control over local matters to a new and distant legislature in which their representatives would be a minority. Thus sections 91 to 95 of the BNA Act allocated the legislative powers of the state to the two different levels of government. Section 91 gave the new federal government the power to make laws for the "peace, order and good government of Canada" (hereafter referred to as the "p.o.g.g. power"), including such specific matters as trade and commerce, taxation, currency, navigation and

CANADIAN GOVERNMENT AND POLITICS

shipping, national defence and criminal law. Section 92 gave the provinces jurisdiction over such matters as "property and civil rights" and "all matters of a merely local or private nature." Needless to say, the boundary line between these two spheres of jurisdiction is not clear, and has been a source of dispute ever since. Section 93 conferred jurisdiction over the sensitive issue of education to the provinces. However, section 93 also guaranteed a separate system of protestant schools in Quebec and separate Catholic systems outside of Quebec, and gave the federal government power to intervene if a province failed to respect these education rights.

The federal form of the new constitution reflected the fact that the new Canadian state encompassed two distinct societies — one English-speaking and largely protestant, the other French-speaking and largely catholic. This religiolinguistic dualism was explicitly incorporated in several important provisions of the new constitution. In addition to the section 93 education guarantees, section 133 made French and English the official government languages of both Canada and Quebec. It required that both languages be allowed in legislative debates and in the courts, and required that the records and statutes of each government be published in both languages. This dualism subsequently gave rise to a French version of the "compact theory" of Confederation — that Canada was formed by a "pact" between its two founding "races" — the French and the English. This version of the compact theory provided the basis for Quebec's claim — as the representative of the French people — to a right to constitutional veto over any amendments to the BNA Act. This right — if it ever did exist — was lost with the proclamation of the **Constitution Act, 1982**. The Meech Lake Accord would have restored it.

The **Constitution Act, 1982**, culminated the political career of the then Prime Minister, Pierre Elliott Trudeau, and changed the original constitution in several important ways. First, it severed Canada's constitutional connection to the United Kingdom, and provided a "made in Canada" amending formula for all future constitutional amendments. Prior to 1982, once the federal and provincial governments had agreed to an amendment, Ottawa still had to request the British Parliament to enact it. The new amending formula requires the approval of both houses of Parliament and seven of the ten provinces with at least fifty percent of the population. This "7/50" amending formula means that a proposed amendment can be defeated by the combined opposition of Quebec and Ontario, since between them they have more than fifty percent of the population. This arrangement did not satisfy the government of René Lévesque, which believed that this stripped Quebec of its traditional right of constitutional veto.[4] For this

I 44 I

THE LIVING CONSTITUTION

reason, Quebec refused to approve the *Constitution Act, 1982.*

The Constitution Act also added the *Charter of Rights and Freedoms* to Canada's written constitution. The Charter enumerates a long list of individual and group rights against both levels of government. The Charter specifically authorizes judicial review; that is, it empowers the Canadian courts to interpret and to enforce the Charter, and to declare laws invalid if they violate these rights.

CONSTITUTIONAL CONVENTIONS

The other component of the Canadian constitution is convention. Constitutional conventions are not written, and can be understood as political traditions that everyone agrees must be followed. A convention usually restricts the way in which a legal power may be exercised. The fact that constitutional conventions are not in the form of written law means that they cannot be enforced by the courts, but this does not make them less important. Some of the most important principles of the constitution are in the form of conventions. For example, nowhere in the written constitution is there any mention of the Prime Minister, the Cabinet, votes of no confidence or "responsible government." Indeed, a foreigner who simply read the BNA Act — without any knowledge of our "unwritten" constitution — would think that Canada is autocratically ruled by the British Queen and her appointed representative, the Governor General.

The truth, of course, is much different. In practice, the Governor General and the Lieutenant-Governors of the provinces are honourary heads of state who basically follow the "advice" (i.e. instructions) of the Prime Minister (or premier) and the Cabinet. The Cabinet, in turn, exercises such authority only so long as it commands the support of a majority of the members of the House of Commons. If the government loses a vote on an important bill, they must resign and (normally) new elections will be held. Thus, link by link, "responsible government" and Canadian democracy is formed. The Crown is responsible to the Prime Minister, who depends on the members of the House of Commons, who must submit to general elections at least every five years.

All of this — and more — is implied by the simple preamble to the Constitution Act, 1867 — that Canada shall have a government "similar in principle" to that of the United Kingdom. In addition to Parliamentary supremacy and "responsible government," the preamble imports the entire British common law tradition into Canada's unwritten constitution. This includes the rule of law and the independence of the judiciary from the

| 45 |

legislative and executive branches of government upon which the rule of law is founded. It also embraces such practices as religious and racial toleration, the freedoms of speech, press, association and assembly, without which parliamentary democracy cannot properly function.[5]

Constitutional convention is thus as important as the written elements of the constitution to the proper functioning of Canadian democracy. Both ultimately are founded in public opinion, in the collective consciousness, customs and morals of the Canadian people. To explain by way of metaphor, Canada's written constitution can be thought of as the skeleton and body of the Canadian state, while convention is akin to the soul. Without the animating spirit of its many conventions, the written constitution would be a dull and lifeless corpse.

I Federalism and the Politics I of Regionalism

Legally speaking, federalism can be defined as the section 91-95 division of the law-making powers between the federal government and provincial governments. It would be wrong to think of federalism as simply a technical or legalistic feature of the constitution. Like democracy, federalism reflects the character of Canadian society. A non-federal Canada is just as unthinkable as a non-democratic Canada. Federalism responds to and channels regionalism, one the strongest forces in Canadian society. Regionalism denotes Canadians' strong sense of regional identity and the long tradition of provincial governments — especially Quebec — trying to protect and promote this identity by maximizing provincial powers and autonomy.

The politics of regionalism manifests itself in two basic ways — either by seeking influence within the institutions of the federal government or by minimizing federal influence in the conduct of provincial government. An example of the first are regional attempts to place their MPs in key cabinet posts and thereby to favourably influence the awarding of federal contracts, economic subsidies, transfer payments and the like. There is a perception — especially in the West — that Quebec leaders have excelled at this activity. This perception in turn has nurtured Western alienation, a sense that Western interests are chronically under-represented in the House of Commons.

This approach — trying to increase regional influence within the federal government — has clear limitations. The enforcement of strict party discipline makes it political suicide for an MP to vote for regional interests against party policy. Also, the sheer numerical dominance of central Canada —

THE LIVING CONSTITUTION

Quebec has 75 MPs and Ontario 99 — makes it difficult for MPs from the Western (86) and Atlantic (32) provinces to exercise much collective influence. One symptom of this problem has been the recent push to reform the Senate to give each province more equal, more effective representation in the second chamber of Parliament. A reformed Senate — in which each province had an equal number of votes regardless of its population — would give the Atlantic and Western provinces a greater voice in the governing process. (Senate reform is discussed below in the Meech Lake section.) Suffice it to say that up to the present, most provinces have invested considerable efforts and resources in the alternative approach of maximizing provincial powers against Ottawa.

With the passage of time since Confederation, the forces of industrialization, urbanization, and the mass media have eroded much of the cultural differences that once distinguished the various regions of Canada. Even Quebec — while still the most distinctive regional culture — is much more like the other provinces than several generations ago. If federalism were simply a reflection of society, then it should have declined as regional difference declined. This is what has occurred in the U.S. In Canada, however, the opposite has happened. This has given rise to the theory that in Canada federalism is as much a cause of regionalism as an effect. Federalism seems to have taken on a life and logic of its own. Provincial governments and provincial politicians have a vested interest in promoting their own powers and indulging in "fed bashing" when things go wrong — blaming the province's problems on the distant and allegedly insensitive government in Ottawa.

This "province building" activity takes both legal and political forms. Because the federal-provincial divisions of powers is part of the written constitution, it has been subject to legal interpretation — judicial review — by the courts.

JUDICIAL DEVELOPMENT OF FEDERALISM

Judicial review has become widely accepted as a necessary corollary to federalism. For a federal distribution of powers to be functional, there must be a mutually acceptable process for settling the inevitable disputes over where one government's jurisdiction ends and the other's begins. The need for a "neutral umpire" to resolve such disputes has been met through judicial review by a final court of appeal. Other federal states — the United States, Australia, West Germany — also use judicial review to resolve jurisdictional disputes.

| 47 |

The Judicial Committee of the Privy Council (JCPC) in London served as Canada's final court of appeal for constitutional issues until 1949. During this time, the JCPC gave a decidedly "decentralist" interpretation to sections 91 and 92 of the BNA Act. The federal government's broad residual power to make laws for "the peace, order and good government of Canada" was whittled away to almost nothing by the JCPC's "emergency doctrine," which restricted Parliament's power to legislate under the p.o.g.g. power to "emergency" situations such as war.

The federal government's unrestricted power to make laws for "the regulation of trade and commerce" was gradually reduced to the much narrower power to regulate only "interprovincial" and international trade and commerce. During this same time the JCPC developed an expansive interpretation of the section 92 powers of the provinces to make laws with respect to "property and civil rights" and "all matters of a merely local or private nature."

The net effect of the JCPC's federalism decisions was to shift a considerable degree of legislative power from the federal to the provincial side of the ledger. Criticism of the JCPC's performance peaked during the 1930s when it struck down a series of new federal laws intended to alleviate the economic hardships caused by the Great Depression. Critics maintained that the JCPC's decisions had made it impossible for the Canadian government to effectively manage a modern, industrial economy.

This dissatisfaction led to the abolition of appeals to the JCPC in 1949. Critics hoped that that the Supreme Court — now liberated from the JCPC's supervision — would develop a bold, new centralist jurisprudence. The centralists' hopes were partially realized. From 1950 to 1976 the Supreme Court did not strike down a single piece of federal legislation. While the Court did not abandon the "emergency doctrine," it developed an alternative interpretation of the p.o.g.g. power — the "national concern" doctrine. This test extends the federal government's jurisdiction under p.o.g.g. to include new, unanticipated policy areas that are of importance to the entire country and are incapable of being dealt with by a single province. Examples include the regulation of aeronautics, telecommunications and environmental protection. This new approach to p.o.g.g. has the potential to expand significantly federal jurisdiction and to correspondingly shrink provincial powers.

A surge of judicial activism in the late seventies saw both federal and provincial laws declared invalid. The Court appeared to try to strike a balance between Ottawa and the provinces, but this did not prevent loud protests of bias from the provinces. Most of the federal laws invalidated during this

| 48 |

period were generally older and less important. The Court upheld the one new federal policy initiative — the Trudeau government's 1976 *Anti-Inflation Act* — as a legitimate exercise of the "emergency doctrine," the first time it had ever been used successfully during peacetime.[6] By contrast, almost all the nullified provincial laws involved recent policy initiatives considered important by their respective governments. Alberta and Saskatchewan[7] saw their taxes on natural resources declared invalid, while Quebec's attempt to regulate cable television was also struck down.[8] While the Supreme Court's federalism decisions during this period were relatively balanced, the provincial perception was one of a judicial bias in favour of Ottawa.

The new "national concern" doctrine, combined with the provinces' perception of a federal bias, made many provincial leaders wary of the Supreme Court. This suspicion was further compounded by the adoption of the Charter of Rights in 1982, which armed the Court with a new and expanded set of constitutional restrictions to enforce against the provinces. This provincial perception of the Supreme Court as a centralizing force and a threat to provincial rights explains the provinces' insistence on the section 33 "legislative override" as a precondition for accepting the Charter of Rights in 1982. It is also behind their more recent demand in the Meech Lake Accord to acquire the power to nominate Supreme Court justices.

NON-JUDICIAL DEVELOPMENT OF FEDERALISM

While British and Canadian judges have shaped the evolution of Canadian federalism, politicians and civil servants, acting outside the courtroom, have been even more influential. For example, the federal government's powers to nullify unilaterally provincial legislation — the powers of disallowance and reservation — have been rendered impotent by the constitutional convention of non-use. These two powers were placed in the BNA Act by centralists such as Sir John A. Macdonald, who favoured "legislative union" and feared that under a system of "pure" federalism the provinces would be too strong. Disallowance and reservation were clearly intended to subordinate the provinces to the new federal government.

In the decades following Confederation, their coercive use by Ottawa provoked such a negative reaction from provincial governments that they came to be viewed as illegitimate federal intrusions into provincial matters. Legally, Ottawa still possesses these powers, but has not exercised them since the 1940s. Public opinion is such that there is no likelihood of their being used again. The development of this convention of non-use significantly enhanced provincial powers in the equation of Canadian federalism.

I 49 I

Another important constitutional convention governing federal-provincial relations concerned the amending formula. The Canadian Founders who drew up the BNA Act did not provide for a general amending formula. They simply assumed that future amendments would be made the same way the BNA Act itself was enacted — by the British Imperial Parliament. A convention was quickly established that the British Parliament would not change the BNA Act except at the request of the government of Canada. The role of the provinces in the amending process was not so simple to define. If Parliament could unilaterally amend the division of powers effected by sections 91-92, the provinces would be at the mercy of the federal government. To prevent this, a practice developed that for amendments directly affecting provincial powers, the consent of all the provinces would have to be obtained before any request was sent to England.

The precise status of this practice — whether it was a constitutional convention or merely a political courtesy on the part of Ottawa — was never clear. Provincial rights proponents insisted that it was a fundamental element of Canada's unwritten constitution. This claim was based on the "compact theory" of Confederation. This theory held that the BNA Act was essentially a contract between self-governing colonies, and that the new federal government was the product of this compact. Since it was the colonies who had made the contract in the first place, it could not be amended without their consent. As noted above, Quebec leaders developed their own version of the compact theory, which held that Quebec in particular had a right to a unilateral constitutional veto. In principle, Ottawa never conceded either of these claims, but in practice usually followed the convention until 1982.

What the federal government lost in disallowance, reservation, and amending powers, it made up through the explosive growth of its spending power and conditional grants after World War II. The federal government's ability to raise and thus spend money far outstrips that of the provinces. In the decades after World War II, the federal government effectively coopted large chunks of provincial jurisdiction by initiating over one hundred new social programs on a conditional, shared-cost basis. Billions of dollars of federal money were made available to the provinces for health, education, and welfare programs on the condition that the money be spent according to federal guidelines. While provincial leaders resented adopting policies and spending priorities made in Ottawa, they were even more reluctant to forgo the large federal grants. Little by little, the federal government has thus bought its way into large areas of provincial jurisdiction without any formal amendments to the constitution. This provincial grievance is one of the issues the Meech Lake Accord sought to address.

"Executive federalism" and its most visible event — the First Ministers Conference — have become mainstays of contemporary Canadian politics, but are nowhere mentioned in the written constitution. Executive federalism denotes the systematic meetings of federal and provincial administrators and politicians to coordinate national policies that straddle both levels of government. Executive federalism has developed independently of the courts, and is generally viewed as a better way to settle federal-provincial disputes — especially disputes involving complex economics and large sums of money. The uncertainty and zero-sum ("winner take all") character of litigation has led many politicians to prefer negotiation and compromise. While judicial review is unlikely to disappear, it is basically a complement to executive federalism, and certainly not a replacement.

To summarize, regionalism is the oldest but still the most vital force in Canadian politics. It is expressed and channelled primarily through the various institutions of federalism. Provincial governments pursue their interests both within the federal government and also against it. Courts have played a significant role in shaping the federal-provincial balance of power. The JCPC's work contributed to the decentralization of Canadian federalism. The modern (post-1949) Supreme Court of Canada has favoured a more centralist interpretation of the BNA Act. Non-judicial developments have been even more important. The decline of disallowance and reservation, the explosive post-war growth of the federal government's spending power, the development of executive federalism and First Ministers Conferences — all attest to the continued vitality of Canadian federalism. The most recent and most dramatic development in this evolution is the 1982 *Charter of Rights and Freedoms.*

I The Charter of Rights I and Freedoms

All liberal democracies are based on the twin principles of liberty and equality. The principle that "all people are by nature equal" means that no person (or group) has a right to govern another without the latter's consent. In the eighteenth century the principle of political equality was used to overthrow the historical claims of priests and kings to rule on the basis of alleged natural superiority. In the twentieth century, it rejects the legitimacy of both left and rightwing dictatorships, including the "dictatorship of the proletariat" as practiced by communist regimes. In practice, political equality means "government based on the consent of the governed," and thus some form

CANADIAN GOVERNMENT AND POLITICS

of majority-rule democracy. Political equality constitutes the democratic element of liberal democracy.

The principle of liberty denotes the "natural rights" of individuals — the rights to life, liberty and security of the person and property. All men and women are understood to possess these rights "by nature" — that is, independently of any specific statute or government. The purpose of government is to protect these rights, and no just government can violate them. The principle of liberty — of individual rights — represents the liberal element of liberal democracy.

There is thus a tension at the core of liberal democracy — a tension between equality and liberty. Equality demands that government be based on the consent of the governed — majority rule. Liberty requires that this same government respect the natural rights of all its citizens. The tension arises when "majority rule" produces policies that do not respect the rights of individuals or groups who are not part of the majority. The balancing of majority rule and minority rights is a practical problem that confronts all liberal democracies.

There have been two principal approaches to giving institutional expression to the principles of equality and liberty in modern liberal democracies: the British parliamentary model, and the American "separation of powers" model. Because of two major differences in the parliamentary and American systems, the courts in each system have very different functions and characteristics. The American model is ultimately based on and organized by a single basic document — a written constitution. By contrast, the Westminster model is based on an "unwritten constitution" — a combination of historically important statutes, the common law, and numerous unwritten conventions and usages. The second difference is that the "written constitution" of the Americans includes an enumeration of the fundamental rights and liberties of the individual against government, known collectively as the *Bill of Rights*. While individuals enjoy basically the same rights and freedoms under the British parliamentary model of democracy, they are not "spelled out" in any single, basic document of government, i.e., they are not "constitutionally entrenched." The results of these two differences is that in the American model of democracy, the courts, and especially the Supreme Court, play a much more explicit and more influential political role.

At Confederation in 1867, the government of Canada was basically modeled after the British parliamentary system. The one important exception was the federal form of the union of the Canadian provinces, and the defining of the forms and limits of this union in a single, written document. This aspect of Canadian government is important, because it thrust upon

| 52 |

THE LIVING CONSTITUTION

the courts the function of judicial review, or "umpire" of the federal system. Federalism aside, both levels of government in Canada were formed after the parliamentary model, which meant legislative supremacy within their respective spheres of jurisdiction.

Accordingly, Canada, until very recently, followed the British approach to the protection of civil liberty — parliamentary supremacy, the rule of law, and the conventions that support them. Inevitably the proximity of the United States has prompted constant comparisons. One of the most eloquent and forceful defences of the Anglo-Canadian approach to protecting civil liberties was given by the dean of Canadian political science, R. MacGregor Dawson. Dawson argued that unwritten constitutional conventions backed by public opinion are a more reliable support for civil liberties than a written Bill of Rights.[10] He was probably thinking of the American experience, where the constitutional requirement of "equal protection of the laws" had failed to prevent a century of mistreatment of and discrimination against Blacks in the American South. Similarly in Canada, the constitutional protection of French language rights in the province of Manitoba had been ignored by provincial governments for eighty years. Written constitutional rights appear to be more secure because their violation can be challenged in the courts. But the courts have no means to enforce their own decisions. Dawson's insight was that even the effectiveness of judicial protection of rights depends ultimately on public opinion. Without such support, constitutional guarantees become mere "parchment barriers," without real effect.

In the wake of World War II and the revelation of Communist and Nazi atrocities, Canadian political leaders became increasingly attracted to the American approach to protecting civil liberties. In 1960 the Diefenbaker government enacted the Canadian *Bill of Rights*. It took the form of a statute, not a constitutional amendment, and applied only to the federal government and not to the provinces. Partly because of dissatisfaction with this document and partly in response to the threat of Quebec separatism during the 1970's, the Trudeau government undertook a program of constitutional reform in 1978.

Prime Minister Trudeau's constitutional agenda included "patriating" the BNA Act, an amending formula, and a new Charter of Rights that applied to both levels of Canadian government. After a year and a half of political manoeuvering, confrontation, and finally compromise, all three objectives were achieved.

The adoption of a constitutionally entrenched Charter of Rights fundamentally altered the Canadian system of government by placing explicit

CANADIAN GOVERNMENT AND POLITICS

limitations on the law-making power of both levels of government. Parliament was no longer supreme; the constitution was. Or almost. Trudeau failed to have the Charter adopted in its original "pure" form. Attachment to the tradition of Parliamentary supremacy combined with provincial suspicion of a centralizing Supreme Court were too strong, and forced an important compromise — the section 33 "legislative override." Section 33 allows a government (federal or provincial) to protect a statute from judicial nullification by declaring that it shall operate "notwithstanding" certain sections of the Charter.[11] Section 33 thus preserves a qualified form of parliamentary supremacy.

THE LEGISLATIVE OVERRIDE CONTROVERSY

Section 33 was — and remains — controversial. Its critics contend that it undermines the Charter. What is the point of constitutionally entrenching fundamental rights and freedoms, say the critics, if a government can violate them by simply invoking section 33? This criticism is valid if we assume that section 33 applies directly to specific Charter rights. While true in theory, in practice this assumption is problematic, because it ignores the crucial role of judicial interpretation in giving effect to the Charter. The Charter is not self-interpreting. Most Charter rights are broadly worded and capable of more than one plausible meaning. Judges must choose among competing interpretations. Unfortunately, different judges often choose different — and contradictory-interpretations. Section 33 critics thus make two false assumptions: that the "true meaning" of Charter rights is either self-evident or can be discovered; and that judges are infallible in discerning this meaning.

The problem of ambiguous Charter meaning and judicial discretion is well illustrated by the most famous Charter case to date — *Morgentaler v. The Queen*,[12] and its "pro-life" counterpart, *Borowski v. The Queen*.[13] Both men challenged the validity of Canada's 1969 abortion law, but for opposite reasons. The 1969 law prohibited abortions except when the pregnancy threatened the "life or health" of the mother, as determined by a committee of doctors at an accredited hospital. Dr. Morgentaler argued that the prohibitory section of the law violated the woman's right to liberty and security of the person. Mr. Borowski argued that the permissive section of the law violated the right to life of the unborn child or fetus.

Both men based their arguments on section 7 of the Charter. Section 7 states:

Everyone has the right to life, liberty and security of the person and the right not to be deprived thereof except in accordance with the principles of fundamental justice.

In other words, both men relied on the same section of the Charter to support completely opposite conclusions. Which argument is correct?

In the end, Morgentaler won, but not for the reasons he wanted. In January, 1988, the Supreme Court ruled 5-2 that the abortion law violated the procedural fairness protected by section 7. Only one justice — the sole woman on the Court — ruled that section 7 gave women a constitutional right to abortion. The two dissenters pointed out that abortion is not mentioned in section 7 and that judges are not free to add unintended meaning to the Charter. A year later, the Supreme Court dismissed the Borowski appeal for technical reasons without deciding the substantive issue of whether a fetus/unborn child is a "person" and thus protected by section 7.

The division of the Court in the *Morgentaler* case illustrates how it is the discretion of the judges and not the actual language of the Charter that often determines the result.

When constitutional language is vague and the Court is divided, it is the judges who are speaking, not the constitution. When in addition the outcome significantly affects important public policy, there is no reason to consider the constitutional issue permanently settled by the decision of nine (or five) unelected, unaccountable judges. In the absence of a clearly worded constitutional requirement, it would make no more sense to allow the Court to prohibit all restrictions on abortion than it would to allow the Court to prohibit abortions altogether. This would be to allow constitutional supremacy to degenerate into judicial supremacy. A society that allowed an appointed court to impose either of these options would cease to be self-governing, that is, governed by the consent of the governed.

Viewed in this light, section 33 seems more positive. It is not a direct attack on rights, but a check on the judges' interpretation of the Charter — a form of "legislative review of judicial review." Just as judicial review serves as a check on legislative error or excess, so the "legislative override" serves as a check on judicial error or excess. Stated differently, section 33 prevents constitutional supremacy from degenerating into judicial supremacy. It places joint responsibility for protecting constitutional rights on legislatures and the courts. The Canadian people, armed with the power of the vote, remain the ultimate judges of the outcome of this partnership.

Canada thus finds itself today almost equidistant between the British and

American models of liberal democracy, with their differing approaches to civil liberties. The debate over which form of liberal democracy is best designed to protect the liberties of its citizens remains very much alive. The truth of this debate most probably lies somewhere between the two contending positions, for as Dawson pointed out:

> Written law and the conventions will normally complement one another, and each becomes necessary to the proper functioning of the other.[14]

THE CHARTER AT WORK

The immediate effect of the Charter was not the creation of new rights, but a new way of making decisions about rights, in which the courts play a more central and authoritative role.[15] Most of the rights and freedoms enumerated in the Charter existed in one form or another prior to 1982. The Fundamental Freedoms (s. 2) and the Legal Rights (ss. 7-1 4) reflect similar rights in the 1960 *Bill of Rights*, which in turn codified the conventions and common law inferred by the Preamble to the BNA Act. Most other Charter rights had an earlier existence in the form of statutes, convention and common law. What the Charter did was to transfer primary responsibility for the articulation of these rights to the courts.

This explains one of the most important effects of the Charter — the creation of a new forum for interest group activity. Historically, Canadian interest groups have concentrated their lobbying activities at the cabinet and senior levels of the bureaucracy, and rarely used litigation as a political tactic. This was predictable. The absence of constitutionally entrenched rights deprived the courts of any supervisory role over legislative policy-making, except for assuring that the limits of federalism were respected. Because of Canada's strong historical attachment to the practice of parliamentary supremacy, attempts to change laws through the courts were viewed as illegitimate. With the advent of the Charter, all this has changed. Interest groups that fail to achieve their policy objectives through the traditional political party and bureaucratic channels can now turn to the courts.

Interest group use of Charter litigation as a political tactic can take several different forms. The most direct is for the interest group to turn its cause into a case and go to court itself. This was the approach used by "Operation Dismantle," a coalition of peace and anti-nuclear groups that challenged, unsuccessfully, the government's decision to allow the United States to test the "Cruise missile" over northern and western Canada.[16] A successful example of direct litigation was the National Citizens' Coalition's Charter challenge to the "anti-PAC" clause of the Canada Elections Act.[17] An Alberta Court of Queen's Bench ruled that the Act's restrictions on election expenditures by "political action committees" unaffiliated with any political party violated the freedom of expression of these groups.

A second way for interest groups to participate in Charter litigation is to pay the legal expenses of individuals who are willing to challenge laws that the groups would like to see nullified. In the two major abortion cases discussed above, both Borowski and Morgentaler had the financial backing of national interest groups on opposing sides of the abortion issue. Campaign Life and the Canadian Abortion Rights Action League (CARAL) spent over $350,000 each to allow their respective "champions" to fight their way to the Supreme Court. A national feminist organization founded in 1985, LEAF (Legal Education and Action Fund) pursues an active strategy of supporting Charter litigants in cases involving sexual equality issues. The federal government's "Court Challenges Program" also provides funds to groups who litigate minority language rights and equality issues under the Charter.

The third and final way for interest groups to participate in Charter politics is to "intervene" in appeal court hearings. An "intervener" is a third party (i.e. other than the Crown and the actual litigant) that the court permits to present legal arguments. Acting as interveners, interest groups can put forward arguments and evidence that support their preferred interpretation of Charter rights. LEAF is a frequent intervener in section 15 equality cases. The Canadian Civil Liberties Association (CCLA) also frequently intervenes in cases raising Charter issues that it considers important. The presence of interveners is usually a good indicator that the case involves political issues that transcend the legal dispute before the court. In the Morgentaler and Borowski cases, for example, there were interveners representing both pro-choice and pro-life positions on the abortion issue.

As recently as 1975, one of Canada's leading historians could accurately state that Canadian "judges and lawyers, supported by the press and public opinion, reject any concept of the courts as positive instruments in the political process. [P]olitical action outside the party-parliamentary structure tends automatically to be suspect — not the least because it smacks of Americanism."[18] The extensive interest group use of Charter litigation — much of it actually financed by government — shows how much has changed since 1982.

Interest groups such as LEAF and the CCLA have also been pleased by another Charter-induced change — a dramatic surge in judicial activism. In a sharp reversal of pre-Charter practice, Canadian judges — led by the Supreme Court — have been much more willing to override legislative decisions and to declare federal and provincial laws invalid. Under the 1960 **Bill of Rights**, the Supreme Court had exercised great self-restraint — the opposite of judicial activism — nullifying just one (quite insignificant) statute in twenty-two years. By contrast, the Supreme Court has nullified eighteen statutes (8 federal, 10 provincial) in the first eight years under the Charter. Another good index of judicial activism since 1982 is the number of victories for Charter litigants before the Supreme Court — 38 (in 102 decisions) compared to just five victories (in 35 cases) under the 1960 **Bill of Rights**.

The main policy impact of the Charter has been in the area of criminal law enforcement, accounting for two-thirds of all Charter decisions. The Supreme Court has given a broad interpretation to the right to counsel (s.10.b) and the right against unreasonable search and seizure (s.8). In a sharp reversal of pre-Charter practice, the Court has established a policy of excluding evidence from a trial if it was obtained in a manner that violated the rights of the accused, no matter how good the evidence. The effect of the Court's activism has been to enhance substantially the procedural defences of those accused of crimes — a result applauded by civil libertarians. The cost has been a proportional decrease in the efficiency of law enforcement and crime control — a trend that worries others.

Beyond the criminal law field, the policy impact of the Charter has been random. Reference has already been made to the Supreme Court's two abortion decisions, as a result of which there was for a long while no regulation of abortion. The Mulroney government had twice tried to introduce a new abortion law, before it insisted on party discipline in the House to accomplish to task. As a result of the National Citizens' Coalition successful challenge to the **Canada Election Act**, there is still no regulation of non-party expenditures during federal elections. This turned out to be important during the November, 1988 election, as it allowed pro–free trade groups to spend millions of dollars on political advertising in the closing weeks of the campaign. This support certainly helped Prime Minister Mulroney and his Tories to their subsequent electoral triumph. In another contentious policy area, the Supreme Court's two "Sunday closing" decisions[19] have contributed to the significant increase in wide-open Sunday shopping across Canada.

Quebec has been the province most affected by the Charter. As soon as the Charter was adopted, the Quebec Protestant School Board challenged the education provisions of Bill 101, the **Charter of the French Language**.

| 58 |

Bill 101 was — and remains — the centrepiece of Quebec nationalist policy. Adopted shortly after the Parti Québecois came to power in November, 1976, Bill 101 was intended to preserve the primacy of French language and culture in Quebec. At the time the Charter was adopted, René Lévesque had bitterly denounced section 23, which was clearly intended to strike down the education policy embedded in Bill 101. "No self-respecting Quebec government," he declared, "could ever abandon the smallest fraction of this fundamental right to protect the only French island in the English-speaking sea of the North American continent."

The education sections of Bill 101 restricted access to English-language education within the province. In 1985 the Supreme Court struck down these restrictions as a violation of the section 23 language education rights of the English-speaking minority in Quebec.[20] Because section 23 is excluded from the scope of the section 33 legislative override, Quebec had no alternative but to accept the Court's decision.

Three years later, the Supreme Court struck down another section of Bill 101 — the "French-only" public signs requirements.[21] This provision prohibited the use of English in commercial signs — billboards, storefront advertising, and the like. Quebec anglophones, especially the 650,000 living in Montreal, considered it oppressive and humiliating, and challenged it as a violation of the Charter right to freedom of expression. Quebec nationalists considered the "French only" rule essential to preserving the "French face" of Quebec, and harshly denounced the Supreme Court's decision. The recently elected Liberal government of Robert Bourassa — contrary to promises it had made to anglophone voters in the 1985 election — gave in to nationalist sentiment and invoked the section 33 legislative override to reinstate the "French only" public signs policy. This override of the Supreme Court's decision infuriated many people in English Canada, and put in jeopardy the ratification of the Meech Lake Accord.

The *Quebec Protestant School Board* decision realized Quebec nationalists' worst fears about the Charter. Coming on the heels of the (perceived) loss of its traditional constitutional veto, the decision further isolated Quebec from the rest of English Canada. To protest its exclusion from the **Constitution Act, 1982**, the Quebec government had boycotted all subsequent First Ministers conferences dealing with constitutional issues.

Quebec's absence was not only regrettable in itself, but also prevented any progress on other constitutional issues such as Senate reform, much to the dismay of its supporters. It was generally recognized that no Quebec government would consent to the **Constitution Act, 1982** until it regained, among other things, its control over the language of education within the

CANADIAN GOVERNMENT AND POLITICS

province. Concern over Quebec's growing isolation and the desire to bring it back within the constitutional fold led to the Meech Lake Accord of April, 1987.

I The Meech Lake Accord I

The Meech Lake Accord is a set of constitutional amendments proposed by Prime Minister Mulroney in the spring of 1987. It was the result of a First Ministers Conference held at the federal government's facilities at Meech Lake, 80 kilometres from Ottawa. The Prime Minister had gained the consent of all ten provincial premiers (a rare feat) for a document whose primary purpose was to gain Quebec's endorsement of the *Constitution Act, 1982*, and thus end its political isolation. As Prime Minister Mulroney triumphantly observed when he announced the Accord: "Tonight Canada is whole again, the Canadian family is together again, and the nation is one again."

The initial reaction to Meech Lake was one of national celebration, especially in Quebec. Quebec Premier Robert Bourassa, who had negotiated the agreement, hailed it as "one of the greatest political victories of [Quebec] history." The Accord was quickly approved by Parliament when it was endorsed by both opposition parties, the Liberals and the New Democrats.

Eight of the ten provinces quickly followed suit, but this initial burst of enthusiasm soon dissipated, as a growing chorus of critics attacked the Accord. The basic thrust of this criticism was that the Prime Minister had bargained away too many of the powers of the federal government, mainly to Quebec but also to the other provinces. The result, according to the critics, would be an enfeebled federal government, incapable of coordinating national policies or protecting the rights of individuals and minorities. Former Prime Minister Trudeau, the architect of the *Constitution Act, 1982*, came out of retirement to spark the attack on Meech Lake.

> Those Canadians who fought for a single Canada, bilingual and multicultural, can say good bye to their dream. We are henceforth to have two Canadas each defined in terms of its language.

Trudeau's stinging attack served as a catalyst for mounting opposition to Meech Lake. The amendment juggernaut was slowed down when new provincial governments with leaders opposed to Meech Lake were elected in New Brunswick and Manitoba. Meanwhile, the chorus of critics was growing. Feminists, ethnic groups, French minorities outside of Quebec,

THE LIVING CONSTITUTION

the English minority within Quebec, human rights activists, civil libertarians, and supporters of Senate reform all found fault with the Accord.

The amending process ground to a complete halt in December, 1988, when the Bourassa government invoked the section 33 power to override the Supreme Court's decision in the *French-Only Public Signs* case. The premiers of the two remaining hold-out provinces, New Brunswick and Manitoba, abruptly canceled scheduled legislative hearings on Meech Lake, and announced that they would not reconsider the Accord until Bourassa repealed his new anti-English measures. Subsequently, the newly elected Liberal premier of Newfoundland, Clyde Wells, announced that he intended to repeal (and did so in April, 1990) that province's earlier approval of the Accord. As the three year deadline for ratification approached — June 23, 1990 — with continuing deadlock, both Mulroney and Bourassa issued dire warnings that national unity was threatened if Meech Lake was not approved.

OPPOSITION TO MEECH LAKE

The controversy over Meech Lake was about both *how* it was made and *what* it would do. That is, critics objected both to its process and its substance. Objections to the process by which the Accord was reached focussed on its closed, secretive and undemocratic character. There was no hint prior to the announcement of the Accord that the First Ministers were considering significant amendments to the Constitution. There was thus no prior public discussion or input from interested groups. Once the Accord was announced, public discussion was irrelevant, as all eleven premiers rejected the idea of any changes, describing the Accord as a "seamless web," to be accepted or rejected as an indivisible "package." While the approval of each legislature was required, this was initially considered little more than a formality, as each premier could invoke party discipline to ensure passage. It was basically a "deal" struck in private between the eleven First Ministers without any public input either before or after. Meech Lake was presented to the Canadian people as a "done deal," to be accepted gratefully or otherwise.

While this approach to constitution making was consistent with the past practice of executive federalism, it did not sit well with the new, more democratic political spirit ushered in by the Charter of Rights. The Charter had the effect of conferring new rights, new status or both on a number of groups in Canadian society. These included women, aboriginal peoples, ethnic groups, French minorities outside of Quebec, and the English minority within Quebec. These new "Charter Canadians" felt they had an important stake in the constitution, and they were angry that it was going

| 61 |

to be changed without any consultation or input from them. This anger was heightened by their perception that the substance of Meech Lake also threatened their recently acquired rights and status.

The substance of the Accord reflects the five demands set forth by the Bourassa government as a condition for Quebec's acceptance of the **Constitution Act, 1982**. These five conditions were: constitutional recognition of Quebec as a "distinct society"; restoring Quebec's historical constitutional veto power; the right to opt out from new federal spending programs in areas of exclusive provincial jurisidiction, with full financial compensation; a role in the appointment of Supreme Court judges; and greater control over immigration into the province.

In its final form, Meech Lake met all five demands, but extended the last four to include the other nine provinces as well. This result is explained by the other provinces' jealous resistance to any special status for Quebec. Since Bourassa's demands were defined as the minimal conditions for Quebec's consent, Prime Minister Mulroney broke the deadlock by extending to all the provinces the special powers demanded by Quebec.

While this compromise made possible the 1987 agreement, had it been ratified by June 1990 it would have produced a decidedly more decentralist form of federalism. It would have meant that no province could be forced to accept a new federal spending program or a constitutional amendment to which it objected. This would obviously have made amending the written constitution more difficult. The provincial power to nominate Supreme Court judges would have made it more difficult for the federal government to exercise any indirect influence over the Court's jurisprudence through the appointment of "centralists" or Charter activists.

The provinces' new power over immigration would have probably been significant only for Quebec, which sought to encourage a high percentage of French-speaking immigrants. The practical effect of the Accord's recognition of Quebec as a "distinct society" with the right "to protect and to promote" this distinctness is uncertain. Its meaning would have ultimately depended on judicial interpretation. Quebec nationalists said — or hoped — that it would have produced the opposite outcome in the two Charter cases nullifying the education and public signs sections of Bill 101. Critics of the "distinct society" clause — especially Quebec anglophones — were against it for this very reason.

Opposition to Meech Lake clustered around several related issues. The most widely shared criticism is that Meech Lake would have fatally weakened the federal government by transferring too much power to the provinces. This criticism remains pervasive among groups who favour and/or benefit from a strong central government and uniform national policies. This group overlaps considerably with a second bastion of anti-Meech sentiment — the various feminist, native, ethnic, linguistic and other minorities who are the primary beneficiaries of the Charter of Rights. These Charter Canadians look to the courts for policy leadership and distrust legislatures, especially provincial legislatures. They felt threatened by the enhanced powers of Quebec and the other provincial governments, not least of all because of the control that Meech Lake would have given them over the nomination of Supreme Court judges.

A third and distinct source of opposition to Meech Lake came from the supporters of "Triple E" Senate reform. The Triple E movement wants to see the Senate reformed to be "elected, equal and effective." Equal refers to an equal number of representatives from each province, similar to the U.S. Senate. Effective means that the reformed Senate would be a meaningful part of the law-making process. Supporters of Senate reform believe that this is the only way that the less populous provinces from the West and Maritimes will achieve fair representation and influence in the federal government. A Senate based on equal representation for each province would mean a significant reduction in the proportion of Senators from Quebec and Ontario. Currently Senate reform is possible under the "7/50" amending formula. Meech Lake would have required unanimity. Senate reformers felt that once Meech Lake was adopted, Quebec would no longer have any incentive to give up its large quota of Senators and would use its new veto to block Senate reform.

I The Old Constitution I
versus the New

The Meech Lake affair can be interpreted as two different constitutions battling for control of the Canadian state.[22] One is the old constitution, with its roots in Confederation. The other dates only from 1982. The old constitution is the constitution of the compact theory — the constitution of governments, federalism, and French-English dualism. Since this constitution belongs to the governments, it can be changed by the governments — by First Ministers Conferences. Under it, constitutional politics is mainly a process of bargaining among political elites. Implicitly this old constitution has always recognized the special status of Quebec. Meech Lake merely makes this explicit through the "distinct society" clause.

The new constitution is the constitution of the Charter. It is concerned

CANADIAN GOVERNMENT AND POLITICS

with individuals and their rights and freedoms. It is also concerned with group rights, but not in the old sense of only the French and English. The new constitution is multicultural, and asserts the equal status of ethnic Canadians and native peoples with the two "founding" peoples. Since this new constitution belongs to "the people," it cannot be amended without their participation and consent.

Meech Lake was made by the partisans of the old constitution. It was attacked primarily by partisans of the new constitution. These "Charter Canadians" object to Meech Lake not only because of its content but also because they were excluded from the process. A constitution that belongs to the people, they argue, should not be amended unilaterally by eleven first ministers.

The fate of Meech Lake suggests just how powerful this new constitutional vision has become. Only ten years ago it would have been unthinkable that a proposal endorsed by all eleven first ministers, plus the leaders of both opposition parties, could not become law. The unthinkable has become the new reality. The old way of conducting political business in Canada — through a closed circle of governmental elites — is being challenged. To the extent that this challenge succeeds, it marks a more liberal, more individualistic, more democratic Canada.

A more democratic Canada, however, risks being a more divided Canada. Because it is individualistic, the new constitution does not attach much value to "provincial rights." Its emphasis on multiculturalism erodes the preferred status of the English and French cultures. And to the extent that it is more participatory, it is less capable of the compromise and accommodation that has kept Canada together for over one hundred years. In a democracy sovereignty rests with the people, not with governments or founding peoples. This more democratic style of politics is likely to reject proposals like Meech Lake and to insist that Quebec be treated "like the others." Are Quebec and the other provinces prepared to accept a new, more equal, less powerful place in Canadian politics? Or will the defeat of Meech Lake rekindle the fires the Quebec separatism?

I Conclusion: Canada's Unresolved I Question: Who Shall Govern?

In the wake of the Charter of Rights and the defeat of the Meech Lake Accord, Canada faces constitutional challenges hardly less difficult than those that confronted the Founders one hundred and thirty years earlier.

THE LIVING CONSTITUTION

Some of these are genuinely new issues, but most are simply new versions of the same issues that shaped Confederation. The challenge of Canadian federalism — the quest to strike an acceptable balance between provincial and federal governments — remains central. This challenge is inextricably linked to the status of Quebec. How distinctive is Quebec, and how should this be recognized in terms of special powers and privileges? In theory, the issue of Senate reform is the question of how best to represent the interests of the less populous provinces within the working of the federal government. In practice, it is really a question of how much of its current influence in Parliament Quebec is willing to give up.

Even the seemingly new issues — such as the Charter and the section 33 controversy — are rooted in the politics of federalism. If Canadians' first loyalties are to their provincial communities, then the section 33 override appears as a legitimate means for provinces to protect their distinctive ways of life from the centralizing and homogenizing influences of the Charter. If, on the other hand, Canadians' primary allegiance is to Canada and the rights enshrined in the Charter, section 33 becomes suspect if not subversive. It is not by accident that the two most ardent defenders of section 33 have been the governments of Quebec and Alberta.

Canada's constitutional odyssey thus continues.[23] Generation after generation, Canadian leaders have tried to negotiate acceptable compromises on such issues as the federal division of powers, an amending formula, national institutions and fundamental rights and freedoms. But beneath this institutional restlessness lies a more fundamental and unresolved question: Who should govern, and for what ends? This is really the constitutional question for every country. Once it is settled, the institutional questions can be more easily resolved.

Unlike the United States, Canada has been spared a violent revolution and a bloody civil war. In one sense, this is an obvious blessing. But in another, it has deprived Canada of a genuine "founding" and a shared sense of common purpose. As Peter Russell has written,[24]

> Canadians have not yet constituted themselves as a people: they have not yet accomplished that profound but essential act of a constitutionally self-governing people — to agree on what they are and want to be as a people.

Unlike other modern democracies, Canada has not chosen the "one state, one nation" model. From the start, we have remained one state, and at least two nations.

| 65 |

The Charter of Rights may be understood as an attempt to solve this challenge — to define Canadians, and thus Canada, as a society of individuals whose primary allegiance is to the rights, principles and policies embodied in the Charter. The problem is that the constitutional vision of the Charter conflicts with several other well entrenched traditions in the Canadian identity: parliamentary supremacy, federalism and — most of all — the historically unique status of Quebec. The Charter thus holds out the promise of resolving Canada's quest for constitutional self-definition, but at the possible expense of losing Quebec. Would Canada still be Canada without Quebec?

Certainly many Canadians would agree with George Grant, one of Canada's best known political philosophers. According to Grant, "The keystone of a Canadian nation is the French fact. . . . English-speaking Canadians who desire the survival of their nation have to cooperate with those who seek the continuance of Franco American civilization."[25] From this perspective, the cure would be worse than the disease.

In reality, the alternatives are probably not this stark. Quebec is willing to live with the Charter, but only with section 33. Quebec wants the Meech Lake Accord, or its equivalent. The Accord has been rejected, for the moment. What compromises and accommodations can be worked out in the coming years remains to be seen. This is the constitutional challenge of the nineties, the next phase of Canada's living constitution.

NOTES

¹ Other acts included in Canada's written constitution are: Manitoba Act, 1870; Rupert's Land and North West Territory Order (1870); British Columbia Terms of Union (1871); Prince Edward Island Terms of Union (1871); Alberta Act (1905); Saskatchewan Act (1905); Newfoundland Act (1949); Parliament of Canada Act, 1875; and the Statute of Westminster, 1931. See the Schedule to the Constitution Act, 1982 for a complete listing.

² This quotation and this theme are taken from Allan Cairns, "The Living Canadian Constitution," in Douglas E. Williams (ed.), *Constitution, Government and Society in Canada: Selected Essays by Alan Cairns* (Toronto: McClelland and Stewart, 1988) pp. 27-42, p. 31.

³ Ibid.

⁴ Under section 41 of the Constitution Act, 1982, certain types of constitutional amendments continued to require unanimous support, thus giving each province a veto. These areas included: the offices of the Queen, Governor General and Lieutenant-Governor; the right to a minimum number of MPs; sections dealing with language rights; and the composition of the Supreme Court.

⁵ The 1982 Charter of Rights entrenched all of these "fundamental freedoms" and democratic rights in the written constitution. It is important to realize that these freedoms existed and flourished prior to the Charter. What the Charter changed was that these rights and freedoms are row subject to judicial interpretation and enforcement.

⁶ *Reference re Anti-Inflation Act,* [1976] 2 S.C.R. 373.

⁷ *CIGOL v. Saskatchewan,* [1978] 2 S.C.R. 545; *Central Canada Potash Co. Ltd. and Attorney General of Canada v. Saskatchewan,* [1979] 1 S.C.R. 42.

⁸ *Public Service Board v. Dionne,* [1978] 2 S.C.R. 191.

⁹ [1981] 1 S.C.R. 753

¹⁰ R. MacGregor Dawson, *The Government of Canada,* 4th ed. (Toronto: University of Toronto Press, 1963), p. 70.

¹¹ The section 33 "notwithstanding" clause can be applied only to the following Charter rights: Fundamental Freedoms (s.2); Legal Rights (55.7-14); Equality Rights (5.15). It cannot be used against Democratic Rights (ss.3-5); Mobility Rights (s.6); Language Rights (ss.16-22); or Minority Language Education Rights (s.23).

¹² [1988] 1 S.C.R. 30

¹³ [1989] 1 S.C.R. 343.

¹⁴ Dawson, *The Government of Canada,* p. 71.

¹⁵ This is the central theme of Peter H. Russell, "The Effect of a Charter of Rights on the Policy-Making Role of the Canadian Courts," *Canadian Public Administration* 25 (1982), 1-33.

¹⁶ *Operation Dismantle v. The Queen,* [1985] 1 S.C.R. 441.

¹⁷ *National Citizens' Coalition v. A.-G. Canada* [1985] WWR 436.

¹⁸ Kenneth McNaught, "Political Trials and the Canadian Political Tradition," in M.L. Friedland (ed.), *Courts and Trials: A Multi-Disciplinary Approach* (Toronto:

| 67 |

University of Toronto Press, 1975) pp. 137-161.

[19] *The Queen* v. *Big M Drug Mart Ltd.* [1985] 1 S.C.R. 295; and *Edwards Books and Art Ltd.* [1986] 2 S.C.R. 713 struck down the federal Lord's Day Act, while *Edwards Books* upheld Ontario's secular "day of rest" Sunday closing law. Notwithstanding the legal result, *Edwards* did nothing to stop the trend toward Sunday shopping in Ontario and other provinces.

[20] *Attorney-General of Quebec* v. *Quebec Association of Protestant School Boards* [1984] 2 S.C.R.66;

[21] *A.-G. Quebec* v. *Ford* [1988] 2 S.C.R. 712; *Devine* v. *A.-G. Quebec* [1988] 2 S.C.R. 790.

[22] This is the thesis developed by Allan Cairns, "The Limited Constitutional Vision of Meech Lake," in K.E. Swinton and C.J Rogerson (eds.), *Competing Constitutional Visions: The Meech Lake Accord* (Toronto: Carswell, 1988) pp. 247-62.

[23] Both this concept and the analysis that follows are taken from Peter H. Russell's essay, "Canada's Constitutional Odyssey," A Lecture delivered at Princeton University, March 7, 1985. Unpublished.

[24] Ibid.

[25] George P. Grant, *Lament for a Nation* (Toronto: McClelland and Stewart, 1965) p. 20.

THE LIVING CONSTITUTION

ANNOTATED READINGS

Cairns, Allan. "The Living Canadian Constitution," in Douglas E. Williams, ed. *Constitution, Government and Society in Canada: Selected Essays by Alan Cairns.* Toronto: McClelland and Stewart, 1988: 27-42. Cairns presents a more sophisticated and detailed analysis of many of the themes and subjects covered in this chapter. Written in 1970, it does not cover the Charter of Rights or the Meech Lake Accord.

_____. "The Limited Constitutional Vision of Meech Lake," in K.E. Swinton and C.J. Rogerson, eds., *Competing Constitutional Visions: The Meech Lake Accord.* Toronto: Carswell, 1988: 247-62. This is the best of analysis of how and why the Meech Lake Accord so divided Canada.

Morton, F.L. "The Political Impact of the Canadian Charter of Rights and Freedoms." *Canadian Journal of Political Science,* (March 1987): 31-55. Morton surveys how the Charter has changed the practice of politics in Canada since 1982.

Gibbins, Roger. ed. *Meech Lake and Canada: Perspectives from the West.* Edmonton: Academic Printing and Publishing, 1988. A collection of essays that captures the various perspectives — both pro and con — on the Meech Lake Accord.

Grant, George P. *Lament for a Nation.* Toronto: McClelland and Stewart, 1965. The most insightful and interesting investigation of Canada's struggle for political self-definition.

Romanow, Roy, John Whyte and Howard Leeson, *Canada Notwithstanding: The Making of the Constitution. 1976-1982.* Toronto: Carswell-Methuen, 1984. This is the best history and analysis of the politics that resulted in the Constitution Act, 1982.

Russell, Peter H. "Introduction," pp. 3-28, in Russell, Knopff and Morton, *Federalism and the Charter.* Ottawa: Carleton University Press, 1989. This is the best introduction to the work of the Supreme Court in the development of Canadian federalism, and, more recently, the Charter of Rights.

| CHAPTER 4 |

THE ATLANTIC PROVINCES:
AN ENIGMA?

AGAR ADAMSON

Atlantic Canada might well be described as a conundrum, or at least as a labyrinth of complexities. On the one hand, there are the statistics, such as unemployment, outward migration, the need for federal grants, the problem of the fishery, and rural poverty, all of which have contributed to the formation of a rather conservative cynical society in a region which may have already experienced its most productive economic days. In other words, Atlantic Canada is a region which has not recently participated fully in the economic growth of the nation.

On the other hand, you have the following description of the region by Dalton Camp who, paraphrasing from the *Report of the Royal Commission on Canada's Economic Prospects* (the Gordon Report of 1957), writes that while Atlantic Canadians

> could never expect to have it quite so good as Canadians elsewhere, there were compensations. These were listed as (1) the close proximity of fishing holes, duck blinds and curling rinks, and (2) the historic, hard-earned right not to work overly much. Gordon's observations outraged Maritimers, and rightly so. They did not wish that kind of information given out.[1]

Reality, as this discussion will endeavour to illustrate, lies somewhere between these two poles.

I The Setting I

In other regions of Canada politics is a fact of life which, like death and taxes, must be endured. But in Atlantic Canada politics is the very bread of life. In the Atlantic Provinces, especially in the three Maritime provinces, politics is followed literally from the cradle to the grave. Furthermore, nowhere else in Canada, with the possible exception of the Territories, are the inhabitants as dependent upon government for employment and social welfare assistance as they are in this region. Similarly, the four provincial governments are, per capita, more dependent on the federal government for assistance than are the other six.

Federal money of one form of another (Atlantic Canada Opportunity Agency [ACOA] grants, equalization grants, Established Program Financing [EPF], DRIE grants, other federal grants, military bases, public works, old age pension, unemployment insurance, etc.) accounts for more than half of the economy of the region. Consequently, Atlantic Canada is deeply influenced by federal policy as witnessed by the reaction to the 1989 federal budget. The "cutbacks" in that budget (base closures, changes within ACOA's budget, changes in certain federal grants, reduced subsidies to VIA rail, etc.) will have a greater per capita impact on this region than on any other section of the nation.

Historically it is true that governments in the region have been reluctant to openly confront the federal government. Similarly, the electorate for some time did not wish to bite the hand that fed it. In fact, 62.2 percent of respondents to a questionnaire distributed to delegates to the 1986 Nova Scotia Liberal Leadership Convention thought that it was more beneficial for that province to have the same party in office in Halifax as in Ottawa than to have different parties in power.[2] Nevertheless, an inspection of recent election results illustrates this region, like the others, has adopted "the Underhill theory" of counterbalance.[3] This theory, simply stated, is that Canadians desire to have a different party in power at the national level than in their province, or as Underhill put it, "Canadians desire to have the opposition in the provincial capitals not in Ottawa." The most recent Atlantic examples of this theory are Prince Edward Island and Newfoundland, both in 1989.

Certain premiers, most notably Brian Peckford but also Frank McKenna,

Clyde Wells and Joe Ghiz, have openly challenged the federal government's stance on a number of issues including natural resource development, free trade, and the Meech Lake Constitutional Accord. Others, like Richard Hatfield, John Buchanan, Robert Stanfield and J.R. Smallwood, preferred quiet diplomacy no matter the colour of the federal government of the day. Which policy has been most effective is open to debate.

I History I

Atlantic Canada is one of the earliest settled regions of the nation but has not benefitted from overseas immigration during the 20th century. Consequently, one is dealing with an established citizenry many of whom can trace their roots back several generations within the same community. Regional loyalties are fiercely maintained as witnessed by the region's reluctance to promote maritime union.[4]

The region has seen many of its inhabitants migrate to other sections of Canada or to the United States. "Going down the road" is a fact of life in Atlantic Canada. The reason for this is the lack of employment opportunities within the region. Recently there has been a reversal of this trend and some people are returning, bringing with them new ideas and new concepts. Within the region, as elsewhere, there has been a shift from the rural to the urban cores. This internal migration has led to the growth of the Halifax metropolitan region, Saint John, and St. John's.

The region has not been blessed with an abundance of natural resources. Historically, the principal resource industries have been the fishery, pulp and paper, base metals, lumber, coal, agriculture, and in the case of New Brunswick and Labrador hydroelectric power. Except for the latter, these resources have been buffeted by world markets and fluctuating prices. The discovery of hydrocarbons off the coasts of Newfoundland and Nova Scotia has given those provinces hope that there is an economic eldorado in their future, but to date these resources remain to be developed.

In Nova Scotia the dream goes on as one correspondent aptly noted: "Energy has become synonymous with opiate to the unemployed in Nova Scotia, where provincial officials assure residents about once a month that one or another of several multi-billion-dollar energy schemes is viable and will create thousands of jobs."[5] They fail to add that most of the jobs will only be in the construction phase of the projects.

Unlike the prairies which are so dependent upon a single crop, wheat, Atlantic Canada is dependent on several crops, though the rise and fall of

THE ATLANTIC PROVINCES: AN ENIGMA?

the fishery can be compared to the rise and fall of wheat in the West. On the prairies, poverty is noticeable when the wheat crop fails. In Atlantic Canada, the poverty is of a less spectacular nature but is more constant and grinds down the inhabitants.

If the West is said to have had an economic handicap, so has the East. Transportation costs, coupled with Sir John A. Macdonald's national tariff policies, made it not only difficult for regional products to be competitive in central Canadian markets, but at the same time the Maritimes lost many of their pre-Confederation foreign markets. Of the impact of the tariff, W.A. Mackintosh wrote, "in the Maritime Provinces the effect was in the direction of accelerating the contraction of exports and of accentuating falling population and declining value of resources in those export industries which could not turn to the domestic market."[6]

In 1867 Nova Scotia was considered to be a "have" province, but because of changes in technology (steam replaced sail, oil and natural gas replaced coal) it soon became a province dependent on federal government fiscal transfers as it had nothing to replace the "lost" industries.

Changes in climate and technology, as well as politics, led to the decision to keep the St. Lawrence River open year round to Montreal, thus damaging the economies of Halifax and Saint John. The construction of the St. Lawrence Seaway further injured the Maritime economy. The three Maritime provinces did not benefit from the opening of the northern and western territories, nor were they compensated for the admission of new provinces. Whether or not they should have been is another question for another time.

The growth of the Canadian population, particularly west of the Ottawa River, means that the Maritimes have lost much of the political clout they had in 1867, particularly in the House of Commons, but also in the Senate, the Supreme Court of Canada, and the federal public service.

I Economic Development I

The issue of economic development is the mainspring of politics and public policy in the four Atlantic provinces. These four provinces have amongst them the highest rate of unemployment in Canada, and the average income is below the national average while the cost of living is as high or higher than the national norm.

A study in 1989 revealed that wage disparity between the Atlantic provinces and the wealthiest provinces had not improved in the previous twenty to thirty years. The unemployment gaps in 1989 were greater than they had been for twenty years and the gap between the Atlantic region and the more prosperous provinces had widened.[7]

The Gordon Report (1957) observed:

> An objective of economic policy should be to integrate and improve the basic economic framework of the Atlantic region, including, in particular, the transportation facilities of the area with a view to facilitating and encouraging economic growth within the region. This is not likely to be accomplished by a multiplicity of uncoordinated measures .... In fact, such aids may tend to prolong the life of industries and activities which may no longer be wholly justified in economic terms. What is needed, we believe, is a bold comprehensive and coordinated approach to the underlying problems of the region."[8]

Although the Gordon Report may not have been well received in Atlantic Canada, its message has been the goal of individual governments since 1957. Unfortunately, the necessary coordinated approach to economic development has been slow to develop. Since 1961 numerous agencies have come and gone before ACOA was conceived in 1987.[9]

ACOA may be the most productive of any of these plans, because instead of promoting the megaproject and inducing industry from outside to locate in the region, ACOA is geared to assist the local entrepreneur and to work with businesses of all sizes located within the Atlantic provinces plus those wishing to locate in the region. ACOA as originally conceived was to be as non-partisan and non-political as possible. Unfortunately evidence illustrates that ACOA quickly became little more than a continuation of previously existing patronage agencies. A major proportion of its five-year budget was distributed prior to the November 1988 federal election and following that election the newly appointed Board of Directors was composed almost entirely of Conservative Party supporters. If ACOA is to be successful and respected by the citizenry it will have to conform to the original concept and be non-partisan. ACOA, if handled properly, has the potential to be the facilitator recommended in the Gordon Report.

Every provincial government, no matter what its political colours or political philosophy, has endeavoured to end the twin problems of unemployment and poverty by providing jobs and programs of economic development. The electorate constantly demands jobs from its politicians not only at the provincial level but also at the federal and even municipal levels. We have witnessed provinces seducing industries to move into the region and

THE ATLANTIC PROVINCES: AN ENIGMA?

have seen little sensitivity to the environment. Jobs today are more important than protecting the ozone for tomorrow's children, and politicians only work in four-year cycles.

It is unfortunate that provincial attempts to promote industry are more noted for their failures (Bricklin Automobiles, Sydney Steel, heavy water, oil refinery, shipyards, and Clairtone) than for their successes (Michelin, McCain's, Volvo). The politician's view is that almost any industry, no matter what its social or environmental impact, is worth the investment because of the employment it creates. The only exception to this statement is Prince Edward Island, which refused to give Litton Industries all the financial assistance they desired and has also refused to purchase electricity generated by nuclear fission in New Brunswick.

The four provincial governments have been active participants in promoting development and "modernization." Each has constructed a process for economic planning. Some of these, like Nova Scotia's Voluntary Economic Planning Council, are a mixture of business and government personnel.

No essay on Atlantic Canada would be complete without a word on the fishery. Just as wheat has fuelled the prairie economy, so the fishery has been the backbone of the rural Atlantic economy, particularly in Newfoundland but also in the Maritime provinces. Fishermen are an independent lot who do not always appreciate government regulations. The fishery is not only a regulated industry but is also a victim of the constitutional division of powers and often the two levels of government are at odds over fishery policy. The provinces (and remember their elections are not always held simultaneously with federal elections) are looking for jobs while the federal authorities, in addition to creating employment opportunities, are concerned with the conservation of the species. Constitutionally, fish do not become a ward of the province until they are landed for processing.

There may be cooperation among the Atlantic provinces on many issues, but one area where there is literally no cooperation is the fishery. This is particularly true of Newfoundland and Nova Scotia. Unfortunately, fish, unlike politicians, do not respect provincial boundaries. As provincial boundaries do not continue to the 200 nautical mile offshore boundary, fishermen from Nova Scotia, for example, fish in the waters off Newfoundland and their "catch" is processed in Nova Scotia. Such actions annoy the Newfoundland fishermen who feel that these are their waters and residents of the other provinces should stay out of them. Naturally, the Newfoundland government sides with its citizens. The upshot is squabbling between the two provinces. It is for this reason that Brian Peckford had the fishery included in the ill-fated Meech Lake Accord.

| 75 |

Several international issues, which Ottawa finds difficult to resolve, for example, the St. Pierre and Miquelon offshore boundary, and overfishing by the Americans and the European Community nations, do not help the situation. In 1990 the fishery was in trouble because of overfishing by both Canadian and foreign fleets, improvements in fish harvesting, including freezer trawlers — demanded by Nova Scotia and disliked by Newfoundland (Ottawa sided with Nova Scotia), a far too rapid expansion of the entire industry in the early 1980's and the high value of the Canadian dollar. In order to solve the domestic problems, Ottawa first must resolve the outstanding international issues, not an easy task.

The policy outputs of the four provincial governments run the full spectrum from economic development to social welfare. Economic development may be the most notable of these, but one must also remember that each province has developed a network of social welfare policies. Of course, in provinces with a weak tax base and many social problems there is still much to be done, particularly in the area of rural poverty.

All four provinces, but especially perhaps Prince Edward Island and Newfoundland, are undergoing a process of political "modernization." The growth of urban centres and the influx of new ideas as well as economic development are leading to changes in political and social attitudes. The rural society, though still important, is not as powerful as it was in the past.

I Maritime Union I

To those who live outside the region the question of Maritime Union is a topic for debate, but in the Maritimes themselves it has a low profile. As the Maritime Union Study (**Deutsch Report**)[10] illustrated, there is little support for such a project amongst Maritimers.

However, the **Deutsch Report** brought about a spirit of cooperation and harmony amongst the three provincial governments. The premiers meet quarterly to debate regional problems and whenever possible to harmonize policy outputs, particularly concerning relations with Ottawa. The Report spawned several of Canada's most notable and useful intergovernmental forms of cooperation. These include the Secretariat which handles the quarterly meetings of the three premiers and coordinates policy and research amongst the three provinces, the Maritime Provinces Higher Education Commission, the University Grants Agency for the three provinces, and the Land Registration Agency. Even in trade, moves are afoot to eliminate barriers between the three provinces. This reform is being spearheaded by

THE ATLANTIC PROVINCES: AN ENIGMA?

Frank McKenna who uses the argument of possible changes in Quebec's position in the federation as the fulcrum for reform. There is more successful interprovincial cooperation in the Maritimes than in any other region of Canada. These attempts to integrate policy and to work together on regional issues have paid many dividends for Maritimers. The political philosophy of the various governments is not a detriment to this cooperation.

Newfoundland, on the other hand, continues to go its own way. Indeed, the Conservative governments of Newfoundland which followed that of J.R. Smallwood made it quite clear that Newfoundland should not be considered as one of the Maritime provinces. Premier Wells may be reversing this trend. Since the political demise of Smallwood there have been few occasions when the Atlantic region has presented a united front at federal-provincial First Ministers' conferences. Furthermore, witness the actions of the Peckford government with respect to the cod fishery, the question of freezer trawlers, or Newfoundland's decision in 1983 to withdraw from the Atlantic Provinces Economic Council.

I Political Culture and Parties I

Given the history of the region one might expect to find political and policy differences amongst these four provinces. In fact, the reverse is true. There is a regional political culture which is the basis for this similarity and which has been apparent for some time. Basically, the prevailing political culture has revolved around the three elements of cynicism, traditionalism and regionalism.

There is some argument whether or not Newfoundland and Labrador's political culture should be grouped with that of the Maritimes. There remain many differences between Newfoundland and the three Maritime provinces, particularly in the area of policy development and federal-provincial relations. Nonetheless, the gradual demise of the outports has eroded many of the distinctive aspects of Newfoundland political culture while integration into the Canadian political community has simultaneously reinforced the pervasive traditionalism and cynicism of Newfoundlanders. It appears that Newfoundland's political culture is converging with that of the three Maritime provinces.

Traditionally, Newfoundland has had one of the lowest political participation rates in Canada while the Maritimes, notably Prince Edward Island, have had the highest. Here, too, one can see a change: voter turnout in the Maritimes, particularly in Nova Scotia, is decreasing somewhat, although it

CANADIAN GOVERNMENT AND POLITICS

is still the highest in Canada, while the percentage of Newfoundlanders who exercise their franchise is increasing.

Traditionalism is a fact of life in Atlantic Canada. Amongst the numerous examples are the fact that Newfoundland kept the Union Jack as its provincial flag until 1980, and Nova Scotia still flies the Union Jack from Province House, the last two dual-member federal constituencies were in Atlantic Canada, Prince Edward Island retained alcohol prohibition until 1948, and the retention of the monarchy was an issue in the 1978 Nova Scotia election. One might add to this list fear of the Free Trade Agreement (FTA) as expressed in the results of the 1988 federal election. True, some of the resentment to free trade was based upon the fact that the issue of what constitutes a government subsidy was left to be resolved after the FTA became operative. If the American view prevails, that any and all government subsidies to industries and workers are contrary to the FTA, Atlantic Canadians will be savagely affected for it will mean an end to government assisted regional development programmes and relocation grants to workers. Nevertheless, and in spite of the fact the region has been adversely affected by Macdonald's national tariff, the region illustrated its conservatism in expressing its support for those who opposed the agreement.

Atlantic Canadians have historically been noted for their relative lack of both political efficacy and political trust. But, there are curious contradictions in the Atlantic provinces' political culture. While the peoples of this region have traditionally both distrusted politics and politicians and felt incapable of effecting political change, they have continued to invest in politics high amounts of physical, intellectual and emotional energy. Residents of these four provinces are more politically attuned than are other Canadians. The result of these tensions has been a political culture which was characterized in the words of the former New Brunswick premier Richard Hatfield as, "an unhealthy cynicism."[11]

Similar evidence is available with respect to regionalism and particularly regional loyalty. Canada may be a country of regions, but with the exception of Quebec nowhere are regional loyalties and love of region so marked in the political process than is the case of Atlantic Canada.

One peculiar aspect of politics in Atlantic Canada is the fact that Atlantic Canadians, unlike those in Western Canada, have never taken the opportunity to produce a regionally based party in order to present a unified voice in Parliament. Atlantic Canadians have always maintained that it was far more appropriate for them to work through the two major political parties than through any third force. Whether or not this has been an advantage is a debatable question. However, it does illustrate the region's political tradi-

THE ATLANTIC PROVINCES: AN ENIGMA?

tionalism. Another example of the region's traditionalism is the fact that third parties, particularly the NDP and its forerunner the Cooperative Commonwealth Federation (CCF), have not found Atlantic Canada to be fertile soil. Only in Nova Scotia has the NDP had continual, although minuscule, support. In Newfoundland the NDP has done well during by-elections, but, as is so often the case with third parties, lose the seat at a subsequent general election.

In New Brunswick both the Parti Acadien and Social Credit have withered and died though the Confederation of Regions (COR) is currently making inroads amongst anglophones in southwestern New Brunswick who, like the COR, are opposed to bilingualism in New Brunswick and indeed in Canada. In Prince Edward Island, at least until the 1986 election, the NDP candidates in some constituencies received fewer votes than there were spoiled ballots. In Newfoundland third parties, with the exception of fights within the Liberal Party in the final stages of J.R. Smallwood's political life, have been relatively unsuccessful.

In Nova Scotia the NDP is currently undergoing a transformation from a party which was based upon trade union support in Cape Breton to one that is supported by the upwardly mobile younger generation in the Halifax area.

Party politics in Newfoundland remain remarkably fluid as that province struggles to build a party system out of a predominently one-party configuration. Many prominent Newfoundland politicians, including Brian Peckford, John Crosbie, Leo Barry, Clyde Wells, have crossed the floor. One of the peculiarities of Newfoundland politics is that it does not seem to be a detriment to move from one party to another, as witness Walter Carter, the Liberal Minister of Fisheries in the Wells cabinet who was a previous Minister of Fisheries in a Conservative government and also a Conservative Member of Parliament. In the Maritimes, on the other hand, to switch parties is virtually a political "kiss of death."

Another example of the region's traditionalism is the overwhelming preponderance of white males in the party elites. Atlantic Canada has been particularly slow to accept the idea of women in politics. Similarly, although there have been Black and native candidates, they have usually run for the New Democratic Party and thus have suffered the same fate as has that party in general.

One of the major reasons for a cynical attitude toward politics in the Atlantic region, and particularly in the Maritimes, is the question of patronage. The tradition of "treating" the voter at election time remains one of the principal forms of patronage in the region. Those who decry these practices (and most of those are either in Upper Canada or in academia) are

❘ 79 ❘

criticized for not understanding the local system and being naive about the political process. Those who reside in the region wonder whether or not it is any worse to buy votes with rum and money than it is to promise new highways, bridges, school cafeterias, hockey rinks, bowling greens, and so forth. One must reluctantly admit that there is a certain validity to their argument. The tradition of "treating" is slowly dying out, though perhaps, as evidence from the Nova Scotia election of 1988 illustrates, not as quickly as one might have expected.[12]

Recent events in Nova Scotia, including police investigations and the approintment of Premier John Buchanan to the Senate, have at least in that province, brought about a public outcry for reform of patronage and a more open system of government. One hopes that these public demands will lead to permanent reforms, but for now, the jury is still out. Other forms of patronage include the practice of punishing a constituency which fails to elect a government supporter, refusal to grant highway access to supporters of opposition parties, and the usual appointments of friends to commissions and boards. One might have added highways workers to this list, but unionization has, to a large degree, brought an end to the traditional Department of Highways personnel changes when the government changes. Of course, highway workers and highway works are different matters, as residents of any opposition constituency will tell you.

One of the side effects, and it may have been a factor in the 1987 New Brunswick provincial election, concerning the punishment of constituencies, is that few rural constituencies wish to be on the opposition side of the House and, consequently, when published polls illustrate to the voter that a certain party is going to win the election they may cause a stampede to the leading party. If this tradition of harassing an opposition constituency continues, perhaps we have another plank in the argument to ban the publication of pre-election public opinion polls.

In Prince Edward Island, as in Newfoundland, the Conservative Party historically receives the support of the majority of Roman Catholics. Thus in Prince Edward Island the parties are obliged to run a Roman Catholic and a Protestant in many of the dual-member constituencies. At one time religion played an important role in Nova Scotia politics, but now modernization seems to have taken precedence and religion is no longer as important a determinant in the recruitment and selection of candidates as it once was, though the Nova Scotia Liberal Party has continued, almost unbroken, its tradition of alternating leaders between adherents of the Roman Catholic and other faiths.

The role of the party leader is significant in all four provinces. The leader,

THE ATLANTIC PROVINCES: AN ENIGMA?

perhaps as is the case in other provinces, is the main electoral asset of the party and is required to have lengthy political coattails.

I Institutional Structure I

The institutional structure of the Atlantic region is similar to that of the rest of the country. Each of the four provinces has a unicameral legislature based upon representation by population. The use of dual-member constituencies — constituency representation based on the Protestant–Catholic factor — has continued in Prince Edward Island and there appears to be little desire by politicians to change to single member districts.

Both the Liberals and Progressive Conservatives have strong bases of support in the four provinces. These two parties, in this dependent hinterland, are more closely aligned with their federal counterparts than is the case in certain other regions of Canada. Historically, the Liberals have been the more successful of the two parties, but an inspection of recent election results illustrates that the parties have become evenly balanced. Forty years ago one might have called this a "one-party dominant" region. Today one cannot make this claim. There is a healthy party system which means there is a viable alternative to the party in power plus vigorous debate in the legislatures.

The legislatures remain true to the British parliamentary system and their own historic tradition. This is not surprising for it must be remembered that Nova Scotia was the first British colony to obtain responsible government in 1847.

The judicial system in all four provinces, but particularly in Nova Scotia because of the **Donald Marshall Royal Commission Report**,[13] are undergoing a form of modernization and much needed reform. In 1990, Nova Scotia appointed an independent prosecutor and all the provinces have a judicial council. Even the appointment of provincial judges is becoming less partisan. These reforms of the judicial system are long overdue. In the past, the judicial system in the region was not respected in the rest of the country because the belief that "not only must justice be done, but justice must be seen to be done" was not always the case, as Donald Marshall Jr. discovered.

I Conclusion I

Many questions remain to be answered concerning the future of Atlantic Canada. These include, the direction of economic development, whether

CANADIAN GOVERNMENT AND POLITICS

the Free Trade Agreement will benefit the region, the success or failure of ACOA to promote jobs, offshore oil and gas development, and the revival of the fishery.

Possibly the most important question is the region's relationship with Ottawa. Atlantic Canada has a weak national voice. True it has had some strong individual representation like Allan J. MacEachen and John Crosbie, but representation by population and a weak Senate has not benefitted these four provinces. It is rather surprising that these provinces are not clamouring for Senate reform, because a Senate constructed as a voice for the regions could benefit Atlantic Canada by giving the region a stronger voice in Ottawa.

There is no question that the region requires financial assistance from the federal government. Without such programs as equalization, transportation subsidies and ACOA, Atlantic Canada would have a lower standard of living than that enjoyed by other Canadians. This is a dependent hinterland. Yet does this state of dependency mean that a form of clientism and federal feudalism prevails?

Political modernization is a fact of life in the Atlantic provinces. But will there be a change of attitude toward politics and politicians? Will there be a groundswell of support to reform the political process, or will cynicism and patronage (even the odd bit of corruption) continue to rule the day? Presumably, politics will continue to be "the best game in town," but will it become more difficult to recruit people to participate in politics? Or will modernization open the door to more women, Blacks and natives in the political process and by so doing bring the region closer to the Canadian "mainstream"? Will changes in society, including the weakening of family ties as people move to urban centres, and more women joining the labour force, make it possible for the NDP to break through and become a meaningful participant in the political process?

One cannot foretell the impact of the FTA in the region, but so far the benefits seem to be few. The problems in the fishery predate the agreement, but if Canada loses the debate on what constitutes a government subsidy, it will mean economic dislocation for the region.

What about French-English relations? Will the COR continue to make inroads in New Brunswick, and perhaps elsewhere, amongst anglophones opposed to bilingualism, or will the realities of Canadian dualism be accepted as part of the price Atlantic Canadians must pay to live in a federation of which they are major beneficiaries?

Finally, what about Atlantic Canadians' standard of living? Will the changes which are already apparent in the political process mean changes in the quality of life? There is no doubt that the residents of Atlantic Canada, despite their economic and geographic handicap, enjoy a remarkable lifestyle. The respect for family and community and "a sense of place" is very pronounced in these four provinces. The residents may dislike Ottawa and "Upper Canadians," but they know their continued existence depends upon federal aid for the region.

There are compensations, as Dalton Camp has stated, for the handicaps experienced by Atlantic Canadians. In spite of all the problems, who has the better standard of living and enjoys the better lifestyle, the Torontonian whose net annual income is $35,000, or the Prince Edward Islander with a net annual income of $15,000? Who is forced to suffer traffic "gridlock," the Montrealer or the Haligonian? Yes, there are compensations for not having it "quite so good" as Canadians who live outside of these four provinces. The major public policy question for the 1990s is, Can this lifestyle be maintained while the political economy is being modernized and will the economic gap between the Atlantic Provinces and the rest of Canada be closed?[14]

CANADIAN GOVERNMENT AND POLITICS

NOTES

[1] Dalton Camp, "The Maritimes Revisited," in Dalton Camp, *An Eclectic Eel* (Ottawa: Deneau, 1981) pp. 113-114

[2] Data collected by the author from questionnaires distributed to delegates to the 1986 Nova Scotia Liberal Leadership Convention.

[3] Based upon a lecture given by the late Frank Underhill at Carleton University in 1960.

[4] Deborah Jones, "N.S. Pins Hopes on Energy Mega-Plans," *The Globe and Mail,* August 19, 1989, p. B5.

[5] *The Report on Maritime Union:* Commissioned by the three Maritime Governments, Fredericton, 1970. The Commission was chaired by John J. Deutsch.

[6] W.A. Mackintosh, *The Economic Background of Dominion-Provincial Relations* (Toronto: Carleton Library Series No. 13, McClelland and Stewart, 1964) p. 153.

[7] *Halifax Chronicle-Herald,* October 3, 1989, p. B3.

[8] *Final Report: Royal Commission on Canada's Economic Prospects* (The Gordon Report) (Ottawa, Queen's Printer, 1957) p. 104.

[9] For details on past attempts to promote regional development see Anthony Careless, *Initiative and Response* (Montreal: McGill/Queen's, 1977), and Donald Savoie, "The Continuing Struggle for Regional Development Policy," in Peter Leslie (ed.), *Canada: The State of the Federation 1985* (Kingston: Institute of Intergovernmental Relations, 1986).

[10] *Report on Maritime Union, op. cit.*

[11] For more details on Atlantic political culture and political parties, see Adamson and Stewart, "Party Politics in the Mysterious East," in Hugh G. Thorburn (ed.), *Party Politics in Canada,* 5th ed. (Scarborough: Prentice-Hall, 1985).

[12] Following the September 1988 Nova Scotia provincial election, successful prosecutions for vote buying were carried out in Shelburne (rum) and Guysborough (gravel) constituencies.

[13] For details on this whole issue see *Report of the Royal Commission on the Donald Marshall Jr. Prosecution* (Halifax: Province of Nova Scotia, 1989).

[14] For a somewhat different viewpoint — with tongue in cheek, see John Fraser "A Modest Proposal Concerning the Atlantic Canada Problem," *Saturday Night,* May 1988. Although the authors tongue is notably in his cheek, many Atlantic Canadians were upset by his proposal to turn the region into one large national park. But then from fiction have many ideas sprung.

THE ATLANTIC PROVINCES: AN ENIGMA?

ANNOTATED READINGS

Mandel, Maurice, ed. *Atlantic Canada Today*. Halifax: Formac, 1987. This work describes in some detail the economy of the Atlantic region including some of the more pressing public policy issues (e.g. the fishery, regional development policies and transportation). The book's forte is economic rather than political.

Savoie, Donald J. "The Continuing Struggle for a Regional Development Policy," in Peter M. Leslie, ed., *Canada: The State of the Federation 1985*. Kingston: Institute of Intergovernmental Relations, Queen's University, 1985. Savoie, a New Brunswicker, presents an analysis of regional development policy, past, present and future, with emphasis on Atlantic Canada. It was Savoie's research which was the foundation to the formation of ACOA.

Adamson, Agar and Ian Stewart. "Party Politics in Atlantic Canada: Still the Mysterious East?," in Hugh Thorburn, ed., *Party Politics in Canada*, Sixth edition. Toronto: Prentice-Hall, 1990. This essay describes in some detail the political culture of Atlantic Canada and also analyzes the political partys of the region.

Alexander, David. *Atlantic Canada and Confederation: Essays in Canadian Political Economy*. Toronto: University of Toronto Press, 1983. Useful background material on the political economy of the region.

Tomblin, Stephen G. "The Council of Maritime Premiers and the Battle for Territorial Integrity," paper presented at Canadian Political Science Association, 1988. This paper, which can be found in the 1988 edition of the CPSA papers, discusses the Council of Maritime Premiers and gives an analysis of the Council's performance and effectiveness.

| CHAPTER 5 |

THE EVOLUTION OF QUEBEC

MARY BETH MONTCALM

Quebec politics has evolved dramatically over the past forty years. Throughout this period, Quebec issues have been high on the national agenda. During the 1960s, Canadians followed the upheaval of the Quiet Revolution; in the 1970s the separatist Parti Québecois came to power. Throughout the 1980s, Quebec figured prominently in efforts at constitutional change. And, in the mid-eighties, the separatists lost popularity and, eventually, power. More recently, Quebec has been captured by an unprecedented entrepreneurial spirit in combination with an apparent return to strong nationalist sentiment. This article will sketch major elements of Quebec's background and trace the broad pattern of change within the province. It will also describe trends in current Quebec politics.

It is argued here that underlying economic changes and overarching economic policy goals have shaped and influenced the path of Quebec politics, especially since 1960. The traditional francophone Quebec way of life, based on farming, became increasingly impossible in the twentieth century as good farmland was used up. The necessity for French-Canadians to find employment in mines and factories, and eventually in cities, undermined the traditional political arrangements within the province. In turn, by the middle of this century the altered Québecois lifestyle required social and political adaptation affecting the governmental level. When people live in cities and seek employment in modern industries, they require modern education, modern hospitals and a wide range of governmental intervention in the social and economic fields. In addition to these changes *within* Quebec, since World War II the province has felt the effect of a major restructuring and reorientation of the Canadian economy. Especially since 1960, this reorientation has forced Quebec governments to intervene so as to bolster the province's fortunes within the North American economy. Governmental efforts to do this underpinned the Quiet Revolution, spurred the nationalist movement and eventually resulted in Quebec's current pro-market sentiment and aggressive capitalist ethic. Indeed, the thread of argumentation throughout this chapter is that major economic changes have shaped policy direction within Quebec. Moreover, it argues that underlying economic change situates the evolution of Quebec politics from the ambitious state interventionism of the 1960s and 1970s through to the clearly pro-business agenda of Quebec governments in the 1980s.

I Traditional Quebec I

From earliest Canadian history, what is now Quebec constituted a distinct society. Settled largely by immigrants from France it had distinctive linguistic, legal and cultural characteristics. Although after the Conquest what is now Quebec was within the sphere of British domination, it remained unique. For French-Canadians centred in Quebec, the Confederation agreement was simply the last of a series of legal frameworks through which they attempted to co-exist with their predominantly anglophone counterparts. The political arrangement struck in 1867 allowed French-Canadians the greatest degree of autonomy of all these agreements; in fact, it was this autonomy which appealed to French-Canadians at the time.

Debates about the terms of Confederation show that French-Canadians hoped it would preserve their culture, religion and traditions. Arguments within Canada East (now Quebec) over whether Confederation was a "good deal" hinged on the preservation of Quebec's autonomy. French-Canadians feared domination by English-Canadians and saw provincial autonomy as a way to prevent this. Delegates from Canada East were divided over whether the terms of the British North America Act afforded enough cultural protection. Some French-Canadian delegates strongly opposed Confederation on the grounds that it entailed too strong a central government and, in the end, only a narrow majority of French-Canadian delegates (twenty-seven versus twenty-two) supported the agreement. But there was little division among French-Canadians as to what was being sought. Even those who supported Confederation saw it as effectively combining a strong central government with preservation of French-Canadians' cultural, legal and religious distinctiveness.

Under the British North America Act, Quebec had no greater powers than other provinces but it differed sociologically and politically for a variety of reasons. While francophones formed the majority within the province, from the outset (and, indeed, prior to Confederation) the English-speaking population played a very powerful role in its business and political life. Anglophones dominated the Quebec economy, had disproportionate political leverage and enjoyed wide educational and cultural autonomy. While French-Canadians headed the government, Montreal's business community carried great weight. In fact, the Montreal-based, and largely English-speaking, business community was integral to the dream of Confederation from the outset and was behind the pan-Canadian railway ambitions which were so central to the drive for Confederation.

In early Confederation, Quebec society was marked by an unusual separation of French-speakers and English-speakers in different spheres. Anglophones figured prominently in the provincial economy and francophones tended to be subsistence farmers; the Roman Catholic Church and middle class French-Canadians (doctors, lawyers, small businessmen, etc.) served as go-betweens for the two cultures. Francophones avoided cities and business partly because within traditional French-Canadian ideology these spheres were viewed as less spiritual than farming, but also because francophones were outsiders in the powerful, but English-dominated, business network.

Over time, however, the separate lifestyles of these two communities became increasingly impossible. By the early twentieth century, good Quebec farmland was occupied and, coupled with the French-Canadian tradition of large families, this required emigration to the cities of the province, to other provinces and to the United States. As well, French-Canadians increasingly moved into industries like lumbering and mining in order to make a living. The influx of French-Canadians into cities, into resource industries and small manufacturing, undermined the separation of the two cultures. In doing so, it undercut the basis for Quebec's traditional political stability.

By the 1940s and 50s, many French-Canadians worked for English-Canadian, and increasingly American, companies; often they did so under harsh and exploitative conditions. The Quebec government, cosy with English-Canadian and American capital, strongly resisted efforts at unionization and labour efforts at decent working conditions. Unsurprisingly, this led to labour unrest, social agitation and political demands for change within the province. The 1940s and 50s were marked by increasing labour militance and major strikes at the Asbestos and Thetford Mines in 1949 and at Murdochville in 1957. In 1949 five thousand Asbestos workers went on strike against the Johns-Mansville multinational. As was its pattern in the face of labour unrest during this era, the Quebec government sided with the company, declared the strike illegal, and used the Quebec provincial police to harass the striking workers.

By the 1950s there was tremendous pressure for social change. Throughout the twentieth century, the province had become increasingly industrialized and urbanized. This led to demands for social and political modernization. Quebec schools still emphasized a classical education for an elite, and illiteracy was extensive among the masses; yet Quebec society needed to be trained for modern industrial jobs. The province needed the co-ordinated social network evident in all modern societies yet the government left welfare measures to private organizations, largely within the orbit of the Roman Catholic Church. The Union Nationale government headed by Maurice Duplessis (1936-39 and 1944-1959) remained opposed to any systematic governmental intervention in the economy and society.

In addition to these obvious social and political pressures for change, the Quebec economy had to readjust to overall economic trends within Canada. These economic trends also demanded altered attitudes on the part of government. At the time of Confederation, Quebec, and especially Montreal, were strategically located within the Canadian economy. Predominant trade links ran east-west across the country and Canada's major trade partner was Great Britain. Over the twentieth century, however, and increasingly after World War II, Canada's economic ties with Great Britain declined dramatically. Instead, Canada became economically linked to the United States. In 1986, for example, fully 77.6 percent of Canada's exports went to the U.S.; only 2.3 percent went to Great Britain (in 1880, 48.3 percent had). This change had wide-ranging ramifications.

Economic integration with the U.S. involved increasing economic concentration in southern Ontario, particularly Toronto. While this has led to problems throughout the Canadian economy, it seriously affected Quebec. As early as the 1950s, business headquarters began relocating from the once-powerful Montreal business community to Toronto, investment in the Quebec economy lagged and Quebec became what has been termed "peripheral" within Canadian and North American business. Combined with the building social unrest within the province and the growing demand for jobs

| 89 |

within Quebec urban centres, this weakening of the Quebec economy created a volatile political situation and increased pressures for government intervention.

I The Quiet Revolution I

With the death of Premier Maurice Duplessis in 1959, the change that had taken place in Quebec's economy and society broke through to the political level. In 1960, Quebeckers elected a Liberal government headed by Jean Lesage and this ushered in an era of interventionist and modern government. According to most observers the break with the past was so dramatic that this era was termed a "quiet revolution." The governmental aspect of this revolution attempted to boost the Quebec economy and improve the situation of Québecois within it.

In order to intervene so as to accomplish these goals, however, the government needed to expand the public sector, bring in modern government techniques (such as co-ordination and planning), and inject financial assistance into Quebec-based businesses which were, on the whole, small and in need of modernized plants.

Especially during the early 1960s (the quiet revolution is often considered to be limited to the 1960-1966 period), numerous new government departments were set up, crown corporations were established to spur activity in most economic sectors and the Quebec government put in place agencies geared at stimulating Quebec-based businesses. During the decade of the 1960s, numerous new government departments were created: Natural Resources (1961), Cultural Affairs (1961), Revenue (1961), Federal-Provincial Affairs (1961), Education (1964), Industry and Commerce (1968), Financial Institutions, Companies and Cooperatives (1968), Immigration (1968), Public Service (1969) and Communications (1969). The government established planning agencies like the Conseil d'orientation économique du Québec (COEQ or Economic Council of Quebec) to assist it in its economic planning strategy. It also established central agencies such the Société générale de financement (SGF or General Finance Corporation) in 1962 and the Caisse de dépôt et placement (or General Deposit and Investment Fund), in 1965. The SGF set up several holding companies in key economic sectors and promoted the industrial transformation of the provincial economy by providing capital for provincially-based industrial projects. The Caisse infused much-needed capital into indigenous enterprises using funds available to the province through the Quebec Pension Plan, the

I 90 I

public service retirement plan and, later, the provincial auto-insurance plan. While neither of these investment agencies appeared especially successful in the 1960s, their continued activity later proved pivotal in the changing character of the Quebec economy. Further, the Quebec government put in place key crown corporations designed to spur economic activity in a variety of economic sectors; for example, in 1964 Hydro-Québec was expanded by the nationalization of private hydroelectric companies and their integration in Hydro-Québec (established in 1944). Hydro-Québec became central in the province's industrial strategy, which relied increasingly on the province's potential to provide hydroelectric power, and even a symbol of the capacity of Québecois to intervene effectively in their economy.

Of course, these innovations vastly expanded the size of the public sector. Between 1959-60 and 1969-70, during which per capita income increased 1.9 times within the province, government per capita expenditures increased 4.5 times. On education alone, spending went from $200 million to over $1 billion between 1960-61 and 1970-71. Growth of the Quebec governmental sector was especially marked in the early 1960s but continued throughout the 1970s and into the early 1980s. In 1961 provincial expenditures on goods and services constituted only 17 percent of the gross provincial product, by 1983 this had increased to 26 percent. Although Quebec governments from 1960 to the early 1980s varied in the degree and character of their interventionism, all of them sought to use the powers of the Quebec state to enhance the Quebec economy. For example, the Robert Bourassa government of the early 1970s, although less overt in its use of the public sector, nevertheless sought to spur the provincial economy by means of massive public works projects.

Initially, the most obvious effect of the new government interventionism was inflation of the size of the provincial public sector and the power of technocrats employed within it. Ironically, while the changes undertaken within the Quiet Revolution sought to spur the private sector within the province, there was little early success in this area. A restructuring of the Quebec business sector did begin but the vast infusion of public money into the provincial economy bore little early fruit. However, in mushrooming the size of the public sector, many of the quiet revolution reforms strengthened a sector of the Quebec populace which saw its future overwhelmingly in provincial terms. Quebec provincial bureaucrats showed limited interest in links with the rest of the country and aggressively sought greater provincial jurisdiction in constitutional battles with the federal level (such as the implementation of the Quebec Pension Plan in place of the Canada Pension Plan in 1965). Moreover, it was public sector workers who formed the

| 91 |

backbone of the separatist movement which grew through the 1960s and became more powerful with the founding of the Parti Québecois in 1968.

I The Turbulence of the 1970s I

The Liberal Party, elected under the leadership of Robert Bourassa in 1970, like Union Nationale governments headed by Daniel Johnson (1966-1968) and Jean-Jacques Bertrand (1968-1970), pursued many of the underlying goals of the Quiet Revolution. Bourassa's appeal in the 1970 election was largely based on his reputation as an economist and on the expectation that he would successfully stimulate the private sector. Under Bourassa, there was a continued effort to spur the provincial economy, but like the Johnson and Bertrand governments the Liberals were less comprehensive in their interventionism than they had been under Lesage from 1960-1966. In fact, the economic strategy of the Bourassa government relied heavily on the pivotal role to be played by the province's hydroelectric resources.

In part, the less comprehensive approach of the Bourassa government reflected conditions affecting most western governments in the 1970s. Especially after 1973 and the world-wide economic crisis caused by the formation of the OPEC (Oil Producing and Exporting Countries) cartel, governments everywhere were less able to plan their economies. Under Bourassa, key crown corporations set up in the preceding decade were increasingly viewed as auxiliary to the private sector; nevertheless, under his government there was substantial public sector investment. His government emphasized large public works projects such as construction of highways, public buildings, the Olympic facilities and the $15 billion James Bay hydroelectric project. As well, it engaged fairly heavily in financial assistance to private Quebec-based firms.

Although the private sector was emphasized under Bourassa, his government also intervened extensively in other aspects of Quebec life. Legal aid and small claims courts were set up, centralized health and social service programs were established, environmental and consumer protection was expanded and Bill 22 was passed in the linguistic and cultural area. Despite these social interventions, the Bourassa government's emphasis on the development of the province's private sector both strengthened Quebec's developing francophone business class and fostered conflict between the provincial government and labour.

In 1971, for example, a strike occurred at *La Presse* which became one of the most bitter in Quebec history and symbolized the frustration experienced

THE EVOLUTION OF QUEBEC

by Quebec's labour movement. In 1972, negotiations for a new contract between the public employee's Common Front and the Bourassa government broke off in bitterness and 200,000 public and quasi-public sector workers marched in protest. By the latter stages of the Bourassa government's tenure, government–labour relations were among the most acrimonious in the country. In 1975-76, for example, Quebec accounted for 41 percent of all work stoppages in Canada.

The difficulties of the Bourassa administration were complicated by the increasingly tense linguistic climate of the 1970s. As Quebec francophones aspired to similar jobs and career opportunities as anglophones, the English domination within the province became a growing political sore point. The Bourassa government faced a serious political dilemma on this issue. English had long dominated the province's private sector and anglophone rights within Quebec had traditionally been much wider than those of francophone communities elsewhere in Canada. The anglophone community was not about to allow its rights to be diminished without objection. Québecois, on the other hand, were increasingly intolerant of the secondary status of the French language within the province. Complicating matters further, by the 1970s Quebec's traditionally high birthrate had dropped to the lowest in the country and the major source of population growth became immigration. But the province's allophone (non-French, non-English) community, recognizing that English was the language of upward mobility within the province, primarily assimilated into the English community. For a host of reasons, including blocked upward mobility and fears of the loss of the province's French character, francophones demanded political intervention on the language issue. While linguistic unrest had been evident in the late 1960s, and had even resulted in a limited government response, pressure for action grew in the 1970s.

The Bourassa government's attempt to deal with the language problem, Bill 22 introduced and passed in 1974, was so clumsy that it managed to alienate almost everyone in the province. French was declared the "official" language of the province; in a move targeting allophone assimilation into the anglophone culture children were required to demonstrate competency in English before being allowed to attend English rather than French schools; and private companies in the private sector were required to obtain "francisation" certificates (indicating that the firm had implemented, or was implementing, French language operation within the firm) if they wished to receive any form of provincial government assistance such as subsidies or contracts.

The English-speaking and allophone communities were outraged at these

| 93 |

restrictions on their linguistic freedoms. Many Québecois, by this time suspicious of the Bourassa government for reasons including financial scandals surrounding the building of the Olympic facilities and alleged corruption, felt measures contained in the Bill were so vaguely worded that they were unlikely to be enforced. The specific formulation of elements of Bill 22 fuelled these suspicions; for example, while firms were to be required to obtain "francisation" certificates, the agency charged with evaluating the degree of francisation was given wide latitude in assessing this.

The Parti Québecois (PQ), founded in 1968 under the leadership of René Lévesque, who had been a popular minister under the Lesage government, profited from the growing opposition to the Bourassa government in response to its labour and linguistic policies and as a result of claims of corruption and economic mismanagement. In the 1970 and 1973 Quebec elections, Bourassa skilfully used the separatist issue against the PQ convincing the electorate that its policies were extremist and likely to lead to political and economic instability. By their third electoral campaign, however, the PQ downplayed the immediacy of the separatist issue and promised, if elected, simply to offer good government and to refrain from proceeding with the separatist (or indépendantiste) option until it received approval to do so in a province-wide referendum. Since many PQ candidates had excellent credentials, their offer to provide good government in place of the scandal-ridden Bourassa government was appealing. As well, Bill 22 had so miffed the anglophone and allophone communities that rather than vote Liberal as they had in the past, in large numbers they voted Union Nationale or not at all (since they remained hostile to the Parti Québecois' indépendantiste option).

The PQ was elected in the 1976 election with a strong social democratic image. Early party platforms stressed the role of the state as a central economic planner and during its first mandate the PQ spoke of its favourable "bias towards workers." Although it never formally challenged the role of the private sector, the PQ portrayed itself as progressive (or left-wing) in social and economic matters. On the language issue it went further than Bill 22, and in Bill 101 declared French to be the province's *only* official language. Yet it continued the Quiet Revolution effort to stimulate indigenous business forces. In fact, many observers of the Parti Québecois era in Quebec politics argue that, in contrast to the central role played by the public sector especially in the 1960s and the PQ's "socialist" image, the party's policies evolved over time becoming increasingly sympathetic to the private sector. Richard French, for example, has noted that PQ policies seemed to fall into three distinct phases. From 1976 to 1979, relations between the indépendantiste government and business were largely conflictual; by the 1979 to 1982 era they were characterized by an attitude of co-existence. By 1982 to 1985 (when the PQ was defeated by the Liberals again led by the politically resurrected Bourassa), the government was clearly pro-business.

In fact, by the late 1970s a shift in the PQ attitude was evident. Although the government had begun with an effort to stimulate the private sector, it attempted to do so while maintaining the prominence of the public sector and an emphasis on state planning. By 1979, at a socioeconomic summit held at Montibello, Premier Lévesque signalled a shift from this approach. At that conference, he indicated that, under his government, the private sector would be the key economic actor. The new attitude of the PQ government was further indicated by two policy documents brought out in 1979 (*Challenges for Quebec*) and 1982 (*The Technology Conversion*). Both signalled the government's shift to a strong pro-market position and together elaborated an industrial policy prepared to pump $1 billion a year into an economy increasingly dominated by francophone and Quebec-based businesses. *The Technology Conversion*, epitomizing the shift to the right and away from direct state intervention, argued that:

[the] responsibility of ensuring sufficient, sustained development lies first of all with the private sector, since most enterprises are in this sector. The gouvernement du Québec [sic] has as one of its prime objectives to create and maintain conditions favourable to the development and dynamism of private initiatives, and feels that the best system of effectively allocating resources remains the market economy.[1]

Among its continuing efforts at economic stimulation, the Parti Québecois government brought in innovative market-oriented policies including a plan to spur stock investments in the province's private sector. This Quebec Stock Savings Plan (QSSP), introduced in 1979 by the PQ Finance Minister (and subsequently leader of the PQ) Jacques Parizeau, granted income tax deductions of 100 percent (and at times up to 150 percent) for investment in Quebec companies and proved a major stimulus the province's financial sector. The government not only assisted development of world-class financial institutions but emphasized efficiency in social programs and fostered development of the province's entrepreneurial climate.

The 1980s: A New Entrepreneurism

The PQ shift to the right occurred for both political and economic reasons. By the late 1970s governmental efforts to spur an indigenous Quebec business class began to pay off. The Quebec-based business community which had been protected and assisted by aggressive government policies since the 1960s demonstrated increasing political strength within the province.

Secondly, in the 1980s, public opinion virtually everywhere in the western world took a turn to the right and the unquestioned faith in public sector intervention, so pervasive in the 1960s, disappeared only to be replaced with an almost equally unquestioning faith in the marketplace and the business community. Like other jurisdictions, Quebec was affected by this ideological shift. Thirdly, in 1980 the PQ "lost" the referendum in which it sought popular approval to pursue discussions with the federal government on the indépendantiste option of sovereignty-association. A number of Quebec observers have suggested that this loss fostered a move from *political* nationalism to *economic* nationalism; in other words, the failure to achieve political independence led to a renewed commitment to pursuing economic independence through the provision of maximum assistance to Quebec-based enterprises. Finally, the 1981-82 recession left Quebec with reduced resources and the province's credit rating was lowered forcing it to rely less on public sector initiatives. Overall, the PQ shift to the right was unmistakeable. Thomas Courchene, who argues that 1981 signalled the changed PQ attitude, commented in 1986 that "the Parti Québecois became, after the referendum, the most business-oriented or market-oriented government in Canada."[2]

The PQ's increasingly pro-business stance alienated many of its key political backers. A crucial element of support had been located in the "new middle class" primarily employed in the provincial public sector. With the rapid expansion of government intervention in the 1960s and 70s, upward mobility had been rapid and many Québecois' careers were linked to continued state growth. By the early 1980s, the PQ demonstrated growing sympathy for the primacy of the private sector and demands of the business community for lessened government intervention. As a result, the government could no longer accede to demands for the continued expansion of the public sector and inflation of wages within it. In an effort to lessen its budgetary problems, the PQ took an increasingly rigid position and even harsh measures in response to labour demands.

In a series of laws passed in 1982-83, the government reduced government

| 96 |

THE EVOLUTION OF QUEBEC

employees' pension benefits, dictated bargaining conditions and salaries, imposed retroactive pay cuts in the public sector, put an end to the public school teachers' strike and arbitrarily determined conditions of work for the subsequent three years of public employees' contracts.

The new sympathies of the Parti Québecois government, although different from the policy orientation of the Quiet Revolution, in fact indicated the success of Quiet Revolution initiatives. Through the 1960s and 1970s, public sector forces functioned largely with the intent of spurring the provincially-based private sector. The SGF and the Caisse, for example, had invested widely in Quebec-based businesses, although without early evidence of success. Throughout the 1960s, the provincial private sector remained sluggish and dominated by English-Canadian and American capital. French-Canadian enterprises were almost entirely reliant on the provincial market. For example, in 1961 only 5 percent of manufacturing export from the province was accounted for by French-Canadian businesses. By the 1970s, however, and undoubtedly as a result of Quiet Revolution policies, the provincially-based private sector began to show some improvement. Data gathered as early as 1974 indicated the increasing clout of Quebec-based business and its growth continued throughout the 1970s and 1980s. Some companies like Provigo, only formed in 1969 as a result of the merger of three Quebec-based and francophone-controlled food wholesale businesses, grew rapidly. In 1977 Provigo expanded its power and size by taking over the larger M. Loeb Ltd. of Ottawa (which included both pan-Canadian and American holdings); in 1981 it acquired National Drug Limited and, as well, virtually all Dominion Stores in Quebec. By the mid-1980s, through its acquisitions and corporate restructuring, Provigo had become a major holding company engaged in the wholesale and retail distribution of food (it was, in fact, Canada's second-largest food distributor), drug products, sporting goods and general merchandise not only in Quebec but throughout Canada. Several other firms in Quebec similarly moved quickly into major international markets. Companies like Bombardier, Lavalin, Power Corporation, Quebecor and Unigesco, many actually only formed in the 1960s, now play major international roles and have spearheaded the new entrepreneurial spirit which has taken over in Quebec. As well, below the level of these larger companies there are a host of small and medium-sized companies which are aggressive in the marketplace. Whereas even in the early 1960s French-Canadian companies were small, backward, in need of capital and largely restricted to the Quebec market, in the 1990s Quebec-based businesses are actively export-oriented and confidently operating in the pan-Canadian, American and international marketplace.

| 97 |

By the mid-1980s, the new power of business in the province was clear. As the 1985 election scenario unfolded, both the PQ and the Liberals staked out their pro-business platforms and competed for prominent business people willing to carry the party banner in the election. The election of the Liberals, historically supported by the business community, signalled the new political power of the private sector. Premier Bourassa himself captured the change from state interventionism to a market-driven economy based on Quebec-based businesses in stating: "The presence of strong, dynamic and well-established Quebec enterprises means that economic power will stay in Quebec hands. But instead of resting with the State, it will be in the hands of Quebec businessmen."[3] Soon after its election, government actions revealed its unambiguous pro-business stance. It appointed three task forces, with membership overwhelmingly from business ranks, to recommend strategies on privatization, deregulation and government reorganization. The government's commitment to a market rationale was further indicated in its aggressive support of the Mulroney government's pursuit of the Canada-U.S. Free Trade Agreement. In 1989, the continued primacy of a right-wing agenda was reaffirmed by two salient events. The Caisse de Dépôt et Placement, by 1989 Canada's largest institutional investor with assets of $32 billion and with a mandate to grease Quebec's economic wheels, assisted a Quebec-based shipping firm, Socanav Inc., to take over the Montreal-based Steinberg grocery chain in the face of a rival bid from a Toronto-based firm. The bid was notable not only for its size but because, as part of the terms of the Caisse's participation, Socanav guaranteed that it would not sell the firm for at least nine years thus ensuring that Steinberg, the province's third largest employer with its head office in Montreal, would remain in the province.[4] Unsurprisingly, this was viewed by some in the Canadian business community as a dangerous example of the Caisse being used largely for political purposes. In contrast, within a few days the government was locked in a bitter dispute with the province's nurses, among the lowest-paid in the country, who had been forced to take recourse to an illegal strike in the face of the government's intransigent negotiating tactics.

The new economic context in Quebec is an outcome of the policy innovations undertaken by Quebec governments since the 1960s. Although the new business optimism within the province is unprecedented insofar as it is primarily francophone in character, it resulted from efforts made by Quebec provincial governments to spur the francophone and Quebec-based business sector. Key roles have been played in this by crown corporations like Hydro-Québec and investment funds like the SGF and the Caisse. In fact, these continue to play major roles in Quebec and international markets and to intervene in order to protect the Quebec economy and its vitality.

Today, Quebec is still marked by a desire to maintain its francophone character and to widen its autonomy from the federal level. This was manifested not only in Quebec's insistence on the ratification of the Meech Lake Accord by other provinces but also in the strong showing of the Parti Québecois in the 1989 provincial election. Although the Liberals were re-elected with 91 seats in the National Assembly to only 30 for the PQ (with an English protest party, the Equality Party garnering 4 seats), there were ominous signs in the election for observers committed to the federalist cause. The PQ, which fell only 10 percent below the Liberals in the popular vote not only did surprisingly well, it did so on what was once again a clearly indépendantiste platform. Furthermore, pro-Meech Lake advocates, including both Premier Bourasssa and Prime Minister Mulroney, unswervingly cast the debate about the Accord in terms by which failure to ratify it by other provinces could only be viewed in Quebec as a rejection of that province's aspirations within the Canadian system. Through these efforts to force the Meech Lake Accord on all Canadians without allowing for any revision, notwithstanding widespread and growing demand for precisely this, key political leaders have put in place conditions which seem likely to exacerbate tensions between Quebec and at least several other Canadian provinces.

Despite these continuing tensions, as Quebec moved into the 1990s the character of its strategy has changed dramatically. Whereas prior to 1960 the attempt to defend Quebec's autonomy relied on a defensive resistance to federal government initiatives, and in the 1960s and 70s on an interventionism which emphasized the primary role of the state, in the 1980s and into the 1990s the hope of Québecois is based on a political nationalism combined with a new economic nationalism and confidence in Quebec-based businesses. Rather than a sole reliance on overt governmental action, the new nationalism emphasizes Quebec-based business forces. Whether Québecois can indeed preserve and enhance their distinctiveness within an acceptance of the liberal and market-oriented world view so strongly resisted by traditional French-Canadian ideology will be interesting to watch as the 1990s unfold. What has become increasingly evident, however, is that the success of many of the Quiet Revolution reforms have combined Quebec's traditional nationalism with a new economic nationalism which may eventually underpin a more viable commitment to political separation from Canada.

[1] Government of Quebec, *The Technology Conversion* (Quebec: Editeur Officiel du Québec, 1982) p. 20.

[2] Thomas J. Courchene, "Market Nationalism," *Policy Options* 7:8 (October 1986) p. 7.

[3] As quoted in Anthony Wilson-Smith and Bruce Wallace, "Quebec's New Entrepreneurs," *Maclean's* 4 August 1986, p. 25.

[4] Barrie McKenna, "Fear, envy of Caisse de Dépôt renewing criticism of its power," *The Globe and Mail* 28 August 1989, pp. B1,15.

ANNOTATED READINGS

Gagnon, Alain-G. and Montcalm, Mary Beth. "Economic Peripheralization and Quebec Unrest." *Journal of Canadian Studies* 17 (Summer 1982): 32-41. Emphasizes the link between political unrest in the province and the peripheral nature of the Quebec economy in North America.

Gagnon, Alain-G. and Montcalm, Mary Beth. *Quebec: Beyond the Quiet Revolution.* Toronto: Nelson, 1990. A concise and thorough analysis of the political economy of Quebec and the long term structural problems within the province's economy, and its relationship to Quebec politics.

Guindon, Hubert. *Quebec Society: Tradition, Modernity and Nationhood.* Toronto: University of Toronto Press, 1988. A collection of essays written by the author, one of Quebec's most prominent sociologists, over a 30 year period. The articles deal with virtually all aspects of Quebec society (class, elites, culture, church, nationalism) and their impact on Quebec politics.

McRoberts, Kenneth. *Quebec: Social Change and Political Crisis,* Third edition. Toronto: McClelland and Stewart, 1988. The book examines the relationship between politics and the operation of government and the relationship between Quebec society and the economy. The historical and, more crucially, the contemporary developments and changes in the economy of Quebec and its effect on the expansion of the role of the state are given special attention.

McRoberts, Kenneth. "Quebec: Province, Nation or Distinct Society?" in Michael Whittington and Glen Williams, eds. *Canadian Politics in the 1990s,* Third edition. Toronto: Nelson, 1990: pp. 98-118. The article examines why Quebec society is distinctive and how a national consciousness has evolved from its distinctiveness.

CHAPTER 6

ONTARIO: CANADA WRIT SMALL

Ontario enjoys a unique status within the Canadian state. One astute observer of the Canadian political scene has suggested that it would be incorrect to even label Ontario as merely one region within Canada.

> Given its central location, the identification of the regional part, Ontario, with the national whole, Canada, is understandable. To illustrate the point in very simplistic terms, it is at least conceivable to imagine Quebec, Newfoundland, or the West separating from Canada. It is inconceivable to imagine Ontario separating: Ontario *is* Canada to a degree that no other region can claim.[1]

While this observation may not be one which is shared by others who populate the various regions within Canada, there can be very little doubt that Ontario is not a province or region like the others. It has a "special status" which is the product of its mirroring the fundamental cleavage patterns within the whole of Canada (ethnic, regional, economic, cultural) and its reflection of significant aspects of the national political process (party system and legislative politics). It is really a microcosm of the nation as a whole. The reflective dimension is only one aspect of the special status, the

ONTARIO: CANADA WRIT SMALL

other aspect is a direct consequence of its centrality within the "core"[2] region of Canada. This centrality gives the province, power, wealth and influence not found in other regions that not only influences its internal provincial politics but also, by almost a process of osmosis, the politics of the entire country. To illustrate this special status and its impact on the national scene, it is necessary to understand the unique economic and political setting of Ontario, its regional make-up, the nature of its party system, the dynamics of its internal legislative decision-making process and the subsequent inter-relationship of these variables upon Ontario's position in the Canadian federation.

I The Setting of Centrality I

Ontario accounts for over 40% of the total value of goods and services produced in Canada. Yet, unlike many of its sister provinces its wealth is not dependent on only one or two dominant economic activities, but rather is widely dispersed and found in most economic sectors which constitute the Canadian economy. Its agricultural sector is heterogeneous and produces total cash values which often places it first in the country. Its manufacturing sector is the strongest, accounting for over one-half of all the manufacturing jobs found in Canada. Its mineral sector ranks first in the country (excluding petroleum products) and it ranks third in forestry.[3]

Ontario's population includes about 35 out of every 100 Canadians. Since it has the largest population base in the state, it sends more representatives to the federal parliament than any other province. Indeed its federal membership in the 1988 House of Commons was three times greater than that of all the Atlantic Provinces (Newfoundland, Nova Scotia, New Brunswick and Prince Edward Island) and exceeded the total of all members sent to Ottawa from Western Canada (British Columbia, Alberta, Saskatchewan and Manitoba). Not only is its total federal representation in Parliament the largest in Canada, but its members also traditionally receive the largest number of cabinet posts, and the most important economic cabinet portfolios in the national government. Its web of influence extends beyond national political power to areas such as finance and media which shape the values and direction of other provinces and regions. This is so because it is home of most of the dominant organizations in these fields: banking, corporate offices, and media (CBC, CTV, magazines, films, etc.).

Yet while in aggregate the figures lead to the conclusion that Ontario is a

I 103 I

wealthy, heavily populated province, in fact Ontario is not economically monolithic or in socioeconomic terms a homogeneous province. Rather, in light of its vast geographic size, it displays within its boundaries a considerable degree of regionalism.

I Regionalism I

Some regions of the province are considerably more economically diverse and subsequently wealthier than other parts of the province (Toronto, South-western Ontario). Other regions of the province are not as fortunate, and, much like the case of other provinces in Canada, are less wealthy and more dependent on one or two economic sectors for their livelihood (Northern Ontario).

The population is not evenly distributed across the province but rather tends to be concentrated along the Windsor to Ottawa corridor. Even within this elongated corridor of population, the Toronto area (the Golden Horseshoe) stands paramount in terms of population (over one-third of the province's population).

The northern portion of Ontario, covers ninety percent of the total area of the land mass, but has only 8.9 percent of the province's total population.[4] Additionally, Northern Ontario itself is not monolithic and can be divided into three distinct sub-regions which vary in size of population, economic activity and ethnic composition. Weller writes that:

> The northeast and the northwest between them comprise the mid-north of the province. This consists of a scattering of small cities and towns, most of them heavily dependent upon the extraction of a single natural resource. The northeast is primarily dependent upon mineral extraction whereas the northwest is primarily dependent upon forest resources. Another clear distinction between the two is the much higher percentage of Franco-Ontarians in the northeast. The third sub-region is that of the far north beyond 50 degrees latitude where the population is very sparse and consists largely of a few widely scattered Indian communities heavily dependent upon welfare and the traditional economy of hunting, fishing and trapping.[5]

Finally, it can be noted that Ontario was and continues to be a magnet for immigrants to Canada. In 1988, for example, almost one-half of all

ONTARIO: CANADA WRIT SMALL

immigrants to Canada (49.1%) chose Ontario as their province of residence.[6] Yet new immigrants to the province have not settled in all regions of the province in equal numbers. Rather, they have primarily chosen the larger cities. This, coupled with the growing proportion of immigrants who come not from the traditional Northern European sources, but rather from Vietnam, Hong Kong, China, the Philippines, India and the Caribbean, has given the urban centres of Ontario a more multicultural and multiracial character than found previously.

I Party System I

The degree of regionalism within the province has influenced the nature of the province's party system. Since 1943 Ontario has become the only province in Canada with a stable three-party system. Since that time the third party has obtained between 20 to 25 percent of the popular vote cast in provincial elections, and since 1967 no third party has obtained less than 16 seats in the legislature.[7] Yet, as in most other provinces of Canada, the party system has been characterized by extended periods of one-party dominance. Indeed in the eighty year period between 1905 to 1985 the Progressive Conservative Party was only out of office on two occasions; 1919-1923, (United Farmers and Labour coalition government) and 1934-43 (Liberal government). More remarkable, however, was the uninterrupted series of consecutive Conservative governments which began in 1943 and ended only in 1985.

However, in spite of this picture of party stability, the actual degree of electoral competition among the parties is and was much greater than the over all aggregate electoral results would indicate. First, the first past the post, simple plurality electoral system utilized in the province greatly distorted the relationship between seats obtained and the actual percentage of the popular vote obtained by the parties. With three parties running two of them split the opposition vote against the government with the net result that a governing party could form a majority government with approximately forty percent of the vote. In the 1990 election the New Democratic Party became the first party in Ontario's history to form a majority government with only 37% of the popular vote. Part of the reason for the vote/seat distortion was a result of the further splintering of the popular vote by other "fourth" parties who received 7 percent of the total vote in the province.

Equally noteworthy has been the tendency, not found in other provinces,

CANADIAN GOVERNMENT AND POLITICS

for the result of an election to produce a minority government. In Ontario, since the beginning of the three party system, there have been four minority governments; 1943-45 (Progressive Conservative), 1975-81 (Progressive Conservative), 1985 (Progressive Conservative) and 1985-1987 (Liberal). Close electoral competition between the parties can also be observed in the brief period between 1985 and 1990 when all three parties formed a government in the province; 1985 (Progressive Conservative), 1985-1990 (Liberal), 1990 (New Democratic). Over all election results also have hidden the degree of regional support that each political party has received in an Ontario election. As Williams observed in his study of Ontario elections during the period between 1974 and 1981 the support for parties has varied considerably by region within the province.[8] Further, he noted the fortunes of the three corresponding federal parties have not been identical with the degree of regional support they have found in provincial elections. This pattern of regional variation has had, not surprisingly, a significant effect on the nature of parties in Ontario and their electoral style.

As the parties cannot rely on the same people to support them in both federal and provincial elections their appeal to the voters has become more pragmatic and less ideological in nature. As Graham White so succinctly noted, the "Ontario economy and society are too complex to permit polarization into two clearly defined political camps"[9] (e.g., Left versus Right).

The net result is that all three parties tend to be more pragmatic than ideological in matters of public policy. This phenomenon, of course, is reinforced by the relative degree of electoral competition found in the province. The lack of any great ideological distance between the parties can be seen at the time of the Liberal–New Democratic accord in 1985 which precipitated the formation of a Liberal party government at the expense of the Progressive Conservative Party which found itself in a minority government position following the election of 1985. The two parties, rather than forming a coalition government, negotiated a "conditional legislative alliance"[10] in a written document which specified agreement between the parties on a host of issues to be implemented during a Liberal government. More significantly the accord was not a radical document but was limited in its policy focus and scope of change.

Three documents that flow from the letter of agreement use the term "reform" over and over again. The reforms are of a limited nature rather than those which students of ideology would regard as fundamentally restructuring the social and economic system. The

ONTARIO: CANADA WRIT SMALL

introduction of the phase "fiscal accountability" in the titles of the second and third documents is testimony to the pragmatic nature of reform.[11]

| Premier, Cabinet, Bureaucracy: | The Apex of Power

At the top of the governmental structure is the premier of the province. In Ontario the individual social background characteristics of a premier have remained relatively little changed since 1867. Of the province's 21 premiers all but one have come from Anglo-Saxon roots; all but one has been protestant, and almost 80% of the time since Confederation the male occupant of the office (there have been no female premiers) has been a lawyer. Also, in spite of the dominance of Ontario's principal city, Toronto, none of the premiers has called Toronto home. Premiers have resided in the smaller towns and cities of the province.[12]

Unlike federal leaders, Ontario premiers have seldom been called upon to provide a "public persuader"[13] role where they have needed to rally the public behind a controversial decision made by the government. They have tended to be "managers" rather than leaders. Their primary role is to look after the store, or, more accurately, to ensure that the economic prosperity of Ontario is not jeopardized. As managers, their relationship with the legislature has tended not to be "hands on" in approach but rather one of watchful attention slightly removed from the actual running of the legislature. In the last few decades "other than attending Question period, premiers spent very little time in the legislature."[14] Further, with the executive reforms initiated in the 1970's by the Committee on Government Productivity (COGP) (a particularly apt name in the Ontario context) the cabinet structure has evolved into an "institutionalized cabinet."[15] This cabinet system in many instances features structure and process concerns (e.g., cabinet committees) which have tended to dilute the power of cabinet in relation to the premier. The gradual erosion of cabinet influence has gone hand in hand with the growth in importance of the province's bureaucracy.

While the administrative apparatus in Ontario employs over 90,000 people, it is the much smaller complement (about 1%) of deputy ministers and senior level officials who have the greatest impact on the initiation, formulation and implementation of public policy. Since the COGP reforms, their position has been enhanced considerably. During the Davis years, from 1971 to 1985, "the political leaders [cabinet] and the senior bureaucracy learned,

| 107 |

in the main, to work together."[16] The traditional idea that administrative and political decisions should be separate was rejected. As Edward Stewart, a man who combined both administrative and political responsibilities as Secretary of the Cabinet for Davis from 1976 to 1985 admonished, "a deputy who claims that political considerations never influenced his or her thinking, or the advice he or she is giving to the government, is either trying to deceive the public or is of limited value to the Premier and ministers he or she serves."[17] The augmented status of the higher levels of the public service was not substantially reduced in the post-1985 years with the ascendancy of Peterson to the office of premier. In Peterson's era all but two cabinet committees had "advisory committees of deputy ministers"[18] and while Peterson only slightly modified the structural components of the executive policy-making process, he "continued to build links to the Ontario mandarinate by giving it a more active role in policy development and paid special attention to its concerns."[19]

| The Ontario Legislature |

The other crucial component in the decision-making process in the province, is, of course, the Legislative Assembly and its members. As with premiers, the background characteristics of the legislators until recently were relatively similar. A study of legislators elected to the 1987 parliament found that seven out of ten came from three professions: Finance, Law, and Education. Additionally, it can be noted that while the percentage of women found in the assembly doubled in the period between the 1985 Parliament and 1987 Parliament they still constituted only 15 percent of the membership in that Parliament.[20]

However, as a result of the 1990 New Democratic Party electoral victory (74 of 130 seats) the occupational and gender composition of the legislature was considerably modified. With 60 first-time elected NDP members the legislature took on a decidedly more blue collar occupational composition, primarily at the expense of those members in the fields of business and law. Fourteen of the party's new MPP's were blue collar workers who came from the auto assembly lines, chemical plants and steel mills of the province[21] (8% of the total legislature). Further, the election produced a further increase in the gender composition of the legislature with 28 women elected (21% of the legislature).

Taken together the social composition of the premiers and legislators would seem to suggest that the Ontario legislature was a relatively homo-

ONTARIO: CANADA WRIT SMALL

geneous upper middle class elite. While the results of the 1990 election modified the occupational composition of the assembly the basic middle class background of the legislature remains. In socioeconomic terms, they certainly are still not representative of the vast diversity of the population in the province. And, while the percentage of women in the legislature has increased over the past few elections, the assembly still remains a predominately male legislature.

Turning specifically to the legislature, its propensity to be a body inclined more towards gradual change and limited influence can be observed in regard to both its size and the impact of the province's party system on its style and operation. The legislature in Ontario has, much like its counterparts in other provinces, changed considerably since the 1960's. The greatest impetus for change came through the Ontario Commission on the Legislature (Camp Commission) which in a series of reports between 1973-75 called for reforms such as an increase in the powers of the speaker and greater party caucus resources. One astute observer wrote that its record had improved considerably in terms of the quality of "its members, its staff and services, its procedure, its committee system and its accountability mechanisms."[22] As White and Levy note,[23] the size of the legislature (130 members: the largest provincial house in Canada) has had an impact on both its structure and operation and its subsequent effectiveness. It has been argued that the degree of executive dominance in the assembly is proportionally less than that found in smaller assemblies. In Ontario only about 20% of the total membership of the House is in the Cabinet. This then gives non-executive legislators greater room for influence than would be found in assemblies where the proportion of cabinet members to the total assembly is much higher. The larger house also permits the assembly to have a more effective and comprehensive committee system which by and large gives adequate representation to all parties in the legislature. Additionally, procedures of the House are influenced by the larger number of members, who thus are able to staff specialized committees, such as estimate committees rather than going to the Committee of the whole, which is the whole house. The larger assembly also gives opposition members a substantial role to play in accountability through mechanisms such as the Public Accounts Committee and question period. Finally, the partisan political behaviour in the House , where generally good inter-party relations are the rule may well be a consequence of its size.[24] Members have more opportunity for cross-party contact in settings such as committees that tend to foster an appreciation of each other's ability regardless of party stripe.

The continuing three-party system has meant the likelihood of a minority

CANADIAN GOVERNMENT AND POLITICS

government is greater than in either a two-party system or in a one-party dominant system where there are few if any elected opposition members (Alberta, New Brunswick). This has meant that members voices are more likely to be heard by the party leaders in order to help ensure a party's electoral success within the province. Further, as there is less ideological distance between the parties than in more polarized provincial political environments (British Columbia) room for moderation and accommodation between the parties in structuring the rules procedures and operation of the house is greater. Party accommodation in changing the rules and procedures of the legislature has been further enhanced in minority government situations. In the 1985-87 period of the Liberal–New Democratic Party accord, legislative procedures were implemented which substantially enhanced the power of legislators at the expense of the executive.

However, in spite of these factors the legislature is still less than perfect in its internal decision-making capacity. In general, as a result of the province's large population, each provincial legislator on average represents approximately 70,000 constituents.[25] While on the one hand, this large number of constituents which the MPP has to serve (constituency service role), has led to increased staff and resources for individual MPP's, it has also meant MPP's in Ontario are to a large degree preoccupied with servicing their constituents. Their focus of attention thus tends to be highly localized, and means that to a considerable extent more province-wide issues tend not to get the attention that they deserve. The legislature as a whole tends to be "preoccupied with issues of limited scope or only local impact."[26] Finally, it may be noted the legislature probably attracts the lowest political interest from its provincial electors of any assembly in the country.[27] This unhappy state of affairs is caused not so much as a result of the legislators tendency to deal with lesser issues, but rather the tendency for Ontarians to view the national government as more important in their daily lives to a greater degree than citizens of other provinces. With the focus of the province's people on the federal level of government the day-to-day events transpiring in Queen's Park tend to be often overlooked, poorly reported, and perhaps greatly misunderstood by the electors.

I Public Policy I

As decision makers the legislature, executive and bureaucracy are responsible for the formulation and implementation of provincial public policy. As can be noted in Table 1 the Ontario government spends the bulk of its money on the provision of social programs (health, education, welfare). In 1987-88 Ontario spent almost two-thirds of its revenues (65%) in social policy fields with two ministries disbursing over four-fifths (83%) of those expenditures, health (50%) and education (33%).

The reasons for the high degree of expenditures on social policy are several. First, provinces have the constitutional responsibility for many of the social policy fields (health, education). Secondly, the federal government stimulated growth in the area by its use of both conditional and unconditional grants to the provinces. Thirdly, extensive industrialization and urbanization within the province have made the provision of social services necessary. Finally, there has been the political will to spend money in the area of social policy.

TABLE 1

PROVINCIAL POLICY: REVENUES AND EXPENDITURES

Expenditures: Policy Fields	%		Revenue Sources	%	
Social Policy	65		Taxation	66	
Health	50		Personal Income Tax	50	
Education	33		Provincial Taxes	50	
Other	17		Federal Transfers		15
Economic Policy	17		Miscellaneous Revenue		4
Debt Payment	11		Trust, Loan Revenue		5
General Government	4				
Justice	3				

Source: George G. Bell and Andrew D. Pascoe, *The System of Government in Ontario*. Toronto: Wall and Thompson, 1988, pp. 33-34.

With the long period of Conservative governments it might have been expected that social policy expenditures might not have been a high priority. This was not the case. The competitive nature of the party system dictated that Conservative governments had to take into account the policy positions of opposition parties. At the very beginning of the modern party system,

George Drew fought and won the 1943 election on a program of sweeping social reforms at a time when the CCF was riding a strong wave of popularity. Since that time all PC governments in Ontario have understood that they cannot allow the initiative on social reforms to pass to the NDP. . . .[28]

| 111 |

Further, social policy expenditures were viewed by Conservative governments as a crucial part of economic policy. For example, welfare policy is "more than a series of responses to the demands of the poor. It must be understood as part of policies directed towards economic stability and management."[29]

Expenditures, of course, require revenue. Table 1 illustrates that Ontario governments receive the largest share of their revenues from taxation (66%) with personal income tax, collected by the federal government being a significant component of those revenues. Additionally, federal transfer payments to the province account for a further 15% of the provinces revenue. This coupled with the observation that over one out of ten dollars (11%) is spend to cover the provincial debt makes federal-Ontario relations a highly salient element in public policy-making in Ontario.

I Ontario in the Canadian I Federation

The history of Ontario-federal relations has been one which has witnessed both periods of harmony and tranquility and bitter conflicts between the two governments. The cyclical nature of the relationship has been readily apparent during the last four decades. In the 1950's, under Premier Frost the relationship was relatively harmonious, yet in the 1960's Premier Robarts had serious conflicts with the national government. In the last two decades, Premiers Davis (1971-1985) and Peterson (1985-1990) were engaged in intergovernmental relations which exhibited an almost equal mix of periods of harmony and conflict.[30]

The differences of opinion between the two jurisdictions are the result of several factors. Rand Dyck has suggested a number of reasons for disagreements between the two governmental entities. Conflict may result from different political parties holding governmental power in Ottawa and Toronto, a situation that in the first 120 years of Confederation was indeed the case over 60 percent of the time. Clashes may be the product of a confrontation between the two largest governments in Canada over such matters as money, power and status. Hostility may be influenced by the leadership personalities of the individual leaders who hold office at either the provincial or national level. Finally, disagreements may result from policy differences between the two governments which are influenced by different regional, economic, ethnic and class differences found in Canada as a whole and in Ontario, as well as the differences in opinion on how best to deal with the

ONTARIO: CANADA WRIT SMALL

United States, a nation whose influence crucially effects both Canada and Ontario.[31] For example while the national government was promoting the Free Trade Agreement with the United States during the 1988 federal election, Premier Peterson opposed the agreement.

While all of these factors have at one time or another had some bearing on federal-Ontario relations Dyck suggests, "Ultimately the most common conflicts between Ontario and the Federal government have related to the question of provincial autonomy and problems of money, power and status."[32] In retrospect, this conclusion should not be seen as an unusual one, when two large and powerful governments come into contact in the arena of intergovernmental relations.

While the battle over power, status and autonomy between the two governments may be a primary cause for disagreement it must be recognized that the struggle does not lead to the conclusion that Ontario is involved in a solely self-seeking "Ontario first" strategy in intergovernmental relations. Such a position would not recognize the policy preferences of the federal government or other provinces. Ontario's traditional bargaining posture is built around bridge-building, balancing the interests of the entire state and requiring the premier to act in a non-partisan statesmanlike role.[33] This bargaining posture is a direct consequence of the province's internal political environment.

Initially, it can be suggested that the regional diversity found within Ontario itself has meant Ontario premiers have been sensitized to the need for balancing Canadian regional interests. Also, because Ontario's citizens have a strong national identification, its provincial leaders must not act in such a way on the national scene that they are perceived by Ontarians as being parochial or putting the province's interests before those of the country. They must be seen as statesmen even if often they are not. Ontario's position must be perceived as one that is constructive and designed to strengthen the nation. Further, the party system which has witnessed long periods of one-party dominance has meant leaders of both the federal and provincial parties, even if they are from different political parties, must accommodate each other if both are to be electorally successful within the province. Finally, Ontario is extremely aware of its dominant economic and political position in the Canadian federation and as it has the largest stake in maintaining the "Canadian common market" it has recognized that it must exercise self-restraint when dealing with the national and the other provincial governments.[34]

The self-restraint (which might well be questioned by residents of other provinces) of Ontario, however, has a special meaning for its relations with the province of Quebec and the federal government. Here, the traditional stance of Ontario's premiers has been one of awareness, concern and indeed of attempting to act as the honest broker between Quebec, the federal government and the other provinces of Canada. The different relationship in regard to Quebec is founded upon historical, economic and cultural factors. Historically, both Ontario and Quebec were part of the original bargain which resulted in the formation of Canada. In recognition of being the founding nations of Confederation, the Ontario premier sits to the right of the prime minister while the Quebec premier sits to his left at First Ministers Conferences. Both to a considerable degree have common economic interests. In the early years of Confederation, both were active in ensuring that the riches of natural resources which flowed from the Canadian Shield, which they both populate, would flow to their respective treasuries.[33] In more contemporary times, both have shared a common interest in fostering and maintaining the manufacturing sector within their provinces and Ontario has at times been involved in an "aggressively provincialist course usually in collaboration with the government of Quebec."[35] The economic link between the two provinces is solidified by the fact that each province is the other's best customer.

Yet, Ontario's position vis-à-vis Quebec is based on more than a self-centred economic interest. As Quebec and Ontario have the largest number of "charter" citizens within their respective provinces (French, English), Ontario in the last thirty years or so has attempted to dampen wherever possible political tensions between the two groups. This has resulted in Ontario premiers attempting, even without full-fledged mass support within the province, to promote linguistic policies which would foster enhanced French-English understanding.

I Summary I

Ontario is in a great many ways a microcosm of Canada as a whole. Ontario's regional nature, its racial and ethnic diversity and its regionally diversified economy are all features which characterize Canada. The stable three party system, the muting of ideological politics, the long periods of one party dominance and periodic minority governments, are all elements which are associated with the national party system. Its internal legislative decision making process with a numerically strong and expert bureaucracy, upper middle class legislators focusing upon matters of regional and local interest, and an executive functioning around an "institutionalized cabinet" with a

ONTARIO: CANADA WRIT SMALL

strong leader at the apex of power, relatively free to deal with the larger issues of state, are all common features of legislative politics in Ottawa. Also much like the national government it has a special interest in Quebec and Quebec's position in the federation.

It is equally apparent the province's wealth, size of population and consequent political power adds immeasurably to its "special status" within Canada. This status is often misunderstood by both its own citizens and the residents of other provinces. On the one hand, people in Ontario, frequently equate Ontario's interests with those of Canada as a whole, a view which often infuriates those outside the province. On the other hand, those who live beyond its boundaries, frequently misperceive Ontario as merely a province or region like all others. The reality of Ontario lies somewhere between. In the final analysis Ontario is a province like no other.

CANADIAN GOVERNMENT AND POLITICS

NOTES

[1] Roger Gibbins, *Conflict and Unity: An Introduction to Canadian Political Life* (Toronto: Methuen, 1985) p. 112.

[2] For the distinction between the "core and the "periphery" see C. F. J. Whebell, "Geography and Politics in Canada: Selected Aspects" in John H. Redekop (ed.), *Approaches to Canadian Politics* 2nd ed. (Scarborough: Prentice-Hall, 1983) pp. 3-27.

[3] See "Ontario" in Rand Dyck, *Provincial Politics in Canada* (Scarborough: Prentice-Hall, 1986) pp. 264-265.

[4] See Geoffrey R. Weller, "Politics and Policy in the North" in Graham White (ed.), *The Government and Politics of Ontario* 4th ed. (Scarborough: Nelson, 1990) p. 276-277.

[5] *Ibid.* p. 276.

[6] *The Globe and Mail*, Wednesday, July 18, 1990 p. A20.

[7] See Graham White, "Ontario: A Legislature in Adolescence" in Gary Levy and Graham White (ed.), *Provincial and Territorial Legislatures in Canada* (Toronto: University of Toronto Press, 1989) p. 31.

[8] See Robert J. Williams, "Ontario's Party Systems: Federal and Provincial" in Hugh G. Thorburn (ed.), *Party Politics in Canada* 5th ed. (Scarborough: Prentice-Hall, 1985) pp. 304.

[9] See Graham White, *op. cit.* p. 31.

[10] R. Krause, R. G. Price and R. H. Wagenberg, "A New Alternative: the Legislative Alliance in Ontario," *The American Review of Canadian Studies* 16, 4 (Winter, 1986) 413.

[11] *Ibid.* p. 419.

[12] Graham White, "Governing From Queen's Park: The Ontario Premiership" in Leslie A. Pal and David Taras (ed.), *Prime Ministers and Premiers: Political Leadership and Public Policy in Canada* (Scarborough: Prentice-Hall, 1988) pp. 159-160.

[13] *Ibid.* p. 161.

[14] *Ibid.* p. 172.

[15] *Ibid.* p. 174.

[16] Edward E. Stewart, *Cabinet Government in Ontario: A View from Inside* (Halifax, Nova Scotia: The Institute for Research on Public Policy, 1989) p. 47.

[17] *Ibid.* p. 49.

[18] Richard Loreto and Graham White, "The Premier and the Cabinet" in Graham White (ed.), *The Government and Politics of Ontario* 4th ed., *op. cit.* p. 100.

[19] Graham White, "Governing from Queen's Park: The Ontario Premiership," *op. cit.* p. 170.

[20] Robert J. Fleming (ed.), *Canadian Legislatures: 1987-1988* (Ottawa: Ampersand Communications Services Inc., 1988) p. 74.

[21] Paul Moloney, "14 New N.D.P. members have held public office," *The Toronto Star*, Sept. 10, 1990 p. A9.

ONTARIO: CANADA WRIT SMALL

[22] Graham White, *The Ontario Legislature: A Political Analysis* (Toronto: University of Toronto Press, 1989) p. 261.

[23] For the impact of size upon the operation of a provincial legislature, see, Graham White and Gary Levy "Introduction: The comparative analysis of Canadian provincial and territorial legislative assemblies" in Gary Levy and Graham White (eds.), *op. cit.* p. 4-7.

[24] *Ibid.* p. 6.

[25] *Ibid.* p. 8.

[26] Graham White, *The Ontario Legislature: A Political Analysis*, op. cit. p. 254.

[27] Graham White, "Ontario: A Legislature in Adolescence" in Gary Levy and Graham White (eds.), *op. cit.* p. 32.

[28] Marsha A. Chandler and William M. Chandler, *Public Policy and Provincial Politics* (Toronto: McGraw-Hill Ryerson, 1979) p. 69.

[29] *Ibid.* p. 182.

[30] Rand Dyck, "The Position of Ontario in the Canadian Federation" in R.D. Olling and M.W. Westmacott (eds.), *Perspectives on Canadian Federalism* (Scarborough: Prentice Hall, 1988) pp. 326.

[31] *Ibid.* pp. 326-328.

[32] These points are covered in Donald W. Stevenson, "Ontario and Confederation: A Reassessment" in Ronald L. Watts and Douglas M. Brown (eds.), *Canada: The State of the Federation 1989* (Kingston, Ontario: Institute of Intergovernmental Relations, 1989) pp. 54-57. Some of the same ideas on the traditional bargaining posture of Ontario are also found in Rand Dyck, "The Position of Ontario in the Canadian Federation," *op. cit.* p. 339-40.

[33] These points are outlined either implicitly or explicitly in Donald W. Stevenson's penetrating analysis of Ontario's position in Ontario-federal relations. See Donald W. Stevenson, "Ontario and Confederation: A Reassessment," *op. cit.* pp. 59-61 and 72.

[34] Garth Stevenson, *Unfulfilled Union* 3rd ed. (Toronto: Gage, 1989) p. 80.

[35] *Ibid.* p. 85.

ANNOTATED READINGS

White, Graham, ed. *The Government and Politics of Ontario*, Fourth Edition. Scarborough: Nelson Canada, 1990. The most informative overall treatment of Ontario dealing with the general areas of environment and political culture, government institutions, politics and policy. An absolutely essential book for those interested in the Ontario political system.

Dyck, Rand. *Provincial Politics in Canada*. Scarborough: Prentice-Hall, 1986. A book that deals with all the provincial governments in Canada. While not explicitly comparative, the treatment of each province, allows for a comparative focus around which the unique nature of Ontario politics can be assessed.

White, Graham. *The Ontario Legislature: A Political Analysis*. Toronto: University of Toronto Press, 1989. A thorough discussion of the Ontario legislature dealing with subjects such as the setting, the participants, the legislature at work (overview, routine proceedings legislation and finances), committees, services to members, accountability and the process of reform.

Levy, Gary and Graham White, eds. *Provincial and Territorial Legislatures in Canada*. Toronto: University of Toronto Press, 1989. While the book deals with the legislatures of the ten provinces and the Northwest Territories and the Yukon, its introductory comparative essay on all sub-national legislatures and the political insights it gives in each of its chapters makes it an extremely valuable book for students of provincial politics.

Stevenson, Donald W. "Ontario and Confederation: A Reassessment," in Ronald L. Watts and Douglas M. Brown, ed. *Canada: The State of the Federation 1989*. Kingston: Institute of Intergovernmental Relations, 1989, pp. 53-74. A brilliant article outlining Ontario's traditional stance in intergovernmental relations and its relationship to Ontario's future position as it is affected by the changing environment (such as Free Trade) facing the province.

| CHAPTER 7 |

WESTERN CANADA

DAVID E. SMITH

| One Region or Two? |

Canada is a country of pronounced geographical and cultural regions. Excluding the North (that is, the Yukon and Northwest Territories), its regions are customarily considered to include the Atlantic Provinces, Quebec, Ontario, the Prairie Provinces and British Columbia. Sometimes, in defiance of the country's most prominent topographical feature, the Rocky Mountains, British Columbia and the three provinces to its east are considered as one region — western Canada. That is the case in this discussion. In addition to the convenience of reducing the number of chapters on regions in a book not devoted to regionalism, there are other justifications for treating the vast area west of Ontario as one unit.

While there are many reasons for treating these provinces as one region, here are some of the main ones. All four western provinces were settled late, primarily after Confederation in 1867. Although Manitoba and British Columbia entered the federation (in 1870 and 1871 respectively) before Prince Edward Island (1873), PEI's institutions and society long pre-dated those of B.C. and Manitoba. As well, and to a unique extent, federal government policies — on immigration, the tariff and railways, for example — determined the development of the four provinces. Partly because of that influence, these provinces share a tradition of suspicion of the federal government and central institutions, one revealed in their electorates' distinctive voting record and support for parties other than the Liberal or Conservative parties. Although all Canadian provinces have depended in varying degrees on the exploitation of natural resources for their wealth, the four western provinces have depended more than the rest, either because, on the one hand, they are less diversified than Ontario and Quebec (who have large secondary-industry sectors), or because, on the other hand, their natural resource base is much greater than that of the Atlantic provinces.

Nonetheless, there are also significant differences among British Columbia and Alberta, Saskatchewan and Manitoba. Again, to begin with geography: the prairies are flat and British Columbia is not, and it was the southern portions of the fertile plains that became the base of Canada's major export in the first half of this century — grain. In turn, the grain economy dictated the pattern of prairie immigration and settlement, the system of land tenure, the location of the railways and roads, and a multitude of other responses, both public and private. British Columbia's mountainous terrain impeded settlement of the interior and confined population to the river valleys and coastal deltas. The forest-clad slopes of the mountains became the base of B.C.'s major resource industry — timber, while the long, indented coastline and the warm Pacific Ocean spawned another lucrative enterprise — fisheries. Contrary to the popular image of the agrarian prairies, the northern half (or Shield portion) of this area is heavily treed, though not with valuable Douglas Fir. Nonetheless, the governments in Edmonton, Regina and Winnipeg have worked hard, though with mixed success, to develop this resource, especially to produce pulp and paper.

Western Canada is well endowed with natural resources below and above, ground. Some, such as coal, are found east and west of the continental divide, while others occur on one or the other side of the mountains: metals in B.C., potash in Saskatchewan, natural gas and oil mainly in Alberta but also in Saskatchewan. The difference in natural resources between British Columbia and the prairie provinces lies less in their variety or location than in the public policies that have surrounded them. Of crucial importance was the decision of the government of Canada to retain the natural resources of the prairie provinces at the time each was created, Manitoba in 1870, Alberta and Saskatchewan in 1905; ownership was transferred to all three only in 1930. Neither British Columbia nor any other province shared in this discriminatory treatment, but, instead, under S. 109 of the **Constitution Act, 1867**, retained possession of their resources when they entered Confederation.

Although more will be said about the resources question later, at this point it is useful to recall that the three prairie provinces were the only provinces to be created by statutes of the Parliament of Canada, in each instance out of the vast territory lying between Hudson Bay and the Rockies that was transferred by Great Britain to the federal government after 1868. By contrast, the colony of British Columbia negotiated its terms of entry into Confederation, and its existing government and territory became part of Canada by action of the imperial (i.e. British) government. The distinctive origin of the prairie provinces explains the antipathy to the federal government more commonly found on the prairies than in British Columbia, and one product of that antipathy — the long search by prairie residents for institutions and processes to protect themselves from further dictation by Ottawa.

Thus, whether western Canada is one region or two depends on the context in which the question is asked. On balance, the topographical differences between British Columbia and the other three provinces are less important to understanding western Canada than the fact that all four provinces share a sense of isolation from central Canada. That isolation is only partly a function of distance; equally significant has been a series of federal policies — economic and cultural — over which westerners believe they have had little influence and which in western eyes neither reflect their values nor contribute to the well-being of their region. Arguably, it is these policies which have provided the strongest stimulus toward creating a western Canadian identity, an observation borne out by a growing tendency in the West for governmental and non-governmental bodies to form a united front when dealing with their national counterparts.

I Setting I

HISTORY: A DIFFERENT KIND OF FRONTIER

Major settlement did not occur on the prairies until after the arrival of the CPR in 1885, while in British Columbia it appeared a few decades earlier but was confined to the southern tip of Vancouver Island. Yet in the previous two centuries European and Canadian traders had regularly crossed the West in search of furs. The North West Company, based at Montreal, and the Hudson's Bay Company (HBC), based in London and given monopoly trading rights after 1670 to the area drained by rivers flowing into Hudson Bay, had established posts and routes throughout the West and North; in 1821 the two companies united under the name Hudson's Bay Company

CANADIAN GOVERNMENT AND POLITICS

and in 1847 that Company secured control of Vancouver Island. The native population had its first encounters with Europeans as a result of this fur trade. Thus, long before the period of mass settlement at the end of the nineteenth century, the West was the scene of a mercantilist trade (i.e. exporting raw materials — in this instance, fur — and importing finished goods). Along with other factors, this trade, via the Hudson Bay route or around the Horn to Britain and Europe, made the West an imperial not a Canadian frontier[1]. In this respect the early history of the Canadian West was vitally different from that of its neighbouring American region. The U.S. frontier stretching from New England to the Carolinas advanced across the continent from east to west enveloping all before it and bringing with it a strong infusion of American institutions and practices. Perhaps befitting a country with sharply defined regions, the Canadian frontier assumed a different character in different parts of the country: in the West, the predominant ethos was derived from the distant imperial power.

The West's experience of government and trade in the hands of the monopolistic HBC, whose decisions were made outside the region, proved but a prelude to similar experiences later, the most obvious parallel being the CPR's singular influence after 1885. Other contacts might be based more closely to home, for instance, the Roman Catholic Church and its missions, whose religious orders often represented the most sustained but not necessarily the most benign contact natives ever had with Europeans. But they, too, were part of an institutional framework that determined the West's early development. In this period the frontier was populated not by independent-minded individuals seeking escape from the confines of civilization but by clerks, clerics and petty bureaucrats.

Confederation, the transfer of Rupert's Land and the North-Western Territory by Britain to Canada, the unrest at Red River in 1869, and the desire by Ottawa to provide for peaceful settlement throughout the West led to the creation in 1873 of the force later known as the NorthWest Mounted Police. Thus another institutional restraint was added to western life, one which with rare exceptions guaranteed an orderly and organized period of settlement. The success of the mounted police depended upon the peaceable nature of the native people and on the pervasive respect both natives and whites held for the law. That respect was intimately linked to British traditions surrounding the courts and judiciary. A major concern in the study of politics is the means by which societies establish their legitimacy; it is no exaggeration to say that the legitimacy of the West's early institutions derived substantially from their British origins.

At least until the First World War, when a strong sense of Canadian nationalism began to become evident in the West, westerners used imperial references to define their development. The Empire offered a set of values for Canadians in other regions of the country too; but in those areas there was also a colonial or domestic experience on which to build. The size and sparse population of the West, whose governing institutions were external to the region and even to Canada, discouraged the development of similar internal unity there. The "separation" of the West from the rhythm of national life, a feature which grew stronger even as Canada expanded westward, was established early because of its distinctive setting.

ECONOMY: BENEVOLENT DEPENDENCY

The dependency which first appeared in pre-settlement days later became an object of public policy, or so it seemed to westerners after they became part of Confederation. Its bedrock was the National Policy, announced by John A. Macdonald in 1887. Initially, that policy was limited to a tariff to protect Canadian industries, but eventually it came to embrace a set of initiatives which included construction of a transcontinental railway and promotion of western settlement. Built with gifts of public money and public land, the CPR received as well preferential treatment in the form of exemption from local taxes and a monopoly on traffic between its line and the international boundary. Prairie farmers needed the railway to haul their grain to distant ports for shipment abroad, but they paid heavily for the privilege. "It was the frontier which paid [for the railway]," wrote Chester Martin in his study of *Dominion Lands' Policy* and to illustrate his claim, he noted that "for more than 650 miles of Ontario mileage for the main line of the CPR, not a single acre of land subsidy came from the Province of Ontario," while Saskatchewan "contributed nearly half the acreage of the whole federal railway land grant system."[2] Under these conditions, which deprived territorial governments of valuable land and resources, no railway could be popular, and hatred of the CPR became an article of faith for western farmers.

At the end of the nineteenth century, when the CPR wanted to build another line from southern Alberta through the Crowsnest Pass and into British Columbia, to tap the coal and mineral traffic of the area, feeling was so intense that the federal government agreed to further subsidies only in exchange for a guarantee from the CPR to fix its freight rates on western goods in perpetuity. These became the famous Crowsnest Rates, widely known as the farmers' Magna Carta. After being temporarily suspended during the First World War, in the 1920s they became enshrined in statute

| 123 |

and, therefore, their abolition required an act of Parliament. This was passed in 1983 only after acrimonious debate within the grain industry, in parliament and between the western provincial and federal governments.

Passion over the Rates suggests another western obsession — railways. For British Columbia, where promise of a railway had been a key condition for its entry in 1871, the CPR symbolized the commitment of Confederation; on the prairies an efficient network of rail lines to serve the thousands of scattered elevators proved indispensable to the success of the wheat economy and to the widely dispersed population dependent upon it. Compared to other areas of the country, where distances were shorter and where alternative means of transportation (e.g. water or road) played a vital role in their economy, the West, and especially the prairies, looked overwhelmingly to rail. This background helps to explain the intense regional feeling which accompanied federal proposals to curtail rail services, either through rail-line abandonment, as implemented in the 1970s, or closure of VIA Rail, as proposed at the end of the 1980s.

To return to the question of resources, as mentioned earlier, Ottawa retained control of the resources, which included the most important resource of the early twentieth century land, because it wanted to promote orderly settlement of the West and it thought this would not happen if each province determined its own settlement policy. In addition to blocs of land set aside to support schools and help finance the railway, other blocs were designated for homesteading. Through an aggressive policy, the federal authorities directed hundreds of thousands of immigrants from Europe, the British Isles and the United States to the West and permitted some who were bound by religion and language to settle as groups. This is the origin of the prairies' unusual collection of ethnic settlements, still evident today in the Canadian census and election returns.

By the 1920s, western settlement had ended and with it the reason for federal control of resources. Ironically, the transfer of resources to the prairie provinces in 1930 coincided with the onset of a decade of severe drought and depression which forced these provinces into near-bankruptcy and consequently renewed dependency on Ottawa, first for relief and then for policies of economic rehabilitation.

Would the 1930 transfer have been made, had the federal government known of the rich reserves of oil and natural gas that lay under the prairies? Fifty years later, when the price of international oil skyrocketed, and Alberta and Saskatchewan stood to gain what those elsewhere called "windfall" profits, the federal government intervened through its National Energy Policy to regulate the domestic price of this resource. Ottawa's argument that a moderated price increase was in the national interest sparked furious dissent in Alberta and Saskatchewan, since no other province had had the price of its natural resources curtailed for any reason.

The dependency of the West on federal policies is a more complex subject than westerners usually admit. On the one hand, unlike the prairie provinces. British Columbia never suffered the indignity of being treated as less than an equal partner in Confederation. Because the development of its forests and mines and hydroelectric power always remained in its own hands, "the province has prospered independently of federal policies."[3] Donald E. Blake, a political scientist who has studied British Columbia's politics, also asserts that "the historical record provides little support for basing grievances on a quasi-colonial past or on federal obstacles to provincial prosperity."

On the other hand, while the federal policies have had a determinative influence on the prairie provinces, it is less than conclusive that they have been detrimental to its well-being. For instance, in this century and except for the decade of the 1930s, when the region's grain industry was ravaged by drought and depression, the prosperity of the prairie provinces — whether measured by per capita income, level of employment or other common indices — surpassed that of half of the provinces of Canada (i.e. those east of the Ottawa River).

It has become part of prairie folk-lore to claim that federal policies have thwarted the economic diversification of the region. Yet recent research disputes this claim and attributes dependence upon a resource economy to a set of intransigent conditions, of which distance from markets and associated transportation costs are the primary discouragement to secondary manufacturing.[4] More heretical still is the view that federal policies — beginning in 1935 with the creation of the Canadian Wheat Board (CWB), which was ultimately to exercise monopoly powers over the marketing and transport of wheat, and continued through a variety of later federal programmes designed to promote regional economic security — have sustained the West and its agrarian way of life. Partial confirmation of this position is found in the recent fears expressed at the effect of the free trade agreement with the United States on the operation of the CWB and on various subsidy and stabilization programmes to support western agriculture.

The federal government may have been benevolent in its treatment of the West, but that has not made the dependence less demeaning to regional pride. It does help to account, however, for the sense of frustration that the receiver and the giver both experience and which manifests itself in a search for political remedies to an unequal relationship. A large part of the discontent arises from the region's inability to assert any significant control

| 125 |

over its economy. That happens because the resources are so important a component of the national economy and because most of them enter international or interprovincial hands, both of which are areas of the constitution under federal jurisdiction.

DEMOGRAPHY: A REGION UNLIKE THE OTHERS

By any demographic measure the western provinces are unusual in Canada. In absolute numbers, as well as in proportion to their individual total populations, each has more native people than any other province. Nonetheless, for most of this century the provincial governments ignored the natives when formulating public policy; in recent years such neglect has not been possible. Developments at different levels of politics account for the change in attitude. First, within the provinces natives are more visible than before due to their migration from reserves and remote areas into the major cities of the West. Secondly, and in the national context, the discussion of native land claims and treaty rights, as well as an enhanced concern generally in Canada for entrenched constitutional rights, has forced the provinces to consider the distinctive claims of these people. Finally, the human rights values promoted by the United Nations and its agencies have been cited as an international standard against which governmental action on behalf of aboriginal peoples is to be judged. As a consequence, westerners are more aware though not necessarily more enlightened than their fellow Canadians about native issues.

Of the nine provinces with populations of mainly British descent, the prairie provinces have the smallest proportion. According to the 1986 Census less than 25 percent of respondents in these provinces, who named a single ethnic origin, called themselves British (the figure for British Columbia was 33 percent).[5] The contrast between B.C. and the other western provinces is even more striking in historical perspective, for British Columbia began as a pre-eminently "British" province (with a minuscule oriental minority who had been brought to Canada initially to help build the CPR), while from the first flood of prairie settlement, a strong European presence qualified assertion of British domination east of the mountains. Before and after the First World War some prairie Anglo-Canadians resisted this non-British influence, and in Saskatchewan went so far as to support the Ku Klux Klan's anti-foreign campaign. By the 1950s, however, the non-British component of the prairie population had become "old ethnics" and ethnic distinctions themselves had almost disappeared. Moreover, in Manitoba and Saskatchewan more recent immigration has been so slight as to leave this situation undisturbed. By way of contrast, 16 and 9 percent of all Canadian immigrants in 1986 lived in B.C. and Alberta respectively, and in those provinces constituted 22 and 16 percent of the provincial population. The characteristics of these new immigrants are different from the earlier settlers too; rather than being isolated in rural locations and engaged in agriculture, they gravitate to the large cities and work at a range of occupations. There is not the space in this chapter to explore the ramifications for regional politics and society of these dramatic changes in immigration patterns, except to note that in provinces like B.C. and Alberta (and even more in Ontario, where in 1986 one in four residents was an immigrant) the "new ethnics" constitute a vigorous force in Canadian society. When combined with deliberate policies to protect ethnic cultures (e.g. multiculturalism), this new force will predictably unleash pressures to diverge from the older western Canadian belief in pluralism on the one hand but common institutions (e.g. schools) and a common language (e.g. English) on the other hand.

In the past, the West has never been receptive to claims made on it by any ethnically defined groups. This tradition is, in part, the source of the hostility some westerners have shown to official bilingualism. In their eyes French-Canadians represent only another ethnic group. While French was a dominant language in the days of the fur trade and even into the early years of Confederation, the population of the western provinces who speak it today is small and concentrated in a few historic communities, such as St. Boniface, Manitoba, Gravelbourg, Saskatchewan and St. Albert, Alberta. This opposition to the federal government's commitment to bilingualism which began with Lester Pearson in the mid-1960s, and accelerated under Trudeau and Mulroney reveals critical differences in political values which helps to explain the strength of regionalism as much as any topographical feature.

One final demographic factor of importance to understanding western Canada relates to migration trends, for they are markedly different in different parts of the region. In the first thirty years of this century, the area of greatest expansion was Saskatchewan and Manitoba. Before the depression and drought, when wheat was undisputed king of the prairie economy, these two provinces, with Winnipeg the commercial and transportation hub of the prairies, experienced rapid growth. But after the depression, Saskatchewan slipped from being the most to the least populous of the four provinces, while Manitoba and its capital stagnated. Since the Second World War the growth provinces have been Alberta and British Columbia, the former primarily because of the expansion of the oil industry and its suppliers, the latter for a variety of reasons not all related to a generally prosperous

CANADIAN GOVERNMENT AND POLITICS

economy (e.g. climate). For instance in the period since 1961, Manitoba and Saskatchewan have consistently lost more people than they have attracted, while Alberta, who looked to oil to lessen its dependence on the unpredictable grain economy, saw its population grow dramatically due to interprovincial migration, gaining 197,000 people between 1971 and 1981, the years of the oil boom, but then losing 27,000 people in the next five years, as the industry went into a slump. British Columbia, more diversified and therefore more protected from similar fluctuations, invariably gained population through interprovincial migration. Alberta and British Columbia also experienced higher rates of natural population increase and greater foreign immigration than the other two western provinces.

The composition of these population flows requires analysis, for the age, sex and ethnic characteristics, among others, of these new arrivals have major implications for public policy and political choices. Similarly, the decline of the two eastern-most provinces of the region has meant these provinces have an older population whose needs and concerns differ from those farther West.

POLITICS: CONFORMITY AND RADICALISM

The old parties of Canadian politics — the Liberals and Conservatives — evolved out of the politics of the United Canadas before 1867. After Confederation they organized elsewhere, as new provinces were admitted to the union, so that by the 1890s, it was possible to speak of a national two-party system at both levels of the federation. That uniformity disappeared at the end of the First World War, when a series of "new," "third," or "minor" parties appeared. To date, the first of these — the Progressives — still holds the title as the most successful third party at a single election in Canadian history, winning 65 seats in the 1921 election and all but six of the prairies' 43 seats. That election was a watershed in national politics, for thereafter the old parties were unable to reassert their absolute control. In the seventy years since, all of the third parties who have fought in national elections can trace their origins to the prairies. This includes the Cooperative Commonwealth Federation (CCF), who from birth saw itself as a national party but who equally depended always upon western agrarian support and organization for success. Similarly, more than half a century later its successor — the New Democratic Party (NDP) — found itself after the general election of 1988 in the same position.

One of the perennial questions of Canadian politics is why third parties took root on the prairies and flourished later in British Columbia but have enjoyed so little success elsewhere in Canada (excluding Quebec's successful third parties — the Union Nationale and the Parti Québecois — and the 1990 NDP victory in Ontario). Clearly, the answer is not simply economic deprivation, or the five provinces east of the Ottawa River who have the most depressed economic indices in the country should be hotbeds of dissent. Instead, they are the regions most loyal to the old parties. Arguably, western Canada's disposition to experiment politically is bound up with the factors already discussed in this chapter: physical and historical isolation, economic dependence and demographic distinctiveness.

The old parties that grew up in central Canada were constructed so as to accommodate the linguistic and religious duality of that area. The search for a balance — between English and French and between Protestant and Roman Catholic — led to what might be termed a politics of culture. While in the West periodic clashes between these sets of interests might occur (e.g. the Riel Rebellions or the Manitoba School Question, when that province in 1890 legislated unilingualism in place of bilingualism), they never provided a sustained basis for political organization. Instead, and because of the region's rapid settlement, economic growth and collapse, and social pluralism, the politics of the West revolved not around culture but around progress and development, or protest, or class, or, significantly, around a rejection of politics altogether.

If there can be such an animal as the politics of administration or bureaucracy, then it took root in a province like Alberta, where one-party dominance became the rule and electoral and legislative competition the exception. In provincial politics, only Saskatchewan in the long-term and Manitoba more recently has witnessed the alternation in power of two parties; since 1952 Social Credit has governed British Columbia for all but three years, when the NDP was in power, and since 1905 only four parties (Liberal, United Farmers of Alberta, Social Credit and Progressive Conservative) have in sequence governed Alberta, for periods of 16, 14, 37 and 19 years respectively.

In democratic systems, political parties are normally viewed as fundamental agents of consensus and unity by bringing together and reconciling the diverse interests of the country. That was the role of the early Liberals and Conservatives (under whatever name they might have used in the colonies); and it is possible to interpret Confederation itself as an achievement of political accommodation. It is because of this crucial function of parties that Canadian history and politics attributes such importance to nationbuilders like Sir John A. Macdonald or nation-maintainers like William Lyon Mackenzie King, who, during their periods as prime minister met and overcame

| 129 |

challenges to national unity. It is in the same context that Mulroney believed that the failed Meech Lake Accord was needed to achieve national consolidation. The failure of the old national parties to win and hold support in the major regions of Canada is a powerful criticism directed at leaders, whether they be Liberals rejected by westerners or Progressive Conservatives rejected (until recently) by Quebec voters. Canadians expect the old parties to fulfil this unifying function; yet in western Canada in the last 70 years, they have performed this task very poorly. Since 1921, there have been 21 elections, following 16 of which a majority of Quebec's members of Parliament sat in the governing caucus; for Ontario and the Atlantic Provinces the number is 14, but for the four western provinces, on only six occasions has this been true. Instead of standing behind the national government, on 15 occasions the West has chosen to support the second major party and third parties. No other statistic so starkly underlines the West's separation politically from the Canadian mainstream.

I Federalism and the West I

THE PROBLEM OF REPRESENTATION

The eternal question of Canadian politics concerns English-French relations or, as often phrased, the question of national unity. Canadian history before 1867, and Canadian politics since then, have focused more intensely on this matter than on any other; in this century, for example, the conscription crises of both world wars, battles over minority language rights, a policy of official bilingualism and Quebec separatist movements have preoccupied the attention of a succession of federal governments. Yet, as this chapter has shown, there is another dimension to the unity question — that of western Canada, which for the last seven decades has repeatedly demonstrated its discontent with national politics. Gradually, that discontent has come to centre on the subject of representation, more precisely on the perceived failure (in westerners' eyes) of national governmental institutions to respond to the West's desires.

The representation problem arises from the stark fact that two-thirds of Canada's population live in Quebec and Ontario, which means that of 295 seats in the House of Commons those provinces occupy 174. No political party wishing to form a government can succeed without strong support in both of these provinces. And, no government party can remain in power unless its policies appeal to those provinces. The crux of the problem lies in

Canada's system of cabinet government which operates on the principle of majority rule whose effectiveness requires stringent enforcement of party discipline. The concentration of power that results from this principle is fundamentally different, say, from that found in the United States, where the executive (the president) and the legislature (Congress) are independent of one another and where, as a result, the president and the congressional parties must engage in complex bargaining to secure the passage of legislation. Much more than in the United States, Canadian government is a question of being in or out of power. And for a long time the West has felt itself to be out of power.

It is for this reason that westerners have in the past experimented with third parties, hoping thereby to deprive either of the major parties of a majority and thus force the resulting "minority government" (the Canadian term for a government that controls fewer than half the seats in the Commons through one party) to respond to regional demands. On balance, however, third parties have failed as dependable instruments of regional pressure on government, although a party like the CCF, with strong social-welfare objectives, did achieve indirect success nationally by forcing governments composed of the old parties to acknowledge these concerns through their legislation (for example, the King Government introduced family allowances, the Pearson Government medicare and the Diefenbaker Government national hospitalization).

More recently, westerners have opted for a new strategy to promote their interests. If non-conformity in the support of parties achieved less than desired, then perhaps (they reasoned) the rules of the game rather than the players should be changed.

That is the origin of the West's, and particularly Alberta's, enthusiasm for Senate reform. Suggestions to reform the upper chamber of Parliament are not new; what is new is the single objective of most recent proposals: to lessen the absolute power of the prime minister and cabinet over Parliament. While their details are complex, the proposals invariably seek to give the provinces a role to play in the selection of senators, thereby removing some or all of that power from the prime minister (where it has rested since Confederation); as well, they usually confer on a reformed Senate some new role in the approval of government appointments and, most importantly, they aim to achieve greater equality of provincial representation in the Senate. Currently, because there are four senatorial regions — the West, Ontario, Quebec, and the Maritime provinces, each with 24 senators, plus 6 senators for Newfoundland and two from the Yukon and Northwest Territories — provinces with small populations (Nova Scotia and New

CANADIAN GOVERNMENT AND POLITICS

Brunswick) have 10 senators each, while provinces with larger populations (the four western provinces) have only six senators.

A reformed Senate, with greater power over the national government, and with better equality of representation (which under any proposed scheme would see increased western representation) appeals to an area of the country which has long complained of the exclusion of its interests from national attention.

As noted, Senate reform is most popular in Alberta. Although discussed elsewhere in the region, it is the Alberta government and provincial interest groups which have most strongly promoted the proposal. Why this is so has yet to be fully explored; the absence of a tradition of competitive parties however, and an entrenched predisposition to see government solely as an instrument of administration, offer initial areas of investigation. It is clear that Senate reform would introduce changes to the form of disciplined party government as it currently operates in the House of Commons. Thus, in the other western provinces, where party competition is more prevalent than in Alberta, such consequences of Senate reform are reasons to treat the proposal with caution.

Similarly, other proposals for institutional reform, such as the introduction of proportional representation (PR), which would see seats in the House of Commons allocated to parties at elections according to the proportion of popular vote won rather than, as now, on a winner-take-all or plurality system, received mixed support in the West, but again with Alberta most in favour. The advantage of PR, in light of recent general election results where the Liberals, for instance, won as much as 24 percent of the vote in Saskatchewan but none of the province's 14 seats, is obvious if representation of voters' opinion is the sole criterion for evaluation. Of course, there are other criteria, among them the belief in the need for strong parties and strong government, which some critics believe PR would undermine.

Because the operation of Canadian federal politics has stifled the representation of western regional interests, the western provinces have long been active in what political scientists call "province-building." In essence, the term refers to "the multifarious activities of provincial governments" by which they seek greater autonomy to advance the interests of their economies and societies.[6] The concept thus encompasses such innovations in Saskatchewan after 1944 as the CCF's central-planning mechanisms and its host of crown corporations to develop that province's economy. Or, again, it applies to the Conservative government's activist involvement in the direction of Alberta's economy after 1970. Province-building has much wider implications than are suggested here, extending for example to the growth of professional bureaucracies in the provinces who possess the expertise to bargain with their counterparts in other provinces and in Ottawa. Although the western provinces are neither the only nor the first provinces to engage in this activity, they have discovered in province-building a route by which they can advance their unique interests; one that is doubly useful since they believe the institutions of the national government to be unresponsive to them.

I Conclusion I

The triumph of Confederation in 1867 rested in the accommodation of English- and French-Canadian interests through a common set of institutions. Out of that achievement emerged an eminently stable government and a free, peaceful and prosperous society. But the original federal bargain adjusted uneasily to change. That was the reason why the central government sought at the outset to control the expansion and development of the West. And it was these assertions of control — of the region's resources, economy and politics — that westerners rejected. The integration of the western provinces into national institutions — both public and private — has been fitful, as the region's distinctive history, economy, demography and politics guaranteed it would be. The cultural basis of the original federation had no counterpart in the West; and because it had no counterpart, the West perpetually felt out of sympathy and out of touch with central Canada whose needs and desires Confederation was designed to fulfil.

CANADIAN GOVERNMENT AND POLITICS

NOTES

[1] See Barry M. Gough, "The Character of the British Columbia Frontier," *B.C. Studies*, XXXII (Winter 1976-77) pp. 28-40; also, R.O. MacFarlane, "Manitoba Politics and Parties After Confederation," Canadian Historical Association (1940) pp. 45-55 at 46.

[2] Chester Martin in Lewis H. Thomas (ed.), *Dominion Lands' Policy* (Toronto: McClelland & Stewart, 1973) p. 74.

[3] Donald E. Blake, "Managing the Periphery: British Columbia and the National Political Community," in R. Kenneth Carty and W. Peter Ward (eds.), *National Politics and Community in Canada* (Vancouver: UBC Press, 1986) pp. 169-83 at 173.

[4] See Kenneth H. Norrie, "Some Comments on Prairie Economic Alienation," *Canadian Public Policy*, II, no. 2 (Spring 1976) pp. 211-24; and "A Regional Economic Overview of the West Since 1945," in A.W. Rasporich (ed.), *The Making of the Modern West: Western Canada Since 1945* (Calgary, 1984) pp. 63-78.

[5] Canada, Statistics Canada, Catalogue 93-109, *The Nation: Ethnicity. Immigration and Citizenship* (Ottawa, 1989) p. vii and Table I.

[6] R.A. Young, Philippe Faucher, André Blais, "The Concept of Province-Building: A Critique," *Canadian Journal of Political Science*, XVII, no. 4 (December 1984) pp. 783-818. See, too, Edwin R. Black and Alan C. Cairns, "A Different Perspective on Canadian Federalism," *Canadian Public Administration*, IX, no. 1 (March 1966) pp. 27-44.

ANNOTATED READINGS

Dyck, Rand. *Provincial Politics in Canada*. Scarborough: Prentice-Hall, 1986. This introductory text is divided into four parts, the last devoted to "The Western Provinces." Each chapter examines the "setting" of a province, its political culture, institutions, evolution and recent politics. Much more detail is included, with the result that the student is presented with the most thorough summary available of the political history of each province.

Conway, J.F. *The West: The History of a Region in Confederation*. Toronto: Lorimer, 1983. A short, sharp, critical analysis of the West in Confederation. While there are numerous references to British Columbia, the argument presented focuses predominantly on the discontents of the prairie provinces. The book's tone is reflected in the subtitle of its Conclusion, "The Politics of Desperation."

Blake, Donald E. "Managing the Periphery: British Columbia and the National Political Community," in R. Kenneth Carty and W. Peter Ward, eds. *National Politics and Community in Canada*. Vancouver: UBC Press, 1986. The analysis of British Columbia's relations with the rest of Canada is a corrective to the western literature that more often focuses on the prairie provinces. Through his examination, Blake suggests that B.C. is both like (and unlike) its fellow western provinces.

Martin, Chester in Lewis H. Thomas, ed. *Dominion Lands' Policy*. Toronto: McClelland & Stewart, 1973. The bases of the prairie West's grievances against the federal government are set out in detail and with a literary style that makes the case memorable and, for some, irrefutable.

| CHAPTER 8 |

FEDERALISM AND FEDERAL-PROVINCIAL RELATIONS

JOAN PRICE BOASE

Since the passage of the **Constitution Act, 1867** (formerly the British North America Act), Canada has had a federal system of government. This means there are two levels of government that can legitimately make laws affecting the Canadian people. The federal or national government can legislate for all Canadians in the ten provinces and two territories, whereas a provincial government's legislation is binding only on those living within the provincial boundaries. Neither level of government has an absolute right to legislate in all areas. The Constitution Act enumerates the areas in which each level of government may legislate, and this is known as the constitutional division of powers. These enumerated powers (primarily in sections 91 and 92) are often referred to as the jurisdictions of the two governments.

The choice of a federal form of government was a deliberate one in 1867, but the Constitution Act that established it reflects an ambivalence towards governing that has persisted. The framers of our constitution looked over one shoulder at the government in the United Kingdom and over the other shoulder at the federal system established in the United States in the 18th century, and attempted to combine what they perceived to be the best elements of the two systems. The result was a constitutional document with ambiguities that only became clearly evident over time, and whose imprecise language was open to different interpretations. While this permitted some necessary flexibility, it also precipitated much federal-provincial wrangling. The ambiguities and the different interpretations resulted from two fundamental tensions in the original constitutional agreement. These were first, the language of the Act which established a federal state reads more as though it were describing a unitary state; and second, the attempt in the Act to reconcile a federal system with a Parliamentary system of government. We will discuss the meaning of these terms separately.

I Unitary, Federal, and I Confederal States

A unitary state is one where all legislative power is vested in a single level of government, which means that one legislature retains total sovereignty over the entire state. Within a unitary state (such as the United Kingdom), there are necessarily lower levels of government — municipal or local governments — that exist to manage local affairs. These governments, however, have had their legislative powers delegated to them from the central government, which always retains the right to rescind the delegated power. For example, in the 1920s, the Parliament at Westminster in London delegated to northern Ireland the power to establish its own legislature in Belfast. Decades later, the British government decided that this experiment had been a failure, and it abolished the legislature in northern Ireland. Subsequently, northern Ireland elected political representatives to the Parliament in London, and retained only local governments — also with their power delegated to them from Westminster.

Legally, in a federal system of government, the central Parliament cannot abolish the provincial or state legislatures, for their power is their own, within their jurisdiction, and is guaranteed by the division of powers in the supreme law of the land, the constitution. In Canada, the relationship between the provincial governments and their local governments is like that between governments in a unitary state. Local governments may make laws binding on their constituents, but this power has been delegated to them by the provincial government, and can always be withdrawn. That is, it does not have a constitutional guarantee.

Clearly, a federal system, with its sovereignty or legislative powers divided between two levels of government, is more decentralized than a unitary system. A confederal system is more decentralized still. A confederal system is one where the individual states each retain their full sovereign powers, but they delegate specified powers to a central body, retaining the right to rescind the delegation and opt out of the confederation. We don't have a clear example of a confederation in the modern world, but the European Community comes close to one, and it is planning to integrate even further in 1992. The various members of the European Community have delegated power over certain economic affairs to a central European Parliament, although each individual state has legally retained full sovereignty. However, as integration proceeds, interdependence among the states increases and this exacerbates the difficulties of opting out.

It is helpful to use the concept of a continuum (a sliding scale) to better understand the relative characteristics of these political systems.

centralized				*decentralized*
U.K.	Can.	U.S.	Can.	EC
unitary	1867-1896	*federal*	1990	*confederal*

The continuum allows us to measure the relative degree of centralization and decentralization of individual states and changes over time. The United Kingdom is situated close to the centralized end, and the EC, while not quite integrated enough to be a true confederal system, is moving in that direction. States move along the bar of the continuum as they become more or less decentralized. The United States, a federal state, is somewhat more centralized (that is, its central government is more dominant) than is Canada, another federal state. In fact, the evolution of Canadian federalism has seen it move sharply along the continuum from the centralized towards the decentralized end.

The ambivalence of the framers of the constitution that has permeated the evolution of the federal system is based on the fact that while they said that they were designing federal structures, they imbued them with many features of a unitary state — and then called the result a Confederation! This label, although a misnomer, has persisted.

FEDERALISM AND FEDERAL PROVINCIAL RELATIONS

I A Parliamentary System I
and Federalism

The second fundamental tension arises from the effort to superimpose a federal structure on a Parliamentary system. The short preamble to the *Constitution Act, 1867* states that the provinces wish to be "federally united ... with a Constitution similar in principle to that of the United Kingdom." The following sections then draft a constitution in many ways more similar to the United States constitution rather than to the United Kingdom, which does not have a written constitution at all! The development of Parliamentary government in Britain was a gradual evolution in governing custom or tradition that led to recognized and accepted constitutional conventions. These conventions (such as responsible government and Parliamentary supremacy) are considered inviolate, and under the preamble to our constitution, they became fundamental (although unwritten) principles in the Canadian system of government.

The convention that is the most difficult to reconcile with a federal — and written — constitution is that of Parliamentary supremacy. It has been said that the doctrine of Parliamentary supremacy means that the government at Westminster can pass virtually any law unchallenged, short of "changing a man into a woman." Clearly, such a doctrine would appear to be the antithesis of a federal system whose very purpose is to divide sovereignty (or legislative powers) between two quite distinct levels of government. Nevertheless, the principle of Parliamentary supremacy has persisted, and its importance to contemporary thinking on government in Canada was very evident in discussions leading up to the adoption in 1982 of a constitutional *Charter of Rights and Freedoms*. The Charter, of course, further restricts Parliamentary "supremacy."

As one might expect, the unclear language and fundamental contradictions upon which our constitutional order is based have led to some very interesting developments in the evolution of federalism and federal-provincial relations in Canada. Before we trace the different stages in this evolution, however, it would be helpful to examine the reasons why the framers of our constitution chose a federal system of government in 1867.

WHY A FEDERAL SYSTEM?

The "fathers of federalism" wanted to establish a new political community in the northern half of the North American continent. At the time — in the middle 19th century — this territory consisted of several colonies of Great

Britain — Prince Edward Island, Nova Scotia, New Brunswick, Newfoundland, British Columbia, Canada (East and West) and an immense tract of land between Canada West and British Columbia, known as the Northwest Territories, and mostly controlled by the Hudson Bay Company on charter from Great Britain. This land was sparsely populated and was valued primarily for its resources and as a link to British Columbia and the Pacific Ocean. It was a challenge to unite these disparate entities into a single nation, and a federal system seemed the only solution to address their individual political, economic and cultural needs.

In the political sense, federation served several purposes. First, it separated the troubled province of Canada, which had been described as consisting of "two nations warring in the bosom of a single state,"[1] into the provinces of Quebec and Ontario. These two provinces and the two well-established political systems of Nova Scotia and New Brunswick formed the new union. It is unlikely that Nova Scotia and New Brunswick would have agreed to union if they had not been able to retain their own political structures. These were the original four provinces and the Act also established a central Canadian government in Ottawa and provided for the admission of other colonies and the expansion of the state west to the Pacific. In so doing, it founded a recognizable political entity north of the American border filling, as Garth Stevenson has said, a "dangerous power vacuum" in British North America, and providing a legitimate resistance to aggressive American expansionism in the West.[2]

In the economic sense, the federal agreement divided the levers of control between the two levels of government. It gave what at the time were considered to be the important levers (for example, trade and commerce, banking, the lion's share of taxation) to the central government, and the unimportant levers (for example, direct taxation, licences, matters of a local and private nature) to the provincial governments. Although the original Act contained a provision (s. 109) that resources would remain under the control of the several provinces, when Manitoba was carved out of the Northwest Territories (1870) and Saskatchewan and Alberta were created (1905), the federal government retained ownership and control of the resources of these three provinces (until 1930). This clearly indicated the intention of developing a federal country economically dominated by the central government and central economic interests.

The Act — and the federal system itself — also addressed the more immediate concerns of the individual provinces, by giving them jurisdiction over all matters that in the 19th century were considered to be the responsibility of local governments and those matters upon which the historical

| 140 |

differences between the French- and English-speaking communities rested. Thus, provincial powers included education, health and welfare, municipal institutions, the administration of justice in the province and concurrent (shared) power over agriculture and immigration. It was anticipated that in matters of a "local and private nature" the provinces would be free to pursue their own priorities, and that the French-speaking majority in Quebec would have the power to ensure the continuation of its cultural and linguistic traditions.

Even in its approach to addressing the particular political, economic and cultural needs of the several provinces, however, the Act exhibits the inherent ambivalence of the fathers of Canadian federalism. Politically, although each province had its own legislature (and some even had upper houses for a while), the federal government retained the power to appoint the Queen's representative in each province, the Lieutenant Governor. The Lieutenant Governor was given the power to reserve provincial legislation subject to review by the federal cabinet and the federal cabinet was given the power to disallow provincial legislation so reserved. This provision clearly circumscribed the doctrine of parliamentary supremacy in the provinces, and legally established a relationship between Ottawa and the provincial governments similar to the colonial relationship between Ottawa and London.

Economically, the fathers also sought to circumscribe the powers conferred on the provinces. While section 92(2) of the Act grants the provinces "exclusive" right to make laws in relation to direct taxation, section 91 states that the Parliament of Canada will have "exclusive" legislative authority over "the raising of money by any mode or system of taxation" 91 (3). Furthermore, section 92 (10)(c) contains the ominous provision that the Parliament of Canada may declare certain "works" wholly situated within a province, to be to the "general advantage" of Canada.[3] The economic ambivalence is further evident in the previously mentioned retention of control over resources in Manitoba, Saskatchewan and Alberta until 1930, thus creating two classes of provinces in the economic sense.

The provisions relating to the preservation of the cultural traditions of the English- and French-speaking Canadians were also subject to ambiguous interpretations, perhaps because the framers were more concerned with protecting the English community within Quebec than the French community outside Quebec. Both languages were to be permitted in Parliament and the legislature of Quebec, its records and journals and in its courts but not the legislatures of the other three provinces. The same bilingual provisions were contained in the Manitoba Act of 1870, but there was little protest when Manitoba declared itself unilingual English in 1890.

I 141 I

The relationship between language and religion has often been a fuzzy one, and although the Act protects denominational schools wherever they existed before 1867, it is silent on the language of instruction. This has created confusion, since in the 19th century, the Catholics in Quebec were almost all French-speaking and the Protestants in Quebec were almost all English-speaking. This was not the case in Ontario, where many Irish Catholics had emigrated, but there were many French Catholic schools as well. The famous Manitoba Schools question in 1890 was based on the unconstitutional denial by the Manitoba government of denominational schools in conjunction with the declaration of unilingualism at the political level. At the same time, the denial of French-language instruction in the schools was a deliberate attempt to obstruct the expansion of French-speaking communities in the west.

SUMMARY

Thus, the ambivalent approach to the development of a political system in Canada began with the attempt to emulate both the British and the American systems by superimposing a federal system on a parliamentary form of government. The problems that arose from this arrangement were compounded by the ambiguous political relationships that were established and by the provisions of the 1867 Act that dealt with economic and cultural concerns. The historical evolution of federal-provincial relations in Canada has been greatly affected by these ambiguities.

I The Evolution of Federal- I Provincial Relations

The ambiguities and uncertainties implicit in the foundations of Canadian federalism have been pervasive in the years of its evolution. As our society experienced social, economic and technological change and demands on governments grew — especially in the second half of the 20th century — relationships between the two levels of government were forced to change and adjust, and they have often reflected the fundamental contradictions. They have also reflected the frequently conflicting perceptions of Canadian federalism that have been held by political leaders. Not unexpectedly, then, the history of the evolution of federal-provincial relations has been a rather convoluted one. Complexity has been added to this convoluted history by our long and often controversial relationship with Britain. Although Canada became in fact a sovereign state under the statute of Westminster in 1931, Britain remained involved in Canadian constitutional affairs in two ways. First, because agreement could not be reached until 1982 on a method of amending the constitution in Canada the British Parliament retained the responsibility for amendments although it exercised the power only on request from Canada. Second, until 1949, a committee of British justices, the Judicial Committee of the Privy Council (the JCPC) remained Canada's final court of appeal, the arbiter of the federal system. The effects of eight decades of the JCPC's decisions have been far-reaching in the development of federal-provincial relations in Canada.

For many years, the conventional wisdom of those who were close observers of the constitutional decisions of the JCPC was that this committee had wilfully and even capriciously tampered with the intentions of the original framers of our constitution.

The early decisions mostly reflected the unitary language of the Act of 1867, and some have referred to this period as one of "quasi-federalism," as the JCPC upheld federal legislation that it perceived to be "national" in nature, but had been challenged on constitutional grounds. During the 19th century, the federal government also frequently used its reservation and disallowance powers, and Canada functioned as a "quasi-unitary" state. Many decisions of the JCPC in the 1890s and subsequently, however, reversed the centralist trend and the powers of reservation and disallowance gradually fell into disuse in the 20th century. Relationships between the federal and provincial governments were irrevocably changed as the JCPC (sometimes with quite innovative reasoning) consistently upheld the broadening spheres of authority of the provincial governments, although federal government actions that were "national" in nature were upheld when an emergency situation (such as war) could be identified.

Much has been written about the decisions of these justices and their propensity for treating the British North America Act simply as a British Statute (which it was) rather than as a Constitutional document (which it also was). It has been suggested that the justices deliberately attempted to impose on the colony their view of "classical" federalism (that is, governments equal in power and functioning in isolation, within their enumerated jurisdictions), even if it did not coincide with the original intentions of the framers of the Act. A perceptive article by Alan Cairns in 1971, however, suggests that the decisions of the JCPC were not capricious but were, in fact, an essential reflection of developing political realities in Canada. Another, and simpler, explanation for the contradictory decisions of the first sixty years particularly, is that the judicial interpretations may also have

| 143 |

occasionally reflected the underlying Canadian ambivalence towards the union: the unitary language, federal structures and confederal title.

Whatever the explanation for the judicial decisions, it is undeniable that political relationships and the federal-provincial balance of power have been fundamentally altered since the agreement in 1867, and jurisdictional competition has become endemic. The original ambiguities have persisted and have emerged as opposing perceptions of Canadian federalism that are manifest in the federal-provincial negotiations that have often dominated Canadian politics since WWII. We will now examine the evolution of federal-provincial relations in the second half of the 20th century.

I Federal-Provincial Relations I Since WWII

Periods of war (1914-1918 and 1939-1945) and crisis (the depression decade of the 1930s) have seen widespread acceptance of the centralization of governing powers and the strengthening of the government in Ottawa — centripetal federalism. However, all other periods of Canadian history, with the exception of the two decades immediately after 1867, have seen efforts by the provincial governments to strengthen their powers vis-à-vis Ottawa — centrifugal federalism. Quebec and Ontario have led the way, and the other provinces, some more enthusiastically than others, have accepted the "provincial rights" argument. The metaphor of a swinging pendulum has frequently been used to describe the alternations from centripetal to centrifugal federalism, and disagreement over the centralist/decentralist balance has often led to discord. Whether the federation is perceived to be too centralized or too decentralized depends on the view one holds of the purpose of the government in Ottawa.

A centralist view of Canadian federalism accepts the proposition that the federal government may identify "national" interests, even in areas of provincial jurisdiction (such as health care, post-secondary education, pensions, day care), and use its enormous spending powers to persuade the provinces to accept federal activity in these areas. The centralist view also believes that Ottawa, as the "senior" government that represents all Canadians, should take the initiative in these areas to ensure all Canadians have an equal standard of services. The decentralist view, on the other hand, adheres to a more classical form of federalism, and argues that the identification of a national interest and pursuit of a national program in a field of provincial jurisdiction has the effect of distorting provincial priorities, since

FEDERALISM AND FEDERAL PROVINCIAL RELATIONS

provincial governments are in a better position to determine provincial needs. This view also believes that the use of the federal spending power to ensure national programs amounts to coercion rather than persuasion, and violates the federal principle. The tensions between these incompatible perceptions have been clearly evident in the post-WWII federal-provincial relationship as the Canadian government identified various welfare programs that it considered to be in the national interest and sought to have them implemented.

These moves by the federal government, and the resistance to them by the larger provinces particularly, have led to a great number of meetings among ministers and officials of the two levels of government. These meetings have come to be known as cooperative or administrative federalism, or in the words of Donald Smiley, "executive federalism."[4] The proliferation of federal-provincial interactions in the second half of the twentieth century is a Canadian phenomenon that has led to our own unique model of federalism. In the practical sense, the result of these interactions has been the development of an interdependence between the two levels of government in virtually all areas of governmental activity. In the political sense, since the provincial governments have been called upon to administer most of the federally initiated and shared-cost programs, consultation and cooperation have become imperative. Provincial bureaucracies have expanded in both a quantitative and qualitative sense and have developed administrative expertise that rivals that of the federal government. Like large bureaucracies everywhere, they are interested in protecting and promoting their own interests, and the provinces have come to expect and demand that Ottawa confer with them before it makes any major moves, even in areas constitutionally assigned exclusively to the federal government. The evolution of federal-provincial relations since WWII is perhaps best demonstrated by a brief examination of the history of shared-cost programs.

THE HISTORY OF SHARED-COST PROGRAMS

It has been suggested that the framers of our constitution demonstrated a lack of foresight when they gave the lion's share of taxation to the federal government, and jurisdiction over social welfare to the provincial governments. In 1867, however, perceptions of the important areas of government were quite different from what they are today, and the division of powers was decided with other priorities in mind. It was not until the depression decade of the 1930s that the great disparity between provincial responsibility and the provincial ability to raise revenue became fully apparent. Much of

CANADIAN GOVERNMENT AND POLITICS

the history of federal-provincial relations since 1940, with its periods of cooperation and conflict, is the history of attempts to reconcile this disparity. That is, the increasing interactions between the two levels of government have most frequently been driven by the need to discuss revenue-sharing arrangements to finance the developing welfare state.

Despite the constitutional difficulties, Canadian governments have developed social programs with a minimum of constitutional change. A major Royal Commission in the 1930s, the Rowell-Sirois Commission, conducted an exhaustive study of dominion-provincial relations and the federal-provincial division of responsibilities and resources. It recommended a broad redistribution of responsibilities and revenue sources and a return to the balance of power as it was originally conceived in 1867. This was to include the transfer to Ottawa of exclusive rights to income and corporation taxes and succession duties to enable the federal government to pursue national planning of essential welfare services. Although a constitutional amendment empowering Ottawa to establish a national unemployment insurance program was obtained in 1940, provincial resistance to the thrust of the **Rowell-Sirois Report** essentially killed any further modification in the division of powers and responsibilities. At a Dominion-provincial conference convened in 1941 to consider the Report, fierce opposition to its proposals for the constitutional centralizing of financial power was expressed by the governments of Quebec, Ontario, Alberta and British Columbia. This ensured that future developments in the area of social welfare responsibility would be a result not of centralized strategic planning, but of ad hoc adjustments and endless federal-provincial discussion and bargaining.

The provincial governments did agree in 1941, however, to give the federal government temporary control over the personal and corporate taxfields, to support the war effort. When the war ended, Ottawa decided that it should retain these sources of revenue, and when the Liberal government called a federal-provincial meeting in 1945 to discuss post-war reconstruction, it was to embark on more than a decade of paternalistic centralism. Ottawa assumed the leadership role in both economic and social welfare policy, although not without provincial resistance, and the realization of its goals required frequent federal-provincial consultation.

The twenty-five years from 1945 to 1970 saw great changes in the relationships among governments in Canada. During the early years of this period, relationships were relatively harmonious, as the acceptance of centralism during the war years carried over into the immediate post-war period. Ottawa achieved dominance by a series of tax-sharing agreements with the provinces that permitted it to collect 75% of all Canadian tax revenue.

Although Quebec and Ontario refused to agree to the tax-sharing arrangements (Ontario agreed to a modified form in 1952) the federal government was able to wield its financial authority and achieve its purposes. It did this by means of grant-in-aid or conditional grant programs that were based on the transfer of large sums of money to the provinces in return for social legislation that met enunciated federal standards. For the most part, the provinces acquiesced, although Quebec under Premier Duplessis and then Lesage refused federal involvement and "opted out" of most of the federal programs, citing interference with provincial autonomy.

By means of these shared-cost conditional grant programs (which the Rowell-Sirois Commission had warned against), the federal government was able to have national standards established in hospital insurance,medical insurance, post-secondary education, the Canada Assistance Plan, vocational education and other areas.[5] In 1965 under Prime Minister Lester Pearson, the Canada Pension Plan was established, and Quebec was permitted to opt out of the plan and create a similar Quebec Pension Plan, and still receive its share of federal funding. The development of these various plans had irreversible effects on the dynamics of federal-provincial relations, as each new agreement followed intense intergovernmental conferences involving officials, finance and other ministers as well as first ministers and their advisers.

The change was gradual, but in retrospect can be seen as inevitable. In the 1940s and 50s, federal-provincial interactions were mostly unstructured and informal, with occasionally more formal first ministers' conferences to discuss financial arrangements and the initiation and administration of national programs. Slowly, the organized machinery grew, however, as the increasing meetings of liaison committees demanded more federal and provincial expertise, and the provincial bureaucratic expertise soon equalled that of the federal government. Federal dominance continued into the 1960s, but the balance was shifting towards the provinces, and tensions and conflicts became more frequent in federal-provincial relations. During this decade, there was a rise in Quebec nationalism and Quebec's many successes in gaining control of a greater share of revenue encouraged the other provinces to become more aggressive in their negotiating and bargaining sessions with Ottawa. There was also a growing awareness at both levels of government of the increasing political importance of many of the areas of provincial jurisdiction. The result was more conflict in federal-provincial bargaining, frequent provincial demands for revenue to match their responsibilities, a gradual dissipation of federal dominance, and increasing federal-provincial interdependence.

| 147 |

CANADIAN GOVERNMENT AND POLITICS

The provinces continued to object to the conditional grant system for both philosophical and practical reasons and demanded more tax room to meet their growing responsibilities, and more provincial control of their constitutionally guaranteed jurisdictions. The federal government was also becoming disenchanted with the shared-cost programs, for the open-ended nature of the approximately 50% financing arrangements meant that the costs of the programs were unpredictable and uncontrollable and they made dependable budget planning difficult. The federal government also came to the realization that while it was perceived as the tax collector, the provincial governments were receiving most of the political credit for the programs. Under the government of Pierre Trudeau in the late 1960s and early 1970s, Ottawa attempted to disentangle itself and to place ceilings on its transfers for some programs. Subsequently, following many intense meetings among the federal and provincial finance ministers, a new fiscal arrangement was negotiated that governed the federal contributions to the established programs of hospital and medical insurance and post-secondary education. An extremely complex law, the **Established Programs Financing and Fiscal Arrangements Act** was passed in 1977, allowing Ottawa to extract itself from its open-ended commitment to the provincial programs by means of a more predictable cash transfer and the granting of an additional share of taxes to the provinces. With the passage of this Act, provincial governments were less constrained in their identification of priorities, there was a real shift of financial power towards the provinces, and by 1983, Ottawa's share of total taxation had dropped to 47%. It is also worth noting that the discussions preceding these changes to our major social programs primarily involved finance ministers, not program ministers. The financing arrangements were considered to be of more importance than discussions of the long-term substantive aspects of these plans.

The long history of the development of shared cost programs ensured that by the 1970s, the machinery of federal-provincial relations was institutionalized. Under Pierre Trudeau in 1976, the Federal-Provincial Relations Office became a central agency of government and the Finance Department, Treasury Board Secretariat and other major federal departments developed their own units of federal-provincial expertise, and many full-time intergovernmental specialists were hired. The provinces established similar machinery. Led by Quebec which created the first Intergovernmental Affairs Office in 1964, the other provinces gradually developed bureaucratic structures modelled on those of Ottawa and Quebec City. Federal-provincial relations had become a major growth industry.

While a knowledge of the development of the shared-cost programs is essential to an understanding of intergovernmental relations in Canada, it is also important to realize that the elaborate federal-provincial machinery is active in almost all policy areas. There are constant meetings, both formal and informal, among ministers, committees of officials, various advisory bodies and councils and individual representatives of different policy areas within the governments. Most of these meetings are amicable although they can be conflictual as well. The many bureaucratic federal and provincial specialists, besides having different policy priorities and institutional concerns, often have personal agendas of status and ambition which lead them to protect and enhance their own and their government's sphere of power.

Although almost all intergovernmental meetings are held in camera (in secret), the federal-provincial meetings with which Canadians are most familiar are the televised annual First Ministers Conferences. These conferences are convened by the Federal Government and the First Ministers and their enormous entourages of advisers meet to discuss an agenda that has been set by the federal government. They have given Canadians a view of relationships among governments quite different from the centralist concept of the post-war years. It is a picture of assertive and well-informed premiers holding their own in discussions with the Prime Minister, who often appears to be just one of eleven. It is interesting to note that federal government representatives in the 1950s and '60s were reluctant to encourage the development of such formal structures for federal-provincial interaction, fearing that they would weaken Ottawa's dominant position. The televised proceedings have shown that their fears were justified.

Whereas the First Ministers' Conferences were primarily concerned with welfare programs and financing agreements in the 1950s and '60s, other policy areas took on higher profiles in the 1970s and '80s. Constitutional issues dominated the agendas from 1968 – '71, followed by the need to address the energy crisis and inflation in the '70s, and environmental concerns in the '70s and '80s. Constitutional issues were dominant again between 1978 and 1982, and these discussions culminated in the passage of the *Constitution Act, 1982*. Throughout these periods, the federal-provincial machinery remained well-oiled and the provincial premiers aggressively sought further decentralization of the federation.

The years of the Trudeau government between 1980 and 1984 were a brief period of renewed central dominance that occurred at great cost to relationships among governments in Canada. The federal government undertook unilateral initiatives on three crucial and divisive issues: energy pricing, constitutional change and what it perceived to be a threat to the national medicare plan. The indignant and hostile reactions of the provincial premiers

| 149 |

to these initiatives took the form of a struggle to determine which level of government should dominate in the federal system. Canadians appeared to be exhausted from the incessant federal-provincial wrangling in 1984, and they gave Brian Mulroney's Conservative party a huge majority in the House of Commons at least partly because of his promise to restore peace to federal-provincial relations.

Peace did come to intergovernmental relations in the first two years of the Mulroney government, as he and his ministers took a less adversarial approach in their relations with the provinces, and acceptable energy accords were reached with the Atlantic and Western provinces. An early First Ministers Conference on the economy was successful, and for a while it appeared that a more cooperative and concilliatory federalism would result. This does not seem to be the nature of Canadian federalism, however, and the hostility is often just beneath the surface, easily triggered by real or apparent federal encroachment on provincial sensitivities.

The Mulroney government came into power during a period of fiscal restraint (although an expanding economy) and in its determination to reduce the federal deficit it reduced federal transfers to the provinces. Conflict arose over who would absorb the cutbacks and who would pay the political price. The Conservatives also antagonized both the West and the East with some of their high-profile policies: the awarding of a controversial aerospace contract to Montreal rather than Winnipeg, VIA Rail cutbacks, high interest rates and the proposal in 1989 to unilaterally impose a very broad goods and services tax. Most of these policies were perceived to favour central Canada — Quebec and Ontario — over the East and the West. A controversial constitutional agreement reached in 1987, the Meech Lake Accord, proved to be very divisive, and federal and provincial representatives criss-crossed the country as the Mulroney government attempted to have the recalcitrant provinces pass the amendment through their legislatures. The Accord, a de-centralizing document, crystallized for many two competitive views of Canadian federalism: a strong central government versus a community of communities approach to federal-provincial relations. Within Quebec, it was perceived as a minimum response to historical demands, while many English-speaking Canadians perceived it as granting an unacceptable special status to Quebec. It died in June, 1990, after an acrimonious federal-provincial conference and amid bitter mutual recriminations. The federal-provincial truce that had been declared in 1984 proved only to be a brief hiatus.

Conclusion

The dynamics of federalism in Canada have evolved enormously since the original agreement was drafted in 1867. Although much of the history of the "high" politics of First Ministers Conferences seems driven by conflict and competition between the two levels of government, it is important to realize that each year there are also hundreds of harmonious federal provincial interactions occurring on the level of "low" politics, among committees, individual bureaucrats and ministers. The success of these latter relationships has allowed the development of a welfare state, produced an irreversible interdependence between the two levels of government and shown that if governments exercise the political will, it is possible to transcend constitutional difficulties and even their own parochial tendencies.

CANADIAN GOVERNMENT AND POLITICS

NOTES

[1] Lord Durham used this phrase in his famous 1840 Report on the problems of Upper & Lower Canada. His suggested solution was a union of the Canada's which occurred in 1840 and they became Canada East and Canada West. This did not resolve the difficulties.

[2] Garth Stevenson, *Unfilled Union: Canadian Federalism and National Unity*, 3rd ed. (Toronto: Gage, 1989) p. 21.

[3] For example, shortly after World War II, the federal government used this section to assume jurisdiction over uranium, so that it could control nuclear energy policy.

[4] See Smiley's discussion of executive federalism in *The Federal Condition in Canada* (Toronto: McGraw-Hill Ryerson, 1987), Chapter 4.

[5] These shared-cost programs meant that the federal government would pay 50 cents of every dollar that the provincial governments spent in these areas, provided certain conditions were met. The Canada Assistance Plan, established in 1966 by the minority Pearson government, was an agreement that Ottawa would match provincial spending on "needy" persons, as defined by the provincial governments.

ANNOTATED READINGS

Cairns, Alan. "The Living Canadian Constitution" and "The Judicial Committee and its Critics," in Alan Cairns, *Constitution Government and Society in Canada*. Toronto: McClelland and Stewart, 1988: 27-85. These perceptive articles, originally written in 1977 and 1971 respectively, are essential reading for students of the historical evolution of Canadian federalism.

Fletcher, Martha. "Judicial Review and the Division of Powers in Canada," in Peter Meekison, *Canadian Federalism: Myth or Reality*, Third edition. Toronto: Methuen, 1977: 100-122. This is an excellent article that traces the important JCPC and Supreme Court decisions and discusses their impact on the legal framework within which the federal and provincial governments operate.

Milne, David. *Tug of War: Ottawa and the Provinces Under Trudeau and Mulroney*. Toronto: Lorimer, 1986. As the title indicates, the focus of this study is on the competitive relationship between the federal and provincial governments. Milne examines the power struggle under the Trudeau government in the early 1980s, and compares it to the brief period of reconciliation under Mulroney's first mandate.

Smiley, Donald. *The Federal Condition in Canada*. Toronto: McGraw-Hill Ryerson, 1987. A scholarly and reflective assessment of the forces at work in contemporary Canadian federalism, and the "continuing constitutional agenda."

Stevenson, Garth, ed. *Federalism in Canada, Selected Readings*. Toronto: McClelland & Stewart, 1989. This book is a collection of essays by scholarly writers past and present, grouped into four sections: the constitutional divison of powers, the social and economic background of Canadian federalism, federalism and party politics and intergovernmental relations: past and present. An excellent anthology of influential articles.

| CHAPTER 9 |

PRIME MINISTER AND CABINET

RICHARD A. LORETO

Notwithstanding the doctrine of parliamentary supremacy, effective decision-making power at the federal level in Canada is exercised by the Prime Minister and Cabinet. Both political institutions occupy the "apex of power" and, therefore, a description and analysis of the role they play in Canadian government and politics is essential.

The executive branch of the national government may be divided into three structural components. They are the Crown or formal executive, the Prime Minister and Cabinet or political executive, and the bureaucracy or public service. The bureaucracy may be subdivided into three types of structures — central agencies, line departments (and other kinds of ministerial portfolios), and a vast array of Crown corporations, agencies, boards, and commissions. In this chapter the focus is on the political executive and those central agencies which support its role in the development of public policies.

Before looking at the functions, structure, and decision-making processes of the political executive and its support agencies, an overview of the role of the federal executive is in order. A departure point is that the repository of executive authority in Canada is the Crown. This authority emanates from both the statutes passed by Parliament and the common law. According to Mallory the latter source is a "residue of common-law powers to legislate, which are the prerogative powers."[1]

The representative of the Crown at the federal level in Canada is the Governor General. The letter of the constitution states that executive authority is exercised by the Governor-in-Council; that is, the Governor General making decisions on the basis of advice from the Queen's Privy Council for Canada.[2] However, written constitutional prescription is substantially at odds with political reality. The British monarch and his or her Canadian representative play an essentially formal and ceremonial role (for example, giving royal assent to government bills or reading the Speech From the Throne at the opening of a parliamentary session). The Prime Minister is the actual head of government and the Prime Minister and the Cabinet, which in formal terms is a committee of the Privy Council, wield the real decision-making power. Although Privy Councillors are appointed legally by the Governor General and retain their title for life, political convention dictates the Cabinet, headed by the Prime Minister and consisting of the ministers appointed by him or her to form the government of the day, is the effective executive body.

The Prime Minister is the leader of the political party which has the support of the majority of the members of the House of Commons. Support for the government party may simply reflect the fact that it holds a majority of the seats in the House or, during periods of minority government, that it has the support (on a contingent basis) of one or more of the opposition parties.

The members of the government party in Parliament, primarily the elected representatives or MPs in the House of Commons and, to a much lesser extent, appointed Senators, constitute the talent pool from which the Prime Minister can appoint Cabinet ministers. As the political head of the department the minister is expected to bring proposals for policy and legislation to the Cabinet and to Parliament. He or she is also generally responsible for the administration of the department and its various programs and services. Support for both of these ministerial roles is provided by numerous public servants who, unlike their elected political master, are appointed to their positions on the basis of merit. The role of the deputy minister is particularly important. The deputy minister, who is usually a career civil servant is appointed as well as transferred and removed by the Prime Minister, is the administrative head of the department. As such he or she is responsible for providing the minister with both administrative and policy advice. The deputy minister and other senior departmental officials are, however, not the only source of policy advice for the minister. Each minister has a chief of staff and other political staff who provide a partisan perspective on the policy responsibilities of the portfolio. These individuals are not civil servants and their fate is closely tied to that of the minister.

| 155 |

Ministers are neither expected to be nor usually can they be experts in their respective areas of policy responsibility. Their role is to function as an agent of public control over the bureaucracy and the resources entrusted to government by the people of Canada. Furthermore, the Cabinet must be a representative political institution. Accordingly, expertise often is secondary to criteria such as race, ethnicity, gender, region, and sectoral economic interests in the selection of a member of the Cabinet.

Cabinet has a collective responsibility for the formulation, coordination, and implementation of government policy. While governments have a number of policy instruments at their disposal,[3] the passage of legislation is a necessary procedural requirement. The government, backed by the formidable expertise of its bureaucracy, initiates virtually all major federal policies. Opposition parties, which lack such staff resources, are normally in a position of reacting to what the government is proposing. The leading role of the government is further reinforced by the convention that only the government can bring in bills which involve the spending and raising of money. While Parliament refines and ultimately approves government legislation, party discipline ensures that the government gets its way for the most part, even in minority government situations. In a minority government situation, of course, the parties' eagerness for an election is a crucial factor.

Several other features of the political executive are worth noting at this point. The first is the distinction between the authority which is the exclusive prerogative of the Prime Minister and that which is exercised by Cabinet as a whole or individual Cabinet ministers. It will be evident below that the position and power of the Prime Minister is preeminent, a condition which is also augmented by his or her status as the leader of the governing party in an era of "leadership politics."[4] Secondly, ministers are not only collectively responsible for government policy, legislation, and budget but they are also individually responsible for administrative and policy matters within their portfolios, including the actions of the public servants who are subordinate to them. Finally, the deliberations of Cabinet are shrouded in secrecy and based on the principle of consensus, two other constitutional conventions.

The remainder of the chapter, which is divided into six parts, examines in greater detail the observations made in this overview. The first part focusses on the role of the Prime Minister. The focus next shifts to Cabinet with particular emphasis on the portfolio structure of the federal government and the representativeness of Cabinet membership. A third part deals with five central agencies that provide substantial support to the political executive, the Prime Minister's Office, Privy Council Office, Federal-Provincial Relations Office, Treasury Board Secretariat, and Department of Finance. Part four traces the evolution of the cabinet committee system, especially developments since the 1960s. The nature of the Cabinet decision-making process, centred on the preparation and approval of Cabinet memoranda, forms the basis for part five. Finally, there are several concluding remarks about the significance of recent trends in the evolution of the political executive in Canada.

I The Prime Minister I

The Prime Minister is clearly the most important person in Canadian politics. Yet, the authority and power of the position rest more on constitutional and political convention than statutory law.[5] In this regard Mallory states that the "office of Prime Minister is entirely lacking in a legal definition of its powers."[6] There is, however, some formal specification of the matters which are the "special prerogative of the Prime Minister." A Privy Council minute, P.C. 3374 of October 25, 1935, essentially stipulates the right of the Prime Minister to make recommendations regarding the dissolution and convocation of Parliament, numerous appointments, and the organization of government.[7]

A central source of the authority and power of the Prime Minister is his leadership of the government party. The strength of this source varies in relation to a fundamental characteristic of political democracy in Canada, namely, the notion that the Prime Minister has a popular mandate from both the party and the people. The legitimacy of the Prime Minster's actions is significantly affected by the ebb and flow in this twofold mandate. A poor showing in the latest public opinion poll does not, however, eviscerate the political power of the Prime Minister. He or she remains the Cabinet's first minister, the chief government spokesperson in the House of Commons, an MP representing the interests of the residents of a specific constituency, and the party leader most able, in a national context, to command widespread media and public attention.[8] Finally, periodic elections provide the supreme opportunity for a Prime Minister to retain (or lose) a mandate from the people.

Substantial power also emanates from the Prime Minister's exclusive right to make certain appointments, advise the Governor General, and determine the structure of government. The Prime Minister appoints both Cabinet ministers and parliamentary secretaries — MPs who assist ministers in various ways (how they do this is the minister's prerogative). These appointments are much sought after since they increase the power, status, and even the income of the ordinary MP. Although the Prime Minister's power to appoint ministers and parliamentary secretaries is constrained by the norm of representativeness and the need to reward loyal party members, it remains an effective means for instilling party discipline and consolidating the Prime Minister's personal support.

The appointment power extends into many other realms. The Prime Minister appoints Senators. Historically these appointments have been a prime source of party patronage (the provisions of the failed Meech Lake Accord would have limited significantly the first minister's prerogative in this sphere). The Prime Minister also puts in place the government's senior administrative team through the appointment of deputy ministers.

Such appointments are usually made with no or minimal consultation with the ministers concerned, thereby allowing the Prime Minister to ensure that a particular blend of political and administrative considerations exists in the leadership of specific policy areas. Finally, the Prime Minister appoints the Crown's representatives in Canada, Lieutenant-Governors at the provincial level and the Governor General; judges (i.e., from the district to superior court levels); and the heads of hundreds of Crown corporations, agencies, boards, and commissions. In sum, the Prime Minister's power to appoint, while not unchecked, is both extensive and a formidable mechanism for asserting control over the operations of government and his or her party.

In formal terms the Prime Minister's choices for various public positions are recommendations to the Governor General (in the case of the appointment of the Governor General the recommendation is to the British monarch). Although the Prime Minister also receives much advice from political and administrative officials on these matters, the recommendations tendered are, in effect, decisions. Advice to the representative of the Crown in Canada, however, goes beyond appointments. The Prime Minister alone can ask the Governor General to dissolve Parliament, a request which is denied only in the most exceptional of circumstances.[9] This gives the Prime Minister control over the timing of elections, yet another device for the maintenance of party discipline as well as personal and governmental power.

The Prime Minister is the only member of Cabinet who can compel changes in the structure of government beyond the boundaries of a single portfolio. Indeed, while advice on such matters abounds, especially from the central agencies examined later in the chapter, an incoming Prime Minister is essentially free to put his or her stamp on the machinery of government. Although legislative approval may be a politically troublesome necessity, departments and other public organizations can be created, disbanded, or amalgamated to reflect shifting political and public policy considerations. Moreover, the Prime Minister may organize Cabinet, both structurally and procedurally, as he or she sees fit. In recent years this has meant the use of Cabinet committees in conjunction with enhanced roles for central agencies. The impact of successive Prime Ministers on the "Cabinet system" is discussed later.

I Cabinet I

While a number of our Prime Ministers have utilized the power of the office to its fullest, one-person rule is not a salient feature of Canadian politics. One-party dominance is, however, a significant trend at both the federal and provincial levels.[10] It is doubtful that these periods of long rule by a single party would occur if other members of the political executive were merely sycophants of the first minister. Hence, Cabinet building is a necessary and a strategic task for any new Prime Minister.

The size of the federal Cabinet has increased gradually over the years in response to both the expansion of government's role in society and the demand for political representation inherent in the demographic, economic, and social changes which have characterized Canada's evolution as a federal nation-state. Sir John A. Macdonald, our first Prime Minister, had a Cabinet of fourteen ministers in 1867. Its size relative to that of Canada's territory and population was large, a reflection more of sectional political imperatives than any notion of increased government involvement.[11] While Cabinets contained as many as forty members during the 1980s, the increase in absolute size has not been in direct proportion to the expanded policy responsibilities of the national government or the heightened demands for a place at the Cabinet table coming from a society which is offically bilingual, highly regionalized, and increasingly multicultural. As a result a Prime Minister is faced with a number of difficult and often conflicting choices regarding the functional and political composition of Cabinet.

One consideration is the type of portfolio that a minister will be given. This decision involves several interrelated legal, political, and functional factors. From a legal perspective ministers fall into one (or sometimes two) of five categories.[12] The first category, which is the largest and most prestigious, consists of ministers who have responsibility for a specific government department and related non-departmental entities (for example, the Minister of the Environment). The next largest category, ministers of the state, can be divided in two. Some ministers of state are responsible for a discrete policy area (for example, Small Business and Tourism), while others have been appointed to assist a departmental minister (for example, Transport or Employment and Immigration). Both forms of the minister of state concept have proliferated since the passage of the *Ministries and Ministers of State Act* by the Trudeau government in 1970. Furthermore, their growth (over one third of the Cabinet members appointed by Prime Minister Mulroney in February 1990 were ministers of state) has largely been in response to the perception, both inside and outside government, that certain clientele groups (i.e., seniors, youth, visible minorities, etc.) require Cabinet representation.[13] The two remaining categories of ministers are relatively small. First, several ministers may be given specialized duties in relation to either legislative matters (usually Government Leader in the House of Commons and Senate, respectively) or the Prime Minister's portfolio (for example, Deputy Prime Minister).

These are Cabinet positions of substance. Second, there is the historic designation of minister without portfolio, which is something of a misnomer in that such ministers are normally given something to do. In recent years the minister without portfolio category appears to have been supplanted by the minister of state concept and even the notion of an associate minister (the Cabinet shuffles announced by Prime Minister Mulroney in January 1989 and February 1990 did not include a minister without portfolio but did include an Associate Minister of National Defence).

Another key consideration is the historical nexus between the functional responsibilities of certain portfolios and the economic interests of certain parts of the country. From this perspective it is appropriate that a minister from Western Canada be in charge of the Department of Agriculture; that an anglophone with links to the financial communities centred in Toronto and Montreal ("Bay Street" and "St. James Street") should be the Minister of Finance; and that only MPs elected in provinces bordering either the Atlantic or Pacific Oceans be entrusted with the task of running the Fisheries and Oceans department

Competence, defined in both political and occupational terms is yet a third consideration. While ministers are, at best, expected to be "enlightened amateurs" rather than experts in their respective policy spheres, major portfolios — Finance, Justice, and the like — must be given to the most capable individuals in the talent pool generated by the electoral process and, to a lesser extent, by appointments to the Senate.

Extending the considerations concerning Cabinet appointments into the realm of socioeconomic factors illustrates further the complexity of the Prime Minister's task.[14] Each province expects to have a voice in Cabinet and, for the most part, this representational norm has been fulfilled. Proportionate representation is also an expectation of the main linguistic and cultural groups, English and French. This reality has influenced the process of Cabinet-building to the extent that francophones have accounted for approximately 30 percent of the ministerial positions. Certain professional and occupational groups have also been well represented. Lawyers, who constitute a minuscule percentage of Canada's population, have held over one half of the Cabinet positions; persons from the business world, over one fifth of the positions. Business representation has been particularly evident in the Cabinet appointments made by Prime Minister Mulroney since 1984. Finally, in terms of class origins, classic studies by Porter[15] and Olsen[16] demonstrate that Cabinet members are drawn primarily from the middle class.

Analysis along socioeconomic lines reveals too that certain groups in Canadian society have been significantly underrepresented. Many of these groups are minorities in numerical terms — native people, skilled and unskilled workers, the poor, so-called "visible minorities," etc. One underrepresented group, women, is actually a majority. Despite this demographic fact, the appointment of seven women to the Mulroney Cabinet of thirty-nine ministers in 1989 is to date the high point of female participation. Since 1984 approximately 15 to 18 percent of federal Cabinet posts have been held by women.

Once appointed to Cabinet, ministers receive assistance from not only the civil servants under their control but also a growing number of so-called "political staff." These individuals — chiefs of staff, executive assistants, communications advisers and the like — are not civil servants. They are supporters of the party in power, personally loyal to their ministers, and exempt from the normal procedures of civil service management (while there is little protection from dismissal, there is a "fast track" route into the civil service after three years of employment).

Political staffs are not new phenomena but their role has certainly changed over the years. During the Pearson era ministers' executive assistants were regarded as an unelected power elite. While the number of aides per minister increased from three to five or six between 1966 and 1978, their power declined. This was due, in large part, to the changes instituted by Prime Minister Trudeau in the cabinet system (i.e., new roles for committees and central agencies such as the Privy Council Office). As a result aides were no longer "alter egos" and "sounding boards" but rather "coordinators and gatekeepers," whose job was "to keep the minister from drowning in the system's swelling flow of information."[17]

| 161 |

The role of political staff changed dramatically when Prime Minister Mulroney assumed power in 1984.[18] After years of Liberal rule in Ottawa and the negative experience of the short-lived government of Joe Clark,[19] a perception that the Progressive Conservative government would have to exert political control over the bureaucracy existed. The solution was more and better political staff playing a more active advisory role. Spending on ministerial staff was immediately increased to $400,000 per minister. A chief of staff, with a salary at the level of an assistant deputy minister, was appointed by each minister in most instances from a list of names compiled by the Prime Minister's Office. While the Leader of the Official Opposition referred to them as 'commissars', an official in the Prime Minister's Office emphasized three roles: to offer political advice to the minister, to manage the minister's office, and to act as a liaison between the minister and the civil service.

These developments concerning a new role for political staff were also evident when the Ontario Liberal party came into office at Queen's Park in June 1985.

I Central Agencies I

Government departments, Crown corporations and other non-departmental entities, and central agencies are the major structural components of the federal bureaucracy. The first two types of government organization usually have sectoral or vertical policy responsibilities (for example, the Department of National Health and Welfare or the Export Development Corporation) and serve clients who are external to government. Central agencies, however, have government-wide or horizontal policy responsibilities and serve internal clients (i.e., politicians and civil servants). In general, these organizations (some of which have the title of department) support both the political executive's responsibility to make, coordinate, and supervise government decisions and the bureaucracy's responsibility to manage the delivery of government programs and services. This part of the chapter focusses on the five central agencies which support the decision-making processes of the Prime Minister and Cabinet. The personnel who staff these organizations have been called the "superbureaucrats" by Campbell and Szablowski.[20]

PRIME MINISTER'S OFFICE

The role of the Prime Minister's Office (PMO) is to provide the first minister with partisan, political advice. It is staffed by political appointees rather than civil servants. These persons are loyal to the Prime Minister personally as well as to the governing party and they expect to leave their positions when a new Prime Minister comes into office, even one from the same party. The PMO is directed politically by the Prime Minister and administratively by a Principal Secretary, a position which carries the rank and status of a deputy minister.

From Sir John A. Macdonald on, Prime Ministers have surrounded themselves with trusted political advisers. However, substantial expansion of the PMO, in terms of both its role and the number of staff, is generally associated with the Trudeau era.[21] In addition, the role and management style of the PMO since the late 1960s has very much reflected the personality and style of its political head. This can be illustrated by comparing briefly the operation of the PMO under Pierre Trudeau and Brian Mulroney, respectively.

According to Tom Axworthy,[22] Prime Minister Trudeau's last Principal Secretary, the notion of a "strategic Prime Ministership" is necessary for success in government and must be supported by a strong PMO. Furthermore, the notion implies that the Prime Minister alone may only be able to deal with five or six major issues over the life of a four-year mandate, while Cabinet's limit is up to twenty-five. Accordingly, it is the task of the PMO to insure a clear sense of priorities, the fusion of politics and policy, a measured capacity to change with events, a clear sense of the constraints which the Prime Minister faces, and the intelligent use of available resources. The PMO also must act as a buffer between the Prime Minister and the Cabinet, the party, the civil service, etc., since the Prime Minister cannot be involved in everything.

Under Axworthy the PMO had five functional divisions: policy, communications, operations, travel, and the Prime Minister's personal office. A "core group" of fifteen senior officers met every day at 8:30 a.m. At 9:15 a.m. Axworthy discussed the most pressing issues with the Prime Minister for about thirty minutes. Weekly planning meetings were also held by each functional division. Several times a year general meetings of all divisions of the PMO took place. Finally, it was Axworthy's responsibility to devise a work plan for each senior officer.

Axworthy's conception of the PMO's specific role has five elements. First, the PMO obtains strategic information (an "early warning system"). While polls are important in this regard, liaising with the Liberal Party caucus was, in Axworthy's judgement, more effective. Second, it sets the political framework. This was done in various ways including "think tank" sessions and the development of the Speech From the Throne. Third, the PMO must forge political coalitions both inside and outside government. Fourth,

FIGURE 1 : Organization of the Prime Minister's Office, 1985

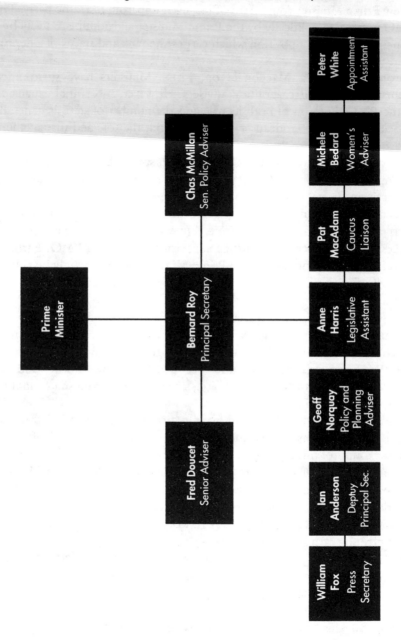

SOURCE : *The Hamilton Spectator*, October 5, 1985, p. A9.

"selling the message" is crucial (for example, the communications program devised for the repatriation and amendment of the constitution in the early 1980s) Fifth, the PMO needs to "service the system"; that is, the PMO acts as a central agency for the network of ministerial political staff. Ultimately, all information must intersect at the desk of the Principal Secretary since he or she is the Prime Minister's chief strategist.

The organization of the PMO during Prime Minister Mulroney's first year in office is depicted in Figure 1. At first glance the structure appears similar to that of the Trudeau years. Bernard Roy, the Principal Secretary and a close personal friend of the Prime Minister, attended all Cabinet meetings as well as those of the Cabinet Committee on Priorities and Planning and briefed the Prime Minister for about an hour daily.

The organization chart in Figure I does not capture the actual workings of the PMO under Bernard Roy. The hierarchy of the Office was flatter under Roy than it had been during the Trudeau years. There were no rigid lines of demarcation among the senior advisers and Roy did not hold daily meetings with them. As a result the PMO, during the first eighteen months of Mulroney's first mandate, was criticized by the media as impotent and excessively concerned with the minutiae of politics not the larger issues.[23]

This approach was not entirely the product of the Principal Secretary's views and actions. Whereas Prime Minister Trudeau pursued a limited and often lofty personal agenda (for example, world peace or the constitution) and left political strategy to staff, Prime Minister Mulroney's perspective is different:

> In Mr. Mulroney's office, the chief political strategist is the Prime Minister, his priorities set by the politics of votes — a calculus of polls and press clippings in which long-term planning is most concerned with what is going to happen next month.[24]

Aucoin characterizes these differences in organizational perspective between the two Prime Ministers in terms of the paradigms of "rational management" (Trudeau) and "brokerage politics" (Mulroney)[25] put it more succinctly : "The informal links between Mr. Mulroney and a number of his old cronies count for more than formal structures, such as the Cabinet committees and the Privy Council Office."[26]

Changes in the structure and operation of the PMO were responsible, to a significant extent, for the transformation from the crisis atmosphere of the first few years of the Mulroney government to the electoral victory in 1988. By the latter part of 1986, for example, Mr. Roy was conducting daily

| 165 |

meeings of senior staff which reviewed the Prime Minister's daily activities and progress on the government's rolling agenda, i.e., the "political agenda from the medium to the long term...."[27] However, the key change occurred in 1987 when Derek Burney, a civil servant with the Department of External Affairs, was put in charge of the PMO. Mr. Burney gave the office a formal structure and centralized its internal flow of information. He held daily briefings with senior staff on the basis of a formal agenda and even assumed responsibility for briefing the Prime Minister prior to Question Period. The appointment of a civil servant as Principal Secretary certainly blurred the lines between politics and administration, but, in retrospect, it was necessary to overcome the problems created by PMO staff who were viewed in some quarters as "a group of frequently ill-informed and disorganized amateurs."[28]

PRIVY COUNCIL OFFICE

In formal terms the Cabinet is a committee of the Queen's Privy Council for Canada. The administrative organization which supports the work of the Cabinet and the first minister is the Privy Council Office (PCO). It is headed by the Clerk of the Privy Council and the Secretary to the Cabinet. The former position has existed since Confederation and it was combined with the latter in 1940.[29] The person who holds these intertwined positions as well as other senior PCO staff are appointed by the Prime Minister from among the ranks of the civil service. Only occasionally are partisan supporters appointed (for example, in 1986 Prime Minister Mulroney appointed Dalton Camp, a well known party adviser as Senior Policy Adviser in the PCO).[29]

The PCO serves the Prime Minister and Cabinet as the principal coordinating agency for the administrative side of government. Furthermore, its role in the development of government policy is intrinsically different from that of the various government departments: it is more concerned with the process of developing policy than the substance of policy (although from time to time this boundary is crossed by PCO staff). This distinction is evident in the specific functions of the PCO. The PCO is responsible for analysing cabinet memoranda, documents prepared by departmental ministers when they require Cabinet approval for a particular course of action; the logistics of Cabinet meetings, i.e., preparation of agendas, scheduling of meetings, the routing of memoranda, and the like; briefing the Prime Minister, Deputy Prime Minister, and the chairs of Cabinet committees; advising the Prime Minister on the appointment of senior civil servants; the documentation of Cabinet and Cabinet committee decisions; advising departmental officials on the preparation of Cabinet memoranda; and monitoring and ensuring the enforcement of Cabinet decisions. In addition, the Clerk of the Privy Council is a key intermediary between the Prime Minister and the civil service.

Prime Minister Trudeau's rational management paradigm changed the traditional roles of the PCO and other central agencies:

> Given the importance attached to the establishment of checks and balances within the decision-making system, it was logical that central agencies would have a critical role to play in providing the prime minister and cabinet with independent analysis of the departmental proposals prepared for submission to cabinet committees.[30]

The notion that the central agencies were counterweights to the departmental bureaucracy necessitated a shift in emphasis from policy process to policy substance. This meant the analysis of departmental proposals in light of the policy priorities and plans of Cabinet; the formulation and analysis of policy options; and an increased "awareness of the need for interdepartmental co-ordination in policy planning and development."[31]

The Mulroney paradigm of brokerage politics (i.e., the accommodation of interests, a transactional management style — where support for a cabinet minister is conditional upon obtaining some benefit, etc.) has swung the pendulum back towards the process end of the scale in the case of the PCO. Parallel with this development is the fact that the "Mulroney paradigm of brokerage politics demands that the powers of the prime minister be exercised to the fullest...," thereby making the first minister the "principal counterweight to ministerial ambitions that are not in accord with his policies, priorities or strategy."[32]

FEDERAL-PROVINCIAL RELATIONS OFFICE

Overall coordination of the complex and multidimensional relationship between the federal government and the ten provincial governments is the responsibility of the Federal-Provincial Relations Office (FPRO). Its political head is the Minister of State (Federal-Provincial Relations) and its administrative head is the Secretary to the Cabinet for Federal-Provincial Relations.

The roots of this central agency extend back to the Cabinet Committee on Federal-Provincial Relations established by Prime Minister Trudeau in 1968. Staff support for this committee was provided by a separate division of the PCO. The committee was disbanded by Prime Minister Clark in 1979 (and was moribund from 1974 on). The staff group, however, evolved into the FPRO in 1975 under a full secretary to the Cabinet and was a prominent bureaucratic actor during the constitutional crises of the 1980s. When Prime Minister Mulroney established his own Cabinet Committee on Federal Provincial Relations in 1986, chaired by the Minister of State, the FPRO became its secretariat. In addition, the FPRO briefs the Prime Minister on federal-provincial matters and serves as the coordinator of the First Ministers Conferences. Notwithstanding these substantial responsibilities, the influence of the FPRO over other federal government organizations has been mixed. In part this is due to the absence of any financial leverage to complement its coordinative role.[33]

DEPARTMENT OF FINANCE AND TREASURY BOARD SECRETARIAT

The two central agencies in the financial sphere, the Department of Finance and the Treasury Board Secretariat, have common historical roots. The Treasury Board, a committee of Cabinet, was established shortly after Confederation. Until 1967 it was chaired by the Minister of Finance and supported by staff from the Department of Finance. The President of the Treasury Board is now the chair and administrative support is provided by a separate secretariat.[34]

The organization of the Treasury Board Secretariat is shown in Figure 2. The administrative head is the Secretary of the Treasury Board and he or she is one of two deputy ministers (the other is the Comptroller General) who report to the President of the Treasury Board. The secretariat's structure mirrors the Treasury Board's role as the government's general manager "concerned with the economical, efficient, and effective use of the government's human, financial, and material resources." This role translates into a number of specific responsibilities: the review of the expenditure plans and programs of departments; the organization of the federal public service and the control of the size of its staff; human resources management policy and practices except in the area of staffing which is assigned to the Public Service Commission; acting as the "employer," for purposes of collective bargaining; general administrative policy; and financial management policies and practices. In 1989 the ministers on Treasury Board met 31 times and its secretariat was involved with 2,749 submissions to the Board, the negotiation of 80 collective agreements, the revision of 125 policies, and another 1,068 items.[35]

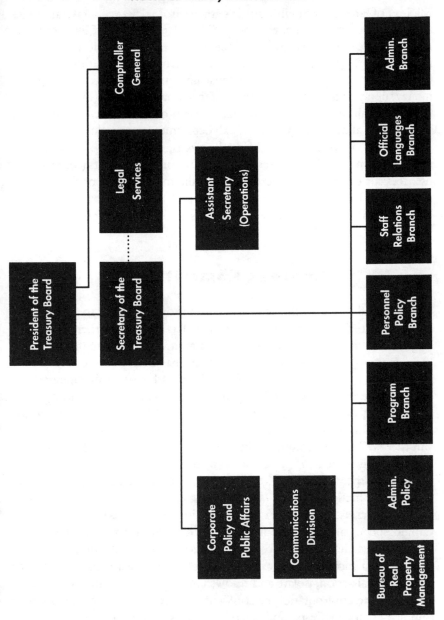

FIGURE 2 : Treasury Board Secretariat

President of the Treasury Board

Comptroller General

Legal Services

Secretary of the Treasury Board

Assistant Secretary (Operations)

Corporate Policy and Public Affairs

Communications Division

Admin. Branch

Official Languages Branch

Staff Relations Branch

Personnel Policy Branch

Program Branch

Admin. Policy

Bureau of Real Property Management

SOURCE : Ian D. Clark, "Treasury Board, Today and Tomorrow,"
A Presentation to the Canadian Centre for Management Development
Annual Seminar for University Faculty (February 22, 1990)

| 169 |

CANADIAN GOVERNMENT AND POLITICS

If Treasury Board and its secretariat fulfill the general manager's role, the Minister of Finance with substantial assistance from departmental staff serves as the government's "chief economist." The Department of Finance is the central agency which advises Cabinet on general economic policy, fiscal policy, intergovernmental financial arrangements, and taxation policy. It influences or controls key economic instruments such as interest rates, the money supply, and the exchange value of the Canadian dollar (in conjunction with the Bank of Canada); the overall amount of government spending as well as the allocations to individual departments; the flow of transfer payments to provinces and individual citizens; the raising of government revenues by means of both taxes and non-taxation instruments (for example, user fees for certain federal services); and the management of the national public debt. In sum, Finance's strong grip on the public money controlled by the federal government ensures that it is a powerful central agency.

I Cabinet Committees I

The increased power of the central agencies is one aspect of the emergence of the "institutionalized Cabinet" at the federal level. Another is a system of formal Cabinet committees. Cabinet committees are, by no means, a new phenomenon.[36] Indeed, the Treasury Board has been in place since 1868. However, it was the outbreak of World War I which first precipitated the extensive use of committees. Ten committees existed by the end of 1939 and the War Committee, chaired by Prime Minister King, effectively displaced the Cabinet during the wartime period.[37]

In theory Cabinet committees improve the efficiency and effectiveness of Cabinet decision making. They do so by making expeditious use of scarce ministerial time. Schindeler[38] translates this broad purpose into a number of specific functions. In his view Cabinet committees relieve the whole Cabinet of certain tasks (for example, meeting delegations) reduce the time Cabinet spends on any one item; reduce the demands on individual ministers (this assumes that Cabinet committee assignments will not proliferate); provide for a more detailed examination of items; ensure coordination of governmental action; isolate and resolve interministerial disputes; provide a forum for the confrontation of conflicting interests, or the cooperation of complementary interests; and deal with issues that no one minister feels inclined to tackle. Moreover, Cabinet committees facilitate the involvement of senior civil servants in policy development at the Cabinet level and often represent a form of symbolic political action (i.e., the creation of a committee

PRIME MINISTER AND CABINET

is a signal to the public or specific groups that the government is concerned about an issue and intends to do something).

All Cabinet committees share four broad features. First, their creation is the prerogative of the Prime Minister. He or she is able, therefore, to determine their role, size, membership, and procedures. Second, they are rarely established by statute (the Treasury Board is the sole exception). This, in conjunction with the first feature, means an incoming first minister has virtually a free hand to redesign the Cabinet committee system. Third, Cabinet committees (except Treasury Board) do not, in a formal sense, make decisions. Instead they make recommendations to Cabinet or another Cabinet committee. The actual role and decision-making power of committees has, however, varied significantly under different Prime Ministers. Fourth, the norms of cabinet decision-making — primarily ministerial responsibility (consensus) and confidentiality — apply to Cabinet committees.

The evolution of the federal Cabinet committee system since World War II has been summarized well by Clark and Matheson.[39] Prime Minister St. Laurent, who followed King, continued to use committees, although full Cabinet met frequently and made all final decisions. Prime Minister Diefenbaker, whose election in 1957 ended twenty-two years of Liberal rule, made little use of committees, preferring the control and tendency towards consensus afforded by frequent Cabinet meetings. It was Prime Minister Pearson (1963-1968), however, who established the basic structural framework of the Cabinet committee system employed by successive Prime Ministers. Pearson set up numerous permanent and ad hoc committees, including the key coordinating committee which he chaired, Priorities and Planning. The flaw of the Pearson system was that while matters were discussed first in committee, they were also discussed at Cabinet. This element of duplication as well as the large number of committees (24) provided little incentive for ministers to make them work.

In 1968 Prime Minister Trudeau built upon the framework set in place during the Pearson years. The number of committees was reduced but they were given more decision-making power. Central agencies, especially the PCO, provided more analytical support to the committees. Indeed, by the end of the first Trudeau era (1968-1979), a new central agency, the Ministry of State for Economic Development (MSED), was created to support the work of the Board of Economic Development Ministers.

Prime Minister Clark made several significant changes during his brief tenure. The first was the establishment of an Inner Cabinet. This structure not only supplanted the Cabinet Committee on Priorities and Planning but also, to a large extent, the full Cabinet which became a forum for political discussion and coordination. Secondly, the number of Cabinet committees was reduced and the committees restructured to correspond to the so-called spending "envelopes" of a new approach to government budgeting, the Policy and Expenditure Management System (PEMS). The PEMS, which was an attempt to integrate the decision-making processes for budget and policy, gave the committees substantial power. A third change was the creation of the Ministry of State for Social Development (MSSD), which, much like MSED, served as the secretariat for a corresponding Cabinet committee. In addition, "mirror committees" of deputy ministers were set up to provide coordination for the committees supported by MSED and MSSD, respectively.

The return to power of Prime Minister Trudeau in 1980 did not result in fundamental changes in the Cabinet committee system. Although the Inner Cabinet disappeared in name, it reappeared in functional terms in the guise of a Priorities and Planning committee which, along with the Cabinet, had the authority to make decisions. The PEMS was not only retained but its procedures were also elaborated. The emphasis on coordination, a hallmark of Trudeau's rational management paradigm which Clark had extended through the creation of MSSD and the adoption of PEMS, advanced yet again by the extension of the ministry of state concept into the External Affairs portfolio. In addition, MSED was renamed the Ministry of State for Economic and Regional Development (MSERD) and its coordinating tentacles reached into the field in the person of a Federal Economic Development Coordinator (FEDC) in each province.

"Back to the future" was an apt slogan for the reforms instituted by Prime Minister Turner during his eighty-day tenure in 1984. Turner's perspective on the Cabinet system was the antithesis of the rational management paradigm forged by his political rival, Pierre Trudeau. The result was the disbanding of MSERD, MSSD, and the ministry of state function in External Affairs; the integration of the FDECs into the Department of Regional and Industrial Expansion; the termination of the mirror committees; and a reduction in the number of both ministers and Cabinet committees (from thirteen to ten).

Prime Minister Mulroney did not alter significantly the Cabinet committee system he inherited from John Turner in September 1984. He also established ten committees including Priorities and Planning which he chaired. The PEMS was retained but its procedures streamlined and the envelopes consolidated. Furthermore, there was no attempt to resurrect the coordinating machinery of the ministries of state which had existed under both

Trudeau and Clark. At the outset of his first mandate, Mulroney made his most substantial changes in the roles played by the central agencies. The paradigm of brokerage politics required that the PMO usurp much of the power of the PCO; the policy of financial restraint required that the Department of Finance keep a tight lid on the spending plans of program departments.

Substantial changes in the Cabinet committee system and the processes of Cabinet decision making were made by Prime Minister Mulroney in the aftermath of his 1988 electoral victory. Three major changes were made in January 1989. First, the roles of certain coordinating committees were significantly adjusted. Second a new coordinating committee and four new sectoral policy committees were established. Third, both the policy focus and the size of the sectoral committees were streamlined. Table 1 identifies the coordinating and sectoral policy committees set up in 1989.

The role of Priorities and Planning continues to revolve around the determination of the government's overall agenda and major policies. However, all other committees except the Treasury Board, which has a statutory mandate, are under its purview. Moreover, the sectoral policy committees only concern themselves with policy (and not budget or routine matters). The "policy reserve" or discretionary money to fund new programs is retained by Priorities and Planning. Finally, the membership of Priorities and Planning has been expanded to eighteen (excluding the chair) in order to make it more representative. This is important because Priorities and Planning, which meets weekly, is, in effect, an "inner cabinet" which has delegated decision-making authority from Cabinet. Cabinet, which meets monthly, has evolved into an "inner caucus," i.e., the ultimate forum to make sure all ministers are on-side.

Expenditure Review is a new coordinating committee. It is chaired nominally by the Prime Minister and effectively by the Deputy Prime Minister. The formal mandate of Expenditure Review is "to ensure that the Government's expenditures continue to be directed to its highest priorities, and that expenditure control continues to contribute to deficit reduction."[40]

The most interesting committee in the configuration announced in January 1989 is Operations, which is chaired by the Deputy Prime Minister and also includes the chairs of seven other Cabinet committees. The Operations committee was first set up as an informal group prior to the 1988 election. Its task then was to end the paralysis at Priorities and Planning generated by disputes between the Minister of Finance and program ministers. While the centralization of control under the Deputy Prime Minister caused some animosity, the exigencies of the pre-election period were paramount.

| 173 |

CABINET COMMITTEE SYSTEM OF
THE MULRONEY GOVERNMENT, JANUARY 1989

Committee	Chair	Number of Members
Priorities & Planning	Prime Minister	19
Expenditure Review	Prime Minister	8
Security & Intelligence	Prime Minister	9
Operations	Deputy Prime Minister	8
Special Committee of Council	Deputy Prime Minister	12
Legislation & House Planning	Minister of Justice	10
Communications	Minister of State (Federal-Provincial Relations)	8
Treasury Board	President of the Treasury Board	6
Sectoral Policy Committees		
Economic Policy	President of the Treasury Board	13
Environment	Minister of the Environment	10
Cultural Affairs and National Identity	Minister of Communications	9
Federal-Provincial Relations	Minister of State (Federal-Provincial Relations)	10
Foreign & Defence Policy	Secretary of State for External Affairs	10
Human Resources, Income Support and Health	Minister of National Health and Welfare	11
Trade Executive	Minister for International Trade	7

Source: Privy Council Office, "Background Paper on the New Cabinet Decision-Making System" (January 30, 1989).

Operations is the most exclusive of the Cabinet committees in that it is an executive committee for Priorities and Planning. Operations meets every Monday and its report is the first item on the Tuesday agenda of Priorities and Planning. Its essential role is agenda management and issues management. In theory it is a process mechanism; in practice it makes decisions (the Prime Minister's presence is tangible in the amalgam of senior ministers and bureaucrats associated with the committee).

The roles of the other coordinating committees require brief comment. Communications focusses on "the most appropriate means of ensuring that policy and program initiatives are effectively communicated to the public and that the overall program of the Government is presented in a coherent fashion."[41] Legislation and House Planning is responsible for reviewing draft legislation and devising the government's legislative strategy. The mandate of Security and Intelligence is evident in its title, and the Special Committee of Council deals with the legal instruments of orders-in-council and regulations. Finally, Treasury Board fulfills the statutory responsibilities discussed earlier. In the budgetary sphere it is only responsible for the expenditures of approved programs (Expenditure Review makes cuts).

Four new sectoral policy committees were created in 1989: Environment; Economic Policy; Cultural Affairs and National Identity; and Human Resources, Income Support and Health. These and the other sectoral committees are oriented to themes in the Throne Speech and are chaired by the lead minister in the policy area. In addition, their membership is more compact (eight to twelve ministers) than that of the sectoral committees employed during Prime Minister Mulroney's first term (as many as twenty-three ministers) However, they are without expenditure authority, a development which some observers regard as indicative of a hierarchy within Cabinet, i.e., those ministers who sit on Priorities and Plannning and Operations, and those who do not.

I Cabinet Memoranda I

A final dimension of the institutionalization of Cabinet is the use of formal, standard procedures for the submission of departmental policy proposals. Once again, the roots of this development reach back to the wartime Cabinet system of Prime Minister King. In recent years a "Memorandum to the Cabinet" consists of two parts. The first is "Ministerial Recommendations," a succinct document which is protected from public disclosure by the tradition of Cabinet secrecy. The second part is a more detailed "Discussion Paper" which is available to the public under the **Freedom of Information Act** and to the Auditor General.[42]

A Cabinet memorandum is a minister's decision-making document. It is also a policy document which contains essential financial and administrative information. A memorandum is employed to obtain approval for policy or program decisions from Cabinet.

The basic procedural model for a Cabinet memorandum encompasses four steps. First, the memorandum is submitted to the PCO, which in turn distributes it to the other members of Cabinet. Second, it is discussed by the appropriate Cabinet committee. Third, either Priorities and Planning or Cabinet receive the memorandum in order to make a final determination. At this point the Prime Minister is briefed by both the PCO and the PMO. Fourth, final approval or rejection of the memorandum is signified in the form of a "record of decision."[43] Prime Minister Mulroney's latest reform of the cabinet decision-making process has several implications for this basic

CANADIAN GOVERNMENT AND POLITICS

model. The role of the sectoral policy committees is only to determine whether the memorandum is consistent with approved policy directions. Priorities and Planning decides whether the proposal is financially affordable. Treasury Board approves the operational plan of a proposal which has received both policy and financial approval.

I Conclusion I

Several trends characterize the evolution of the political executive at the federal level in Canada. The first is the preeminent position of the Prime Minister whose power rests on the prerogatives of the office, the support of political and administrative organizations, and the contemporary emphasis by the media and others on "leadership politics." Secondly, the Cabinet system has undergone a continual process of institutionalization, i.e., the emergence of powerful central agencies, a Cabinet committee system, and formal procedures for Cabinet memoranda. Implicit in this trend is the search for improved policy planning, coordination, and assessment. A final trend is the dialectical relationship between institutional rationalization and the vicissitudes of politics. Any overview of the roles of the Prime Minister and the Cabinet cannot do justice to the complex and problematic nature of the decisions taken by men and women seeking consensus within the formal and informal parameters of government.

NOTES

[1] J. R. Mallory, *The Structure of Canadian Government*, revised ed. (Toronto: Gage, 1984) p. 34.

[2] *The Constitution Act, 1867*, SS. 9-16.

[3] Kenneth Kernaghan and David Siegel, *Public Administration in Canada: A Text* (Toronto: Methuen, 1987) pp. 126-128.

[4] Leslie A. Pal and David Taras (ed.), *Prime Ministers and Premiers: Political Leadership and Public Policy in Canada* (Scarborough: Prentice-Hall, 1988).

[5] Robert J. Jackson and Doreen Jackson, *Politics in Canada: Culture, Institutions, Behaviour and Public Policy*, 2nd ed. (Scarborough: Prentice-Hall, 1990) p. 77.

[6] J. R. Mallory, *op. cit.* p. 77.

[7] Fred Schindeler, "The Prime Minister and the Cabinet: History and Development," in Thomas A. Hockin (ed.), *Apex of Power: The Prime Minister and Political Leadership in Canada*, 2nd ed. (Scarborough: Prentice-Hall, 1977) pp. 29-30.

[8] David Taras, "Prime Ministers and the Media" in Leslie A. Pal and David Taras, *op. cit.*

[9] J. R. Mallory, *op. cit.* pp. 48-63.

[10] Richard Van Loon and Michael Whittington, *The Canadian Political System: Environment, Structure and Process*, 4th ed. (Toronto: McGraw-Hill Ryerson, 1987) p. 368.

[11] J. E. Hodgetts, *The Canadian Public Service: A Physioloay of Government 1867-1970* (Toronto: University of Toronto Press, 1973), Chapter 3.

[12] Robert J. Jackson and Doreen Jackson, *op. cit.* pp. 288-289.

[13] John A. Chenier, "Ministers of State to Assist: Weighing the Costs and Benefits," *Canadian Public Administration*, Vol. 28, No. 3 (Fall, 1985) pp. 404-406.

[14] Richard Van Loon and Michael Whittington, *op. cit.* pp. 440-452.

[15] John Porter, *The Vertical Mosaic: An Analysis of Social Class and Power in Canada* (Toronto: University of Toronto Press, 1965), Chapter 13.

[16] Dennis Olsen, *The State Elite* (Toronto: McClelland and Stewart, 1980), Chapter 2.

[17] *The Globe and Mail,* September 5, 1978, p. 8.

[18] *The Globe and Mail,* October 18, 1984, p. 1.

[19] Paul W. Fox and Graham White (eds.), *Politics: Canada*, 6th ed. (Toronto: McGraw Hill, 1987) pp. 494-499.

[20] Colin Campbell and George J. Szablowski, *The Superbureaucrats: Structure and Behaviour in Central Agencies* (Toronto: Macmillan, 1985).

[21] Robert J. Jackson and Doreen Jackson, *op. cit.* p. 307.

[22] Based on a presentation made by Thomas Axworthy to the Department of Political Science, University of Toronto, January 14, 1985.

[23] *The Globe and Mail,* March 5, 1985 p. 3; June 22, 1985, pp. B1-2.

[24] *The Globe and Mail,* March 5, 1985, p. 3.

[25] Peter Aucoin, "The Machinery of Government: From Trudeau's Rational Management to Mulroney's Brokerage Politics" in L.A. Pal and D. Taras, (eds.) *op. cit.* pp. 50-68.

[26] *The Globe and Mail,* September 2, 1986. p. 4.

[27] *Ibid.* p. A 5.

[28] *Ibid.* October 21, 1987, p A 5.

[29] Robert J. Jackson and Doreen Jackson, *op. cit.* p. 309.

[30] Peter Aucoin, *op. cit.* p. 54.

[31] *Ibid.*

[32] *Ibid.* pp. 61-62.

[33] Richard J. Van Loon and Michael S. Whittington, *op. cit.* pp. 492-493.

[34] W.L. White and J.C. Strick, *Policy, Politics and the Treasury Board in Canadian Government* (Don Mills: Science Research Associates, 1970) pp. 1-16.

[35] Ian D. Clark, "Treasury Board, Today and Tomorrow." A presentation to Canadian Centre for Management Development Annual Seminar for University Faculty, February 22, 1990.

[36] J.R. Mallory, *op. cit.* p. 110-112.

[37] *Ibid.* p. 112.

[38] Fred Schindeler, *Responsible Government in Ontario* (Toronto: University of Toronto Press, 1969) pp. 53-55.

[39] Ian D. Clark, "Recent Changes in the Cabinet Decision Making System in Ottawa," *Canadian Public Administration,* Volume 28, No. 2, (Summer, 1985) pp. 185-201, and William A. Matheson, *The Prime Minister and the Cabinet* (Toronto: Methuen, 1976) pp. 83-91.

[40] Privy Council Office, "Background Paper on the New Cabinet Decision Making System" Ottawa, January 30, 1989.

[41] *Ibid.* p. 2.

[42] Richard Van Loon and Michael Whittington, *op. cit.* p. 476.

[43] Robert J. Jackson and Doreen Jackson, *op. cit.* p. 300.

ANNOTATED READINGS

Aucoin, Peter. "The Machinery of Government: From Trudeau's Rational Management to Mulroney's Brokerage Politics" in L.A. Pal and D. Taras, eds. *Prime Ministers and Premiers: Political Leadership and Public Policy in Canada.* Scarborough: Prentice-Hall Canada, 1988: 50-68. Provides a conceptual framework for the comparative analysis of the Cabinet systems under Trudeau and Mulroney.

Clark, Ian D. "Recent Changes in the Cabinet Decision-Making System in Ottawa." *Canadian Public Administration,* Volume 28, No. 2 (Summer 1985): 185-201. Overview of the evolution of the Cabinet system from King to Mulroney's first term.

Loreto, Richard and Graham White "The Premier and the Cabinet" in G. White, ed. *The Government and Politics of Ontario,* Fourth edition. Toronto: Nelson, 1990: 79-102. Examination of the political executive in Ontario, with particular emphasis on the changes made by Premier Peterson.

Matheson, William A. *The Prime Minister and the Cabinet.* Toronto: Methuen, 1976. Detailed historical and political analysis of the Cabinet system up to the initial years of the Trudeau era.

Mallory, J.R. *The Structure of Canadian Government,* Revised edition. Toronto: Gage, 1984. Emphasizes the legal, historical, and institutional dimensions of the political executive as well as the other branches of government.

CHAPTER 10

THE FEDERAL PUBLIC SERVICE: STRUCTURE AND PERSONNEL *

STAN DRABEK

Once Parliament debates and ultimately passes legislation, what then happens? How is legislation or policy implemented and administered on an on-going basis? What structures and processes are involved? Who are the people involved in the process of implementation and administration? This chapter will try and answer these and other questions concentrating, for the most part, on the operations of the federal government. The public service[1] is probably one of the most talked about but least understood aspects of the total Canadian governmental structure.

Examining the role of the federal public service is a study in public administration. For this purpose we can define the public service as an organized group capable of implementing programs and policies as well as providing advice on the development of policy to their political masters, the cabinet ministers. Public servants operate in a framework that is at one and the same time non-political (non-partisan) and anonymous.

---

*   The author would like to thank Scott McAlpine for his comments on a draft of the chapter.

At this point it might be wise to remind the reader of points discussed elsewhere in this volume that may have some bearing on this chapter. Canada is a federal state with a constitution dividing legislative powers between the federal and ten provincial governments each of which has its own public service structures and personnel.[2] This division of powers largely determines whether the federal or provincial public service administer a particular policy. For example, the federal government determines and administers defence policy while provincial governments deal with educational issues. In some cases, such as concurrent powers where powers are shared between the governments such as agriculture, then both federal and provincial governments and their public services are involved.

Canada's bilingual nature also affects the nature of the federal public service. Accommodating this factor in terms of providing services to both French-speaking and English-speaking people as well as in terms of the resultant effects on personnel hiring practices continues to be a contentious issue.

Another important element in the nature of Canada is its vast geographical size. Most Canadians talk about regions of the country and remark on the distances between their home-town and "far-off Ottawa." How this geographical factor influences the administration of national policies as well as the question of whether regional differences (the West, the Maritimes) are taken into account when implementing policies are important questions in the study of the Canadian federal public service.

Finally, the growth of government is another important theme in our study. For a long while people demanded that governments play an increased role in society. There were demands for consumer protection, expanded educational and social service policies and lately the protection of the environment. Government involvement in these areas has meant an expanded role for the government and its public servants who make decisions which affect the lives of many people in different ways.

I Organizational Structures I

Since government is involved in a myriad of activities, the most efficient organizational principle is to create specialized organizations entrusted with the task of achieving the objectives of government. Specialization means the allocation of responsibilities, the division of work and the arrangement of personnel in different types of structures to do this. There is no one single organizational structure for the federal public service, rather, various organizational structures exist for different purposes. Differences among the various types of organizations stem from internal structuring, the question of accountability (to parliament and to Cabinet ministers) and the freedom of action or autonomy given to the organization.

In general, the operational structures of the Canadian federal government can be categorized under the following headings:

- Departments (i.e. Agriculture, National Revenue)
- Regulatory Agencies (National Transportation Agency, Canadian Radio-television and Telecommunications Commission)
- Crown Corporations (Canadian National Railways, Canada Post Corporation)

DEPARTMENTS

Political scientists find it difficult to describe exactly what a government department is. Perhaps J.E. Hodgetts provides the best definition. He describes it as, "an administrative unit comprising one or more organizational components over which a minister has direct management and control."[3] Departments are structurally pyramidal in form with operational staff at different hierarchical levels performing different functions. The pyramid usually peaks in the position of Deputy Minister who is administrative head of the Department. In turn, the Deputy Minister is responsible to the Minister who has the political responsibility for the department's actions to his Cabinet colleagues and to the House of Commons.

Government departments are established by statute and have an intended function to perform and a program or set of programs to administer. Departments are a means to achieve a goal such as the provision of social service programs by Health and Welfare Canada. Over the years as programs and government involvement have expanded, the number of government departments has grown. Depending upon the exact definition of a department, there are at least twenty-five departments.

As programs expand and the administrative goals of an organization broaden, departments tend to undergo a series of reorganizations in response. The historical development of the former Department of Trade and Commerce is illustrative. After several reorganizations over the years, the organization's most recent manifestation is as the Department of Regional and Industrial Expansion.

Some political scientists[4] categorize government departments according to their functions so that they refer to:

- vertical departments
- horizontal departments

Vertical departments (also called line departments), such as Agriculture, are directly involved in administering programs which respond to the needs and expectations of the public or of a particular segment of the public.

On the other hand, the functions of horizontal departments are directed at providing assistance to other government departments (such as the Department of Supply and Services) or else the co-ordinator of governmental policy activities (for example, The Treasury Board Secretariat). Because of their influence and strategic role in the decision-making process, some of these "horizontal" departments also carry the designation of central agencies (i.e. the Department of Finance, Privy Council Office). Central agencies tend to be the elite parts of the federal public service or bureaucracy and are the centres of power and decision-making.

The regional geographic nature of Canada, its distances and its linguistic differences, mean an administrative decentralization of activities. Some government programs involve direct contact with the public and this means "on the spot" administration rather than the provision of that service from one distant office located in Ottawa. For example, there are unemployment insurance offices located in many Canadian cities and immigration offices located at border points as well.

These are referred to as the field offices while the headquarters of a department is usually located in Ottawa. Field offices are examples of applying national policies to the different geographic regions of Canada.

Our other two operational structures mentioned above — regulatory agencies and crown corporations — constitute a category called crown agencies or what Hodgetts has referred to as "structural heretics." Each of these categories has specialized structures to perform their intended functions which differentiate them from ordinary government departments.

REGULATORY AGENCIES

Regulatory agencies are involved in performing the function of regulation which the Economic Council of Canada has defined as "the imposition of constraints, backed by government authority that are intended to modify the behaviour of individuals in the private sector significantly."[5]

Regulatory functions usually fall under two headings:

- direct regulation
- social regulation

Direct regulation is mostly economic in nature and is concerned with such things as the nature of return on investment and regulations concerning the entry or exit of firms to and from specific industries such as those in the natural resources sector (a function of the National Energy Board). Social regulations aim at attaining broad social objectives in widely disparate areas such as transportation safety (National Transportation Agency) or Canadian content regulations in the Canadian media (Canadian Radio-television and Telecommunications Commission). In a way social types of regulation can also be considered direct in nature since they have economic effects on the private sector.

To accomplish its specified task, a regulatory agency performs adjudicative (quasi-judicial), legislative (law-making) and administrative roles. These roles create the unique organizational structure of a regulatory agency. In addition these roles demand an organization that is specialized, impartial and independent of direct political control. These demands mean that an ordinary government department structure does not fit the bill. One might say that regulatory functions and regulatory agencies are created "to take something out of politics."

Structurally speaking, regulatory agencies do not necessarily follow the hierarchical model. Many agencies such as the National Energy Board have a board (currently 12 members) consisting of appointed members including a Chair. Terms of appointment usually range from three to ten years. This board becomes the ultimate decision-making level in the organization and is roughly parallel in nature to the departmental Deputy Minister. Rather than having a Minister directly responsible for the regulatory agency there is a "designated" Minister in Parliament who fields and passes on questions which arise in the House of Commons about the operations of the regulatory agency to that agency. For example, this is the function of the Minister of Energy, Mines and Resources with respect to the operations of the National Energy Board. Finally, because of its regulatory nature and its semi-autonomous nature and lack of direct ministerial control, a regulatory agency is not subject to the same amount of parliamentary and governmental supervision and control as is a regular government department. Regulatory agencies tend to be more flexible than departments in their operations and in their implementation of government policy.

In recent years governments have made proposals to decrease the existing number of rules and regulations administered by regulatory agencies especially those dealing with the airline and trucking transportation sectors. This would result in the down-sizing of some regulatory agencies. The process of down-sizing and the elimination of rules and regulations is referred to as deregulation. For example, the National Transportation Agency is proposing to "modernize and streamline" the rules and regulations applying to international charter services.[6] The rationale for deregulation is to let the market decide the nature of the business sector in question. Fewer rules, fewer governmental demands for information and increased competition will, according to the proponents, mean cheaper costs (fares) and allow new businesses to compete in sectors previously protected by rules and regulations. Critics of deregulation claim, however, that increased competition will result in a situation where small companies will suffer and the larger ones dominate the sector concerned. To the critics, deregulation also means that large companies are unlikely to provide all necessary services but only those which stand a chance of being profitable. Finally, the critics argue that public safety will suffer in the absence of rules and regulations emphasizing this important point.

A further step in the process of deregulation is the concept of Sunset Laws. The idea here is to require each regulatory agency, for example, to justify its existence after an operational period of say five years. If it cannot argue for its continued existence, then it is dissolved by the government. So far this idea has not really taken hold in Canada.

CROWN CORPORATIONS

Crown Corporations have been an important factor in the historical development of Canadian government. Who hasn't heard of Canadian National Railway (CNR), the Canadian Broadcasting Corporation (CBC) and until its recent change of ownership, Air Canada? Like their regulatory agency counterparts, crown corporations are complex and specialized organizations structured to meet particular objectives. One point of disagreement crops up in any analysis of crown corporations. How many federal crown corporations are there? Figures range from 336[7] to 454[8] depending upon definition. In other words there is no definitive count.

Historically the reasons for the establishment of crown corporations have been wide and varied. They range from rescuing a series of bankrupt railways (the creation of CNR); maintaining Canada's cultural independence (the CBC); providing a "window" on the natural resources sector (Petro-

Canada); and the "maintenance" of railway passenger services (VIA Rail).

Many, but not all,[9] crown corporations resemble private businesses in terms of structure and personnel administration (hiring, promotion etc.). The main difference is in ownership. Private investors own shares in a private business organization such as Bell Canada Enterprises. It is the federal government in the name of the people of Canada which owns the shares of a crown corporation.[10]

As is the case with other governmental organizations, crown corporations are subject to classification. The "official" classification is found in the Financial Administration Act as amended in 1984. This Act establishes a regimen of accountability to parliament for three categories — Schedule B, CI and CII. In general, the more the financial need of the corporation the more rigorous the accountability requirement.

Schedule B corporations are involved in basic administrative research or information and advice provision (National Research Council, Canada Employment and Immigration Commission). They rely heavily on government funding and are, therefore, subject to the most accountability and control.

Schedule CI corporations are those which generally compete with private enterprise in various areas but which also rely on government funding (appropriations) to make up operating deficits (Canada Mortgage and Housing Corporation, VIA Rail). They are also subject to demands of accountability and control but less so than Schedule B corporations.

Schedule CII corporations are the least subject to governmental control. These corporations compete directly with private business corporations (CNR competes with Canadian Pacific in the railway freight business) but they are financially viable and much less dependent on government financial assistance. They have, in effect, managerial autonomy (Canadian National Railway, Petro-Canada and Air Canada when it was a crown corporation).

Financial need and accountability is but one method of government control. Another method is the ability of the government to issue directives to Crown corporations "in the public interest after consultation with the corporation's board of directors." An example might be a directive to the crown corporation to make a profit whenever circumstances dictate. Schedule CII corporations, unlike the others, submit only their capital budgets and corporate plans for approval. Schedule B and CI corporations must also submit their operating budgets to the government for approval.

Students of crown corporations also pay a great deal of attention to appointments made by governments to the Board of Directors of these companies. What criteria are used? Does the federal nature of Canada affect the choices? The answer is definitely yes in the case of the Bank of Canada where the Bank of Canada Act specifically provides for regional representation on the Board of Directors.

Usually appointments to the boards of crown corporations are made up to three years. These appointees are part-time directors usually working with the full-time chief executive officer and other members of management. The appointments of the chief executive officer of a crown corporation also rests with the government of the day.

When filling vacancies on the board of directors of crown corporations, governments tend to appoint the party faithful. For example, when Air Canada was still a crown corporation, the Mulroney government appointed loyal Conservatives. These appointments included Frank Moores, a former Conservative Premier of Newfoundland, and David Angus, a former chairman of the PC Canada Fund — the fund-raising arm of the federal Conservative party. Liberal governments in the past did the same thing.

This continuing pattern of appointment is referred to as patronage, with all its negative connotations. These appointments are considered rewards for "service to the party." However, given the top calibre and legal and business background of most of these appointments, perhaps the term "political appointments" would be more descriptive and accurate. One could also argue that private corporations are subject to patronage appointments to their boards of directors because of things such as "the old boys network."

It is quite noticeable, however, that the government often makes sure that board appointments do reflect the geographic divisions of the country. For example, the 1989 Annual Report of Petro-Canada based in Calgary reveals the following representation:

Alberta	5	Newfoundland	1
Ontario	2	Nova Scotia	1
Quebec	2	Manitoba	1
New Brunswick	1	British Columbia	1

Of the five Alberta representatives on the board of directors, two are management personnel, the Chief Executive Officer and the President and Chief Operating Officer.

CROWN CORPORATION ISSUES

Over the years, the major issue concerning crown corporations has been that of managerial autonomy versus that of being an instrument of public policy. Lately, another issue has arisen — that of privatization.

Managerial autonomy versus instrument of policy. Managerial autonomy refers to an "arm's length" relationship between the government and the corporation and usually refers to Schedule C II or similar corporations. These corporations are most similar to the private firms they compete with and consequently, the argument is that they be allowed to pursue their own paths. This includes the right to make a profit. Several crown corporations including CNR and, more recently, the Canada Post Corporation have shown profits and have paid dividends to the government.

Arm's length also means little or no government interference in the organization's business decisions. This has been achieved in the case of CNR in part by its abandonment of underused branch lines. These decisions are meant to make operations more profitable even though they may have political repercussions. From a business perspective, arm's length is also justified by the fact that the publication of detailed information about budgets might undermine the competitive position of the corporation in its sector.

On the other hand, the instruments of policy approach stresses the fact of government ownership. In this view the crown corporation should be used as another method of implementing the government's social and economic policies. Government directions, not arm's length relationships, are the standard procedure. It would mean the provision of services at cost or even at a loss where there was a political demand as in the case of VIA Rail and railway passenger service in some parts of the country.

A specific use of the instrument of policy approach was the Liberal government's establishment of Petro-Canada as an entry into the American dominated oil and gas industry so that Canada might have some control over its resources and prices. From a policy perspective Petro-Canada was also a way of expediting and developing offshore resources which otherwise might not have been developed by the private sector. However, the Conservative government of Brian Mulroney has moved Petro-Canada from the instrument of policy approach to an arms-length approach with a mandate for making a profit, thus becoming a candidate for privatization.

Privatization. In the last number of years, neoconservative philosophy and marketplace economics have influenced the policies of many governments in the world. Canada is no exception. One result is an increasing call for privatization of crown corporations.

Privatization refers to the sale of a crown corporation to the private sector. This can be done in one fell swoop, such as was the case with the Northern Transportation Agency, or in stages as in the recent privatization of Air Canada. Underlying the trend to privatization is the belief that government should not be involved in activities where the private sector could make money. The government, according to this view, should not use corporations to implement policy. Profitability of a crown corporation clearly indicates to the supporters of privatization that private enterprise could provide that service. As such money-making crown corporations are prime targets for privatization and at the same time the easiest to sell to the private sector.

Decisions on privatization are based on political factors. Governments such as the one led by Mulroney, oriented to the marketplace economy, have tended to accelerate the process of privatizaton. A future government may veer back to the instrument of policy approach.

I Personnel Relations I
and Administration

Without people, organizations such as government departments cannot function. The staffing of government organizations — the human element — is an important issue, especially given the demographic and geographic differences of Canadian society as well as the development of specialized departments and agencies which administer government policies and provide policy advice on these matters. Who are these public servants?

In this section we will highlight some of the more important and interesting aspects of federal government personnel administration. Because of space limitations, companion topics such as the specific role of the Public Service Commission in the hiring and placement of public servants and its role as the guardian of the merit principle as well as the Treasury Board Secretariat in the classification of public service and its role in the collective bargaining process will have to be left aside.

This section will concentrate on the historical development of the patronage/merit approaches to personnel administration in the federal public service; the question of representative bureaucracy (especially francophone, female and minority representation); and finally the question of political rights for public servants and its effect on the idea of a neutral public service.

PATRONAGE/MERIT APPOINTMENT SYSTEMS

No analysis of the public service is complete without reference to the patronage/merit issue. For a good number of years after the federation of 1867, patronage (rewards for the party faithful) was the personnel administration system. Given the uncomplicated and generally clerical nature of government activities of the time, few disputed the use of this system. Changes in government usually meant changes in public service personnel.

Nevertheless, these wholesale changes in personnel and the growth of government activities and the development of the specialized nature of government created a growing demand for a highly skilled and more politically neutral public service which would be able to work with any government in power. Thus the demand for a merit system of personnel administration.

Merit, is somewhat difficult to define in operational terms. Some claim that merit should have a flexible meaning which will change with fluctuating demands and circumstances. Nevertheless, an accepted statement of the merit principle is that:

1. Canadian citizens should have a reasonable opportunity to be considered for employment in the public service and,
2. Selections must be based exclusively on merit or fitness for the job.[11]

The first step in this direction was taken with the passage of the 1908 *Civil Service Act* which established the Civil Service Commission dedicated to the implementation of the merit system of appointment. However, the 1908 Act only applied to the "inside" (Ottawa) part of the bureaucracy which was, by chance, the smaller part of the federal civil service in terms of numbers. Only with the passage of the 1918 *Civil Service Act* was the cycle complete and that Act pointed the federal service firmly in the direction of political neutrality, efficiency and the merit system.

During the decades after the passage of the 1918 *Civil Service Act*, merit really meant the elimination of patronage and the establishment of a politically neutral public service. Only with the increase in government activities, the demand for specialization due to technological development and the influence of the scientific management school of administration did the meaning of merit expand to include efficiency and later representativeness. At the same time, there were complaints that the application of the merit system had resulted in the cumbersome application of too many controls to protect the public service.

Efficiency received a strong boost from the studies of the Royal Commission on Government Organization (Glassco Royal Commission) in 1962-63. The Commission stressed the need for economy in the provision of public services and its motto was "let the managers manage." The Glassco Commission then added flesh to the bones of the definition of the merit

THE FEDERAL PUBLIC SERVICE

principle. Over time efficiency and capability finally overtook political neutrality as the guiding factors of the merit principle. Recently other factors have added more depth to the meaning of merit particularly in terms of a representative bureaucracy.

REPRESENTATIVE BUREAUCRACY

The question of which Canadians "should have a reasonable opportunity" to be considered for employment is part of the merit principle as well as the broader question of representative bureaucracy. In general representative bureaucracy is defined as being one which mirrors and is reflective of the various components of Canadian society. The aim is to represent as many groups of people in relation to their proportion of the population. Ultimately this would make the public service more responsive to all aspects of society.

The first move in this direction occurred during the 1960s with the impact of the Quiet Revolution in Quebec and the report of the federal Royal Commission on Bilingualism and Biculturalism both of which stressed francophone grievances about their inadequate level of participation in the federal public service itself and especially in the higher and policy-making positions such as Deputy Minister.

The Liberal government of the day, under Lester Pearson, accepted the thrust of the argument by the Royal Commission that more francophones should be hired for public service positions particularly policy-making positions. The government promised to proceed with plans to ensure that the federal public service would reflect in numbers and accountability those Canadians whose mother tongue was French. Further impetus for this effort came from the federal *Official Languages Act* of 1969 which declared English and French to be the official languages of the public service. Attempts were also made to make service more bilingual especially in Ottawa and in the policy-making positions.

Progress towards a bilingual representative bureaucracy is a matter of interpretation. To some progress is slow in terms of numerical representation. Others look at the question from an entirely different viewpoint. The issue raises a series of intertwined and complex questions. On one side, the argument stresses that the public service should be numerically more reflective of a country's population and therefore more responsive to the groups represented in the population. With at least 25 percent of the Canadian population being French-speaking, administrative and policy decisions must take this into account particularly since values and attitudes can differ between the two linguistic groups. Another viewpoint claims that the

| 191 |

push for a bilingual public service takes away, to some extent, the idea of a bureaucracy based on the merit principle. In other words, merit is sacrificed for representativeness. One might ask here whether bilingualism itself could not be considered another factor in the overall definition of merit.

A more recent counterpart to the question of francophone representation is that of female representation. Under-representation of women in the federal public service does exist and, like francophones, especially at policy-making levels. However, it must be noted that because of the historical importance of francophone-anglophone linguistic relations over the years the barriers to numerical representations were easier to overcome and were overcome earlier than is the case with female representativeness.

Yet the forces of women's rights groups and public opinion have led the government to quicken the pace of accommodating more women in the public service. In the late 1980's, for example, an increasing number were promoted to the influential policy-making positions of Assistant Deputy Minister (ADM) and Deputy Minister (DM), a development which would have been unthinkable even ten years earlier.

To ensure continued opportunity for women and other groups (indigenous people and handicapped people), the government introduced in June 1983 an affirmative action program. The declared aim of this program was to eliminate barriers in hiring practices which would otherwise exclude these groups from employment as well as to correct any other procedures which would place these groups at a disadvantage in other personnel administration matters such as classification, promotion or pay.

Affirmative action also includes the concept of employment equity or equal opportunity. Everyone should have equal access to a job and the opportunity of working one's way up the career ladder. Without doubt, the Canadian *Charter of Rights and Freedoms* has helped promote affirmative action and especially section 15 of the Charter which guarantees "equal protection and equal benefit of the law without discrimination." Applied to the public service program of affirmative action/employment equity, it means that "preferential treatment for groups which have historically suffered from discrimination does not constitute reverse discrimination."[12]

Supporters of strong affirmative action programs indicate that only a quota system will solve the problem of representation. If there is to be representation of a minority group, then that group's representation in the public service should approximate its percentage of the population. Critics of this approach maintain that it undermines the merit system and also prevents people outside a defined minority or disadvantaged group from being appointed or promoted. This is the stuff of strong debate.[13] Nevertheless, in the Canadian federal public service there is no quota system in place for women or minority groups. What is in place is a series of targets established by the Treasury Board Secretariat which public sector managers should be working toward in order to ensure a more representative bureaucracy. What all this amounts to is an indication that the merit principle as defined earlier in this chapter is an ever changing one whose implementation is enhanced by expanding the equality of access to public service employment and equity programs.

But one might ask at this point whether the fine words on representative bureaucracy have been translated into practice. According to statistics provided by the Public Service Commission, francophone participation in the federal public service (as defined by the Commission) increased slightly from 27.2% in 1977 to 28.2% in 1987. At the same time, however, francophones constituted only 20.8% of the management category which includes the top executive levels of the bureaucratic structure.[14]

Statistics concerning female representation in the public service also indicate an upward trend no doubt influenced lately by affirmative action/employment equity programs. Female participation in the public service increased dramatically from 27.3% in 1967 to 42.4% in 1987.[15] Figures for the management category indicate that only 10.6% of the category is female.[16]

From these statistics, it would appear that progress towards a more representative bureaucracy is slow. True, the percentage of francophone, female and other minority representation is increasing in the general population of the public service. However, representation in the top decision and policy-making levels still has a way to go and it is here that improvements must be concentrated.

POLITICAL RIGHTS OF PUBLIC SERVANTS

Our final point of analysis in this section deals with the political rights of public servants. This is an off-shoot of the discussion of the political neutrality of public servants discussed earlier in the section on merit. Political neutrality traditionally meant that federal public servants should be seen but not heard. To serve all political parties in government meant being above suspicion of partisanship which in turn meant that public servants would not be allowed to participate in political activities.

Given the desire for a politically neutral public service, the *Civil Service Act* of 1918 prohibited public servants from engaging in partisan political activity of any kind. Violation of this prohibition meant dismissal. Public

CANADIAN GOVERNMENT AND POLITICS

servants could, however, vote. These restrictions on partisan political activity weren't changed until the *Public Service Employment Act* of 1967.

This Act allowed public servants (with the exception of Deputy Ministers) to run for political office if the Public Service Commission felt that their employment would not be compromised. If elected, the public servant had to resign from the public service. Over the years a small number of public servants have taken advantage of this provision and been allowed to run for office.

The 1967 Act also permitted employees to contribute to the political party of their choice and attend political meetings but they could not work for the campaign of a candidate or party nor work against a candidate or party. These provisions still restrict the political rights of public servants and it raises the question of whether there should be a half-way house in terms of the right for public servants when other people have full political rights.

A decision made by the Federal Court of Appeal in July 1988 however, has enlarged, to a certain extent, the realm of political rights of public servants. The case dealt with the prohibition in section 32 of the *Public Service Employment Act* of working for or against candidates and political parties. In its decision the Court indicated that the prohibition infringed on the *Charter of Rights and Freedoms* provisions for individual rights and specifically indicated that the prohibition was "too vague, ambitious and open to discretionary application."[17] Consequently, the prohibition can no longer be enforced.

I Concluding Observations I

The federal public service is in a constant state of flux. Departmental structures come and go. New functions such as environmental protection policy mean the establishment of new departmental organizations. Governments create, enlarge and then down-size regulatory agencies. Crown corporations are being sold off to the private sector.

Personnel administration or human resources management has changed from an emphasis on political neutrality and the application of the merit principle in terms of efficiency to a wider application of the merit principle so as to include representation, responsiveness, equal access and equity. This means that more people are given the opportunity of becoming public servants. A wider meaning of merit may also provide for the widening of political rights of public servants equal to those of the ordinary citizen.

What does the future hold for the federal public service? One issue comes to mind immediately. Size. How large should government be? It is a philosophical discussion, to be sure, between those who believe that the best government is one that governs least and others who insist that government must be involved in the economy and society to protect citizens from economic and social exploitation.

Privatization, deregulation and the recent hesitancy of governments to undertake new activities all indicate that the growth of the public sector for the next while will be slow and best. No doubt government will undertake new activities but the wholesale expansion of the past few decades has been braked by public attitudes and the problem of finances. Any future expansion of the public sector will have to rely on the force of public opinion and its reflection in the priorities of political parties.

The future federal public service will be leaner in overall numbers, more representative of the Canadian population as a whole, more responsive but as in the past departments, regulatory agencies and crown corporations will continue to exist and the implementation and administration will continue at a high level.

NOTES

[1] The term civil service also appears in the literature but presently most writers use the term public service. Another term used to describe the entire public service is bureaucracy.

[2] It should also be remembered that local governments such as Calgary, Windsor and Toronto also have their own public service.

[3] J.E. Hodgetts, *The Canadian Public Service: A Physiology of Government 1867-1970* (Toronto: University of Toronto Press, 1973) p. 89.

[4] For example, see G. Bruce Doern, "The Cabinet and Central Agencies" in G. Bruce Doern and Peter Aucoin (eds.), *Public Policy in Canada* (Toronto: Macmillan, 1979) p. 27-61.

[5] Canada, Economic Council of Canada, *Responsible Regulation*, An Interim Report by the Economic Council of Canada, November 1979 (Ottawa: Minister of Supply and Services Canada, 1979) p. xi.

[6] Canada, Office of Privatization and Regulatory Affairs, *Federal Regulatory Plan* (Ottawa: Minister of Supply and Services Canada, 1989) p. 336.

[7] Treasury Board of Canada Secretariat, *Crown Corporations and Other Canadian Corporate Interests* (Ottawa: Minister of Supply and Services Canada, 1984) p. 3.

[8] Source: John W. Landford and Kenneth J. Huffman, "The Unchartered Universe of Federal Public Corporations" in Robert S. Pritchard, ed., *Corporations in Canada: the Calculus of Instrument Choice* (Toronto: Butterworths, 1983) pp. 233-273.

[9] Advisory crown corporations such as the Economic Council of Canada have different organizational structures than the commercially oriented ones such as CNR.

[10] There is another type of organization called a mixed corporation in which government and private enterprise are owners. A good example is Alberta Energy Corporation which is 35% owned by the government of Alberta.

[11] R.H. Dowdell, "Public Personnel Administration," in K. Kernaghan (ed.), *Public Administration in Canada*, 4th ed. (Toronto: Methuen, 1982) p. 196.

[12] K. Kernaghan and D. Siegel, *Public Administration in Canada: A Text,* (Toronto: Methuen, 1987) p. 489.

[13] For a discussion of this question, see Public Service Commission, *Equality of Access: Equal Opportunity and the Merit Principle* (Ottawa: Public Service Commission, 1982).

[14] Canada, Public Service Commission, *Annual Report 1987* (Ottawa: Minister of Supply and Services, 1988) p. 31.

[15] Public Service Commission, *Annual Report 1987,* p. 15 and 30.

[16] *Ibid.* p.84.

[17] Canada, Public Service Commission, Press Release, "Political Activities of Public Servants Federal Court of Appeal Decision on Section 32 of the Public Service Employment Act," August 1988.

ANNOTATED READINGS

Students may find it difficult to locate books which deal specifically with the federal public service. There are, however, a number of Canadian public administration texts which contain a wealth of material on some of the issues covered in this chapter. Two of the more recent and comprehensive texts are: K. Kernaghan and D. Siegel, *Public Administration in Canada*: (Toronto: 1987 Methuen) and R.F. Adie and Paul G. Thomas, *Canadian Public Administration: Problematic Perspectives*, 2nd edition (Scarborough, Ont.: 1987 Prentice-Hall). At a more sophisticated and theoretical level there is J.E. Hodgetts, *The Canadian Public Service: A Physiology of Government* (Toronto: University of Toronto Press 1973) which is still influential and applicable even though published almost twenty years ago.

For some of the specific issues mentioned in the chapter, the student should consult, amongst others, Allan Tupper and G. Bruce Doern, *Corporations and Public Policy in Canada*, (Montreal: The Institute for Research on Public Policy: 1981); Lloyd Brown-John, *Canadian Regulatory Agencies* (Toronto: Butterworths, 1983); and R.H. Dowdell "Public Personnel Administration" in K. Kernaghan (editor), *Public Administration in Canada: Selected Readings*, 4th edition (Toronto: Methuen: 1982) pp. 190-196 or Part V in the 5th edition of the same text published in 1985.

| CHAPTER 11 |

TIES THAT BIND:
PARLIAMENTARY MEMBERS
AND THEIR CONSTITUENCIES

RICHARD G. PRICE AND MAUREEN MANCUSO

Since 1867 there have been several noteworthy changes in Canadian politics which involve the relationship between elected representatives and those they represent. These changes which effect the link between the two include the rise of disciplined parliamentary parties, extension of the franchise to women and non-property holders, selection of political party leaders by provincial and national party convention, simultaneous constituency elections, and the prominence of the mass media as participants in the electoral and governing processes. Yet one thing has not changed: MPs and MLAs continue to represent territorial units called ridings or constituencies and do so with considerable vitality and enthusiasm.

In a study conducted for *Parliamentary Government*, MPs agreed that constituency work forms a major part of their responsibilities: those contacted estimated that they spent from fifty to eighty percent of their time on constituency issues.[1] Clearly, being able to respond to the needs and wishes of the constituency is a pivotal facet of a legislator's job. Members of Canada's parliaments and territorial assemblies typically respond to their constituencies and constituents in three ways:

SYMBOLIC RESPONSIVENESS: Parliamentarians communicate with individuals and groups via newsletters or quarterly reports, and demonstrate their constituency commitment by congratulating individuals for personal achievements. Such messages to students, community volunteers, husbands and wives celebrating anniversaries, and so on represent a member's search for personal support.

SERVICE RESPONSIVENESS: The growth of government in the post-depression period has resulted in MPs and MLAs becoming ombudsmen or rectification agents who are called upon to intercede with bureaucracies to rectify a wrong imposed by bureaucrats.

ALLOCATIVE RESPONSIVENESS: In order to promote the economic and cultural interests of their constituents, representatives serve as project boosters. They assist municipalities in obtaining funds for important capital projects (marinas, arenas, government offices) and help businesses qualify for government grants, projects, or contracts.[2]

This commitment to constituency responsiveness by MPs and MLAs results from characteristics inherent in two separate but overlapping milieus: the recruitment environment — the sphere of selection, election, and re-election — and the legislative work environment — the sphere of debate, question period, and committee deliberation (See Figure 1). Experiences in these environments serve, by encouraging effort spent on the constituency, or by discouraging efforts spent elsewhere, to enhance and strengthen constituency responsiveness. We will illustrate how career forces and parameters interact to keep the attention and activities of Canadian parliamentarians focused on their constituencies.

I The Recruitment Environment I

The recruitment environment includes three harmonious, reinforcing institutions: a political culture which emphasizes the virtue of local representation, a selection process in which federal and provincial candidates are nominated by local constituency parties, and an electoral system in which one candidate represents each constituency and victory requires only a plurality of votes.

FIGURE 1 : Legislative Environments and Constituency Representation

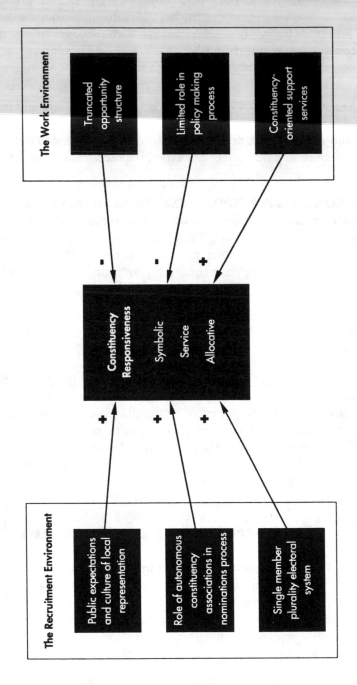

PUBLIC EXPECTATIONS:
A CULTURE OF
LOCAL REPRESENTATION

Observers of Canadian politics have long argued that federal and provincial politics are conducted in a maze of political cultures or psychological and perceptual environments. For Pammett and Whittington, "political culture is viewed as being composed of attitudes, orientations, values, beliefs, emotions, images and in functional terms it is viewed as a determinant of political action or behaviour."[3] These psychological orientations focus on four objects: the political community (province, federation, territory or nation), the regime (the government and constitution of Canada), the authorities (the people and positions who comprise the government) and especially one's view of oneself as a political participant. Local political culture is a cultural-representational linkage of immediate interests, involving citizen expectations of elected members and elected member perceptions of citizen expectations.

According to repeated studies conducted by the Canadian Institute of Public Opinion, there is little question about what Canadians expect from their elected leaders. Average citizens expect members to vote according to the views of their constituents, and believe that Canada would be better off if leaders were more responsive to the views of ordinary Canadians (see Table 1). Additionally, a public opinion poll commissioned in 1982 by the Canadian Studies of Parliament Group buttresses these results. Of all persons contacted nearly 50% said MPs should vote as their constituents would vote while 30% said MPs should use their own judgement. Only 8% thought MPs should vote as their political party required. When asked what Members of Parliament should consider their first duty, 62% said it should be looking after the needs of constituents, 18% said serving as a watchdog on government activities and spending, 7% said passing laws and 6.5% mentioned party loyalty.[4] The Canadian people clearly believe a member's first responsibility is to his or her constituents. They expect MPs (and by extension MLAs) to emphasize those aspects of their jobs which involve service and allocative responsiveness.

Members' perceptions of their own duties similarly emphasize constituency responsibilities. In a panel study of new members of the House of Commons (1974-78), Price, Clarke and Krause asked MPs to reflect upon and describe their own view of the job of a member prior to receiving their party's nomination. Over two-thirds of all freshmen defined their future job in terms of constituency work — being an ombudsman, communicating

| 201 |

with constituents, representing constituents. This emphasis on service and allocative responsiveness overshadowed such activities as attending House debates, committee work, caucus responsiveness:

- I'm an ombudsman. It involves representing constituents to government and the government to your constituency.
- To take the concerns or problems of my constituents and direct them to the proper departments for solution.
- To solicit cabinet ministers for projects in my riding, represent the riding generally, and legislate.
- Getting answers back to people. There is a lot of satisfaction in helping people with their problems.[5]

TABLE 1

PUBLIC'S PERCEPTION OF MPS' AND LEADERS' RESPONSIBILITY TO THE PUBLIC

Panel A: Members of Parliament Should Vote According To:

	Own View	Constituents' View	Undecided
	%	%	%
1981	29	61	10
1976	34	58	8
1972	29	63	8

Panel B: Canada Would Be Better Off If Nation's Leaders Followed The Views Of The Public

	Better Off	Worse Off	Other
	%	%	%
1986	59	15	26
1976	60	13	27

What is especially interesting about these results is that they reflect constituency-oriented attitudes of new members before they have discovered, as will be discussed, that their opportunities in the legislature itself are rather limited. From the beginnings of their legislative careers, members appear to be focused on their constituencies.

Reports of similar MLA perceptions of constituency expectations appear in Levy and White's recent public *Provincial and Territorial Legislatures in Canada.*[6] In Prince Edward Island, constituency demands on members' attention are high:

> Islanders expect to have direct personal access to their MLAs; despite their part-time status, legislators are always 'on call.'... Islanders just take for granted that if they walk into the office that you're there.

In Ontario, much of a member's resources are devoted to servicing the constituency:

> MPPs' personal staff spend most of their time on constituency business, as opposed to more broadly based policy concerns. Similarly, though resources certainly are available to assist members in their roles as legislators, far more services cater to the needs of the members as local representatives, as ombudsmen, as constituency case workers, and ultimately as incumbent politicians seeking re-election.

And in Newfoundland, the bonding between representative and represented is strong and clearly acknowledged:

> [The] role as intermediary between citizens and government officials (both elected and appointed) is one in which many members find satisfaction. In the province of Newfoundland it has historically been the most commonly noted function of an MLA. Members devoted a substantial portion of their time and effort to dealing with the problems and requests of their constituents; for the most part these demands emanate from individuals rather than from groups.

Federal and provincial representatives agree with their constituents that elected members should primarily serve the interests of constituents. Although members cannot always vote as their constituency would prefer, they make up for it by "taking care of the folks back home" through careful deployment of personal and staff resources. This shared commitment to local representation is the first tie that binds parliamentarians and constituents.

| 203 |

LOCAL CONSTITUENCY ASSOCIATIONS
AND THE NOMINATION PROCESS

Nominees for federal and provincial legislatures are currently selected from a field of politically active local aspirants by autonomous constituency parties which are responsible for scheduling and supervising nomination meetings and, between elections, for trying to maintain a schedule of partisan activities attractive to members.[7] These two features — community involvement of candidates and the significant role of the local party— constitute the second tie binding members to constituents.

Recently, Barrie and Gibbins reported the results of an exhaustive study of all 3,083 individuals who served in Parliament (that is, the House of Commons and/or appointed Senate) between 1867 and 1984.[8] Slightly less than one-half of all parliamentarians (48%) were elected to the House of Commons with no prior elected political experience and just less than one-quarter (22%) went directly from municipal politics to the House of Commons. Thus, between 1867 and 1984, 70% of all MPs entered the House of Commons with minimal elected political experience.

This rather notable absence of pre-parliamentary office-holding (especially provincial incumbency) among MPs does not, however, imply a lack of local or community involvement. Indeed, exactly the opposite is the case for both MPs and MLAs. In a case study of members of the 28th Parliament, Kornberg and Mishler reported that most MPs were very much products of their own constituencies. The average MP had lived in the constituency for 34 years, and had become active in political party work at the age of 29. Almost two-thirds (62%) have held one or more party offices at the constituency, provincial, or federal level, and four-fifths (83%) had been active party workers when first nominated for public office. The level of party organization cited as most important in securing nomination was the constituency party (46%).[9]

Provincial members have reported similar backgrounds. In a survey of all MLAs, Clarke *et al.* reported that 82% resided in their riding at the time of election, nearly four fifths (79%) had worked for a political party previous to election, one-half had held local office (municipal office or school board), and one-quarter (25%) had been both active party workers and local office holders.[10] MPs and MLAs appear to be firmly rooted in the life of local party organizations and the community as a whole when they seek elected office. This pre-parliamentary integration of members into the communal and partisan fabric of their constituencies influences their responsiveness to constituents.

This integration is encouraged and enhanced by the centrality of the local constituency organization in the selection process. Constituency associations developed slowly after Confederation, but by 1930 — at least at the federal level — both the "Liberal and Conservative parties officially had constituency associations in every constituency across Canada in order to field virtually complete slates of candidates in each general election."[11] Similarly, at the provincial level, MLAs are typically nominated by independent constituency parties. The process of nomination and re-nomination brings candidates into contact with two special groups of constituents upon whom MPs and MLAs can rely for current information about local issues and problems. These two groups are core partisans and local party activists.

John McMenemy has argued that core partisans serve as local party ambassadors who communicate party stereotypes to friends, neighbours, and business associates. Core partisans were defined as:

> those Canadians who express either a "fairly strong" intensity in their party identification, who voted for that party in at least two recent, consecutive federal elections four years apart (1980 and 1984) and who have publicly manifested their political personality by engaging "sometimes" or "often" in one of several standard gladiatorial activities (trying to convince friends to vote as they do; attending a political meeting or rally; contacting public officials or politicians; spending time working for a political party or candidate). Thus, in 1984 the core partisans of the three parties constituted 16% of the electorate.[13]

These core partisans also perform an important representational function: they provide MPs and MLAs with solicited and unsolicited advice about constituency needs and opinions. This putative relationship between members and constituents occurs because nomination campaigns are themselves intense, combative, competitive experiments in personal organization with a single victor. Winning one's party nomination thus involves mobilizing core partisans. Once nominated and elected, MPs and MLAs cannot simply poll constituents when circumstances require. Accordingly, it is quite natural that they turn to core partisans for guidance, opinions, and judgements about current constituency sentiment.

Nested within this pool of core partisans are local party activists, a considerably smaller group of men and women who maintain continuous contact with their representative. Recently William Irvine confirmed that "in Canada, as in Britain, MPs are in much closer contact with the politically active segment of their constituencies than they are with 'everyone.' "[13]

Activists differ from their "inactive" neighbours in several respects. They are, for example, more likely to contact their MP and believe their MP has actually helped them. Their assessment of their local MP's work is more positive: they perceive the MP as available and helpful to the riding, good at explaining government activities, getting projects for the riding, and working in Parliament. Not surprisingly, their predictions of the future work of their members are more favourable than those of average voters.[14]

Because representatives often emerge from the ranks of party activists or core partisans it is not surprising that they tend to share with these individuals constituency-oriented beliefs and perceptions about their job as legislators. Roots in the community and prior involvement in the party constituency association produce legislators who focus on constituency concerns. Continuing contact with local party activists only serves to sharpen that focus.

THE SINGLE MEMBER PLURALITY ELECTORAL SYSTEM

Countries vary widely in the type of electoral systems used to recruit legislators. These differences range from Israel, for example, where the entire country is a single constituency, to Canada where each representative has his or her own area to represent. Canada's single member plurality system constitutes the third recruitment "tie" linking members and constituents. No two constituencies in Canada, either at the provincial or federal level, are the same, or even very much alike. Each constituency, since it is represented by one and only one member in the legislature, thus comes to expect that its representative should respond to its unique needs, problems, opportunities, and interests.

Because Canada's electoral formulae (federal and provincial) do not require constituencies to contain an equal number of voters, members from different ridings find themselves called upon to represent areas with widely varying populations. House of Commons constituency populations range from a low of 25,000 to a high of 144,000, and even within each province, the size of federal constituencies varies greatly (see Table 2). At the provincial level as well, the average number of constituents per member varies dramatically, from a low of 3,788 per MLA in Prince Edward Island to a high of 68,274 constituents per Ontario member (see Table 3). The effect of population size per se on representational relationships between members and constituents is worth emphasizing. Service responsiveness in Prince Edward Island means, for example, that Island MLAs are expected to personally satisfy constituent requests, complaints and problems. Contrariwise, in Ontario the

TIES THAT BIND

public expects someone in the constituency office, Queen's Park Office, or the Member to rectify a constituent problem. Moreover, size of constituency begets size of staff. That is, in larger provincial jurisdictions legislators confronted by massive service and allocative demands have responded by increasing office, staff and constituency resources sufficient to address demand.

TABLE 2

POPULATION DIFFERENCES IN HOUSE
OF COMMONS CONSTITUENCIES
(1988)

Province	Number of MP's Elected in Each Province	Average Population of Constittuencies	Range in Population of Constituencies
British Columbia	32	90,105	67,317 to 108,492
Alberta	26	90,993	65,664 to 110,520
Saskatchewan	14	72,115	65,469 to 83,186
Manitoba	14	75,930	65,812 to 84,572
Ontario	99	91,936	58,268 to 144,226
Quebec	75	85,914	51,719 to 119,812
New Brunswick	10	70,944	54,607 to 88,128
Nova Scotia	11	79,743	62,822 to 96,481
Newfoundland*	7	81,193	80,984 to 106, 299
Prince Edward Island	4	31,661	29,794 to 34,627
Yukon and the NWT	3	25,247	20,198 to 30,296

* Excludes Labrador

TABLE 3

AVERAGE CONSTITUENCY POPULATION
IN PROVINCIAL LEGISLATURES

Ontario	68,274
Quebec	52,205
British Columbia	47,607
Alberta	29,515
Manitoba	17,784
Nova Scotia	16,150
Saskatchewan	14,944
New Brunswick	11,886
Newfoundland	10,841
Prince Edward Island	3,788

| 207 |

Federal and provincial constituencies vary also in their social, economic, and cultural attributes. According to Eagles, federal constituencies differ from each other in many respects including, for example, proportion of residents who are French, immigrants to Canada, employed as a manager of one's own business, employed in agriculture, unemployed, home owners or apartment dwellers and total family income.[15] That Canadian legislators are sensitive to their own constituency context is demonstrated by the following constituency descriptions offered by MPs:

> 1.8% of all Mineral Production in Canada (1982). Mostly rural. Hunting and Trapping. Largest riding in Canada. Formerly known as the Northwest Territories. (Jack I. Anawak, Nunatsiaq)

> Canada's most highly industrialized riding. Constituents include workers at Steel Co. of Canada, Westinghouse, Dofasco...Constituents comprise a virtual United Nations of Ethnic backgrounds including Anglo-Saxon, Italian, Polish, Ukrainian, French, Yugoslavian .... (Sheila Copps, Hamilton East).

> Basically an agricultural community, but also fishing, lumbering, and many small businesses. 34 municipalities, 12 community councils, 7 Indian Reserves. (Brian K. White, Dauphin–Swan River).

> Urban with many professionals and entrepreneurs. (Honourable Michael Wilson, Etobicoke).[16]

The potential for legislative responsiveness (symbolic, service and allocative) is thus a consequence of population size, the complexity of local constituencies, and sheer number of government programmes capable of generating demands for personal assistance. The responsiveness of MPs and MLAs to demands for help is influenced by two personal considerations: the desire to be re-elected, and the perception that constituency responsiveness (and service or constituency service work in particular) is associated with being re-elected.

While elections like the 1984 federal, the 1987 and 1990 Ontario, and 1987 New Brunswick are dramatic and capture the attention of the media, they are not typical results. The prevailing pattern is for governments to be re-elected and hence for incumbent MPs and MLAs to be returned to office. For example, there were 117 provincial elections between 1945-1986, but only 28 changes in government (a turnover rate of only 24%).

During the same period the average percentage of provincial legislative seats changing hands was approximately 19%.[17] In short, in Canadian politics the message is clear: incumbents tend to be retained and government parties tend to be re-elected. While there are no systematic studies of retirement patterns in Canada, evidence suggests that few members leave office voluntarily. Most seek re-election and do not return to the legislature only when voters deny them the opportunity. In 1979, for example, 96% of all freshman members elected in 1974 sought re-election. The percent of Ontario MPPs seeking re-election in 1981 was reported to be 89%.[18]

As professional politicians (full-time and part-time) MPs and MLAs recognize the enormous electoral importance of party, leader image, and issues. In order to protect themselves from modest swings in public opinion legislators try and establish a "personal vote" or electoral following by engaging in and advertising their constituency activities. This personal following, in the minds of members, is associated with constituency work. For example, 90% of all MLAs surveyed in 1972 agreed that "the services a provincial legislator performs for constituents are important in getting re-elected."[19] The anticipated electoral benefit of constituency work is perhaps best summarized by Drummond and Fletcher:

> In parliamentary systems such as those currently operative at the federal and provincial levels in Canada, where backbench legislators must take a largely reactive posture in the policy-making process, the importance of individual members resides primarily in two roles: service to constituents and the personal attraction of electoral support. There is considerable evidence that legislators see these roles as interdependent ... Doing constituency service work may not guarantee re-election, but the failure to do so will ensure defeat.[20]

The single member plurality electoral system emphasizes the accountability of MPs to their constituents. Since the tradition of party discipline deprives members of an opportunity to vote in accord with constituency opinion(s) and sentiments, incumbent members seek to create a personal constituency following by providing symbolic, service and allocative favours for their riding. The electoral system, then, constitutes the third recruitment tie binding representatives and their constituencies.

I The Work Environment I

The second set of ties that bind Canadian representatives to their constituencies arise as a direct result of the structure of the legislative work environment. A number of institutional factors serve to reinforce links with constituents and the constituency. These include the limited possibilities for career advancement within the legislature itself, the peripheral role accorded MPs and MLAs in the policy process, and the network of constituency-oriented support services provided to legislators. The first two factors, by restricting legislators' opportunities in the national or provincial arena, help to focus their attention on their constituencies, which remain their exclusive domains. The third factor enhances this trend, by encouraging legislators to spend more time and effort on their constituency.

The principle of party discipline is the main organizational feature of the legislative work environment.[21] Institutional arrangements within the Canadian parliamentary system elevate parties over individual politicians. Legislators are conditioned to accept party voting as an essential feature of the parliamentary system, and to believe that the media and the public will be harsh judges of those who defy their party leadership.[22] Legislators owe their election to their respective political parties as much as to their own personal efforts and in today's media age electoral success hinges to a great extent upon the image and popularity of the party leader. When Canadians choose an MP or MLA they also, implicitly in theory but quite explicitly in practice, choose a government. This fusion of the choice of executive and legislative candidates fosters a "team mentality" rather than the "every man for himself" mentality nurtured in most systems that have a formal separation of executive and legislature.[23] Virtually every aspect of a legislator's interactions within the legislative work environment is mediated by partisan considerations.

CAREER STRUCTURE AND OPPORTUNITIES

In order to encourage active and constructive contributions to the attainment of party goals, a party leader must provide incentives, both material and psychological, to individual legislators.[24] One of the main incentives available is the prospect of advancement in the ranks. Party leaders have at their disposal a number of positions which carry with them additional remuneration and perquisites. There are far more of these positions available to the Prime Minister and the Premiers than available to the Leaders of the Opposition parties.

On the government side, the most obvious of such positions are cabinet portfolios, which carry with them not only additional compensation, but heightened public exposure and influence in the policy-making process. The number of ministerial positions to be handed out is a prerogative of the Prime Minister and Premiers. The 1990 Mulroney cabinet stood at 39 and the size of provincial cabinets varied from 11 in Prince Edward Island to 30 in Ontario.

Only a fraction of the government backbenchers will ever find themselves elevated to cabinet. The remainder, however, still have open to them a number of other positions on the nebulously defined parliamentary career ladder. These include Speaker and Deputy Speaker, House Leader, whip, parliamentary secretary and committee chair. Most of these positions offer additional pay allowances, with the notable exception of committee chairs in the House of Commons (see Table 4). In the federal legislature, some 70 government MPs can expect to raise themselves above the level of ordinary backbencher during a parliament.[25] The number of remunerated positions available will vary from province to province, and from premier to premier.

On the opposition side fewer prestigious and remunerated positions are available to ambitious legislators. The only formally recognized positions (other than party leader) that carry with them an additional stipend are whip and Opposition House Leader. A few senior opposition MPs can expect to chair legislative committees in the House of Commons and one opposition member will ordinarily be named chair of the Public Accounts Committee in the House as well as all of the provincial assemblies. Appointment to the shadow cabinet provides an informal distinction, and is seen by many as an indication of eventual ministerial appointment should their party assume power, but in reality, no party leader makes such a guarantee. Thus opposition members experience even more restricted career mobility than do government members, especially since Canada's electoral history is marked by long periods of one-party dominance.

The small number of elevated positions available in Canadian legislatures, combined with the large number of potential aspirants to those positions, might be expected to cause fierce competition amongst legislators for the "plum" jobs. In many cases, however, individuals realize or are made to realize fairly quickly that they are not cabinet material — they may be too old, too young, from an over-represented region, too ethnic or not ethnic enough, lacking in education or political instincts, or otherwise deficient in one of the many attributes that must be balanced in appointing cabinet ministers and other highly visible and easily criticized legislative posts. But even the most peripheral backbencher is central to his or her constituency's

|211|

TABLE 4
ALLOWANCES FOR CANADIAN LEGISLATORS

Additional Allowances	House of Commons	Senate	NFLD	N.S.	PEI	NB	Quebec	Ontario	Manitoba	Saskat.	Alberta	B.C.	NWT	Yukon
Prime Minister (Premier)	$68,400		$49,588	$45,535	$46,000	$46,561	$57,811	$50,640	$26,600	$52,300	$50,157	$45,000	$62,655	$30,496
Cabinet Ministers	$45,800		$35,952	$35,290	$35,300	$31,042	$41,294	$30,094	$20,600	$36,610	$40,841	$39,000	$56,415	$22,260
Speaker	$45,800	$28,900	$35,952	$35,290	$7,400 +$2,600 tax free	$31,042	$41,294	$22,214	$15,500	$20,920	$40,841	$39,000	$15,000	$7,420
Opposition Leader	$45,800	$22,300	$35,952	$35,290	$35,300	N.A.	$41,294	$35,267	$20,600	$36,610	$40,841	$39,000	N.A.	$22,260
Leader, other parties	$27,600			$17,650	N.A.	N.A.	$19,270	$17,696	$15,600	$18,305	$7,243		N.A.	$4,452
Deputy Speaker	$24,000		$11,978	$17,650	$3,700 + $1,300 tax free	$15,521	$19,270	$6,458	$3,500	$4,845	$20,240	$19,500	$6,000	$5,565
Opposition House Leader	$22,300		$17,966	$2,000	$3,500		$19,270	$11,495	$2,500	$7,845		$6,000	N.A.	
Chief Whip, Government	$12,400	$7,100	$5,650	$85/mem.	$3,000	$1,500	$19,270	$11,495	$2,500	$7,845		$6,000	N.A.	
Opposition Whip	$12,400	$4,600	$5,650	$85/mem.	$3,000	$1,500	$16,517	$7,878	$2,500	$7,845		$6,000	N.A.	
Deputy Chair, Committees of the Whole	$9,900							$6,458	$2,500	$3,923	$10,210	$3,000	$3,500 + $65/day	
Asst. Dep. Chairman, Committees of the Whole	$9,900													
House Leaders, other parties	$9,500							$8,652						
Whip, other parties	$7,100			$85/mem.			$8,259	$6,458		$3,923				
Deputy Whip, Government	$7,100						$8,259	$7,878		$3,923		$3,000		
Deputy Whip, Opposition	$7,100						$8,259	$5,682		$3,923				
Leader of the Government		$45,800												
Deputy Government Leader		$14,000												
Deputy Opposition Leader		$8,800												
Chairman of Standing Committees			$5,989	$1,000			$13,765	$5,036		$3,923			$3,000 + $65/day	
Chairman of Select Committees		$3,500 max.		$1,500			$5,506 $13,765 (Govt. only)							
Caucus Chairman				$85/mem.								$6,000	$2,000 + $65/day	

N.A. = not applicable
Revised from Commission to Review Allowances of Members of Parliament, Supply and Services, February, 1989, pp. 8-9.

political life. Those who may never make it big in the legislative work environment can become very big indeed in the world of the riding.

ROLE OF LEGISLATORS IN THE POLICY PROCESS

Canadian legislators also suffer from restrictions on the extent to which they are able to play an active and meaningful role in setting and implementing the legislative agenda. The legislative autonomy of MPs and MLAs are increasingly being displaced as sources of communication and information for the executive by interest groups, which possess specialized information vital to the operation of the machinery of government, and by the media, which are able to focus public discussion more effectively than individual legislators. In an age of electronic communication, cabinet need not depend upon backbenchers to relay information to and from the electorate — a short televised address or telephone opinion poll is far more efficient.

Constitutional provisions ensure that only ministers may introduce legislation involving the raising of revenue or expenditure, and thus backbench members are prohibited from initiating bills of any significant consequence. While any member may introduce a private member's bill, the opportunity to do so is limited and, despite the reforms of the McGrath Committee which established that at least six private member's bills must be debated and voted upon each session, the success rate for these bills remains pessimistic.

The committee system holds out the most attractive prospect for individual legislators interested in meaningful contribution to the policy process. In the House of Commons the recent introduction of a legislative committee structure has provided backbench members with more to do, but the committees' effectiveness is still hampered by timing: bills go to committee only after they have been approved in principle in second reading. Some committees have succeeded in forcing the government to alter provisions of major legislation, but such rare instances do little to comfort members who remain frustrated with the limited impact they have on the shaping of policy. In an attempt to increase their effect on the policy-making process, federal committees have in recent years been granted permanent staff, increased support services and the right to travel to collect information essential to their investigations, but they continue to be plagued by problems of high membership turnover, absenteeism, and thus instability.

Provincial legislatures experience the same difficulties, but the smaller size of many assemblies adds logistical constraints which further hamper the effectiveness of a committee system. The provinces have often suffered a

| 213 |

severe shortage of private members on one side of the House — the backbone of a viable committee structure — especially in a minority government situation or when one party has an overwhelming majority. Smaller legislatures also find that resolving issues in Committee of the Whole negates the need for an active committee system. Thus, even in the one arena in which backbenchers are theoretically freed from constitutional and partisan restrictions on their ability to affect policy decisions, problems of structure and efficiency limit further the degree of influence they can bring to bear.

The other avenue down which members might seek to influence the direction of party policy is caucus. These closed-door meetings of party members normally occur once a week, and it is in these sessions that members are unleashed from the fetters of party solidarity and can voice their opinions and views candidly, without fear of recrimination. But once the door is opened, the expectation is that even those who disagree with the party position will be supportive in public. As the case of Progressive Conservative MPs David Kilgour and Alex Kindy (who voted against the Mulroney Government Goods and Service Tax) demonstrates, boat-rockers are discouraged or even expelled. Dissent within the ranks leaves the leader vulnerable to attacks from the other side and the media. Within opposition parties tolerance for disagreement is somewhat greater than in the government, as there is no fear that dissenters could bring the government down.

Members of the government caucus are ordinarily accorded the privilege of hearing legislative proposals before they are introduced into the House. While this preview does not ordinarily result in changes to legislation, it does serve as a means of drumming up support from within the caucus and provides a forum in which government members can discuss proposals and policy initiatives with cabinet ministers.[26] Government backbenchers can use this forum to make suggestions and voice concerns over proposed legislation. But in practice, not all ministers regularly seek the advice of their backbenchers and some treat caucus more as a warm-up than a policy-making tool. Opposition members are of course denied this channel of potential influence altogether.

Very few legislative decisions are made by individual private members. Party discipline and the requirements of cabinet government combine to restrict policy-making influence to a small cadre of members, and even the mechanisms which purport to spread such influence more widely are not always effective. No such limitations affect MPs and MLAs in their constituency offices. Riding association executives may have an important say in choosing who is to be nominated, but in terms of prestige and influence, the representative is the local kingpin. Legislators who become frustrated

TIES THAT BIND

with a party or government which limits their input can find they have a great deal of effect in the constituency arena. Some MP's may never have their views heard in the legislature to their satisfaction, but they are almost assured of front page coverage back home, no matter what issue they addresses, and a single letter on MLA stationery may easily be enough to extricate a constituent from a bureaucratic tangle. MPs and MLAs in their constituencies play to a receptive and favourable audience rather than a legislature which can seem largely indifferent to their contributions.

SUPPORT SERVICES

Legislators are provided with allowances which permit and encourage them to spend time servicing their constituencies. In addition to their salaries, members of all Canadian legislatures receive an expense allowance, which is intended to defray the costs incurred by members in performing their representative functions. These costs which arise from the responsibilities of their elected position include the cost of a second home, apartment or hotel room; meals while in transit; hospitality in Ottawa for visiting constituents; and increased clothing costs. In the House of Commons in 1990 this allowance was $19,900, and in the provincial assemblies it ranged from $7,322 in Saskatchewan to $17,820 in the Northwest Territories.[27]

Additionally, all legislatures provide some funds to help cover the expense of travel between constituency and legislature. Without this allowance, many members would be unable to return regularly to their constituencies, without great costs to themselves. These travel allowances normally detail specific provisions for travel by air, bus, boat, or train. In addition, all jurisdictions except PEI, Newfoundland, New Brunswick, and the Yukon provide for a car allowance. The House of Commons covers travel through a point system: each member receives 64 points per year; one round trip between Ottawa and a member's constituency, via any mode of transportation, uses up one point. The most generous travel plan is found in Alberta, where legislators are afforded the luxury of unlimited air and bus travel within the province. Ontario ensures unlimited travel for members by bus or train, as well as an unlimited mileage allowance for driving within the constituency or between the constituency and Queen's Park. In the House of Commons and the legislatures of Quebec, Ontario, and British Columbia, members are permitted to transfer some of these travel perks to their spouse or other family members.[28]

Members of most legislatures are also furnished with the funds necessary to set up and staff an office in the constituency. These offices have proven to be vital in the performance of a representative's duties and as a communication link with the electorate. A constituency allowance ensures that members are able to rent office space, pay utilities, purchase office supplies and equipment, and hire support staff. Only the legislatures of PEI, New Brunswick, Newfoundland and the Yukon do not provide such a constituency allowance. Elsewhere the allowances vary in terms of generosity and restrictions. The House of Commons is the most supportive of its members in their constituencies: MPs receive up to $11,450 for the operation of an office, and $2,000 (new MPs) or $1,000 (re-elected MPs) for the purchase of furniture and equipment at the beginning of each parliament; $25,100 of their $125,400 staff allowance must be spent on employees in the constituency; they also enjoy free mail and telephone privileges and have access to electronic mail networks. The provinces are not as generous: there are no free mail or telephone privileges in Nova Scotia, and many other legislatures will pay for these services only upon submission of receipts. Despite these variations, most of the provincial legislatures encourage and support the efforts of their members in the constituency.

The variation in the degree to which the legislatures are willing to help defray constituency expenses is almost certainly related to differences in constituency size. An Ontario MPP represents on average about 68,000 constituents, and Quebec MNAs have constituencies of approximately 52,000. In the Atlantic provinces, and in Manitoba and Saskatchewan, the average is only about 18,000 constituents, and in PEI only 3,700.[29] Legislators from Ontario and Quebec thus face higher and more frequent demands for services in the constituency. The same is true for the House of Commons, where the average constituency size is around 85,000. The House has also formally recognized the problems for constituency service which are caused by spatially large or densely populated constituencies. For several years now these types of constituencies have been accorded "special status" — members representing them have been granted additional allowances to help them in their constituency work, and also have been permitted to exceed established limits on election expenses.[30] In combination, these geographic and electors supplements currently provide additional allowances to more than one-half of the members of the House.

I Conclusions I

Factors in both the recruitment and legislative work environments help to encourage Canadian legislators to concentrate their efforts on their con-

TIES THAT BIND

stituency. In the recruitment environment, three factors serve actively to attract and retain in the constituency the attention of legislators. Both members and their constituents share cultural expectations of strong responsiveness to local community concerns. The influence wielded by party riding associations and members' involvements with them, constantly renew the link between legislator and local activist. Finally, an electoral system which specifies a one-to-one mapping between constituencies and representatives, and allows significant variation in constituency size, population and composition, forces legislators to remain cognizant of the unique characteristics and interests of their particular riding.

In the legislative work environment, circumstances conspire to deflect legislators' efforts away from full-time parliamentary policy work. By default, these negative inducements reinforce the commitment to constituency service. The slim possibility of advancement within the parliamentary ranks suggests to many legislators that their discretionary time and effort is better spent in an arena where they are almost guaranteed to be appreciated. The limited opportunity for backbenchers to affect the policy process in the legislature sharply contrasts with their power to perform "bureaucratic miracles" at home. And a system of allowances that facilitates and supports constituency work and expenditures helps to make local community work attractive.

This matrix of forces is relatively stable. It remains to be seen, however, whether constituencies' increasing demands for more responsive legislative behaviour from their representatives — especially as expressed by voting the "riding line" rather than the party line — will lead to an eventual relaxation of the strict party discipline that continues to overshadow most activity in the legislative work environment. Ironically, such a development might weaken responsiveness: members who find themselves freer to vote against party dictates and pursue meaningful policy initiatives may no longer need to turn to the constituency out of frustration with their limited role in policy-making. Nevertheless, barring significant electoral reform, the ties that bind members to their constituents, especially in the recruitment environment, can be expected to remain strong and lasting.

CANADIAN GOVERNMENT AND POLITICS

NOTES

[1] Bob Miller, "On the Front Lines," *Parliamentary Government*, Volume 6, No. 2, 1986, p. 3.

[2] Malcolm E. Jewell, "Legislator-Constituency Relations and the Representative Process," *Legislative Studies Quarterly*, 8 (August, 1983) pp. 303-304.

[3] Jon H. Pammett and Michael S. Whittington, "Introduction: Political Culture and Political Socialization," in Jon H. Pammett and Michael Whittington (eds.), *Foundations of Political Culture* (Toronto: Macmillan, 1976) p. 2.

[4] Toronto *The Globe and Mail*, September 10, 1982, pp. 1-2.

[5] Richard G. Price, Harold D. Clarke and Robert M. Krause, "Socialization of Freshman Legislators: The Case of Canadian MPs," in Pammett and Whittington (eds.), *op. cit.* pp. 211-238.

[6] Gary Levy and Graham White eds., *Provincial and Territorial Legislatures in Canada* (Toronto: University of Toronto Press, 1989). See chapters on Prince Edward Island, Ontario, and Newfoundland.

[7] This discussion does not extend to the territorial legislature of the Northwest Territories, which features no political parties.

[8] Doreen Barrie and Roger Gibbins, "Parliamentary Careers in the Canadian Federal State," *Canadian Journal of Political Science*, 22 (March, 1989) pp. 137-145.

[9] Allan Kornberg and William Mishler, *Influence in Parliament: Canada*, (Durham: Duke University Press, 1976). See Chapter 2, "The MPs: An Overview" pp. 58-101.

[10] Harold D. Clarke, Richard G. Price and Robert Krause, "Backbenchers," in David J. Bellamy *et al* (eds.), *The Provincial Political Systems* (Toronto: Methuen, 1976) p. 219.

[11] Roman R. March, *The Myth of Parliament* (Scarborough: Prentice-Hall, 1974) p. 51.

[12] John McMenemy, "Getting to Know the Parties by the Company We Keep: Local Sources of Party Imagery" in Alain G. Gagnon and A. Brian Tanguay (eds.), *Canadian Parties in Transition* (Scarborough: Nelson, 1989) p. 312.

[13] William P. Irvine, "Does the Candidate Make a Difference? The Macro-Politics and Micro-Politics of Getting Elected," *Canadian Journal of Political Science*, 15 (December, 1982) p. 767.

[14] *Ibid.* pp. 768-69.

[15] Munroe Eagles, "Local Effects on the Political Behaviour of Canadians" in Alain G. Gagnon and James P. Bickerton (eds.), *Canadian Politics: An Introduction to the Discipline* (Peterborough: Broadview Press, 1990) pp. 285-307.

[16] John Bejermi, *Canadian Parliamentary Handbook* (Ottawa: Borealis Press, 1989) pp. 93, 182, 485, 491 and 91.

[17] Peter McCormick, "Provincial Political Party Systems, 1945-1986," in Gagnon and Tanguay (eds.), *op. cit.* pp. 152-185.

[18] For analyses of the effects of incumbency see three articles by Michael

Krashinsky and William J. Milne. They are "Some Evidence of the Effect of Incumbency in Ontario Provincial Elections," *Canadian Journal of Political Science*, 16 (September, 1983) pp. 489-500; "Additional Evidence on the Effect of Incumbency in Canadian Elections," *Canadian Journal of Political Science*, 18, (March, 1985) pp. 155-165, and; "The Effect of Incumbency in the 1984 Federal and 1985 Ontario Elections," *Canadian Journal of Political Science*, 19 (June, 1986) pp. 337-343.

[19] Harold D. Clarke, Richard G. Price and Robert Krause, "Constituency Service Among Canadian Provincial Legislators: Basic Findings and a Test of Three Hypotheses," *Canadian Journal of Political Science*, 8 (December, 1975) pp. 520-542.

[20] Robert J. Drummond and Frederick J. Fletcher, "Political Communication and Orientation to Legislators Among Ontario Voters," in Harold D. Clarke *et al.* (eds.), *Parliament, Policy and Representation* (Toronto: Methuen, 1980) p. 104.

[21] Once again, with the exception of the "partyless" Northwest Territories.

[22] Paul Thomas, "Parliamentary Reform Through Political Parties," in John C. Courtney (ed.), *The Canadian House of Commons: Essays in Honour of Norman Ward* (Calgary: University of Calgary Press, 1985) p. 46.

[23] Bruce Cain, John Ferejohn, and Morris Fiorina, *The Personal Vote: Constituency Service and Electoral Independence* (Cambridge, Mass.: Harvard University Press, 1987) p. 214.

[24] Thomas, "Parliamentary Reform Through Political Parties," p. 45.

[25] C.E.S. Franks, *The Parliament of Canada* (Toronto: University of Toronto Press, 1987) p. 45. This figure is of course dependent upon the size of cabinet and the frequency of cabinet shuffles and the turnover of parliamentary secretaryships.

[26] Franks, *The Parliament of Canada*, p. 45

[27] Honourable Gerry St. Germain, P.C., Chairman and the Honourable Francis Fox, P.C., Q.C., Commissioner, *Commisison to Review Allowances of Members of Parliament* (Ottawa: Minister of Supply and Services, August, 1989) pp. 8-9.

[28] The details of the various travel allowance schemes in operation in the provinces and the House of Commons can be found in: Robert J. Fleming (ed.), *Canadian Legislatures* (Ottawa: Ampersand Communications Services Inc., 1988) p. 104-108.

[29] Levy and White, *Provincial and Territorial Legislatures in Canada*, p. 8.

[30] For a complete discussion of the specifics of these additional allowances see John C. Courtney, "Parliament and Representation: The Unfinished Agenda of Electoral Redistributions," *Canadian Journal of Political Science*, XXI:4 (December, 1988) pp. 682-684.

ANNOTATED READINGS

Courtney, John C., ed. *The Canadian House of Commons: Essays in Honour of Norman Ward.* Calgary: University of Calgary Press, 1985. An excellent collection of original essays dealing with such timely subjects as debate and question period in the House of Commons, changes in procedure, parliamentary reform, the election expenses act and 1984 election.

Franks, C.E.S. *The Parliament of Canada.* Toronto: University of Tronto Press, 1987. Required reading for students interested in Parliament. Most of this text, quite properly, deals with the House of Commons and focuses upon different models of parliamentary government, parliamentary parties, members backgrounds, committees, workload and reform.

Kornberg, Allan and William Mishler. *Influence in Parliament: Canada.* Durham: Duke University Press, 1976. A penetrating case study of the 28th Parliament dealing with the evaluation of the House of Commons, members, patterns of participation and the acquisition of political influence.

Levy, Gary and Graham White, eds. *Provincial and Territorial Legislatures in Canada.* Toronto: University of Toronto Press, 1989. Essential reading for students interested in provincial and territorial assemblies.

White, Graham. *The Ontario Legislature: A Political Analysis.* Toronto: University of Toronto Press, 1989. A comprehensive analysis of legislative politics in Queen's Park, Canada's largest legislature outside Ottawa. Topics include a thorough discussion of the participants, the legislature at work, committees, services to members, and the process of reform.

| CHAPTER 12 |

PUBLIC POLICY AND
POLICY-MAKING IN CANADA

STEPHEN BROOKS

Almost every aspect of policy-making in Canada
remains shrouded in ignorance if not mystery.

— Richard Simeon, 1976

In the decade and a half since the above pronouncement was made the study
of public policy has emerged as one of the more fashionable areas of
Canadian political science. More courses are offered in it, more students take
them, and more political scientists direct their research energies toward
public policy than was the case when Richard Simeon lamented the ignorance in which policy-making in Canada was shrouded. Along with the field
of public administration, it has probably been the fastest growing sector in
the discipline. Whether this flurry of interest and activity has helped to pull
back the shroud, revealing the lineaments of the subject that lies underneath,
is another question. But before we consider what is known about Canadian
policy-making, we need to answer some basic questions about our subject.
What is public policy? And why do some matters become policy issues,
attracting the attention of governments, the media, and societal groups,
while other matters do not?

CANADIAN GOVERNMENT AND POLITICS

One of the most-cited definitions of public policy is that of American political scientist Thomas Dye. According to Dye, public policy is "whatever governments choose to do or not to do."[1] Policy involves, then, conscious choice that leads to deliberate action — the passage of a law, the spending of money, an official speech or gesture, or some other observable act — or inaction. No one would disagree that a concrete act like the passage of a law counts as policy. But can inaction reasonably be described as policy? The answer depends on whether or not the failure to act takes place in the context of political controversy.

To understand this, consider the following real-life example. In January of 1988 the Supreme Court of Canada struck down the federal abortion law on the grounds that it violated the "security of the person" guaranteed by s.7 of the *Charter of Rights and Freedoms*. A year and a half later (as this is written) the government still had not introduced a new abortion law, leaving a policy lacuna into which "pro-life" and "pro-choice" factions poured their energies. Abortion did not, then, cease to be controversial when the Supreme Court ruled the existing law uncontroversial. On the contrary, the controversy swirling around this issue gained renewed momentum, as various groups perceived an opportunity to influence whatever policy might ultimately be decided by the government and by the courts.

The government's long delay in introducing a new law was sheer political prudence, given that any legislative solution would leave many people intensely unhappy. Inaction, in this case, was a deliberate policy on an issue where compromise was viewed as defeat by both the pro- and anti-abortion sides.

Government inaction sometimes results from unawareness that a "problem" exists. For decades carcinogenic PCBs (polychlorinated biphenyls) were used, stored and disposed of without much care being taken. There was no public policy on the handling of these deadly chemicals before it was realized that there was reason for concern. When the public became alerted to their cancer-causing properties, the use, transportation and elimination of PCBs — and the same is obviously true of other hazardous substances — became policy issues. Government inaction before then obviously had health consequences for those who were exposed to PCBs, and certainly allowed the accumulation of stockpiles of what today is the most widely known and feared of toxic chemicals. But this was not deliberate inaction. There was no public policy on PCBs, just as there was no policy on the production and handling of many other industrial chemicals, because there was no significant level of awareness that a problem existed. It makes no sense to speak of policy where an issue has not yet been formulated in problematic terms. Once it

PUBLIC POLICY AND POLICY-MAKING IN CANADA

has, however, inaction by policy-makers becomes a deliberate policy choice.

Conscious choice, therefore, must be a part of any definition of public policy. But is policy necessarily what policy-makers say it is? In other words, if we want to determine what public policy is on some issue should we direct our attention to official government pronouncements, or to the actual record of what has and has not been achieved? The dilemma is a real one, as the following two examples show:

- Since 1889 Canada has had an anti-combines law whose ostensible aim is to limit undesirable concentrations of corporate power in the Canadian economy. During the 100 years since its passage there have been only a handful of prosecutions under this legislation, and fewer convictions. Meanwhile, the concentration of corporate power has increased enormously. Can we reasonably claim, therefore, that there exists a policy of ensuring adequate competition among Canadian producers? A law exists, but the actual record of implementation and achievement has caused many critics to question whether we have the symbol without the substance of policy.

- Canada is constitutionally a bilingual country. The official equality of French and English is guaranteed by the Constitution Act, and given more concrete form through the principles set forth in the *Official Languages Act.* Despite these guarantees, the rate of francophone assimilation outside of Quebec has continued to be high. And as far as the language of work in the federal government goes, the Commissioner of Official Languages regularly comments on the overwhelming predominance of English. Critics like the Parti Québecois have been even more dismissive of Ottawa's official policy of bilingualism. Is language policy what the government says it is, or should it be judged by the results-oriented criteria that its various critics deploy?

The number of such examples could be multiplied almost without limit. We should not, however, exaggerate the problem of what criteria we should use — official statements, or actions and effects? — in determining what is policy on some issue. No one takes all official pronouncements at face value, just as we would not assume that an individual's motives and intentions are always what he or she claims them to be. Vagueness and ambiguity are oftentimes deliberate, and are always part of the recipe for political longevity

CANADIAN GOVERNMENT AND POLITICS

in democratic political systems. The bottom line on determining what actually constitutes public policy in some field comes down to this: both official claims and concrete actions should be looked at carefully, and one should be prepared to find that actions often speak louder than words.

But the determination of policy is even more complicated than this. It often happens that a government's most sincere efforts misfire, failing to achieve the goals expected of them and perhaps even aggravating the situation they were intended to improve. Consider a policy of government controlled rents. Critics of rent controls have long argued that such a policy in fact hurts the lower income groups it is intended to benefit, by discouraging developers and investors from building new rental accommodation for the low end of the market. As the supply dwindles, prices inevitably are pushed up. If and when this happens are we justified in saying that government housing policy favours the less affluent? But even more common than policy misfires are those frequent cases where government action simply fails to accomplish its intended goals. In fact, a programme, or law, or regulation hardly ever "solves" a problem in the sense of eliminating the conditions that inspired controversy and demands for action in the first place. When problems do disappear this is more likely to be the result of changing societal conditions — including when they are pushed below the surface of public consciousness by other problems — than a direct consequence of government policy.

We have mentioned the case of official pronouncements that do not coincide with the observable actions of government, or which bear little resemblance to the facts of whatever situation they ostensibly address. When this happens, and it frequently does, we should not jump to the cynical conclusion that policy is just "sound and fury which signifies nothing." Gestures, symbols and words are important components of the political process. They are often valued in their own right, and their capacity to reconcile and to divide should not be underestimated. The "distinct society" clause of the Meech Lake Accord, which recognized Quebec as a distinct and predominantly francophone society within Canada, turned out to be the most contentious feature of the Accord outside of Quebec. It was not so much that non-Quebecers perceived that the constitutional recognition of Quebec as a distinct society would have material consequences. Instead, it was the symbol of special status for Quebec that was objected to by many, and which led opponents of Meech Lake to label it a sell-out to Quebec. Governments influence the allocation of symbolic values in society; what Raymond Breton calls the "symbolic order." And as in the case of material benefits and burdens, satisfying one group's symbolic aspirations may mean denying those of another group.

The Agenda and Discourse
of Policy-Making

But there is another, more general sense in which the symbols, gestures and words manipulated by policy-makers are important. They constitute the *political agenda*, defining what is relevant in public life, how issues are defined, whose views should be taken seriously, and what sort of "solutions" are tenable. A statement by a political leader, a law, media coverage of a group's policy demands or of some situation or event all provide an affirmation of the relevance of a problem and of the values and conflicts associated with it. If we may be excused a bit of jargon here, political issues and policy problems are constructed out of the conflicting values and terminologies that different groups put forward when they compete for something that cannot be shared so as to satisfy all of them fully. These issues and problems do not exist apart from the words and symbols used to describe them. They are constructed in the sense that political issues and policy problems do not possess an inevitable character that is inherent in them. Whether we even recognize them as political issues and policy problems, and what comes to mind when they are presented to our attention, both depend on the particular forces that shape the political agenda in a given society. These forces change over time and so, therefore, does the political agenda. As American political scientist Murray Edelman observes, "conditions accepted as inevitable or unproblematic may come to be seen as problems; and damaging conditions may not be defined as political issues at all."[2]

Once we accept that the political agenda is not an inevitable product of social and economic conditions, we are then confronted with the question of why some of these conditions become formulated as problems and others do not. This leads to a consideration of the various agents of cultural learning — the family, the schools, the mass media, the workplace — which together generate the ideological parameters of society. To understand the practical importance of cultural learning, consider the following examples.

In liberal democratic societies like Canada and the United States we learn (most of us, anyway) that achievement and opportunities are relatively open to those with ability and a willingness to work hard. Consequently, most people do not perceive economic inequality as a serious problem. In another ideological setting the fact that the bottom 20 percent of income-earners in Canada account for about 1 percent of earned income (not counting social security transfers), while the top 20 percent account for about 50 percent of earnings, might be viewed as a problem.

225

Still on the topic of inequality, until a couple of decades ago the extensive and profound differences in the career opportunities, incomes and social roles of men and women were not generally seen to be a problem. As cultural attitudes have changed, the unequal social conditions of males and females have become a prominent item on the political agendas of virtually all industrialized democracies. Gender politics and the policy debates that surround such issues as abortion, pay equity, affirmative action for women, pornography, publicly subsidized day-care and sexual harassment are constructed out of the arguments, claims and demands for action put forward by women's organizations and their spokespersons, and the counter-arguments, claims and demands of others who feel compelled to respond to their definition of the problem. The same can be said of any policy issue. What emerges from such exchanges is a *policy discourse* — an unfolding tapestry of words and symbols that structures thinking and action — that is constructed out of the multiple definitions (or denial) of the problem.

The capacity to influence this discourse is more than half the battle. Every group, organization and individual with the least bit of political acumen knows this, so that their first line of attack is often through the mass media. Governments have a distinct advantage in the struggle to shape the contours of policy discourse. Not only do they have virtually guaranteed access to the public through mass media coverage of official statements, press conferences and other orchestrated efforts to communicate a particular message (and influence public opinion), they also are able to tell their story through paid advertisements — the federal government has for years been the largest single advertiser in Canada — and through government information services directed at households and organizations. The messages governments communicate, particularly when they touch on controversial issues, are often greeted with cynicism by the media and the public. But even then they receive a hearing. One reason for this is the official authority of their source. Even if the government's message is not considered to be credible, its capacity to influence the outcome of an issue means that the information it disseminates is not likely to be ignored. Cynicism, vocal opposition and an unsympathetic media are not enough to close off the channels through which government can influence policy discourse. The 1989 introduction of the widely unpopular Goods and Services Tax (GST) was followed by an extensive campaign of paid advertising and information sent directly to businesses and households, intended to increase public acceptance of the GST. Only a couple years earlier Ottawa had spent tens of millions of dollars on brochures and other information distributed to households, "explaining" the benefits that the Free Trade Agreement (FTA) with the United

States would bring to Canada. It is never easy to determine exactly what sort of impact these policy advocacy campaigns have on public opinion. But the very fact that the problems, positions and information contained in such campaigns are being communicated makes them automatically a part of policy discourse on an issue.

Despite the formidable information and financial resources at their disposal, governments are a long way from being able to control either the policy agenda or the particular policy discourse that develops around some issue. Indeed, much of the time governments are on the defensive, reacting to the claims, demands and interpretations put forward by opposition political parties, by societal groups, and by the media. Whose "problems" reach the political agenda, and whose arguments, interpretations and proposals are taken seriously in the policy-making process, are largely determined by the social power of the interests advancing them. In fact the capacity to influence policy discourse would seem to be one barometer by which the power of different interests could be measured.

But this is too simple. Politics in the capitalist democracies is open-ended enough that ideas and reforms which very clearly are not favoured by the powerful often are woven into the fabric of policy discourse and institutionalized through public policies. One would be hard pressed to explain the policy successes of the women's movement, and the arguments associated with gender-based differences in such matters as employment and pay, from the standpoint of dominant class interests. Or consider the entry of aboriginal rights, of visible minorities, and of the handicapped into modern political discourse. These are groups that lie far from the epicentre of social and economic power in Canadian society. Despite this, they have been able to influence the agenda of politics and the actions of governments in this country. Moreover, there are some policy areas that never reach the public agenda in a way that mobilizes powerful social and economic interests. Therapies for treating the mentally-ill and approaches used in dealing with criminals and victims are policy domains where scientific expertise may carry greater weight than usual because the issues involved do not capture the sustained attention of the public. We should not assume, therefore, an automatic and perfect correspondence between the ideas that get onto the political agenda and which become embodied in state actions and, on the other hand, the pecking order of social and economic interests in society.

Policy discourse is not, however, a wide open mêlée in which every voice has an equal opportunity to be heard. It has become popular to speak of *systemic bias*, a term intended to capture the selectiveness of the policy system. Some points of view, it is claimed, never get articulated and some

CANADIAN GOVERNMENT AND POLITICS

policy outcomes are virtually precluded by the biases inherent in the cultural and institutional warp and woof of society. At one level this is obviously true. For demographic, historical and political reasons language has a prominence in Canadian politics that it does not have in the United States. Conversely, individual rights and freedoms occupy a more significant place in American political discourse than they do in Canada and most other capitalist democracies. In saying, then, that any society and political system have particular biases we have not said much — or at least not much that is very interesting. The more interesting question is what these biases reveal about the sources and distribution of power, and about the capacity of different social and economic interests to influence the actions of government. Let us turn now to the relationship between power and public policy in Canada.

I Power and Public Policy I

In *How Canadians Govern Themselves*, a booklet published by the Canadian government, the Honourable Eugene Forsey observes that "government is our creature. We make it, [and] we are ultimately responsible for it...."[3] What governments do, what policies they pursue and with what means, are ultimately determined by those who elect them. We may call this the *democratic ideal*. It starts from the simple and irrefutable premise that governments are elected by the people in periodic elections. They cannot afford to be complacent and unresponsive because of the possibility that voters will replace them with the candidates of some other party. The power to determine public policy — at least its broad contours and direction — lies with the people, by whose consent governments act. While formally accurate as a description of the Canadian system of democratic government, it is completely unreliable as a guide to where the real power to shape policy lies. If it does not lie with the "people," where does it lie?

There is no single answer to this question. Instead, there are several *realist* versions of policy-making that offer different answers to the questions of who influences policy, when, and how. They may be grouped under the following four labels: *pluralism; public choice; Canadian political economy* (CPE); and *statism*. Each of them views political power as being concentrated in many fewer hands than is suggested by the ideal of democratic government. Together they constitute the main theoretical explanations of how power and public policy are related in Canada. We will look at each of them in turn.

1. PLURALISM

Groups and their efforts to influence government action are at the heart of pluralist explanations. Whatever the issue is, the major players are likely to be organizations representing — or at least claiming to represent — the interests of groups that perceive themselves as having a stake in how government deals with some problem. Policy, then, is the outcome of a competition between organized groups. Governments are not neutral by-standers in this process. They have their own interests to promote and defend: bureaucrats' interests in the size of their budgets, in the preservation and perhaps expansion of their programmes and responsibilities; politicians' interests in re-election, in their own career advancement, and in whatever personal ideals they may want to promote. Nevertheless, the pluralist explanation of power and public policy is fundamentally a *society-centred* approach to understanding policy-making. It locates the principal forces shaping state action in the societal milieu in which policy decisions are made.

Any serious effort to come to grips with policy formation must explain why it is that some interests are more successful than others in shaping the political agenda and government action. Pluralists do not suggest that the competition between groups is an equal one. Business interests are especially likely to be singled out as dominant players. As the American political scientist, E.E. Schattschneider observed thirty years ago, "The flaw in the pluralist heaven is that the heavenly chorus sings with a strong upper-class accent....The system is skewed, loaded and unbalanced in favor of a fraction of a minority."[4] Theodore Lowi argues that policy-making "is biased not so much in favor of the rich as in favor of the established and organized."[5] (As it happens, business interests are always among the best-organized in capitalist societies, with superior resources and access to policy-makers.) Charles Lindblom speaks of the "privileged position of business," which he attributes to a combination of superior financial resources and lobbying organization, greater access than other groups to governmental officials and, most importantly, propagandistic activities that — directly through political advertising and indirectly through commercial advertising — reinforce the ideological dominance of business values in capitalist democracies.[6] Lindblom has recently stressed the importance of the market economy as a "prison" that limits government's room for manoeuvre. Governments are necessarily concerned with how their actions will affect "business confidence," because a sharp or prolonged fall in capital investment will have a negative impact on both the economy and their popular support (to the extent that they are held responsible for the economy's fortunes).[7]

But even though many contemporary versions of pluralism maintain that

| 229 |

economic interests dominate in the political marketplace, politics and policy-making are never reduced to strictly economic or class terms. Other lines
of political conflict, including ethnicity, language, religion, gender, region,
and ideology, are viewed as having a significance that is not necessarily less
than class. It depends upon what is at stake and which interests are mobilized
to act. What is certain, however, is that pluralist theory does not view these
non-economic divisions as merely class conflicts dressed up in ways that make
them difficult to recognize.

The cutting edge of recent pluralist work on policy-making in Canada has
used the concept of *policy communities*[8] or, in the case of industrial policy,
sectoral policy networks[9] to analyze the process of policy formation. The focus
of these studies are the specific constellations of state — bureaucratic and
political — and societal interests that mobilize around a particular issue. Paul
Pross has used the term *sub-governments* to convey the fact that within any
policy community only a part of the state system is likely to be involved in
the determination of policy. These concepts — policy communities, sectoral
policy networks, sub-governments — are intellectual descendants of a longer
pluralist tradition associated with "iron triangles" (developed in the United
States, these are the webs of congressional committees, administrative
agencies and societal actors that dominate policy-making in a particular field)
and with "clientelism" (the mutually dependent relations that develop
between state actors and the particular societal interests that benefit from
the programmes they administer).

2. PUBLIC CHOICE

Public choice theory represents the colonization of traditional political
science concerns by economics. Those working within this approach attempt
to explain political behaviour, including the policy decisions of governments,
in terms of a theory of individual choice developed in microeconomics. The
central figure of microeconomic theory is, as veterans of introductory
economics courses may be aware, *homo economicus*. Like their economics
cousins, *homo politicus* also operates on the basis of rational self-interest,
seeking to maximize satisfaction at the least cost within the limits imposed
by the information they have at hand. What keeps competition in the political
marketplace from degenerating into a no-holds-barred mêlée is the existence
of rules — the constitution, laws — that constitute a web of incentives and
constraints influencing an individual's choices. And as in the economic
marketplace, the "wrong" rules will distort the behaviour of individuals,

resulting in outcomes that are inefficient from the standpoint of society as a whole.

The appeal of the public choice model for students of policy-making lies in its purported theoretical rigour. It provides a set of sharp analytical tools for understanding how policy is determined. Foremost among these tools is public choice theory's strict insistence on the individual as the basic unit of analysis. The state is viewed in terms of the individual politicians and bureaucrats who occupy particular positions within it, and whose coalitons and conflicts are determined by rational calculations of individual self-interests. Politicians seek to be elected, and once elected, to maintain themselves in power (their motivations for wanting to hold office are beside the point). Bureaucrats seek promotion and/or more control over the environment in which their organization is situated. Expansion, increased budgets, new policy tasks, and capturing chief responsibility for a policy field are all strategies that may be used to achieve these bureaucratic goals.

It is important to keep in mind that the state does not act in a single-minded way. The bureaucracy, for example, is divided into "spender" organizations with large budgets, for whom financial restraint means placing limits on the goals that individual bureaucrats pursue, and "savers" who operate under a very different system of incentives for behaviour. The incentive system of individual bureaucrats also varies according to the societal interests that "consume" the services they provide, their regional focus, and their function. These divisions lead to competition and bargaining within the bureaucracy. This is also true of the elected government. Behind the facade of unity that typically characterizes single-party government in Canada (coalition governments introduce another level of complexity), the fact that the re-election prospects of individual members of the government are tied to different constituencies (regional, special interest, and ideological), and to the various parts of the state bureaucracy they oversee, ensures that they, too, are involved in this process of bargaining within the state.

The behaviour of those within the state — the choices open to them and the strategies they pursue — is influenced by the actual and anticipated actions of special interest groups, the media, and various segments of the electorate. The behaviour of collective agents like political parties, the media and pressure groups is explained in terms of the self-interested motives of those who comprise these groups. For example, one of the major Canadian contributions to public choice theory describes political parties as "loose coalitions of individuals who are prepared to work together for the election of a slate of candidates. Presumably the members believe that if the party they support were to form the government their personal interests would

| 231 |

CANADIAN GOVERNMENT AND POLITICS

be better served than if some other coalition were in office."[10] Special interest groups are successful in influencing public policy to the extent that the individual members who comprise them perceive that the costs of investing in collective action are exceeded by the individual benefits they receive from group membership (what we might call the *group cohesion condition*), and to the extent that the relevant policy-makers perceive that their own capacity to pursue what is important to them would be advanced by meeting the group's demands or hindered by resisting the group's pressure activities (the *credible threat condition*).

Like pluralism, public choice explanations view policy-making as a highly competitive process. They share such terms as "logrolling," "bargaining," "accommodation," and "exchange." Moreover, their portrayal of the state as being a mediator of competing claims, as well as having its own internal divisions to work out, is broadly similar. Though methodologically different, pluralist and public choice theories view the political work through much the same lens. It is a world in which political competition is unequal, but real competition does exist and the distributional outcomes that public policy determines or reinforces are fairly open. This stands in marked contrast to the next explanation we will look at, that provided by Canadian political economy (CPE).

3. CANADIAN POLITICAL ECONOMY

The label "political economy" has meant different things in Canada at different times. It currently is associated with a *class analysis* of Canadian politics and policy-making, which draws on concepts developed by Marxian academics and on problems and interpretations that bear a more distinctively Canadian stamp. Class analysis is characterized by four main elements. These are:

(1) the division of society into classes, an individual's class position being determined by his or her relationship to the means of production;
(2) the pre-eminence of class as the basis for political and economic conflict;
(3) the inequality of classes, with society divided into dominant and subordinate classes; and
(4) the bias of the state in favour of the dominant class(es), which in a capitalist society will be those who control capital.

Together these four elements do not constitute a rigid theoretical code. Indeed, there are wide variations in the importance that those working within this framework attach to such non-economic factors as culture, technology and the role of individuals. Canadian political economy (CPE) does not reduce all politics to a question of economic class. But CPE does make the material conditions of society — "the processes by which material requirements are satisfied"[11] — the touchstone for its analysis of politics and policy-making. In the words of one of Canada's foremost contemporary political economists, Wallace Clement, "While the economic provides the context, it is the political and the cultural/ideological that write the text of history, the particularities of each nation, and the possibilities for the future. The script is one in which human actors have significant freedom of action."[12]

The self-declared openness and eclecticism of contemporary CPE have not changed the fact that class analysis forms the mainstream of this theoretical approach. Applied to policy-making, this means that the state is viewed as an agent for reproducing the class inequalities that exist in society, as well as being contested terrain where class conflicts — between dominant and subordinate classes, and between different segments of the dominant class — are played out. The state's sympathies are not, according to class analysis, neutral, and the overall pattern of public policy supports the general interests of capital. The reason for this is that policy-makers usually believe such policies to be in the public interest; also, failure to maintain some minimum level of business confidence leads to economic downturn, the consequences of which are reduced popular support for the government and losses in the state's ability to finance its activities. This second factor is an important structural constraint on policy-makers in capitalist societies.

A couple of features of this model need to be stressed. First of all, for the state to serve the general interests of capital, it is not necessary that policy-makers be drawn from the dominant class. In fact, some argue that the fewer the personal ties between the state and the dominant class the more effective will be the state in maintaining the interests of this class. This is because the reality of capitalist domination will to some extent be hidden by the appearance of government that is not in the hands of the members of any one class. Second, policy-makers are receptive to the demands of subordinate classes. Their readiness to implement reforms that may in fact be opposed by powerful business interests does not result from any special vision on their part as to what concessions must be made to save the capitalist system from the shortsightedness of individual capitalists. Instead, it results because governments are subject to popular pressures through elections, and because those who manage the state are unlikely to be concerned about the reactions of only one or a few segments of the business community. Governments therefore are willing to act in ways that offend parts of that community. This does not mean that policy-makers are more astute about what needs to be done to maintain the capitalist system than are the capitalists themselves. It does mean, however, that their concern for the overall level of economic activity — a factor that influences both the popular support of governments and the capacity of the state to finance its activities — frees policy-makers from the narrower interests of particular parts of the business community.

It would be a mistake to think that policy-makers consciously ask themselves, "What do we need to do to preserve the capitalist system?" They do not need to consciously pose this question because their conception of the "national interest" coincides with the general interest of capital. As Ralph Miliband explains, "if the state acts in ways which are congruent with the interests and purposes of capital, it is not because it is driven out of dire compulsion to do so, but because it wants to do so."[13] Ideology reinforces the structural mechanisms described earlier, to ensure that the interests of the business community are not treated like those of a mere special interest group.

4. STATISM

Statism is a rather awkward sounding label for those explanations of policy-making that stress the independence of policy-makers. By "independence" we mean the ability and inclination of elected officials and bureaucrats to act as they see fit, irrespective of the pressures and demands coming from societal groups. The role of permanent bureaucratic officials has been particularly emphasized, and indeed this approach to policy-making is sometimes referred to as bureaucratic politics.

As Leslie Pal observes,

> Modern public policy is increasingly, it appears, a bureaucratic affair, conceived and developed within the state, proposed as part of departmental agendas, and implemented by state authorities. Recent work has therefore focused on the influence of bureaucracy on public policy. This influence may be understood more broadly as the effect of autonomous state forces on public policy formation and implementation. While different models emphasize different forces, their common ground is a belief in the independence of state

and political institutions — from bureaucracy to political parties — from other social forces.[14]

The sources of bureaucrats' influence on policy include the following:

- Technical expertise
- Control over information
- Links to those groups who depend on the programmes the bureaucrats administer
- Permanence and stability, compared to the transience of governments and cabinet ministers
- Claim to be apolitical, detached from the hurley-burley of interest group and party politics

These are formidable resources. But they do not tell us why bureaucrats would want to impose their particular stamp on policy, influencing what gets done and not simply how it is done.

The question of bureaucratic motivation has been most thoroughly plumbed by public choice theorists (see the earlier discussion of public choice), starting with Anthony Downs' *Inside Bureaucracy*.[15] Bureaucrats are portrayed as budget-maximizers, the reason being that a bureaucrat's pursuit of individual goals is tied closely to the resources and prestige of his or her bureau and of the programmes that it administers. Bureaucratic politics, then, results from the fact that permanent officials are motivated to pursue their own organizational goals, and they have the resources that enable them to translate these bureaucratic preferences into policy.

So why do we label this section "statism" instead of simply "bureaucratic politics"? The answer is that the goals, ambitions and ideas of elected officials — goals, ambitions and ideas that are not merely responses to the demands made on them by societal groups — also influence state actions. State officials, both elected and bureaucratic, are capable of developing and putting into effect their own conception of the "public interest." Even more fundamentally, perhaps, public officials have a powerful influence on what problems are recognized as worthy of the state's attention, and on how the policy response to a problem is framed.

The influence of the state on society, and not the other way around, has been the subject of a small mountain of theoretical and empirical studies over the last decade. In Canada, the statist framework was given a major boost by Alan Cairns' 1977 article, "The Governments and Societies of

| 235 |

Canadian Federalism."[16] Cairns argued that "Canadian federalism is about governments, governments that are possessed of massive human and financial resources, that are driven by purposes fashioned by elites, and that accord high priority to their own long-term institutional self-interest.... It is abundantly clear," he goes on to claim, "that the massive impact of government on society at the output stage does not require a prior massive impact of society on government at the input stage."[17] Just how autonomous the state is from society, and in what circumstances, are the questions posed by this state-oriented approach to policy-making.

More recently, Cairns has suggested a way of viewing politics and policy-making that fuses the pluralist and statist perspectives. He uses the concept of the *embedded state* to capture the modern reality of government that has been "invaded" by society. Cairns argues that "The overall tendency is for the state to pick up and recognize more and more identities and cleavages that are reinforced by their association with the state." Whether the original impetus for state intervention is found in the demands made by particular social interests or in state officials' own attempts to achieve political or administrative goals is less important than the fact that once a state-society linkage is embodied in policies and structures, the affected societal interests have become "embedded" in the state. The divisions and identities that vie for recognition are imported into the state system. Cairns argues that policy-making in Canada and in other liberal capitalist societies has become more difficult because state expansion both contributes to and is influenced by the increasing fragmentation of society.

I The Pattern of Public Policy I

The preceding section surveyed four general approaches to answering the question of why governments behave the way they do. For students of politics this is certainly a vital question. It also happens to be the most contentious one, as the diversity of theoretical explanations demonstrates.[18] Only somewhat less contentious are the questions of *what* government does, *how* it does it, and with *what consequences*. These address what are more formally labelled the scope, means and distributional dimensions of public policy. Together, they provide the basis for comparing the pattern of public policy and the role of the state in different societies, and for charting — and understanding — the course of historical change within a society. We turn to them now.

1. THE SCOPE OF PUBLIC POLICY

We know, without the need for elaborate demonstration, that governments do more today than they did in the past. They pass more laws and regulations on a wider range of subjects than before; they spend a larger share of national income; they tax in more ways and at higher levels; and they employ more people to operate the machinery of government. The scope of their activities range from the municipal by-laws requiring dog owners to carry a "stoop-and-scoop" when walking their pooch, to laws affecting the most vital aspects of our lives.

Recently, however, the growth of government has been stalled, and even reversed, in some political systems. The *welfare state* — symbol of the expanded scope of government's functions — has for years had a tarnished image. Asked whether they think the current size of government is too big, most Canadians agree. "Big government" has for decades ranked as the number one threat to Canada's future in the eyes of Canadians, with "big labour" a distant second and "big business" an even more distant third. Bureaucracy-bashing is a popular blood sport among conservative and populist politicians whose ideologies and policies strike a sympathetic chord among those who believe that society is "overgoverned."

The appropriate scope of government activities is largely a matter of personal preference. Take something as mundane as the random stopping of automobiles by police to check for drunk drivers. Some people object to this practice on the grounds that it violates the individual's freedom — not the freedom to drive while intoxicated, but the freedom from arbitrary detention by the state. Others — probably most Canadians — are willing to tolerate the possibility that innocent people may be pulled over and questioned by the police, and possibly even asked to take a breathalyzer test, as a reasonable infringement on individual freedom that contributes to public safety.

Should the state be in the business of redistributing wealth between groups and between regions? And if so, to what extent? Is the expenditure of public money on the promotion of bilingualism an appropriate use of taxpayers' dollars? Is a law that restricts the freedom to advertise in languages other than French, as exists in Quebec, a justified intervention by the state in society?

The easy answer to all of these questions would be "Yes." If the political process results in a particular policy then this choice is by definition an appropriate one. The reason is that policy choices are political matters, so that the only sensible standard for deciding whether a policy is appropriate or not is whether it has been arrived at according to the generally accepted rules of the political system. But in fact things are not so simple. Can the rules that permit and promote certain outcomes, and discourage or even preclude others, be wrong? Most people would have no hesitation in condemning a political system that excludes certain people on racial grounds and which therefore permits apartheid policies as in South Africa. Closer to home, the feminist movement argues that the dominant culture and social structures in Canada are patriarchal. Policy-makers, they contend, typically do not perceive the systemic gender discrimination that pervades society as a problem. If governments fail to take the actions necessary to redress the social and economic inequalities between men and women, are we justified in saying that governments are not doing enough (or that they are doing the wrong things)?

Trying to determine whether the scope of what government does is appropriate or not inevitably forces us to confront our own political values. The extreme *relativist* position asks only whether a policy is determined in accordance with the constitution and the other rules that govern political life in a society. Such a position would lead us to accept as legitimate any policy and any level of state intervention in society. Does the state have any business in the bedrooms of the nation? In the boardrooms of the nation? These would be reduced to matters of personal taste like the choice between classical music and heavy metal. And to some extent these are, obviously, matters of taste.

But we cannot — and as a practical matter we do not — abandon all efforts to judge the "goodness" of the state's activities and the limits of its reach into the economy and society. These activities may be out of sync with current social attitudes, either because of changing societal values or because policy has evolved in response to forces that result in a widening gap between the scope and profile of state activities, on the one hand, and the standards by which most people justify these activities, on the other. Moreover, there are certain social and political values that are less controversial than others. Consider a bromide like promoting health. Who disagrees with this vague objective? Disagreement begins when we go beyond platitudes to decide how these goals are best achieved.

Is the goal of promoting health better served by a predominantly private health care system, as in the United States, by a state-controlled system as in the Soviet Union, or by a system that combines elements of private fee-for-service health care with state financing as in Canada? It may seem that the question of the best means is an essentially technical one. But as we will see, the choice of means, like judgements on the scope of public policy, is influenced by ideology.

2. THE CHOICE OF POLICY INSTRUMENT

Ends and means are inseparable. To choose a particular goal requires that a plan of action, the means for achieving that goal, be developed and put into effect. The successful attainment of chosen goals, including the policy objectives of governments, depends on the choice of instruments for achieving them. This all sounds very rational and calculated. In the real world of policy-making, as in other realms of life, the process by which these instruments are chosen is much messier. The selection of means is influenced by how things have been done in the past; by vested bureaucratic, political and societal interests; by chance, including the individuals involved in a decision; and by ideas and beliefs that may or may not be well founded. In addition to this it appears that means sometimes precede, and determine, the ends of policy. The statist and public choice theories, discussed earlier, are especially likely to locate the sources of decisions about what to do in the structures of government and the motives of the political and bureaucratic officials who operate within them.

The instruments of public policy have changed dramatically over time. Public ownership was relatively rare in Canada's early history. The vast majority of publicly owned corporations have been created since 1960 (about 60 percent of federal Crown corporations and 75 percent of provincial ones). The extent and types of taxation have also undergone major changes. As the scope of public policy expanded, governments resorted to an increasing variety of taxes. Direct taxes on income, payroll taxes, and special health insurance taxes — none of which existed at Confederation — have become major sources of revenue for governments. The tax system has become one of the chief instruments for the pursuit of governments' economic, social, and even cultural policy objectives. Direction regulation, usually under an independent regulatory agency, has also increased dramatically. Over 40 percent of all federal and provincial regulatory laws have been enacted since 1950.

In recent years controversy has surrounded all of the most common tools of public policy. Sometimes the issue has been whether the goals associated with a particular policy instrument — Canadian culture and the CBC; Canadianization of the petroleum industry and Petro-Canada; regional economic assistance and the Department of Regional and Industrial Expansion — are worth pursuing. More often, however, debate has centred on whether there is a better, i.e., less costly, way of achieving given policy objectives. This debate has been fueled by the arguments of economists, some political journalists, and business organizations about the alleged inefficiencies of publicly-owned businesses, and the economic distortions

| 239 |

produced by regulation. Taxation, subsidies and spending programmes have also come in for heavy criticism for the same reasons; i.e., that they do not accomplish the goals which they ostensibly are supposed to promote. Even governments have gotten into the act. One of the first actions of the Conservative government elected in 1984 was to establish the Task Force on Program Review to "produce an inventory of government programs with special concern for identifying duplication, waste and inefficiencies."[19] Canada's Auditor General acts as a sort of permanent critic on the instruments of policy, annually commenting on whether federal departments, agencies and crown corporations — his precise targets vary from year to year — are providing "value for money" in their performance. The Liberal government of Quebec produced its own broadside against inefficiency in 1986, establishing task forces on deregulation, privatization and government functions and structures.

The evaluation of how well a particular policy instrument achieves what is expected of it is not a simple task. To begin with, the government's goals may not be terribly clear, and may even be confused and contradictory. But even assuming that we can identify these goals with some precision, the only readily available standard for measuring how well they are being achieved is an economic one. It is fine to talk about "justice," "equity," "national identity," "the quality of life" and other such non-economic values. But the fact that these values do not carry price tags — indeed the very reason why governments involve themselves in the promotion of these things is often because the unregulated marketplace does not produce them at politically acceptable levels — creates a problem in assessing their worth. Measuring the "output" of policy is a necessary part of an evaluation of the instrument used to achieve it.

Let us assume that both of these formidible problems can be dealt with satisfactorily. The goals of policy are clear and their economic value is determined. All that is left is the question of whether the value of these goals could be achieved more efficiently using some other policy instrument. Even this is not a simple matter. We know, in this case, the costs and the benefits associated with the existing policy instrument — the publicly-owned CBC for example. But we are much less certain about those that would be associated with an alternative means for producing the same levels of cultural and nationalist values achieved by the CBC. Experience elsewhere may provide relevant comparisons. In fact, however, these assessments are more likely to be based on theoretical assumptions and models — such as those deployed by economists — which themselves are open to the charge of ideological bias.

PUBLIC POLICY AND POLICY-MAKING IN CANADA

3. WHO BENEFITS, AND WHO PAYS?

Entire books are written on this subject, without there being any consensus on the distributional impact of public policy. The very term "welfare state" implies that wealth is to some degree transferred by the state from those who can afford to pay to those in need. And there is no doubt that the various taxation and spending policies of governments affect the distribution of wealth. How much and to whose advantage are disputed issues. The majority opinion, however, sides with the conclusion of Canadian economist Irwin Gillespie: "In Canada, at least, a larger state has not led to a more egalitarian state."[20]

By itself, the tax system does not redistribute income from Canadian society's more affluent classes to its most impoverished ones. This is because several important taxes — notably sales and excise taxes, property taxes, and health insurance premiums — are regressive. They take a larger share out of the incomes of lower income-earners than they do from higher income-earners. The fact that the personal income tax is progressive — the rate at which one is taxed increases with one's income — and that governments typically rebate part of the personal cost of regressive levies like the sales and property taxes to lower income earners, do not eliminate the regressive impact of total taxation. On the other hand, it is clear that the total effect of the money transfers received under income security programmes and of public spending on education, housing, health care, transportation and a host of other programmes favours the poor. In 1986, the bottom fifth of income-earners in Canada accounted for 1.1 percent of earned income, but 6.3 percent when all sources of income were taken into account.[21] Or to put this another way, in 1981 the lowest 20 percent of households by income received 29.1 percent of all money transfers by governments,[22] thereby demonstrating the redistributive impact of government social policies.

Governments in Canada also act in ways intended to affect the distribution of wealth between regions. These regional subsidies take three main forms:

> (1) equalization payments from Ottawa to the less affluent provinces, intended to ensure "that provincial governments have sufficient revenues to provide reasonably comparable levels of public service at reasonably comparable levels of taxation" (**Constitution Act, 1982**, s.36[2]);
> (2) income transfers from Ottawa to individuals, like Unemployment Insurance, that are a major source of income in communities where employment opportunities tend to be seasonal, and

| 241 |

(3) federal and provincial industrial assistance programs that subsidize businesses in economically depressed regions.

As in the case of policies geared toward redistributing income between individuals, there is no agreement on the impact of these regionally focussed policies. The approximately $7.5 billion a year that Ottawa transfers to the economically weaker provinces in the form of equalization payments certainly enables them to finance a level of services that would otherwise be beyond their fiscal means. And the fact that certain regions benefit more than others from the UI system involves regional redistribution. But some have argued that these transfers impose a burden on the national economy, without "solving" the problems that underlie the weak economies of the provinces that benefit from them. Regional industrial assistance programmes have come in for the same criticism. Moreover, their impact on the regional distribution of wealth needs to be viewed alongside the economic consequences of the billions of dollars worth of other industrial subsidies, including tariffs, which have bestowed their greatest benefits on the economies of Ontario and Quebec — often at the expense of other regions.

Government's impact on the distribution of economic well-being does not stop at individuals and regions. In all industrial societies, Canada included, the state is in the business of protecting a vast range of producer and occupational groups from the unregulated workings of the market. Canadian economist Thomas Courchene calls this the "protected society."[23] It is a society in which any group with political clout is able to persuade the state to protect its narrow interests, at the public's expense. Courchene's concept of the protected society recognizes that both society's privileged and its disadvantaged elements may be "welfare recipients." Indeed, the Conservative government's own Task Force on Program Review described Canadian businesses as "program junkies,"[24] addicted to the billions of dollars worth of subsidies that successive governments have been willing to dole out to them.

All of the distributive effects of policy discussed to this point have involved material benefits and burdens. But as Raymond Breton observes, "public institutions and their authorities are involved in the distribution of symbolic as well as material resources."[25] We need only think of the outraged reaction of anglophone Quebeckers to the Quebec government's 1989 decision (Bill 178) to invoke the notwithstanding clause of the **Charter of Rights and Freedoms** (s.33[1]) after the Supreme Court of Canada had ruled that Quebec's restrictions on the language of signs violated the freedom of expression guaranteed in the Charter. It is doubtful that any English businessperson or consumer had suffered a material loss because of this restriction, and in fact the Quebec government had turned a blind eye to most violations of the *affichage* provisions in the language law. But for English-speaking Quebeckers, and for many Canadians outside the province, what was offensive about the Quebec government's action was that it seemed to relegate English and anglophones to an inferior status within Quebec society. As Montreal-born novelist Mordecai Richler said during the 1989 Quebec election campaign: "I was born here, and Montreal is my home. It seems strange to me that suddenly my language has become illegal."

I Conclusion I

There is little doubt that we know more about policy-making in Canada today than when Richard Simeon lamented the "ignorance" and "mystery" that surrounded this subject. Policy studies have proliferated enormously since then, coming from political scientists, economists, sociologists, legal scholars and historians. This revitalization has been due to three main developments; two of them intellectual and the other practical.

On the intellectual side, the concept of the *state* has been retrieved from the obscurity and negligence in which it was mired during the years leading up to Simeon's lament. The state — or "government" as it was more likely to be called — was not taken very seriously as an independent agent affecting politics, but was generally viewed as a place where societal interests slugged it out. The dominance of society-centred approaches to understanding politics left the state and public policy largely in the hands of public administration and legal-constitutional studies. These tended to be dry and descriptive, revealing little about the inner dynamics of the state or about its relationship to society. Which leads us to the second intellectual source of policy studies' revitalization, namely, their liberation from the dusty confines of traditional public administration. Before this could happen, the inadequacies of society-centred explanations of politics needed to be more widely recognized. When this happened, political scientists, sociologists, historians and economists increasingly turned their research energies on the state and policy-making.

Both of these intellectual developments have been related, to some degree at least, to the changing political scene. The 1970s in particular was marked by a growing belief that capitalist democracies were facing some sort of crisis. Terms like the "fiscal crisis of the state," "crisis of democracy," "bureaucratic leviathan," and "ungovernability of society" expressed various diagnoses of what ailed government. The concern with crisis has abated — not disappeared — since then. But the intrusiveness of government in society, and what Alan Cairns calls the invasion of the state by society, have become such obvious facts of modern life that no reasonable analysis of politics can fail to look closely at the state and its actions.

Although we know more about policy-making in Canada today than when Simeon surveyed the field, we are no closer to agreeing on the answers to the fundamental questions posed in this chapter. This does not mean that no progress has been made in understanding policy-making, unless progress is equated with the stifling of controversy. Answers are often elusive, but they are impossible if we do not ask the right questions. The fact that so much ground is being tilled by contemporary students of public policy, using a variety of methodological and theoretical implements, should alone be reason for optimism.

NOTES

[1] Thomas R. Dye, *Understanding Public Policy* 3rd ed. (Englewood Cliffs, N.J.: Prentice-Hall, 1978) p. 3.

[2] Murray Edelman, *Constructing the Political Spectacle* (Chicago: University of Chicago Press, 1988) p. 12.

[3] Eugene Forsey, *How Canadians Govern Themselves* (Ottawa: Supply and Services Canada, 1982) p. 2.

[4] E.E. Schattschneider, *The Semi-Sovereign People* (New York: Holt, Rinehart and Winston, 1960) p. 35.

[5] Theodore Lowi, *The End of Liberalism* (New York: W.W. Norton, 1979) p. 280.

[6] Charles Lindblom, *Politics and Markets* (New York: Basic Books, 1977), especially chs. 13-16.

[7] Charles Lindblom, "The Market as Prison," in Thomas Ferguson and Joel Rogers (eds.), *The Political Economy* (Armonk, New York: M.E. Sharpe, 1984) p. 3-31.

[8] Paul Pross, *Group Politics and Public Policy* (Toronto: Oxford University Press, 1986).

[9] Michael Atkinson and William D. Coleman, *The State, Business and Industrial Change in Canada* (Toronto: University of Toronto Press, 1989).

[10] Michael Trebilcock *et al, The Choice of Governing Instrument* (Ottawa: Economic Council of Canada, 1982) p. 10-11.

[11] Wallace Clement and Glen Williams (eds.), *The New Political Economy* (Montreal: McGill-Queen's University Press, 1989) p. 6.

[12] *Ibid.* p. 7.

[13] Ralph Miliband, "State Power and Capitalist Democracy," an essay read at Carleton University, Ottawa, July 1984, p. 6.

[14] Leslie A. Pal, *State, Class, and Bureaucracy: Canadian Unemployment Insurance and Public Policy* (Montreal: McGill-Queen's University Press, 1988) p. 94.

[15] Anthony Downs, *Inside Bureaucracy* (Boston: Little, Brown, 1967).

[16] Alan Cairns, "The Governments and Societies of Canadian Federalism," in Cairns, *Constitution, Government, and Society in Canada* (Toronto: McClelland and Stewart, 1988). This was Cairns's 1977 presidential address to the Canadian Political Science Association.

[17] *Ibid.* pp. 153-154.

[18] We have not even brushed the surface of the internal debates within these perspectives. For a brief discussion of these see Stephen Brooks and Andrew Stritch, *Business and Government in Canada* (Toronto: Prentice-Hall, 1990), ch. 3.

[19] Canada, Task Force on Program Review, *An Introduction to the Process of Program Review* (Ottawa: Supply and Services Canada, March 1986) p. i.

[20] W. Irwin Gillespie, *The Redistribution of Income in Canada* (Ottawa: Carleton University Library, 1980) p. 173.

[21] Statistics Canada, *Income after tax distributions by size in Canada*, cat. 13-210

annual, p. 13.

[22] This does not include the value of "services in kind" like public education and health services.

[23] Thomas J. Courchene, "Towards a Protected Society: The Politicization of Economic Life," *Canadian Journal of Economics*, 13 (November 1980).

[24] Task Force on Program Review, *Economic Growth: Services and Subsidies to Business*, p. 15.

[25] Raymond Breton, "Multiculturalism and Canadian Nation-Building," in Alan Cairns and Cynthia Williams (eds.), *Politics of Gender, Ethnicity and Language* (Toronto: University of Toronto Press, 1986) p. 30.

PUBLIC POLICY AND POLICY-MAKING IN CANADA

ANNOTATED READINGS

Banting, Keith, ed. *State and Society: Canada in Comparative Perspective.* Toronto: University of Toronto Press, 1986. This is a collection of essays prepared as one of the research studies for the Royal Commission on the Economic Union and Development Prospects for Canada. It includes an outstanding and provocative chapter by Alan Cairns, entitled "The Embedded State: State-Society Relations in Canada."

Brooks, Stephen. *Public Policy in Canada: An Introduction.* Toronto: McClelland & Stewart, 1989. This a textbook aimed at students who have some background in Canadian politics and government. It examines the theories, environment, and institutions of Canadian policy-making, and surveys several policy fields.

Cairns, Alan C. *Constitution, Government, and Society in Canada.* Toronto: McClelland & Stewart, 1988. This collection of essays brings together a number of seminal works that Cairns has written over the years on the Canadian constitution, federalism, the electoral system and parties, and Canadian society.

Campbell, Robert M., and Leslie A. Pal. *The Real Worlds of Canadian Politics: Cases in Process and Policy.* Peterborough, Broadview Press, 1989. Through their examination of six case studies covering a broad range of policy issues, Cambell and Pal succeed in conveying the complexity and diversity of policy-making. The "real worlds" examined in this book are worlds that differ in terms of the processes, actors, institutions and political discourse that are relevant to understanding policy outcomes.

Pal, Leslie A. *Public Policy Analysis: An Introduction.* Toronto: Methuen, 1987. How to analyze, understand and evaluate public policy are the subjects of this book. Pal's objective is to "equip even the neophyte to analyze virtually any Canadian public policy at any level of government." The bibliographic guide at the end of the book is bound to be a useful research tool for students writing papers on policy and policy-making.

CHAPTER 13

ORGANIZED INTERESTS

JOY ESBEREY AND GRACE SKOGSTAD

It's that time again! Red, blue, orange and green posters vie with realtors' boards on lawns and vacant lots. Strangers are anxious to shake your hand at bus stops and in shopping malls. An election is under way and democracy in Canada is alive and well — or is it? On a side street placard-carrying citizens walk up and down outside an abortion clinic. Canada Post delivers another sack of petitioning letters to a minister's office. Consultants in a public affairs company supply well-prepared analyses of forthcoming policy proposals to clients. A 'professional lobbyist' makes a luncheon 'date' with a junior bureaucrat. A senior civil servant finishes a 'consultation' session with an important Chief Executive Officer. Which is the 'real' world of democracy?

The Legitimacy of Interest Group Activity

Although interest groups have always been a part of the Canadian political system, their proliferation in the post-Second World War period heightened concerns about their appropriateness. The legitimacy of individuals or firms coming together in groups to press their concerns and interests on governments is somewhat suspect largely because democracy in western industrialized countries developed in association with a specific form of representative activity. The latter includes a geographically based right to vote and the monopolizing of the decision-making process by the elected representatives of the people. Of the variety of channels that link citizens in advanced industrial democracies to their rulers, only the electoral process has unquestioned legitimacy. Within this framework, ideologically coherent, disciplined parties were accepted because they made the electorally based legislative process more efficient.

A number of factors and developments have served to undermine this link between democratic government, on the one hand, and political parties and territorially based representatives, on the other. First, the geographically stable, economically integrated local communities on which representative democracy had been based were no longer the norm.

In today's sprawling rural ridings and commuter-based urban areas, people within the same geographical constituency no longer share an identity of interests. Territorially based loyalties are everywhere being replaced by other identifications, rooted in the group characteristics of occupation, language, ethnicity, or shared commitments to particular issues. As our society has become more pluralist, elected representatives are less and less able to represent the diverse interests of their constituents and these same constituents are more and more likely to form organizational links with like-minded Canadians that cross constituency boundaries.

Second, parties no longer appear to be fulfilling their necessary role in furthering representative democracy in Canada. With the exception of the big 'set piece' occasions — leadership conventions and elections — when individuals are actively recruited and encouraged to play a role, political parties are largely peripheral to most people's lives. Party financing is no longer dependent upon individual membership fees; their financial needs are met mainly through corporate donations and subsidies from taxpayers. The failure of parties to distinguish themselves along lines of principle, and the associated rise of brokerage parties may have reinforced the need for group activity. Further, long periods of one party dominance may have weakened the perceived possibility of changing policy through the electoral process and encouraged the politics of pressure.

The legitimacy of organized interests can be defended on grounds other than the decline in popular esteem of political parties. First, interest group activity can be seen to be rooted in the basic democratic rights of freedom of association and freedom of expression.[1] Second, the right of groups to advocate or petition is "deeply rooted in our tradition,"[2] originating in the historical British struggle for the "redress of grievance." Together these two themes are encapsulated in the U.S. Madisonian doctrine that the "autonomous expression of interests [through freely organized groups]" is "a hallmark of liberal democracy."[3]

Organized interests can also be defended as necessary to meet the needs of the modern interventionist government. The creation of the welfare state in the post-Second World War period and the intervention of governments in the marketplace created a need for expertise which could only partially be met by increasing the size of the public service and by creating independent advisory bodies, like the Economic Council of Canada. Much of the knowledge required for modern government is not in the public realm, but with private interests which relay this technical information to governments by being drawn directly into the policy-making process.

However, even while a widespread disillusionment with the electoral process can help to justify a role for organized interests in the political process, there remains uneasiness with the extent to which interest groups are an appropriate supplement to or substitute for political parties and elected representatives. The concerns are three-fold. The first is that the substitution of the group for the elected representative diminishes the influence of the individual Canadian, replacing as it does the MP as an intermediary on behalf of individual constituents. The reality, of course, is that individual MPs have very little influence in the political system.

The second concern is that while MPs are concerned to promote the public good and the national interest, interest groups are by definition promoting specialist interests, likely at the expense of the public interest or good. The criticism is weakened by the very real difficulty elected representatives have in identifying just what is the public interest. If it is only the sum of special interests, then it is difficult to deny groups a role in public policy formation. If the interests of the whole community are greater than the sum of particular interests, then allowing public officials to define this holistic interest smacks of elitism. This difficulty in defining the public interest is exacerbated by the distortion which our electoral system creates between the wishes of individual citizens expressed in the popular vote, and the translation of these wishes into parliamentary seats.[4]

The third source of uneasiness with an enhanced role for interest groups and thus with their legitimacy rests on the claim that the processes which form interest groups are not characterized by the same openness and widespread access as the legislative and electoral processes. If "it is not enough that democracy exists, [but] must be seen to exist," then interest group activity is marred by the fact that much of it is shielded from public

ORGANIZED INTERESTS

view by the same secrecy that is the characteristic of the Canadian executive process. Indeed, in sharp contrast to the public visibility of the behaviour of political parties during elections and of elected representatives in the House of Commons, interest group influence is usually contingent upon groups accepting the confidentiality of government-group discussions and being willing and able to engage in "quiet, behind the scenes consultations."[5] In this closed environment, it is not difficult for the public to suspect that deals are being made and special interests are being substituted for the public interest.

By far the greatest controversy concerning interest group activity centres on the question of providing equal access for all interests. Diametrically opposite views prevail here. On the one hand, a president of the Retail Council of Canada has argued that "Almost every special interest group, be they disabled, the poor, the native people, have formed their own pressure groups" and "legislators and civil servants pay at least as much attention to these groups as to the older established lobbies of business and labour."[6] On the other hand, an activist associated with the Status of Women has argued that although groups representing women, labour, minorities, and the unemployed exist, they are "virtually ignored."[7]

To help settle the dispute as to whether all interests enjoy the same opportunity to affect government policy, it is useful to note that before interests can even influence policy, they must first be organized. Some interests face greater obstacles to organizing collectively than do others. Where potential group members who share common concerns are divided on other grounds — by geography, ideology, ethnicity, or language, for example — their mobilization within one association will be more difficult. Thus, consumers, spread out across the country, find it difficult to build cohesive organizations. So have Nova Scotia's individualist fishermen, divided by the species they catch, the waters they fish (inshore, nearshore, offshore), and their partisan attachments.[8] By contrast, group formation is much easier where potential members are concentrated geographically and/or economically, and/or united by a common history, ethnicity, or language. Thus the communal traits and historical legacy that farmers in Quebec share have allowed them to build a very strong farm organization that wields considerable political influence. Likewise, the significant economic concentration and vertical integration among processors of forestry products, have combined with the geographic concentration of the industry to foster very strong industry associations.[9]

Governments have sometimes actively sponsored the formation of groups that have lacked the resources or motivation to organize themselves; groups

CANADIAN GOVERNMENT AND POLITICS

representing the poor, women, official language minority groups, and East Coast fishermen are all examples. These government-sponsored groups, however, do not enjoy the same degree of autonomy and security as do groups with independent financing. Thus, the National Action Committee on the Status of Women, a recipient of government operational grants since the implementation of the Report on the Royal Commission on the Status of Women in 1973, had its funding seriously cut back by the Mulroney government in 1989, after it had campaigned strenuously in the 1988 election campaign against the Progressive Conservative Party's Free Trade Agreement with the United States.

Besides providing core funding, governments can assist group organization by legislating compulsory membership in organizations. When it incorporated the Canadian Bankers Association (CBA) in 1900, the Canadian government required all Canadian banks to belong to the CBA, and in doing so, enabled the bankers to build one of the most effective interest groups in Canada.[10] Similarly, the Quebec government has empowered the Quebec farmers association, the Union des producteurs agricole, with a legal mandate to represent Quebec farmers and to require all farmers to pay membership dues to it. Such government initiatives have enabled these groups to build organizations that are much more autonomous of governments than are those that are dependent upon governments for their core funding.

The issue of disparities in the ability of interests to organize and subsequently influence public policy is at to the heart of the debates about the appropriate role of organized interests in the political system. Relevant to this debate is the distinction which can be drawn between groups which engage in policy advocacy or lobbying, on the one hand, and groups which can be said to participate in policy-making, in terms of either formulating or implementing public policies, on the other.[11] The two activities reflect the different roles which interest groups play in policy communities.

I Policy Advocacy and I Policy Participation

The idea of an autonomous government policy-making process and an independent interest group system, with the latter attempting to influence the former from the outside, is not an accurate picture of the policy system in practice. A more appropriate recognition of the interconnection of the two systems, especially in sectoral policy areas, is captured by the concept of a policy community.[12] A policy community includes "all actors or potential actors with a direct or indirect interest in the policy area or function who share a common 'policy focus' and who, with varying degrees of influence, shape policy outcomes over the long run."[13] Members of a policy community share a "concern with one area of the policy problem, interaction with each other's ideas, proposals and research ... and know each other well personally."[14] That is, policy community members are internally integrated and share certain beliefs and values to a lesser or greater degree.

A policy community, in turn, subdivides into two segments: the sub-government and the attentive public.[15] The sub-government consists of the decision-makers; the attentive public, of those who follow and attempt to influence policy but do not participate in policy-making on a regular basis. Thus, the farm policy community concerned with dairy policy would include the sub-government of public officials in the federal and provincial agriculture departments and on government agencies, who, along with dairy producers and processors, have been mandated to devise and implement dairy policy, while the consumer associations and other interested onlookers form the attentive public.

Government agencies or departments will virtually always be part of the sub-government that makes policy in a given policy area. Interest groups may or may not be. A major distinction can be drawn between groups which remain part of the attentive public and those which form part of the sub-government. Groups that are part of the attentive public approach public decision-makers as lobbyists and policy advocates from the outside, while those that are part of the sub-government can be said to be participants inside decision-making circles. The line between advocacy and participation is not an easy one to draw, as groups are often invited to serve on advisory bodies, only to have their advice go unheeded. Generally speaking, however, policy advocacy entails attempting to influence what will or will not be a matter of public policy, the content of the policies being made, and the manner in which policies are implemented or put into effect. By contrast, policy participation entails the direct participation of interest groups in the process through which policy is formulated or implemented.[16] Groups may be policy advocates at one time and on one issue, and policy participants at another time and on another issue. Although this cleavage between groups that are part of the sub-government and those that are not is the most fundamental division among groups, groups in the attentive public will also vary in terms of their degree of influence on public policy.

A group which hopes to influence policy-making should be aware that there is more involved than attracting media or parliamentary attention. It

| 253 |

is essential that the group understands how the political system works. At a basic level we can identify three stages of the policy process during which a group could have input. The first stage (often pre-parliamentary), involves setting the agenda and concerns what will or will not be a matter of public policy; the second, focuses on determining the content of public policies (a stage at which parliament's ratification is normally necessary); and the third, concerns implementing and enforcing public policies (post parliamentary). It may be assumed that groups will differ in their attitudes and effectiveness at each stage. Consider, for example, the question of determining the agenda: generally speaking, the efforts of groups in the attentive public will be directed toward trying to get issues on to the political agenda: groups that are part of the sub-government will be more interested in ensuring that the status quo prevails and to that end, they are likely to spend more time trying to keep issues that could disrupt the status quo off the public agenda.

Knowing that there are three stages in policy making is one thing, exercising influence at each stage is something else. For this a group must also possess information of the types which Coleman (1988:48-9) has labelled policy process, policy specific, and political impact knowledge. The first type of information relates to knowledge of how the system works: knowledge which Stanbury (1978: 183-94; 1986: chap. 7) identifies as important for timing (when) and targetting (who). Policy specific expertise is normally technical in nature and includes information about the likely economic, structural, and other consequences of suggested policy options. Groups must be able to present specific, highly detailed proposals in a language comprehensible to public officials. Political impact knowledge relates to the political costs and benefits of various policy proposals. Elected officials are especially concerned about the votes that will be gained or lost if a group's proposals are acted upon, and need assurance that the reaction of the wider public will be favourable.[26] Both kinds of information are critical to group input into the formulation of government policy, and are equally significant at the stage of policy implementation. With the legislature delegating more and more of the details of legislation — the regulations through which it is implemented — to the bureaucracy, groups with considerable expertise can play a constructive role advising the administration of possible difficulties and resistance, and sometimes participating in the policy delivery process. That same policy expertise can allow groups to delay, divert, and obstruct programs.

As expertise and impact presume that policy is actually being made, we need to stress the importance of understanding how issues and policies get onto the political agenda, or conversely, why some issues, including important

ORGANIZED INTERESTS

problems, are kept off the public agenda. While the question admits no easy answer, it would appear to be more difficult to get issues *into* the public arena than to keep them *out*. In part, this is because, in liberal democracies, solutions to problems will be assumed to lie in the private sector. Moreoever, elected politicians have a number of ways of shelving or undermining issues that do not accord with their own priorities. They can offer symbolic responses that put the issue on the back burner, by sending it off into the wilderness of committees of inquiry, research studies, or consultative processes. However, it is increasingly difficult for officials to keep issues off the public agenda, as groups have become skilled at enlisting the support of the mass media, and changes to committees of the House of Commons have made Parliament a more effective forum to bring group concerns front and centre.

The obstacles to injecting items onto the public agenda highlight the advantage that accrues to groups who can find a sympathetic hearing for their proposals among elected or appointed officials. This means that groups whose own goals coincide with those of public officials are likely to be more effective. But because only a finite number of issues — certainly not more than a handful — will directly engage the attention of elected politicians, the advantage clearly lies with groups that are served by the status quo. Their attennae must be alert to any policy proposals "brewing" in the attentive public or sub-government that would disrupt the status quo by removing or changing existing beneficial policies. Probably even more so than for groups seeking to introduce policy change, such groups require process knowledge — information about all the steps and stages of the policy process, each of which provides a point where proposals can be stopped, reversed, delayed or speeded up.

Although the Canadian policy process is more structured and hierarchical than that in the U.S., where there are multiple points of access and opportunities for "decisions to be made and unmade at many different locations,"[19] it, too, places considerable strain on groups' resources as time and energy must be spent monitoring the progress of issues through the system. Who the key actors are varies depending upon the policy issue under consideration and upon the policy community. Thus, Andrew Roman[20] suggests that the policy initiators are found deep in the bowels of the public service; they are the "privates" and "corporals" at the lower end of the public service pay scale. Stanbury[21] agrees, advising interest groups "to plant the seed of [their] own ideas very early in the process" since "most new ideas begin very deep in the civil service machine." On the other hand, James Gillies,[22] a former Cabinet Minister, suggests that in a limited number of significant issues when a minister and cabinet collectively are determined to follow a particular line of action, the influence of even the most senior departmental public servants is limited. The point is that no one policy process is necessarily like another. Although public servants, the cabinet, members of parliament, other interest groups, the media, and the public are generally members of most policy communities, how and when they affect policy proposals will differ from issue to issue. Thus, policy process knowledge will need to be rather sophisticated.

Alarmed in the mid 1970s with their ignorance of the government's agenda and frustrated at being surprised with issues which they believed they should have foreseen and forestalled,[23] business and professional groups have since taken a number of measures to enhance the sophistication of their process knowledge. One root has been to hire a professional lobbyist or public affairs consultant company. Such companies proliferated in the 1980s as they were used by groups to provide "an early warning system" about forthcoming government policies."[24] The costliness of such consultants — "flat retainers of $1500 to $4000 or more a month plus expenses" were the going rate in 1989 among the elite such as Bill Lee's Executive Consultants Ltd.[25] — rules them out for all but those groups with considerable financial resources. A more frequent route taken by groups, especially business groups, to strengthen their informational needs has been to restructure their organization to create government affairs divisions staffed by individuals whose sole responsibility is to monitor government and media sources. The smaller groups may be reduced to culling such news-sheets as the Southam newsletter on key government activity affecting business and industry: *The Public Sector*.

I The Organizational Development I of Groups

What sorts of interest groups are best able to obtain these various kinds of information, judged necessary to successful policy advocacy and policy-participation? The advantage would appear to go to those groups that are organizationally developed[27] or institutionalized.[28] Organizationally developed associations possess a permanent structure able to (1) generate the policy specific and political impact information required by governments and with the staff to lobby government officials full time; (2) communicate effectively with members so as to build the cohesion necessary for political mobilization; (3) represent members diverse interests by informing them of developments and getting their feedback; and (4) build favourable relations

ORGANIZED INTERESTS

with the public. All these capacities are necessary for effective lobbying. Participation in policy making normally requires, as well, that the interest group have a representational monopoly — that is, that it be the only group recognized by potential members and government alike to speak on behalf of a particular interest. The latter condition is necessary because governments will normally require it — in order to avoid the allegations of bias from excluded groups and the political costs that will surely ensue if participant groups are not fully representative of the particular interest.

Organizations that represent business interests are among the best developed or most institutionalized, as the Canadian Bankers Association (CBA) illustrates. The CBA employs about 100 people who provide expertise on financial affairs and financial institutions, engage in public relations, maintain close contacts with government officials in Ottawa and in the provincial capitals, and interact closely with the individual bank members. It can be ready on short notice to provide the government with the political and technical information needed to devise banking policy and it can assure government that, as the sole organization that represents Canada's banks, its proposals have the support of the Canadian banking community. The consequence is that the CBA has been drawn into the sub-government that devises and administers many policies of significance to the financial community.[29]

A sharp contrast can be drawn between the organizational development of the CBA and that of most non-business groups. Take for example, the groups that seek to represent the interests of social welfare recipients. There is not one association that represents social welfare recipients, but several, including the National Anti-Poverty Organization, the National Council of Welfare, the Canadian Council on Social Development (CCSD), and a host of other consumer groups that are concerned with additional issues. In contrast to the financial security and autonomy which the CBA enjoys, these organizations are all dependent upon the Canadian government for their funding. Moreover, none of them has sufficient staff resources to generate the expert information necessary for appreciable input into government policy. Their differences hamper any efforts to mount a united front before government. This disunity and the groups' limited capacity to represent the poor has meant that social welfare groups have individually and collectively been politically ineffective in the late 1980s and early 1990s in thwarting the national Conservative government's agenda for social welfare reform.[30]

The Impact of Government Structure on Groups

We have already noted a number of ways in which the organization of the government has an impact on groups. You will read elsewhere of reforms in the structure of the legislature and executive. Here we would emphasize the fact that the dispersal of authority within the executive has rendered more difficult the task of interest groups attempting to trace the course of a proposed bill or policy through the cabinet structures and the bureaucracy. Pross[31] argues that despite the monitoring costs this bureaucratic diffusion creates, it is not without benefits for groups. The dispersion of authority among bureaucrats places them in competition with one another, he argues, and one way in which they compete to secure approval for their policies is by forging links with client groups affected by these policies. Pross argues that officials thus seek the support of interest groups and draw them more closely into the policy community as a way of legitimizing policy initiatives to other (competitive) officials.

The dispersion of authority among officials at the national level is compounded by the federal system which divides authority between the two levels of government. Fragmented authority has varying effects for groups and governments.[32] For governments, divided jurisdiction and dispersed bureaucratic authority undermines their ability to devise coordinated and coherent policies. This is likely to be especially problematic when governments are faced with well-financed organizations with goals of their own. In such circumstances, fragmented authorities will be highly vulnerable to group pressure. For groups, the effects of dispersed authority are less clear. On the one hand, the fragmentation of authority across governments and within governments may create multiple veto points at which pressure can be placed to block disliked policies. Conversely, groups unable to secure support for their policies at one level of government may be given a second "kick at the can" if they can bring onside the other level of government and persuade it to pursue its goals. On the other hand, federalism may make it more difficult for regionally dispersed interests to build strong national organizations, and it increases lobbying costs when both levels of government must be targetted.

In short, the influence of interest groups is importantly affected not only by characteristics of the groups themselves, but equally, by characteristics of the governments with which they interact. How authority is organized within the political system — within governments and across the levels of government — affects the ability of groups to realize their goals. This can

ORGANIZED INTERESTS

be illustrated by examining two policy communities in action. The first example demonstrates how business interests were challenged, but ultimately prevailed, when a traditionally relatively closed policy community was opened to allow access to new actors. The second example reveals the dynamic and fluid nature of interest group structures and policy communities in the late twentieth century, as a new government institution, the Supreme Court of Canada, has become an important target of interest group activity.

I Interest Groups In Action I

Finance is at the heart of policy-making and the use of the tax system as a tool for achieving important national objectives puts it at the heart of the common good/special interest debate.

In the same way, control over finance is at the heart of democracy and the major vehicle of responsible government in our political system. A government unable to win legislative support for its budget has no option but to resign. The drama of resignation and the annual ritual surrounding "budget night" give a false impression of tax policy-making. It is more accurately seen as an ongoing process which is adjusted by specific amendments which are treated calmly and with little media attention — an ideal situation for interest group activity.

The very complex and technical nature of tax policy also lends itself to being dealt with through a process of quiet negotiation with interest groups.

David Good[33] has described the tax policy community as "a close knit system of individual participants who are collectively responsible for the federal government's concern in taxation." At the core, in the sub-government, are politicians and public servants, in an approximate ratio of 1:5. Business groups and experts in the field (the tax professionals — lawyers, accountants, investment specialists) also wield considerable influence in this policy process. The attentive public is relatively small, especially among the media and general public, reflecting the widespread belief that tax increases are inevitable and that there is little that can be done about them.

When tax issues break out of this closed policy community into the limelight, we get a brief insight into the way interest groups participate in this policy arena. At the same time, we must emphasize that the very visibility of these examples underlines their atypical nature.

In the early 1960s, elements in the business sector put pressure on the Diefenbaker government to undertake tax reforms directed to relieving the

I 259 I

burden placed on them. The government responded by creating a Royal Commission. Such commissions have served more as a symbolic response than as a major source of policy initiatives, so it was not suprising that business groups chose not to put their case to the Carter Commission.[34] They were already well represented in the tax community and the Commission Chairman was a respected figure in the business world. In these circumstances, inaction seemed an appropriate response but it ignored the fact that the royal commission introduced a new, external actor to the policy field. When the Carter Commission delivered a report calling for radical changes which would have imposed a greater tax burden on selected industries, the process took on a new complexion. The issue of tax reform was now on the public agenda and it would be difficult to confine it to the closed world of the tax policy community.

Even in these circumstances, however, it is difficult for policy advocates without status in the community to effect change. The situation was further complicated by an election which brought to power the Pearson Liberal government. The latter found itself presented with a set of solutions "that it hadn't asked for and would have preferred to avoid altogether."[35] The Pearson Liberal government responded with its own stalling tactic — a White Paper presented by Finance Minister Benson and another round of opinion gathering on it. The industry, which had already gone public in a media based "orchestrated campaign of alarm," was now also very active in the parliamentary committee's public hearings on the issue.[36] They were also able to forge a close alliance with provincial premiers and members of parliament with a constituency interest.

Although the proposed reforms would have indirectly benefitted the general taxpayer, there was no strong coalition of interests to sustain the pressure for reform. In contrast, "the business and financial interests, who had a great deal at stake, were far more adept at using the political system to their own advantage ... [and] with their vast resources, they simply dominated the debate ... They used every avenue available to them."[37]

A major tactic used by the mining industry to build public and government support for their renunciation of the government's tax proposals was to threaten a capital strike (a refusal to invest), and to warn of the ensuing loss of jobs. With the electorate thus onside, provincial governments were quick to follow, and eventually so was the national Liberal government, which had, in any event, not been totally committed to reform. The case demonstrates the privileged position that business enjoys in liberal democracies. As long as governments look to business to create the employment and economic growth which are necessary to re-election, governments will be in a weak

ORGANIZED INTERESTS

bargaining position vis-à-vis business.[38] In the foregoing case, the government was able to save face by the mining sector agreeing to incremental changes at subsequent phases of tax reform. But the case also demonstrates how the federal system of Canada can be exploited by groups which can use the two-tiered system of government to form alliances with provincial governments in order to pressure the national government.

Before we leave the tax field, we should briefly consider a case which appears to contradict the foregoing view that interest groups are most effective when they participate in the policy process as part of the sub-government within the policy community.

In his budget speech of May 23, 1985, Finance Minister Michael Wilson announced that the government was limiting increases in pensions for seniors to three percent below the rate of inflation. Five weeks later ... the Finance Minister reinstated fully-indexed pensions for seniors.[39]

The ability of "grey power" groups, like the National Pensioners and Senior Citizens Federation, to enlist the media and parliamentary support that proved effective in achieving this change of heart suggests their success as policy advocates. However, the outcome can as readily be explained by factors external to grey power groups. One factor important to the Finance Minister's reversal, and which is unlikely to recur, was the Prime Minister's sensitivity to his low credibility during his first term in office. The Minister of Finance's proposal directly contradicted Mr. Mulroney's statement during the 1984 election campaign that universal and fully indexed pensions were a "sacred trust" and his unequivocal promise "to reinstate complete indexing."[40] Thus, we suggest that this case demonstrates the importance of groups being accepted as legitimate and integrated members of the policy community, able to influence decisions as they are being made, and not forced to mount rearguard actions at the eleventh hour.

I Organized Interests and I the Supreme Court

The entrenchment of *The Charter of Rights and Freedoms* in *The Constitution Act, 1982*, provided organized interests with a new target. Since then, the Supreme Court's decisions with respect to national defence, minority language, trade union activity, and abortion have illustrated the new policy role of the Court.[41] Here, the Canadian experience would seem to replicate that in the United States and West Germany, where entrenched rights and judicial review have existed for some time and where the courts have become an important arena of interest group activity.

The decision which the Supreme Court of Canada rendered in *Morgentaler v. the Queen* in January 1988, and which struck down Canada's abortion law as a violation of the Charter of Rights, had been preceded by considerable interest group activity. Pro-choice groups had fought hard to get the case before the Supreme Court, where their interventions were countered by groups representing the pro-life position. The high salience of the issue prompted the formation of umbrella organizations (the Canadian Abortion Rights Action League, the Coalition for Reproductive Choice, Campaign Life) to coordinate the activity of many existing women's and civil libertarian groups — a move we have described earlier as one toward greater organizational development.

The *Morgentaler* case[42] allows speculation as to the differing opportunities and constraints which the legal process, as compared to the bureaucratic-legislative process, presents to group activity. In contrast to the scope for influence which the political process provides for "groups that can win hearts and minds," the legal process is more rational. Court cases are not popularity contests, not even jury trials. Cases are won or lost on the legal merits of the case. Further, the capacity of the legal system to respond to group goals is essentially negative: the court strikes down an existing statute, leaving a vacuum that it cannot fill. While the absence of a law can meet the goal of a group seeking to have the law removed (as in the *Morgentaler* case), courts are less useful forums for groups seeking to fill a policy vacuum.

The legal system affords a further limitation. As long as our courts hold that groups do not have "standing," an interest group wishing to achieve policy goals through the courts must act through a "front man," the complainant. This can be a two-edged or blunt sword. The aims, strategies, tactics, perception of the problem, and so on of the complainant can diverge from those of the group. The complainant can therefore be an asset or a liability; if the latter, the cause as a whole may be undermined. Moreover, the court's verdict will generally apply only to the specific case of the specific individual in the specific circumstances. The case will establish a precedent and have an indirect effect on any subsequent actions, but the decision is neither retroactive nor automatically applied to all similar cases unless the law itself is declared invalid — a much rarer event than is generally believed.

What then is the value of using the judicial system to pursue group aims? The major value of legal action would seem to be that of agenda setting.

Judicial decisions can force politicians to act in a situation in which they prefer inaction.

This would seem to be a primary objective of the interest group, LEAF (Women's Legal, Education and Action Fund) which has carefully selected cases which test the meaning of the equality sections in the Charter to bring before the courts. However, to the extent that judicial decisions force issues back into political channels — as the *Morgentaler* decision did — groups successful before the courts cannot count on prevailing in the political arena. In the latter, the technical expertise required for drafting legislation and regulations means that the medical and legal professions are more likely to be consulted than either the pro-choice or pro-life groups. And once the issue moves into the legislative forum, the victory will go to those groups best able to deploy their resources (membership cohesion and conviction, finances, organizational structure) to maximize their political clout. And once again, the vulnerability of groups like LEAF which are highly dependent upon government funding, is exposed.

I Conclusion I

The legitimizing of interest group activity in Canada has been an incremental process. We moved from regarding them as a "hidden," if not "evil" empire, to accepting their legitimacy, and even desirability. The latter view is captured by the preamble to the **Lobbyist Registration Act** proclaimed in June 1989:

> WHEREAS free and open access to government is an important matter of public interest;
>
> AND WHEREAS lobbying public office holders is legitimate activity;
>
> AND WHEREAS it is desirable that public officeholders and the public be able to know who is attempting to influence ...
>
> NOW THEREFORE, Her Majesty, by and with the advice and consent of the Senate and House of Commons of Canada enacts as follows: ...

The links between the "whereas" clauses, however, are not self-justifying. The fact that free and open access is important is a separate issue from the wider question of how interest groups should be integrated into the political and policy-making process. We have mentioned earlier that the Canadian

CANADIAN GOVERNMENT AND POLITICS

political system is based on representative and responsible government and both these aspects need to be considered in the case of interest group activity.

The election process provides a vehicle by which we can hold our representatives in the legislature and in government responsible for their actions or inactions. How can we hold interest groups to account for their contributions to policy-making? If we are dissatisfied with a tax reform proposal we can, in theory, change the political actors in the policy community, but if the other actors in the sub-government remain unchanged, what have we achieved? A related question concerns the degree to which interest group spokespersons themselves protect the concerns of their own members in the face of pressures to compromise within the community.

The situation is no less ambiguous if we restrict ourselves to the representative dimension of interest groups. With a few exceptions,[43] analysts have not seriously addressed the imbalance in access which exists between business groups and other interest groups, including public interest groups. Policies which affect all Canadians, such as the GST, are "sold to us" by public relations firms and advertising agencies, while those which affect specialized groups, such as investors, are settled after discussion with representatives of the latter. Failing a development that allows the affected citizenry to be consulted on tax issues, McQuaig[44] suggests that we must question the appropriateness of allowing special interests to be consulted on the issues that directly affect them. The justification for such consultation — that it concerns technical issues which must be ironed out to ensure the effective and efficient application of laws — is not sufficient to offset the potential conflict of interest position in which groups that participate in such consultations are placed. Even on highly technical matters, groups are unlikely to be completely value-neutral and objective; they will find it difficult to place the public interest ahead of that of their clients.

The solution seems to lie with more far-ranging reforms that move interest group activity into the open, public arena. The latter would remove its clandestine feature and thus defuse much criticism. Whether these changes take the shape of corporatist arrangements which would formalize the role of interest groups as decision makers (as Coleman suggests),[45] or whether the process should remain informal and consultative is an issue that Canadians will have to decide for themselves. The point to be stressed is that the issue of interest groups in politics did not end when their existence was publicly recognized. The question of the most appropriate structure for democratic interest group input is yet to be resolved.

NOTES

[1] Roger Scott (ed.), *Interest Groups and Public Policy* (Melbourne: Macmillan, 1980) p. 240.

[2] See "Submission on Bill C-82, The Lobbyists Registration Act" *Canadian Bar Association*, April 19, 1988. pp. 1-2.

[3] Rod Hague and Martin Sarrop, *Comparative Government: An Introduction* (London: Macmillan, 1982) p. 79.

[4] Alan C. Cairns, "The Electoral System and the Party System in Canada, 1921-1965," *Canadian Journal of Political Science*, 1:1, pp. 55-80.

[5] Kenneth Kernaghan and David Siegel, *Public Administration in Canada* (Toronto: Methuen, 1987) pp. 410-11.

[6] Alistar McKechan, "Lobbying and Interest Group Representation ... A Comment," in William A. Neilson and James MacPherson (eds.), *The Legislative Process in Canada* (Montreal: Institute for Research on Public Policy, 1978) p. 221.

[7] Johanna den Hertog, "Lobbying and Interest Group Representation: A Comment" in William A. Neilsen and James MacPherson, *ibid.* p. 218.

[8] A. Paul Pross and S. McCorquodale, "The State, Interests, and Policy Making in the East Coast Fishery" in William D. Coleman and Grace Skogstad (eds.), *Policy Communities and Public Policy in Canada* (Toronto: Copp Clark, 1990).

[9] See William D. Coleman, *Business and Politics: A Study of Collective Action* (Montreal: McGill-Queen's University Press, 1988) pp. 210-14; and Wyn Grant, "Forestry and Forest Products" in William D. Coleman and Grace Skogstad (eds.), *ibid.*

[10] William D. Coleman, "The Banking Policy Community and Financial Change," in William D. Coleman and Grace Skogstad (eds.), *ibid.* Chapter 4.

[11] See William D. Coleman, *Business and Politics: A Study of Collective Action op. cit.* pp. 48-50.

[12] See, A. Paul Pross, *Groups Politics and Public Policy* (Toronto: Oxford University Press, 1986); R.A.W. Rhodes, *The National World of Local Government* (London: Macmillan, 1987); and Stephen Wilks and Maurice Wright, "Conclusion: Comparing Government — Industry Relations: States, Sectors and Networks" in Wilks and Wright (eds.), *Comparative Government–Industry Relations* (Oxford: The Clarendon Press, 1987) pp. 275-313.

[13] William D. Coleman and Grace Skogstad (eds.), *ibid.* p. 19.

[14] John Kingdon, *Agenda, Alternatives and Public Policies* (Boston: Little Brown, 1984) p. 123.

[15] A. Paul Pross, *Group Politics and Public Policy op. cit.* p. 98.

[16] William D. Coleman, *Business and Politics: A Study of Collective Action op. cit.* p. 48.

[17] *Ibid.* p. 48-49.

[18] W.T. Stanbury, "Lobbying and Interest Group Representation in the Legislative Process," in Neilson and MacPherson (eds.), *op. cit.* pp. 183-94.

[19] Jeffrey Berry, *The Interest Group Society* 2nd ed. (Boston: Scott Foresman/Little Brown, 1989) p. 193.

CANADIAN GOVERNMENT AND POLITICS

[20] Andrew Roman, "Lobbying and Interest Group Representation, ... A Comment," in Neilson and MacPherson, *op. cit.* p. 214-15.

[21] W.T. Stanbury, "Lobbying and Interest Group Representation in the Legislative Process," *Ibid.* p. 179.

[22] James Gillies, *Where Business Fails: Business-Government Relations at the Federal Level in Canada* (Montreal: Institute for Research on Public Policy, 1981) p. 49.

[23] John Sawatsky, *The Insiders: Government, Business and Lobbyists* (Toronto: McClelland and Stewart, 1989) p. 50-51.

[24] James Gillies, *op. cit.* p. 73.

[25] John Sawatsky, *op. cit.* p. 50-51.

[26] William D. Coleman, *Business and Politics: A Study of Collective Action, op. cit.* pp. 48-49.

[27] *Ibid.* Chapter 3, and Coleman and Skogstad (eds.) *op. cit.* Chapter 1.

[28] A. Paul Pross (ed.), *Pressure Group Behaviour in Canadian Politics* (Toronto: McGraw-Hill Ryerson, 1975) pp. 1-22.

[29] William D. Coleman, "The Banking Policy Community and Financial Change" in William D. Coleman and Grace Skogstad (eds.) *op. cit.*

[30] Rodney Haddow, "The Poverty Policy Community in Canada's Liberal Welfare State," in Coleman and Skogstad (eds.) *op. cit.* Chapter 9.

[31] A. Paul Pross, "Parliamentary Influence and the Diffusion of Power," *Canadian Journal of Political Science*, 1985, 18-2, pp. 235-66.

[32] Hugh G. Thorburn, *Interest Groups in the Canadian Federal System* (Toronto: University of Toronto Press, 1985).

[33] David A. Good, *The Politics of Anticipation: Making Canadian Federal Tax Policy* (Ottawa: School of Public Administration), Carleton University, 1980) p. 3.

[34] M.W. Bucovetsky, "The Mining Industry and the Great Tax Reform" in A. Paul Pross, *op. cit.* (1975) p. 93.

[35] Linda McQuaig, *Behind Closed Doors* (Markham: Penguin, 1987) p. 181.

[36] M.W. Bucovetsky, *op. cit.* pp. 94-95.

[37] Linda McQuaig, *op. cit.* p. 179.

[38] Charles Lindblom, *Politics and Markets* (New York: Basic, 1977).

[39] Elizabeth Riddell-Dixon and Greta Riddell-Dixon, "Seniors Advance, The Mulroney Government Retreats: Grey Power and the Reinstatement of Fully Indexed Pensions" in Robert J. Jackson, Doreen Jackson and Nicholas Baxter-Moore (eds.), *Contemporary Canadian Politics* (Scarborough: Prentice-Hall Canada, 1987) p. 277.

[40] *Ibid.* p. 276.

[41] F.L. Morton, "The Political Impact of the Canadian Charter of Rights and Freedoms," *Canadian Journal of Political Science*, 1987, 20:1, pp. 31-55.

[42] Robert M. Campbell and Leslie Pal, *The Real Worlds of Canadian Politics* (Peterborough: Broadview Press, 1989).

[43] William D. Coleman, *op. cit.* 1988, 1990.

[44] Linda McQuaig, *op. cit.* p. 112.

[45] William D. Coleman, *op. cit.* 1988, pp. 276-85.

ANNOTATED READINGS

Coleman, William D. and Grace Skogstad, eds. *Policy Communities and Public Policy in Canada*. Toronto: Copp Clark Pitman, 1990. Examines policy communities and policy networks in such sectors as banking, agriculture in Ontario and Quebec, the forestry and environmental land use in British Columbia, the East Coast fishery, occupational health and safety in Quebec, and social welfare to illustrate the variety of relationships that exist between governments and groups in Canada.

Pross, A. Paul, ed. *Pressure Group Behaviour in Canadian Politics*. Toronto: McGraw-Hill Ryerson, 1975. A collection of various case studies which reflects the then dominant "lobbyist" approach to examining interest groups and governments.

Pross, A. Paul. *Group Politics and Public Policy*. Toronto: Oxford University Press, 1986. Argues that interest groups are essential to democratic politics. Pross explains the proliferation of interest groups and changes in their policy role and impact in response to changes in the structure and functioning of the national government. The concept of policy community is elaborated.

Sawatsky, John. *The Insiders: Government, Business, and the Lobbyists*. Toronto: McClelland and Stewart, 1989. An outsider's view of the professional lobbyists and public affairs consultant companies whose influence has grown since the 1980s.

Thorburn, Hugh G. *Interest Groups in the Canadian Federal System*. Toronto: Universitiy of Toronto Press, 1985. Examines how federalism affects the distribution of power among organized interests and structures, how they seek to influence governments. Thorburn argues that interest groups find it difficult to cope with executive federalism and Canadian federalism more generally. The reciprocal impact of interest group activity on federal-provincial relations is also examined.

| CHAPTER 14 |

MASS MEDIA IN CANADIAN POLITICS: A SURVEY OF CONTEMPORARY ISSUES

WALTER C. SODERLUND

As we enter into the last decade of the twentieth century, few would take the position that mass media do not play an important role in Canadian politics. While there are no explicit arguments that mass media have come to occupy a position as the "fourth branch of government,"[1] nevertheless it is obvious to anyone who attempts to understand how Canadian politics works that media constitute a factor of the first order of importance. While from the time of Confederation, media, in the form of newspapers, clearly played a role in the political process,[2] that role was essentially one of "spokesperson" for leading politicians. Today the relationship between mass media and politicians is a good deal more complex and their overall role as an intermediary between government and society is far more important. It is the nature of this multi-faceted relationship that this essay seeks to explore.

In explaining the functions performed by mass media in the Canadian political system, it is first necessary to discuss in a broad context the relationship between mass media systems, political systems, and the societies which they serve.

The seminal work in this area is *Four Theories of the Press*, by Fred Siebert, Theodore Peterson and Wilbur Schramm,[3] which outlined the characteristics of mass media behaviour in terms of authoritarian, communist, social responsibility and libertarian systems. While this initial typology has been revised and refined, the crucial point remains unaltered: that there is a high degree of congruence between the mass media system found in a society and the character of its political system. In fact, we would argue that the nature of the mass media system is one of a relatively few key indicators (others being free and fair elections, a multi-competitive political party system, and an independent judiciary), of the level of democratic attainment extant in a particular society. Further, if there is a degree of non-congruence between the mass media system and the political system in a society, the trend in mass media tends to be predictive of the direction of change in the political system.

Two scholars, Robert Picard and William Hachten, have extended the original formulation of four theories of the press. While there are differences between them, it now appears that consensus has developed around the proposition that there are in fact five distinct types of mass media systems: authoritarian, communist, revolutionary, developmental and western.[4] It is important to understand the differences among these five types of mass media systems, as they both clarify the functions performed by mass media in Canada and highlight the uniqueness of this type of media system.

Even the most cursory international comparative study of mass media points to the conclusion that in most political systems around the world the press is not "free," but rather is "controlled" by governments to perform certain functions held to be important those governments.

The key to understanding authoritarian media systems is that governments seek to restrict the dissemination of news that they find not to their liking. Thus censorship tends to be the means by which control over mass media is exercised. Mass media can function independent of government, but they must be careful not to present material which would offend the government. There is obviously some room for manoeuver on the part of bold journalists in authoritarian systems, but the price paid for overstepping the permitted boundaries can be high: fines, imprisonment, exile or even, in some circumstances, death.

In communist systems the prohibition on dissemination of offensive material is replaced by the belief that mass media have a positive role to play in the creation and maintenance of the "new" societal value system. Thus in communist systems, the mass media are consciously used as organs of pro-government propaganda in a coordinated effort aimed at achieving social control. In short, the party line becomes the media line. Mass media practitioners are seen as functionaries of the state. Independence, beyond that specifically authorized by the government is unthinkable.[5]

| 269 |

Revolutionary media systems are transitional phenomena, operating during a period of time when the established order in a society is being challenged. Often located physically outside the boundaries of the country they are intended to serve, they combine uncensored news reporting with revolutionary mobilization.

Developmental media systems are also transitional, but function over a much longer period of time. They are characteristic of ex-colonial, developing areas of the world (in shorthand terms, the third world), where problems of nation-building in circumstances of post-colonial dependency have left governments supposedly too fragile to survive the stinging criticism of an unfettered press. The mass media in the developmental model, are seen, therefore, as championing the cause of development, while pulling their punches in reporting government failures and corruption. Obviously developmental systems are potentially subject to great abuse, as the line between "authoritarian" and "developmental" justification for restrictions on press freedom can in practice be difficult to draw.

Western media systems are those characterized by the functioning of a "free press," defined by Hachten as "the right of the press to report, comment on, and criticize its own government without retaliation or threat of retaliation."[6] While western systems operate within the context of laws governing libel and slander, there are no specific restrictions on journalists, and in the United States, for example, journalists are extended "special status" (by the Constitution and judicial interpretation), beyond that enjoyed by ordinary citizens. As the criminal prosecution of Canadian journalist Doug Small following April 1989 budget leak made evident, no such special status exists for journalists in Canada. In fact, testimony by an RCMP investigator at the Small trial created a major embarrassment for the government as he testified the government insisted Small be charged in order to "teach journalists a lesson."[7]

Western media systems are based on the assumption that, while damage may be done by false reporting, in the final analysis, truth will win in the open marketplace of ideas. Of course, in those relatively few societies in which a "free press" functions, journalists have tended to internalize the norms of "fairness, accuracy and lack of bias."[8] Critics of western systems tend to argue that journalists have also internalized the value systems of the political and economic elites of that society, thereby effectively reducing the number of points of view which compete in the open marketplace of ideas.

I Roles of Mass Media in I
Democratic Systems

Canada has a democratic political system that is well anchored in Anglo-American traditions and, not surprisingly, its mass media system is western in character. This observation having been made, how can we describe the functions of that mass media system in its political context.

In a key work, Bernard Cohen isolated six "role conceptions" of the media in democratic political systems:[9] the press as "informer," the press as an "interpreter," the press as an instrument of government (i.e., a "supporter" of policy), the press as "critic" of government policy, the press as "advocate" of its own alternative policy, and the press interacting with government as an actual "policy maker."

In order to understand these various roles, let us examine Figure 1.

FIGURE 1 : Roles of Mass Media in Democratic Systems

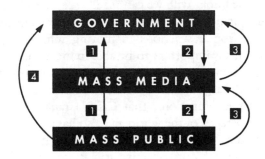

1   Role of "informer" and "interpreter" of events to government and mass public

2   Role of "supporter," "critic" and "advocate" of policy

3   Role of "informer" and "interpreter" of mass public responses to government policy through reporting of polls, letters to the editor, and coverage of demonstrations, etc.

4   Direct channel of communication between mass public and government

The "informer" and "interpreter" roles of mass media constitute the core of daily news activities. Finding news and and reporting it with some degree of objectivity, accuracy and sensitivity to their audiences is the essence of what journalists are paid to do. While it is fairly obvious that, while most citizens have to rely on mass media for information about that which occurs outside the range of their own experience, politicians themselves are voracious consumers of mass media information. Thus, mass media offer information and interpretation to two important constituencies in the democratic process, the citizenry and the government.

The remaining four roles of the press relate to the decision-making process. In this context, mass media can either "support" or "criticize" government policy. Indeed, in the 1988 federal election, *The Globe and Mail* and *The Toronto Star* adopted differing editorial positions with respect to the Free Trade Agreement with the United States. The press may also offer policy alternatives of its own (the "advocate" role), as *The Globe and Mail* did suggesting that the government link its foreign aid to Central America to those countries which respected human rights and complied with the Arias Peace Agreement signed in August, 1987. The role of the press as "policy maker" entails the press interacting with government in the actual formulation of policy, although I am aware of no example of this in the Canadian context.

As democratic theory assumes a "responsiveness" on the part of the government to the public will, we can readily see how inordinately difficult it would be for a democratic system to work without a media system which is relatively free from restrictions in moving information and opinion. Moreover, it is equally important to be able to move that information from the level of the citizenry to the government as it is to move it the other way. While no one would argue that the Canadian system has achieved perfection in carrying out these functions, that Canada ranks as one of the better functioning democracies of the world and also has a mass media system that operates within the context of democratic norms goes without question. Lest, however, we break our collective arm attempting to pat ourselves on the back, let us attempt to examine in some detail, four areas of concern in the overall context of the media and Canadian politics: (1) freedom of the press, (2) media ownership, (3) foreign media penetration, and (4) the quality of international reporting in the country.

I Freedom of the Press I

Freedom of the press is not an either/or proposition. There are some restrictions on press freedom in every political system. The important question to ask, therefore, is not "whether" there is freedom of the press, but rather how much press freedom exists and what type of restrictions on press behaviour apply.

In democratic political systems restrictions on the press can be viewed in the context of three types of control: governmental (legal and quasi-legal), social (attitudinal) and economic (ownership).

Among academics who have devoted time and energy to analyzing questions associated with freedom of the press, John Merrill ranks as one of the most important. Merrill's latest work in this area focuses on the concept of "inclination to control"; that is "the inclination of governments to have a restricted or disciplined press."[10] In the course of his research Merrill developed a "Control Inclination Index" consisting of six factors relating to restrictions placed by governments on journalistic practice: (1) in-country licensing, (2) international licensing (3) identification or accreditation, (4) university education as a prerequisite for entry into the profession, (5) in-country codes of ethics, and (6) international codes of ethics.

As is evident, these are all subtle rather than overt measures of control, and it is not surprising that democracies such as the United States, Canada, the United Kingdom and Sweden tend to rank among those countries where inclination to control is least, while communist and authoritarian political systems such as Cuba, the People's Republic of China, Iraq and Syria demonstrate the greatest propensity to control the press.

With respect to specific legal/constitutional restrictions on press freedom in Canada, Arthur Siegel has done an admirable job in documenting the situation. Siegel points out that the earliest press in Canada functioned in the classic authoritarian tradition: "The press was to be used as an aid to governing. Journalism was tolerated rather than encouraged. The press was to be closely controlled, and operated in the interests of the governors."[11] In the evolution of Canada's media system from authoritarian to democratic, Siegel cites the importance of the legal traditions of Anglo-American democracy, specifically the Peter Zenger case in the colony of New York in 1734. The outcome of this case, that "truth" was a valid defence against the charge of seditious libel, was used a century later in Nova Scotia in a case involving similar charges brought against journalist Joseph Howe. Established in these legal precedents is the "watchdog" or "critic" role of the press.

According to Siegel, the fact that Canada's "media system is American in style, while our political system is British in character,"[12] leads to some important differences which tend toward the restriction of press freedom in Canada. Siegel argues that the tradition of cabinet secrecy and legislation such as the *Official Secrets Act* (the latter used in a 1978 prosecution of the Toronto *Sun*[13]), inhibit press freedom. While "freedom of the press and

| 273 |

other media of communications" listed among the *Charter of Rights and Freedoms* (1982), case law, which defines what this freedom means in practice, is scant.[14]

There also appears to be consensus that Canadian libel laws are much stricter than those in the United States. For example, a sports columnist writing in *The Detroit Free Press*, was alleged to have libeled the attorney representing hockey player Bob Probert. The attorney chose to sue the newspaper in Windsor, where *The Free Press* is widely available, rather than in Detroit. Likewise, the Prime Minister of the Bahamas chose to sue the American television network NBC in Toronto, where an allegedly libelous NBC news story was distributed on cable, rather than in New York where it originated.

Further, subtle restrictions on press freedom could result from the fact that the Canadian Broadcasting Corporation (CBC), as a publicly owned entity, receives the bulk of its operating revenue from the government, as well as having its Chair appointed politically. During the Quebec separatism crisis of the late 1970s, Federal Cabinet Minister, Andre Ouellet, criticized Radio-Canada for alleged support for separatism on the part of the French arm of the CBC. In that Radio-Canada defended itself and was defended by others, the impact of these charges on political reporting is not clear. It is of course true that in many democratic societies, where traditions of impartiality and insulation from political pressure are not as well established as they are in Canada, governments can excercise control over content. In Jamaica, for example, hiring, promotion and firing decisions in public broadcasting have been made on the basis of political affiliation.[15]

The case in which Global TV reporter Doug Small was charged with possession of stolen property following his reporting of budget details from a stolen government document (not stolen by him, but passed to him) is of too recent a vintage to allow full assessment of its implications for press freedom in Canada. Nonetheless considering the RCMP testimony cited earlier, it is impossible not to see the case in this light. It is interesting that in the case of this "budget leak" that the "normal" response to such an event, namely the resignation of the Finance Minister, was not only abandoned, but instead, the government broke new ground in "controlling" press behaviour with respect to reportage of information deemed "secret" by the government. In terms of Professor Merrill's concept of inclination to control, such efforts, regardless of the motivation of the government in laying charges, has to be seen as a disturbing development in the area of press freedom in Canada.[16]

MASS MEDIA IN CANADIAN POLITICS

I Media Ownership I

As our discussion of the possible abridgement of freedom of the press arising out of government ownership of the CBC should make clear, there is a relationship between press freedom and ownership. And, in the Canadian case, it has *not* been government ownership which has been of primary concern.

Ownership of Canadian mass media is a mixture of private and public types. Ownership of electronic media is characterized by public (CBC) and private radio and television networks and stations coexisting in an uneasy, competitive relationship.[17] Print media, on the other hand, are privately owned, with the trend over the past three decades strongly in the direction of chain ownership. It is this phenomenon of chain ownership, which has reached near saturation in Canada, combined with "cross ownership" (control of both print and electronic outlets in the same market by the same group), that has caught the attention of those concerned with possible abuses of power latent in these conditions.

The primacy of economic forces over political decision-making is a well-established tradition in Canadian scholarship. The works of John Porter and Wallace Clement explicitly framed Canadian media as a part of the interlocking "corporate elite," functioning as a legitimizing voice for the continued rule of the dominant class.[18]

The evils of chain ownership *per se* were first given widespread attention in the **Report of the Special Senate Committee on Mass Media**[19] (the Davey Committee Report), which recommended legislation to curb further consolidation of ownership of the country's newspapers. Approximately ten years later, the Royal Commission on Newspapers[20] (the Kent Commission) was created to examine the newspaper industry in the wake of the closing of competitive newspapers in Ottawa and Winnipeg, by two of Canada's largest newspaper chains. Fundamental to both the Davey Committee and Kent Commission inquiries is the underlying assumption that chain ownership is inherently evil. Its evil rests in the consolidation of power in a relatively few hands, the assumption that this power will be used to restrict the amount of competing information available, and consequently that democracy will be ill-served.

How valid are these fears? Just as in the case of government ownership of mass media, potential abuses on the part of corporate chain owners are a reality. However, in Canada, while it is arguable that particular chains may not be committed to bringing the highest quality news to their readers, there is very little empirical evidence which suggests that the economic power of

I 275 I

chains has been used in concentrated ways to affect media content. For example, in studies of media coverage of three federal elections, chain ownership as a variable in predicting substantive issue, party and leader coverage was extremely weak.[21]

The reluctance of chains to flex their economic muscles, we argue, stems from two considerations. The first relates to notions of fair play and non-bias alluded to earlier. Journalists are principled and their profession has norms of appropriate behaviour leading to the situation where they simply cannot be bought and ordered about by owners. The second, is that the motivation for ownership of mass media outlets is primarily economic, not political, and chain ownership is attractive economically because it spreads the costs of news acquisition, as well as many other costs, over a large number of units, thus increasing profitability.[22] To the extent that flaunting ideological positions will tend to alienate readers with opposing views, and that profitability is dependent on circulation (for advertising revenue), the reality of the situation is that Canadian newspapers have become progressively less politically identifiable during the second half of the twentieth century, when, paradoxically, chain ownership has increased dramatically.[23] While we certainly would not argue that concentration of ownership of the magnitude found in Canada is "healthy" politically, there are no more than scattered instances where media output of chain owned papers appears dictated by the will of the corporate owners.

A second way in which ownership may influence media product is through hiring, promotion and firing decisions. In fact, in communist political systems, it is argued that western media cannot be "free" precisely because they are privately owned and owners will of course hire and promote those who agree with their point of view and fire those who they find out of step with their values.

This is an important area of concern as there are distinct "value structures" (corporate cultures) existing in all formal organizations. Moreover, these corporate values are important as they do play a role in the recruitment and subsequent upward mobility of personnel, as well as in their dismissal. Potential employees, as well as employers, try to match up individual desires with corporate expectations. As in courtship, when both feel comfortable, a relationship is struck. Once a hiring decision has been made, on-the-job socialization further solidifies the set of corporate values with which the recruit was at least in basic agreement.

While this set of processes no doubt does restrict the number of "radical" or "revolutionary" voices employed by major media operations, by and large the "watchdog" role of the press appears so strongly incorporated into mass

MASS MEDIA IN CANADIAN POLITICS

media norms of operation that government or corporate misdeeds will not go unreported.

Taking press freedom and press ownership together, we see that ownership (whether government or private) does to some degree almost necessarily infringe on freedom of the press. It also appears that the intelligent response to this situation is the recognition that *any* scheme of ownership is open to abuse, and it is abuse (whether by private or public owners) which needs to be challenged squarely and forcefully, whenever it occurs.

I Foreign Media Penetration I

Being located next to the United States has tended to be a mixed blessing for Canada. Although until 1776 the two countries shared a similar colonial history, the American Revolution divided British North America into what are now the United States and Canada, granted that Canada did not emerge as a distinct political entity until 1867. The relationship between the United States and Canada has always reflected the asymmetry of power stemming from a 10 to 1 population ratio. In order to preserve a political entity separate from the United States, Canadian politicians have had to engage in nation-building strategies. High on the list of institutions which were used for the purposes of nation-building were those of the mass media.[24]

Nation-building in Canada has had to contend with a problem of dual-directional pull. On the one hand, there is the obvious need to protect Canada from the onslaught of American-based media; on the other hand, there is the need to combat more localized loyalties imbedded in provincial identification, especially in the province of Quebec. It is the first of these problems that concerns us here.

In that mass media are primary transmitters of culture, it was feared early on that American media institutions would simply spread American culture across the border into Canada. While this never materialized as a major problem during the era of newspaper primacy, this was not to be the case with respect to broadcast media. Radio was introduced in Canada in 1922 and spread very rapidly across the country. Politicians and concerned citizens alike were both impressed and alarmed with the potential of this new medium of communication. Regulation of broadcasting spectrum use began almost immediately and the CBC was created in 1936, specifically with nation-building in mind.[25] In spite of regulations written into subsequent Broadcasting Acts and warnings issued by a host of Royal Commissions, historically Canadians have tuned into American programming in large

CANADIAN GOVERNMENT AND POLITICS

numbers, and even Canadian networks and stations feature American programming to attract audiences. Quotas for Canadian media content were finally introduced in 1959.

Despite the long-standing efforts aimed at curbing American media influence, the penetration of American culture and values into Canada in general and its impact on the political process specifically, has continued. In the Third World the kind of cultural intrusion characteristic of the American-Canadian relationship has been termed "media imperialism" or "electronic colonialism," defined by Thomas and Brenda McPhail as

> the dependency relationship established by the importation of communications hardware and foreign-produced software, along with engineers, technicians, and related information protocols, which unconsciously establish a set of foreign norms, values, and expectations which may alter the domestic culture and socialization process.[26]

In the case of Canada and the United States there is no direct attempt to target Canadian audiences for American media programming. Cultural intrusion results rather from the "spill-over" of American signals across the border, and the fact that over one-half the Canadian population lives within 320 kilometres of the border, which puts them within easy range of radio and television signals originating in the United States. The development of cable and satellite distribution systems only intensifies the problem. The fact that the United States is the most prolific information-producing society on earth, makes virtually inevitable the conclusion that Canadian cultural values, and consequently a separate identity, are being seriously undermined.

Of course, the reality that Canadians like to watch and listen to American programming means that, to a large extent, we as media audiences are as much a part of the problem as is the availability of American signals. Thus, it is important to note that while Canadians complain of American influence (a Gallup poll of August 1989 reported 60% of respondents "felt Canadian life was too influenced by Americans"[27]), in the area of communications, viewing and listening to U.S. programming is voluntary.

While we should not be surprised that Canadian life in general has been affected by the importation of American culture through mass media, what is truly interesting is the degree to which mass media has "Americanized" Canadian political processes. I use the word "interesting" because Canadian politics *per se* is not a subject of great importance for American media. In that studies have shown repeatedly that Canada ranks relatively low on the

MASS MEDIA IN CANADIAN POLITICS

scale of American news priorities, it is not American media content which is the culprit. The problem appears to be that American television style — particularly the "science of packaging electoral candidates for sale on television," has crossed the border, resulting in what is little short of a revolution in the process whereby political leaders are recruited, campaign for office, and are evaluated and elected by their constituents.

The consequent focus on leadership has significantly "presidentialized" the Canadian parliamentary system. Complex issues tend to get neglected due to the difficulty in dealing with them in the TV news format, in which a long story may run three minutes. Leaders have to be able to summarize their positions to fit the "30 second clip" format. In such circumstances, style tends to prevail over substance.

Also of great concern is the impact of polls on the political process, especially the media's reporting of them during electoral campaigns.[28] Contrary to conventional wisdom on the subject, which indicates that polling results do not impact on the outcomes of elections, I feel quite strongly that — given the circumstances where poll after poll (in the 1988 election twenty four polls were published as opposed to twelve in 1984) reports one party substantially in the lead, and in addition these poll results become, if not the leading issue in the campaign, at least a leading issue — the outcome of the election will be affected. As a consequence, the media adviser, the advertising executive and the pollster have in large measure replaced traditional political party operatives as key members of a campaign staff. Thus, paradoxically, the area of politics, which should be among the most insulated from the impact of American media, has been "Americanized" through the adoption of an American media style on the part of Canada's own media institutions.[29]

I International Reporting I

The quality of international reporting in Canada is especially important because for most citizens it is extremely difficult to get access to information on developments outside the range one's own personal experience other than through mass media channels. As a consequence, for most of us, what we know of the world is based on what we read in the newspaper, hear on the radio, or see on television.[30] Thus there is an immense responsibility on the part of the media to report accurately and in a proper context to Canadians what is happening in the world.

CANADIAN GOVERNMENT AND POLITICS

Assessments regarding the quality of international reporting in Canada, by and large, have not been very complimentary. Academic judgements such as those offered by Joseph Scanlon[31] and Denis Stairs,[32] plus the reports of the Davey Committee and the Kent Commission have pointed out serious problems with respect to Canadian reporting of international news. Criticisms focus on three major areas: (1) overall lack of interest in and coverage of international news, (2) a heavy reliance on foreign (mainly American) wire services for material and (3) a neglect of specific Canadian foreign policy aspects of international news.

Before assessing the current status of international reporting, it is first necessary to discuss standards of evaluation more generally. Indeed, gaining consensus as to the quality of mass media in a democratic society such as Canada is not an easy task, partly because, as Edwin Black has argued, standards of evaluation tend to be subjective.

> Critics do not, and cannot possibly, agree on the essentials of Canadian society or even how it should be conceived or defined. Everyone conceptualizes truth, the role of the citizen, government, courts, business, and the role of mass communications differently. Unscrambling the particular criteria that critics use goes a long way to explaining why policy solutions to the problem of news quality in Canada are a long way off.[33]

The entire print sector and a substantial portion of the electronic media in Canada are privately owned, and while it is reasonable to expect these owners to display some measure of "social responsibility," it is probably unrealistic to expect them to produce media product geared in large measure to elite tastes (academic and other), when their audiences tend to have different tastes. Thus, there is a real question regarding how much and what type of international coverage should be considered adequate, and it appears that at least some past criticism can be seen as based on unrealistic expectations.

The author, working in conjunction with a number of different colleagues over the past decade, has attempted to assess the performance of various Canadian media (print and broadcast) with respect to international reporting. While I would not want to argue that problems identified previously have disappeared, it is certainly my contention that both the quantity and quality of such reporting has increased fairly dramatically.

While I have done little work on Canadian mass media much before the 1960s, one project on which I am currently working, a comparative study of press images of Cuba's Fidel Castro in *The New York Times* and *The Globe and Mail* in 1953 and 1956, points out rather dramatically that, with respect to at least this international story, the 1950s were not the "golden age" of international reporting in *The Globe*. Of 82 press items coded in 1953 from July 27th (following the Moncada Barracks raid) to the end of the year, and from December 1st (following the landing of "Granma") to the end of the year, 76 (or 93%) of these items appeared in *The New York Times*, while only 6 (or 7%) appeared in *The Globe and Mail*. Moreover, of the six stories appearing in the Canadian newspaper, all were straight "hard news" reports appearing on inside pages, only one was longer than 15 paragraphs, and all were American wire copy.[34] Even those Canadians who read the nation's most prestigious newspaper very carefully, would have been largely ignorant regarding these important formative events of the Cuban Revolution.

More recent studies comparing Canadian and American press coverage in the same area of the world (Central America and the Caribbean) show considerable improvement in the ratio of Canadian to American reporting. For example, in press coverage of the Nicaraguan revolution from 1978 through 1980, the ratio was 64% of coverage in three leading American newspapers (*The New York Times*, *The Washington Post*, and *The Christian Science Monitor*) to 36% in three matched Canadian papers (*The Globe and Mail*, *The Citizen*, and *Le Devoir*).[35]

For events occurring in Central America in the 1980s the ⅔–⅓ ratio appears relatively stable. However, for events in the Caribbean (both English- and French-speaking), Canadian reporting fares better. In the case of the Grenadian election of 1984, Canadian and American coverage in a matched sample of six newspapers in each country was about equal.[36] What is even more interesting, the Haitian election crisis of 1987-1988 elicited greater coverage in six Canadian newspapers (53%) than it did in six American newspapers (47%). Greater interest on the part of Canadian newspapers, while paramount in the French-language press, was not restricted to these newspapers. The percentages of editorials and feature columns in Canadian newspapers compared favourably to those in American papers. It is true, however, that much material appearing in Canadian newspapers still originates from American wire services.[37]

The concern regarding the lack of coverage of specific Canadian foreign policy questions also needs to be reassessed. In a major study of foreign policy coverage in six Canadian newspapers in the fall of 1982, it was found that there were nearly nine foreign policy items per day in each newspaper coded: frankly far more than the researchers had expected.[38] Moreover, Canadian daily newspaper editors themselves believe reporting on international events in the country is nothing to be ashamed of; 78% rated it in the

| 281 |

CANADIAN GOVERNMENT AND POLITICS

"good," "very good," and "excellent" categories, while approximately half felt that it had improved over the past five years.[39]

Coverage of international news on Canadian television has not been as thoroughly studied (at least not in a comparative framework), but in one study comparing American and Canadian network news it was found that the same criteria for news worthiness were employed in both countries (armed conflict, terrorism, riots etc.). American TV news tended to focus more heavily on the USSR and the world's hot spots, while Canadian news offered coverage a wider range of countries and world events.[40]

Our overall conclusion is that during the 1980s, Canadian international reporting has in fact improved dramatically in every area in which it had previously received criticism. Getting a specifically Canadian viewpoint on the news remains the most problematic. While leading newspapers have placed more foreign correspondents abroad, wire copy still tends to originate with American wire services.

I Conclusion I

Canada is a country with a large physical territory (second largest in the world), a population that is relatively small (about 26 million), is characterized by strong regional and cultural/linguistic cleavages, and happens to share a border with one of the world's two superpowers. In short, it has its share of problems.

While this is the case, Canada also has benefited from the successful implantation of Anglo-American democratic traditions. It has also developed important norms of non-violence and political compromise, along with the structures and attitudes conducive to a free press.

As this essay should have made clear, the author is of the opinion that, on the whole, Canada's mass media systems have served the country well; in fact much better than the assessments of many media critics would lead us to believe. However, this having been said, the current status of the relationship between mass media institutions and the political process they service is not without its problems. It is also very important to convey to students the reality that these problems, while differing as to specifics, will never be "solved" in the sense that they will disappear.

The related issues of press freedom and media ownership interact continually in ways that might prove deleterious for democratic governance, and it is important to be aware that abuses can arise in circumstances of government ownership/control as well as in the context of privately owned systems. Likewise, problems of Canadian national unity, compounded by the existence of strong cultural and regional sub-identities and the at times painful reality of living next to the United States, are neither likely to go away nor otherwise be resolved, whatever enlightened policies may be decided upon by the Canadian government.

The best that we can hope for are mass media structures that attempt to cope with the set of problems which face Canada and report on and analyze these problems to the best of their ability. It is my judgement that with respect to domestic political reporting, this has been done at least as well as is the case in other leading democracies, for example, Britain and the United States. In the area of Canadian reporting of the highly complex international news scene, the situation is not as problem free. There is room for improvement, especially a need for a greater commitment on the part of Canadian mass media institutions to bear the cost of getting more Canadian journalists into the field, thus lessening the current reliance on American wire services. Even is this area, however, one can conclude that the current situation is better than it was, and trends are running in the right direction.

It is a cliché to say that a society has the kind of mass media system it deserves. In the case of Canada, we have a society that deserves no less than an excellent mass media system, and while there are problems associated with the operation of that system, by and large it is an excellent one.

NOTES

[1]Douglas Cater, *The Fourth Branch of Government* (Boston: Houghton-Mifflin, 1959).

[2]P.B. Waite, *The Life and Times of Confederation, 1864- 1867: Politics, Newspapers, and the Union of British North America* (Toronto: University of Toronto Press, 1962).

[3]Fred Siebert, Theodore Peterson, and Wilbur Schramm, *Four Theories of the Press* (Urbana: University of Illinois Press, 1956).

[4]Robert G. Picard, *The Press and the Decline of Democracy: The Democratic Socialist Response in Public Policy* (Westport, Conn.: Greenwood Press, 1983); and William A. Hachten, *The World News Prism: Changing Media, Clashing Ideology* (Ames, Iowa: Iowa State University Press, 1987).

[5]Hachten, *The World News Prism*, pp. 24-27.

[6] *Ibid.* p. 19.

[7]"Officer gave biased testimony, Crown says in budget-leak trial," *The Globe and Mail*, April 21, 1990, p. 2.

[8]L. John Martin and Anju Grover Chaudhary, *Comparative Mass Media Systems* (New York: Longman, 1984) p. 8.

[9]Bernard Cohen, *The Press and Foreign Policy* (Princeton: Princeton University Press, 1963) pp. 17-47.

[10]John C. Merrill, "Inclination to Control Press and Attitudes on Professionalization," *Journalism Quarterly* 56 (1988) pp. 839-844.

[11]Arthur Siegel, *Politics and the Mass Media in Canada* (Toronto: McGraw-Hill Ryerson, 1983) pp. 85.

[12] *Ibid.* p. 20.

[13] *Ibid.* pp. 67-69.

[14]Robert Martin and G. Stuart Adam, *A Sourcebook of Canadian Media Law* (Ottawa: Carleton University Press, 1989) pp. 73-74.

[15]Aggrey Brown, "Jamaica" in S.H. Surlin and W.C. Soderlund (eds.), *Mass Media and the Caribbean* (New York: Gordon and Breach, 1990) pp. 16-18.

[16]Allan Hutchinson, "The Budget Leak: How free should the press be?" *The Globe and Mail*, June 1, 1989, p. 7.

[17]W.C. Soderlund, W.I. Romanow, E.D. Briggs, R.H. Wagenberg, *Media and Elections in Canada* (Toronto: Holt, Rinehart and Winston, 1984) pp. 99-116.

[18]John Porter, *The Vertical Mosaic: An Analysis of Social Class and Power in Canada* (Toronto: University of Toronto Press, 1965) pp. 462-490; and Wallace Clement, *The Canadian Corporate Elite: An Analysis of Economic Power* (Toronto: McClelland and Stewart, 1975): pp. 270, 324.

[19] *The Uncertain Mirror: Report of the Special Senate Committee on Mass Media* (Ottawa: Queen's Printer, 1970).

[20] *Report of the Royal Commission on Newspapers.* (Ottawa: Minister of Supply and Services, 1981).

[21]Soderlund, *et al.*, *Media and Elections* pp. 90-91.

MASS MEDIA IN CANADIAN POLITICS

[22]Michael F. Charette, C. Lloyd Brown-John, W.I. Romanow, and W.C. Soderlund, "Acquisition et fermeture de journaux par des chaines de journaux: effets sur les tarifs de publicité," *Communication/Information* 6 (1984) pp. 50-54.

[23]Frederick J. Fletcher, *The Newspaper and Public Affairs* Volume 7, Research Reports, Royal Commission on Newspapers (Ottawa: Ministry of Supply and Services, 1981) p. 20.

[24]Thomas L. McPhail, *Electronic Colonialism: The Future of International Broadcasting* 2nd ed. (Beverly Hills: Sage, 1987).

[25]Soderlund, *et al., Media and Elections* pp. 106-108.

[26]Thomas L. McPhail and Brenda McPhail, "The international politics of telecommunications: resolving the North-South dilemma," *International Journal* XLII (1987) p. 294.

[27]"American Influence worries us," *The Windsor Star*, August 8, 1989, p. 1.

[28]R.H. Wagenberg, W.C. Soderlund, W.I. Romanow, and E.D. Briggs, "Campaigns, Images, and Polls: Mass Media Coverage of the 1984 Canadian Election," *Canadian Journal of Political Science* XXI (1988) pp. 117-129.

[29]Soderlund, *et al., Media and Elections*, pp. 127-130.

[30]William L. Rivers and Wilbur Schramm, *Responsibility in Mass Communication* rev. ed. (New York: Harper and Row, 1969) p. 14.

[31]T. Joseph Scanlon, "Canada sees the World through U.S. eyes: One Case in Cultural Domination," *Canadian Forum* 54 (1974) p. 230.

[32]Denis Stairs, "The press and foreign policy in Canada," *International Journal* 31 (1976) p. 230.

[33]Edwin R. Black, "The Quality of News Media" (Paper presented at the Annual Meeting of the Canadian Communication Association, Université Laval, June 1989) p. 2.

[34]W.C. Soderlund, "Western Press Coverage of Fidel Castro: The Early Years, 1953 and 1956" (Paper presented at the Conference, "Thirty Years of the Cuban Revolution: An Assessment," Halifax, November 1989).

[35]W.C. Soderlund, "Press Images of the Nicaraguan Revolution, 1978-1980: A Canadian-American Comparison" (Report prepared for The Canadian Institute of International Peace and Security, January 1989) p. 5.

[36]W.C. Soderlund, "The 1984 Grenadian Election: A Comparison of Canadian and American Press Coverage" (Paper presented at a Joint Meeting of the Canadian Communication and International Communication Associations, Montreal, June 1987).

[37]W.C. Soderlund and R.C. Nelson, "Canadian and American Press Coverage of the Haitian Election Crisis," in Surlin and Soderlund, *Mass Media and the Caribbean* pp. 373-389.

[38]T.A. Keenleyside, B.E. Burton, and W.C. Soderlund, "La presse et la politique étrangère Canadienne," *Etudes Internationales* XVIII (1987) p. 520.

[39]W.C. Soderlund, R.G. Price, and R.M. Krause, "Canadian Daily Newspaper Editors' Evaluation on International Reporting: A Report of Survey Data" (Paper presented at the Annual Meeting of the Canadian Communication Association, Université Laval, June 1989).

[40]S.H. Surlin, W.I. Romanow, and W.C. Soderlund, "TV Network News: A Canadian-American Comparison," *The American Review of Canadian Studies* XVIII (1988) pp. 469-472.

ANNOTATED READINGS

BOOKS

Black, Edwin R. *Politics and the News*. Toronto: Butterworths, 1982. Informed and interesting discussion by journalist turned professor of political science.

Fletcher, Frederick J. *The Newspaper and Public Affairs*. Volume 7, Research Reports, Royal Commission on Newspapers. Ottawa: Ministry of Supply and Services, 1981. Report assessing how well the newspaper industry has fulfilled its political roles.

Kesterton, Wilfred H. *A History of Journalism in Canada*. Toronto: McClelland and Stewart, 1967. The standard work on the history of the press in the country.

Martin, Robert and G. Stuart Adam. *A Sourcebook of Canadian Media Law*. Ottawa: Carleton University Press, 1989. In an era where Canadian politics is becoming "legalized," an extremely useful compliation of media laws and cases which bear upon them.

Peers, Frank W. *The Politics of Canadian Broadcasting, 1921-1951*. Toronto: University of Toronto Press, 1969, and *The Public Eye: Television and the Politics of Canadian Broadcasting*. Toronto: University of Toronto Press, 1979. Taken together, the definitive history of Canadian broadcasting.

Rutherford, Paul. *The Making of the Canadian Media*. Toronto: McGraw-Hill Ryerson, 1978. Readable history of the country's mass media.

Siegel, Arthur. *Politics and the Media in Canada*. Toronto: McGraw-Hill Ryerson, 1983. The only text focusing on all aspects of the relationship between politics and media.

Soderlund, Walter C. and Walter I. Romanow, E. Donald Briggs, and Ronald H. Wagenberg. *Media and Elections in Canada*. Toronto: Holt Rinehart and Winston, 1984. Treats mass media coverage of Canadian elections, focusing on 1979 and 1980.

Taras, David. *The Newsmakers: The Media's Influence on Canadian Politics*. Toronto: Nelson, 1990. An excellent up-to-date text focusing on the question "Who determines media content?"

GOVERNMENT DOCUMENTS

The Uncertain Mirror: Report of the Special Senate Committee on Mass Media Volume I. Ottawa: Queen's Printer, 1970. The Davey Committee Report. A benchmark from which to assess the current status of Canada's mass media.

Report of the Royal Commission on Newspapers. Ottawa: Ministry of Supply and Services, 1981. The Kent Commission Report. Thorough, but controversial, investigation of the newspaper industry, highlighting issues of ownership.

Report of the Task Force on Broadcasting Policy. Ottawa: Ministry of Supply and Services, 1988. The Caplan-Sauvageau Committee Report. Extremely complete investigation into the status of the country's broadcasting industries, focusing of the development of new policies.

CHAPTER 15

CANADIAN POLITICAL PARTIES

ROBERT M. KRAUSE

Political parties in Canada have not received universal praise for their ability to organize and articulate the aspirations and opinions of the general public over the past few decades. Rather they have been subject to severe criticism that they have been ineffective vehicles for the representation of interests emanating from the Canadian people. Some critics would argue that political parties are declining in influence in the political system. John Meisel for one, believes this state of affairs is caused by a host of long term and short term factors. The long term factors which have led to the decline of parties are: the rise of the bureaucratic state, pluralism and the rise of interest group politics, incipient corporatism (representation based on economic interests), federal-provincial diplomacy, the rise of electronic media, investigative journalism, opinion polling, the dominance of economic interests and one party dominance. The short run factors, which he attributed to the Liberal style of government under Trudeau are: the disdain of parliament, confusing the public, decline in ministerial responsibility and plebiscitary tendencies.[1]

While this list of causes for the decay of Canadian parties is extensive it is not exhaustive. In an examination of the overall arguments of supporters of the "decline of party" thesis, Gagnon and Tanguay summarize the findings into four major propositions.

1. Canada's major parties have failed to accommodate the country's diverse regional and cultural interests and are being superseded (or should be) by more effective institutions.

2. Long term changes in Canada's socioeconomic structure have rendered political parties less important as organizations for the representation of interests.

3. The traditional parties have failed to respond to changes in the values and political orientations of post-war generations of voters and are now being partly displaced by other forms of representation.

4. The new technology of politics — polling, consulting, the use of the electronic media have made party organizations less relevant to the winning of election campaigns. The new arts of political marketing reinforce the traditional leadership fixation of Canadian politics, again to the detriment of parties themselves.[2]

While these observations taken together with those of Meisel paint a rather dismal picture of Canadian parties, it must be recognized the picture may well be overdrawn. First, the indictment against political parties seems to assume prior to their decline parties were indeed fulfilling their representational roles. That is political parties accommodated the diverse regional and cultural interests across the nation; met changes in individual values and orientation; and were structured in such a way that they were effective representational organizations whose electoral "technology" was relevant and congruent with the election campaigns they conducted. All of these assumptions are, of course, highly suspect. Secondly, the decline of party thesis tends to single out Canada's "major parties" (Progressive Conservative, Liberals) as those in decay and by implication assumes Canada's third party (New Democratic Party) is relatively unaffected. Finally, the decline of party thesis tends to assume that parties as organizations are basically incapable of changing to meet the challenges facing them. In short they have a limited capacity for change.

Therefore, it can be suggested all the questions on the viability and effectiveness of Canadian political parties may not have been addressed. To more fully appreciate the status of Canadian parties a re-examination of the question is in order. A re-examination which utilizes three different perspectives on the nature of political parties: the party in the electorate, the party as an organization and the party as government. The first approach, party

CANADIAN GOVERNMENT AND POLITICS

in the electorate, examines the nature and extent of a party's electoral support and the strength of that support. The second approach, party-in-government, recognizes parties are influenced by their role in organizing the government agenda. The final perspective, party as organization, views parties from the perspective of how they organize to fulfil their electoral role. By using all three perspectives a more complete understanding of the present status of Canadian parties may well be revealed. One that leads to a fuller understanding not only of the forces which have negatively influenced parties, but also those forces which may have arrested the decline of parties or have had a more positive impact on the role and status of parties.

I Parties and the Electorate I

Support for a particular political party is a matter of individual choice. It is a question of party identification. All parties portray an image of what they stand for and the differing party positions on issues and attitudes towards groups (e.g.: labour, business) produce a generalized picture in the voter's mind which shapes their party identification and their subsequent voting behaviour. The party images fashioned in the voters mind are produced by both short and long term factors in the environment. In Canada contemporary studies of voting behaviour have shown that Canadian political parties lack a strong and committed mooring in the populace and there is, therefore, a high degree of electoral volatility.[3] While the question of how and why an individual is psychologically attracted to a party (party identification) is of importance for an understanding of voting behaviour, the more crucial question is how the overall aggregation of individual support is reflected in party standings which make up the party system.

I The Canadian Party System I

While there are many ways of classifying party systems one of the most useful ways is simply to classify them according to their competitive status. By this criterion it is relatively easy to see the Canadian party system is multi-party competitive with a two-and-a-half party system being the norm since 1921. It is a party system in which the two older parties (Liberals and Progressive Conservatives) receive support from approximately 80% of the Canadian electorate and a third party (New Democratic Party) obtains the remaining 20% of the vote. Yet, while this more or less three party pattern can be

CANADIAN POLITICAL PARTIES

construed to operate at a national level, such a conclusion is in actuality somewhat misleading. It detracts from the reality that by the late 1980's Canada had an overlapping two party system. A system in which two parties (Liberals and Progressive Conservatives) are the dominant parties east of the Ottawa River and two different parties (Progressive Conservatives and New Democrats) are the dominant national parties in Western Canada and British Columbia. Only in Ontario, and since 1988 in Manitoba, do the regional two party systems overlap with all three parties being relatively competitive.[4] Additionally, the three parties do not always enjoy a monopoly of support from the Canadian voting public. In the 1988 federal election 5% of Canadians voted for parties other than the three major national parties. Support for "other" parties was not evenly distributed across the country but was found principally in three provinces (Alberta — 17%; British Columbia — 7%, New Brunswick — 5%). Two parties, the Reform Party in Alberta and in British Columbia and the Confederation of Regions Western Party in New Brunswick, were the major beneficiaries of "other" party support in those provinces. While the Confederation of Regions party was primarily a party which advocated no bilingualism, the Reform party, the stronger of the two, was much like other third parties whose roots were established in Western Canada, in that it was in opposition to the practice of party politics in Canada (advocated less party discipline and more referendums) and national economic policy (advocated less government spending).

To further add to the weakening of electoral support for the three national parties has been the growth of support in Quebec for the Bloc Québecois which arose after the 1988 election. Here, as a direct consequence of the failure in passing the Meech Lake Accord, disenchanted Quebec conservative and liberal members of parliament left their parties and formed a new group (eschewing a party classification) dedicated to achieving political independence for the province of Quebec.

Not only does the electoral strength of national parties vary among regions and provinces but it can also be observed that in some of the provinces other parties which are non-competitive or nonparticipants in the federal arena are major parties in their respective provinces and have formed provincial governments (e.g. Social Credit in British Columbia and Parti Québecois in Quebec) Further, and not surprising in light of the overlapping nature of the national two party systems is the finding that Canada's third party, the New Democratic Party and its predecessor (CCF) has formed at one time or another a government in every western province in Canada (British Columbia, Manitoba, Saskatchewan) except that of Alberta, and formed a

CANADIAN GOVERNMENT AND POLITICS

government in Ontario in 1990. Thus, the Canadian party system is highly competitive, fragmented and subject to competing powers from provincial parties. It is a nationally regionalized party system.

The effect of regional patterns of party support has considerably influenced the formulation of party platforms. It has meant as Brodie observed, that parties house within them regional "policy cleavages."[5] Often times there is a much difference within a party, as between the parties, on what a parties policy position should be. For example, Conservatives in Alberta, who live in a gas and oil producing province, favour a high price for gas and oil, while their party counterparts in Ontario, who reside in a province deficient in those resources, favour a low price.

Regionalism of party support has also tended to diminish the impact of the class cleavage, around which more ideologically distinct policy proposals could be fashioned. Regional party viewpoints, a consequence of the diverse cleavage patterns found within the country (cultural, religious, ethnic, economic), make class appeals to voters extremely difficult. The end result is that frequently policy positions put forth by the parties are extremely vague and in ideological terms less distinctive.

The impact of the party system is such that each of Canada's federal parties, NDP, Progressive Conservative, Liberal, are subject to different competitive pressures varying by region which ultimately influence how each of them operates in the political system. Most crucial, however, is the simple fact that only two of the parties (Liberals and Progressive Conservative) have had the necessary electoral support to form a national government. This is not an insignificant fact in understanding the operation of Canadian parties in the national political system.

I Parties in Government I

Parties are influenced by their role in the governing process. To some this governing role is of paramount importance in shaping the behaviour and structure of parties and the party system. From this vantage point a party system will change over time in response to the objectives and vision of the party in power (particularly as outlined by its leader) as it governs the country. This perspective places heavy emphasis on parties themselves as major agents in shaping the nature of the party system. Indeed one proponent argues parties "not only respond to change" but they "initiate and determine events as well."[6] As a consequence, their organizational structure changes to meet the governmental objectives they have set. In short "party

CANADIAN POLITICAL PARTIES

structures ... imitate ... governmental objectives."[7] From this observation flows the proposition that Canada has witnessed "three different models of party government, each characterized by different approaches to political leadership and the mobilization of support ...."[8] In the period which lasted from Confederation until 1921, the party system was affected by the prerequisites necessary for building a state. That is building a political, administrative and geographic identity for the country which would bring together the parts of the country into a single territory. Here, leadership was provided by proven parliamentarians, chosen by the caucus (elected members), who used patronage as the means by which they could link local areas with the central government and achieve the objective of state building. Starting in 1921 and lasting till 1957, the party system changed as a result of the new governmental objective of nation building. The objective was to unite a sociocultural entity, where citizens would identify with each other. Party emphasis moved from a concern with local constituencies to those of region. Here leadership was provided by known politicians selected through managed leadership conventions. Rather than a politics characterized by the judicious usage of patronage the emphasis shifted to a brokerage style of politics where ministerial and regional politics became the order of the day. Finally, the third type of party system emerged in 1963 when leadership was conferred on challengers who were fundamentally party outsiders chosen from leadership conventions which were more open to party member participation. The emphasis moved away from politics based on a brokerage style of politics to one where the building of a national agenda was transmitted to the voting populace directly by means of the mass media, especially television. It thus became a party system characterized as one based on "electronic politics and personal parties,"[9] a party system in which mobilization of the electorate was achieved by direct appeals to voters by the leader through television and radio without the need to rely on intermediaries (regional ministers) to get the message across to the voting public. This party system, by virtue of not having to rely on intermediate middle men (brokers), gave the leader a pre-eminent position in fashioning the party message and program, and made for all practical purposes the party an extension of its leader.

I The Party as Organization I

Both the party in the electorate and the role of a party in government influence the organization of a political party. In the former case several studies have shown that the regionalized nature of the Canadian party system has produced a relationship between federal and provincial parties of the same name, as one characterized as being more "confederal" (decentralized) than "integrated" (centralized) in organizational characteristics.[10] In essence this means that both the provincial and federal wings of a party are relatively autonomous in their own geographic area. While the New Democratic Party is more organizationally integrated (centralized) in the relationship between its provincial and federal wings than the two other parties it too is still not a fully integrated party. Equally as significant as the party system is the impact of the governing role of a party on its organization.

We have under the previous section seen how parties since 1963 have placed more emphasis on the leader within a party, utilizing electronic means to mobilize voters. The emphasis on party leader appears to have its greatest impact on the structure of the parliamentary wing of the party (elected party members). The party leader is now less dependent upon regional representatives or regional ministers for policy advice within the confines of the legislative party. Additionally, the media attention and concentration on the leader as the principal spokesperson for the party gives the leader a level of visibility that few (if any) in a party can match. However, the effects on the extra-parliamentary wings of the parties (the general membership) is less clear.

The extra-parliamentary structure of a party consists of three principal organizational levels: local, provincial and national. The local level of the party is composed of all the party's local riding associations. The principal tasks of a local constituency organization is to act on behalf of the party in both the pre-election and election period and more crucially to nominate a candidate for parliament when an election is called. The provincial level of the party is a coalition of all the local constituencies within a province whose major function is to coordinate and give direction to the local ridings within the province. Finally, the national level of the party through its national executive oversees the overall political agenda of the party as a whole.

Paradoxically, while parties have become even moreso than in previous years extensions of their leaders, their extra-parliamentary organizations have never been stronger or more viable than they are presently. This is most apparent if one views recent changes in both the national and local constituency organizations of Canadian parties. Turning first to the central party organizations which are responsible for the conduct of the day-to-day business of the parties it can be noted they have grown both in size and financial resources. As Wearing notes, by 1986 the Progressive Conservative party had a permanent paid staff of 125, the Liberals employed 41 and the

NDP had 12 national staff members. To facilitate their central party operations in Ottawa the parties' yearly budgets ranged from half a million dollars for the NDP to almost one million seven hundred thousand dollars for the Liberals to a whopping four million dollars for the Progressive Conservative Party.[11]

While these figures do show variation among the parties in the availability of resources for their extra-parliamentary organizations it does not detract from the point that the national party organizations of all three parties are thus better equipped from both a staff and resource standpoint than ever before to lend institutional support for party activities such as fund raising, internal information dissemination and membership contact. Also the ability of the national offices to assist their candidates in the task of candidate support during election periods have also been greatly enhanced since 1963. The strengthening of the financial and personnel resources of the three parties has given them increased expertise, better planning capabilities, and continuity to more effectively conduct by-elections, election campaigns and day-to-day operations.

❙ Local Constituency ❙ Organizations

Along with the enhanced capabilities of the parties' central organizations there have been refinements at the local riding level which have improved their operating capacity. In one sense this has been a consequence of the growing strength of the central party organizations. The constituency members have become more assertive in ensuring that their voices will be heard in the wider party beyond the riding. While it is true that the national party has a vested interest in ensuring that their local structures have strong viable organizations, the grass root members have also begun to recognize that with the emphasis on the leader and the utilization of electronic media politics they are being by-passed to a considerable degree in the electoral operations of the party. As a result local party activists have been more vigorous in calling for a larger participatory role in the affairs of the party as a whole. They appear to be far less willing to accept only the traditional electoral tasks usually assigned to them. Part of the reason is the *Election Expenses Act* which has given the parties at both the local and national level larger and more stable financial resources. At the riding level the parties are less dependent on the national parties for funding. While there are variations in local finance among parties, occasioned by either whether the local party has an incumbent or not, or the degree of financial transfer between the national and local level, the local organizations have since the passage of the Act become more viable than was the case prior to it.

They now have more funds to mobilize both party members and voters in election periods, but also, in the period between elections. Whereas, prior to the passage of the Act, local constituencies often remained virtually dormant in the period between elections they are now more inclined to be active than passive.

Campaign Organizations

The ability of a party leader to appeal directly to individual voters is dependent to a great extent upon the leaders' and parties' ability to gauge correctly the issue and policy orientations of the electorate. It is here public opinion polling plays its greatest role. Polling gives the marketing and advertising experts the information needed to plan, develop and implement the parties' media campaigns. While governments employ polls when in office, to probe the strengths and weakness of existing and proposed policies, it is generally parties' usage of polling data in conducting their electoral campaigns which has produced the greatest amount of criticism. Indeed it has been proposed as a prime factor in the decline of parties. Part of the reason for the view is based on the premise that parties by-pass their general membership in the formulation of party platforms when they go to the voters. Party platforms are the result of polls rather than the result of party policy conferences or views emanating from the general party membership. This criticism, however, ignores the reality of how party platforms were formulated in the period preceding the era of public opinion polls. In the golden age of brokerage politics prior to 1963, the old line parties seldom involved their general party members in the development of party policy. While the New Democratic Party has a better record in this regard, it can still be noted that the selection of issues and programs to be stressed and highlighted in an election campaign were in the hands of the leader and the campaign organization rather than the general membership. Further, the criticism ignores the question of who constitutes the party. A party is not composed solely of card-carrying members.

Indeed card-carrying members of the three national parties do not fully mirror the socioeconomic characteristics of the general population that they purport to represent. They are a unique substrata of the general public. Party activists in all three parties come from a higher socioeconomic stratum than

CANADIAN POLITICAL PARTIES

members of the general public. In terms of age they are generally more middle-aged than the general population. Additionally, they tend to be much like their elected parliamentary counterparts, male dominated, especially at the higher executive levels of the party. Further, the motivation for members to formally join a party are not all policy or ideologically driven. For some the initial motivation to join a party is "purposive" (interested in policy and ideology) but for others the motivation is "material" (interested in patronage and economic benefits for themselves) while for still other activists the motivation is social ("solidary" motivation). Coupled with the initial motivational pluralism found among party activists is the complimentary reality that a party member's motivation for joining a party may well change during the time of a party career. In short their "sustaining" motivations for remaining within a party may differ from their "initial" motivations which led them to join the party. Where once an individual may have had a purposive motivation for joining the party (policy), it may well be a solidarity motivation which motivates their continued participation.[12] Therefore, it can be proposed that political motivations (initial and sustaining) of party members, which influence their policy predisposition and objectives, may well differ from those same predispositions and policy objectives of the general population and their subsequent claim that they alone can fully articulate the interests of their local area may be open to some doubt. Going beyond the more limited circle of formal party members, it can be proposed that a party may well be considered to be all those who regularly identify with and support the party. Thus public opinion polling allows parties to go beyond its structured membership and glimpse the opinions of all its members.

Additionally, there are other positive features of polling which critics of contemporary parties have often ignored. First, it has strengthened parties central organizations by enhancing their research capabilities. Polls have required a centralization of information gathering and dissemination which has given the extra-parliamentary national offices more accurate data on the issue preferences of Canadians than they possessed previously. Parties are able to understand that there are a wide range of interests which may vary by nature, scope and intensity across the country. For some individuals for instance, the question of job creation may be most salient while for others language questions may be more pressing. While critics of parties would often prefer that parties' electoral platforms be narrower and more specific, the polling data obtained allow them to more realistically reflect a wider range of interests than they would without polling information.

Secondly, polls give parties the capacity to better understand the total scope and complexity of an issue. For example, it permits the party to better appreciate that on issues such as day care and abortion single women, married women with children, women without children, single mothers, etc. may have differing opinions on those and other issues. Again, parties are thus better equipped with polls to represent the interests of the populace. Finally, it can be suggested, polls assist the party in obtaining better candidates for office. Polls assist local party organizations in obtaining a better understanding of local interests and the type of candidate best suited to represent those local interests.

At the level of parties' campaign organizations all of Canada's three national parties have since 1963 used polls in devising their campaign strategies. Historically Canadian parties first employed an American firm or expert to conduct their polls. This was done because of the lack of experience and expertise within their own ranks. Structurally the polling experts sat uneasily off to the side within a campaign organization which is traditionally composed of individuals selected primarily on the basis of representational criteria (geographic and positional). However, over time as the campaign organization became more sensitized to the utility of polls in conducting their election campaigns, the polling experts and their appendages (advertising, communication, marketing experts) became central to the campaigns, and expertise based on solely representational criteria was less important in structuring the campaign organizations. As the organization became more familiar with polling it finally hired a Canadian polling firm. While this has been the general process in Canada it has not occurred at the same speed within all parties and consequently the impact of polling, upon which "personal and electronic" politics is built, has not been uniform across the three parties.

The Liberal party was the first national party to utilize polling as an essential element in its campaign organization in 1963. The impetus for polls came from the leader of the party, and Prime Minister Lester Pearson and his advisers. And, as it was the governing party in Canada from 1963 until 1984 (excluding the brief Progressive Conservative Government of 1979/80), it grew to be highly dependent upon polling techniques for the conduct of its election campaigns. However, with its loss of power in 1984 the party has attempted to more properly balance its polling emphasis with more broadly based traditional representative criteria for inclusion within its electoral organization.

The Progressive Conservative Party followed a similar path to that of the Liberal party but with two striking differences. First, it employed polls after the Liberal initiative and more crucially used polls extensively while it was an opposition party. In the Conservative party the legitimacy of polls was more easily accepted by the general membership since it was recognized as necessary if the party was to remain competitive with the Liberals. However, on becoming a governing party in 1984 the Progressive Conservatives have not had the same doubts on the effects of polls on the campaign organization as have the Liberals. The ease of adoption to polling was partly the result of the fact that, when the party was in opposition, it was the government in several of the provinces and consequently strong regional voices were heard in the national campaign organization which tended to dilute the more one dimensional polling focus found in the Liberal Party.

The New Democratic Party illustrates a different picture from that of either the Conservatives or the Liberals. First, the New Democratic Party lagged behind the other two parties in the utilization of polls within its campaign organization. It was not until 1988 with its use of American polling experts that the party seriously engaged in the new era of polling techniques. However, much like the Liberal party the party as a whole has not taken kindly to a reliance on polls in its campaign organization. More specifically, the labour movement which has traditionally had a large and audible voice within the party has felt threatened that its counsel has been and will tend to be muted.

I Conclusion I

This examination of Canadian parties has attempted to temper the argument that national political parties are in a continual state of decline. Political parties in Canada still perform the same tasks that they have rendered the political system since the time of Confederation. Parties still are responsible for nominating candidates, running election campaigns, selecting issues, pushing policies and structuring how power is organized in Parliament. The proposition concerning the causes for the decline of parties may more accurately be considered as factors which have modified and altered the way parties operate within the political system. What they illustrate is that parties have changed, but it does not necessarily follow that they are in decline. As noted, the role of party in government can dramatically affect the nature of a party and the party system. This suggests that parties have the capacity to change the political environment within which they operate. As Meisel observed one of the short-run causes for the demise of parties was the Liberal style of government under Trudeau. This may or may not be true but it does highlight that if a party and leader in government has the capacity to cause

CANADIAN GOVERNMENT AND POLITICS

a decline in parties capabilities it may well be argued that a party and leader can also cause the opposite effect. More specifically it can be suggested that the passage of the Election Expenses Act of 1974 had a significant impact on strengthening the organizational capacity of parties that was lacking in the years prior to its enactment. At both the level of the central party organization and the local constituency, parties today have a more viable capacity to more fully represent the interests of Canadians than they possessed previously. Further the parties' campaign organizations are, with the use of modern techniques such as polling, better able to comprehend, plan and execute effective campaigns than was the case prior to 1963. Finally, it is not only the major parties electoral organizations (Progressive Conservative, Liberals) which have been subject to change but all three parties. The New Democratic Party has not been an island unto itself.

While there are, indeed, indications that Canadian parties have the potential and means to alleviate their perceived shortcomings it would be misleading to suggest that all is well for Canada's three principal parties. As has been observed earlier the three parties face challenges from new political forces (Reform Party, Bloc Québécois) which may well alter the three party system found at the federal level. The new party system may produce a realignment of existing parties, a coalition with newly emerging parties, or indeed may feature more than three parties.

In sum it can be seen that political parties in Canada are influenced by their relationship to the electorate, their role in the government and their organizational characteristics.

Each of their roles is not independent of the other. The net effect is that all three roles interact with each other, and more significantly produce variations within parties and among parties which over time make them adaptative organizations which are to some extent always organizations in transition.

NOTES

[1] See John Meisel, "The Decline of Party in Canada" in Hugh G.Thorburn (ed.), *Party Politics in Canada* 5th ed. (Scarborough: Prentice-Hall, 1985) pp. 98-114.

[2] See Alain G. Gagnon and Brian Tanguay, "Introduction: Canadian Parties in Transition" in Alain G. Gagnon and Brian Tanguay (eds.), *Canadian Parties in Transition* (Scarborough: Nelson, 1989) pp. 3-8.

[3] See Lawrence LeDuc, "The Canadian Voter" in this text.

[4] See Darrel R. Reid, "The Election of 1988 and Canadian Federalism" in Ronald L. Watts and Douglas M. Brown (ed.), *Canada: The State of the Federation 1989* (Kingston: Institute of Intergovernmental Relations, 1989) p. 40.

[5] M. Janine Brodie, "Tensions from Within: Regionalism and Party Policy in Canada" in Hugh G. Thornburn (ed.), *Party Politics in Canada* 5th ed. (Scarborough: Prentice-Hall, 1985) p. 80.

[6] David E. Smith, "Canadian Political Parties and National Integration" in Alain G. Gagnon and Brian Tanguay, *op. cit.* p. 144.

[7] *Ibid.* p. 131.

[8] R.C. Carty, "Three Canadian Party Systems: An Interpretation of the Development of National Politics" in George Perlin (ed.), *Party Democracy in Canada: The Politics of National Party Conventions* (Scarborough: Prentice-Hall, 1988) p. 15.

[9] See R.K. Carty, pp. 24-28.

[10] See D.V. Smiley, *The Federal Condition in Canada* (Toronto: McGraw-Hill Ryerson, 1987) pp. 103-104, and Rand Dyck, "Relations Between Federal and Provincial Parties" in Alain G. Gagnon and A. Brian Tanguay, *op. cit.* pp. 186-219.

[11] Joseph Wearing, *Strained Relations: Canada's Parties and Voters* (Toronto: McClelland and Stewart, 1988) pp. 182-186.

[12] For a discussion of motives for initiating and sustaining political activity when joining a party in Canada see: Allan Kornberg, Joel Smith and Harold D. Clarke, *Citizen Politicians: Canada* (Durham, N.C.: Carolina Academic Press, 1979) pp. 87-93. For a discussion of how motivations change over time within a party see, Harold D. Clarke, R. Price, M. Stewart and R. Krause, "Motivational Patterns and Differential Participation in a Canadian Party: The Ontario Liberals," *American Journal of Political Science*, 22 (February, 1978).

ANNOTATED READINGS

Gagnon, Alain G., and Brian A. Tanguay, eds. *Canadian Parties in Transition: Discourse, Organization, Representation.* Scarborough: Nelson, 1989. A collection of original essays dealing with both the nature and function of Canadian parties and their changing role in the political system.

Perlin, George, ed. *Party Democracy in Canada: The Politics of National Party Conventions.* Scarborough: Prentice-Hall, 1988. A series of well-written analytical articles pertaining to national leadership conventions.

Thorburn, Hugh G., ed. *Party Politics in Canada,* Fifth edition. Scarborough: Prentice-Hall, 1985. A collection of readings dealing with the historical background of parties, the party system, the three national political parties, and parties in the provinces.

Wearing, Joseph. *Strained Relations: Canada's Parties and Voters.* Toronto: McClelland and Stewart, 1988. An excellent overview of Canadian parties and their relationship to the voting public. The conclusion presents the question, Are Canadian parties fit to govern? and is a well-constructed argumentative chapter worth a second reading.

CANADIAN POLITICAL PARTIES

| CHAPTER 16 |

THE CANADIAN VOTER

LAWRENCE LeDUC

The re-election of a Progressive Conservative federal government in 1988 seemed to many observers to represent a consolidation of important changes in the Canadian electorate rooted in the Mulroney landslide of 1984. The conventional interpretation of Mulroney's success was that the long era of Liberal dominance in Canadian federal politics which had begun with the collapse of the Diefenbaker government in 1963, or perhaps even earlier with the post-war King and St. Laurent governments, was decisively ended. Yet there is much in this seemingly simple interpretation of events that is at odds with what political scientists know about the attitudes and behaviour of the Canadian electorate over the last three decades. Volatility and change are hardly new to Canadian electoral politics. National surveys of the Canadian electorate, conducted regularly with each election beginning in 1965, portray an electorate which has changed relatively little in its fundamental characteristics and outlook, yet is easily susceptible to sudden and often dramatic swings in voting choice.[1]

Before Mulroney did so in 1988, no Canadian federal government since 1953 had succeeded in winning a second consecutive parliamentary majority in an election. Of the dozen federal elections which have taken place since Louis St. Laurent achieved his second majority in 1953, half have produced majority governments and half have been minorities. Within each category, exactly half of the elections held have been won by the Progressive Conservatives (1957, 1958, 1962, 1979, 1984 and 1988) and half by the Liberals (1963, 1965, 1968, 1972, 1974, and 1980). In every one of these elections except 1958, "third" parties have polled at least 20% of the total vote, often in the process gaining enough parliamentary seats to deny a majority to the winner. For thirty years, elections in Canada have been anything but orderly, predictable affairs.

Figure 1.

Percent of National Samples Agreeing That "Members of Parliment Tend to Lose Touch with the People Soon After They are Elected" or That "The Goverment Doesn't Care What People Like Me Think", 1965-88

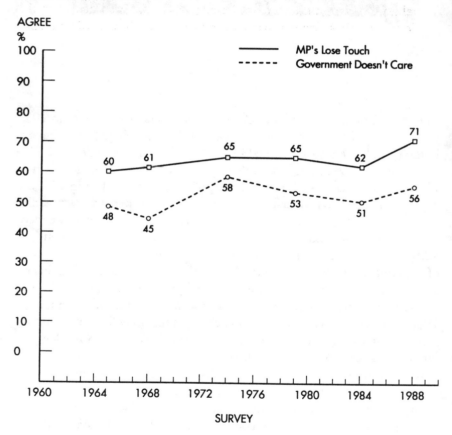

Canada has not been an easy country to govern, and its rulers have been rewarded with political defeat nearly as often as with victory. In these dozen elections which form the modern Canadian political era, five federal governments have been gone down to electoral defeat (St. Laurent in 1957, Diefenbaker in 1963, Trudeau in 1979, Clark in 1980, and Turner in 1984), and one more has come precariously close (Trudeau in 1972). Although the Liberals were the governing party for nearly two-thirds of the period since 1957 (20 of 31 years), their hold on power was only rarely more secure than that of their opponents. Even those governments which have enjoyed considerable political success have often found their standing with the mass public to be at risk. The most popular federal political leaders of the modern era — Diefenbaker and Trudeau — both faded quickly in public esteem during their early years in office, turning majority governments into minorities within four years of an overwhelming election victory. Virtually every federal government in the past two decades has found itself behind in the public opinion polls after less than two years in office.[2] In spite of his record majority achieved in the 1984 election, Brian Mulroney has fared little better in the affection of the public than his predecessors. At the beginning of 1988, the Conservatives stood third in the Gallup poll, preferred by only 28% of a national sample. Only 25 percent of that sample felt that Brian Mulroney was the best choice for Prime Minister.[3] The Liberals, led by the same John Turner who had brought his party to such a crushing defeat in the 1984 election, enjoyed a comfortable lead in the polls during much of Mulroney's first term in office, even though only 11% felt that Turner would be a better Prime Minister. Within but a few months of his 1988 election victory, Mulroney's Conservatives again found themselves trailing their adversaries in many polls.

I Volatility and Discontent I

The reasons for continued volatility in Canadian politics may be found in Canadians' attitudes toward government and in the nature of the Canadian party system. Studies of the Canadian public have long disclosed a highly negative view of the political world, and extensive discontent with government, parties, and politicians.[4] Many Canadians further believe that they have little say in the affairs of government, and that their representatives begin to "lose touch" with the people soon after being elected to office (Figure 1). Nevertheless, there has been a clear tendency to place much of

CANADIAN GOVERNMENT AND POLITICS

the blame for the problems of the country on the shoulders of those in power. Canadians of course are not in any sense unique among citizens of Western democracies in expressing discontent with government. But, while such prolonged discontent can sometimes lead to a withdrawal from the political process or the formation of protest movements, in Canada it has more often been manifested in a willingness to "throw the rascals out" when the opportunity arises.

The Canadian party system to a considerable degree magnifies and encourages this tendency toward volatility in elections. While most Canadians express some degree of allegiance toward a political party, relatively few are strongly partisan. In the 1984 national election study for example, only 23% of those surveyed were found to be "very strong" supporters of any political party, about the same proportion as were found in a 1965 study. Many Canadians hold different party attachments at the federal and provincial levels of government, a tendency that also explains some of the volatility in federal elections.[5] This phenomenon has increased in recent years, as distinct provincial parties such as the Parti Québecois in Quebec or Social Credit in British Columbia gained support. In the 1984 study, fully 35% of the national sample identified themselves with different parties at the federal and provincial levels. But even at the federal level alone, substantial numbers of Canadians are found to have changed their party identification at one time or another, sometimes over fairly short periods of time. Between 1974 and 1980 for example, a national panel study estimated that 41% of the electorate had either changed or abandoned their party identification over the six year period.[6]

These patterns are suggestive of the precariousness of the base of public support on which the parties depend. Using a classification scheme developed in *Political Choice in Canada*, we estimated in 1980 that slightly over a third of the Canadian electorate could be thought of as "durable" partisans — reasonably dependable, fairly strong, supporters of a particular party — while about two-thirds were "flexible" partisans, a voting group whose political allegiances were much more susceptible to change.[7] Flexible partisans are more likely to change their vote from one election to another and more likely to be influenced by short-term factors associated with particular issues, leaders, or events. While the existence of the durable partisans produces an element of stability from one election to another, the flexible partisans are a continuing potential source of sudden and unpredicatble change. In each of the last two elections, about two-thirds of the electorate continued to be made up of flexible partisans, thus tilting the electoral balance heavily in the direction of volatility and change.

TABLE 1

MULTIVARIATE ANALYSIS OF THE PROGRESSIVE CONSERVATIVE VOTE, 1979 AND 1988 FEDERAL ELECTIONS

	1979		1988	
	*r	Beta	r	Beta
REGION				
Atlantic	.04	.10	-.01	.03
Ontario	.15	.21	-.15	-.02
West	.20	.25	.06	.11
RELIGION				
Catholic	-.20	-.20	.01	-.09
Other non-Protestant	-.16	-.06	.03	.03
No religious affiliation	-.02	-.10	-.05	-.06
SOCIAL CLASS				
"Working class"	.00	-.03	-.07	-.04
Income (household)	.04	.05	.08	.06
Union membership (household)	-.02	-.04	-.04	-.07
Education (yrs)	.04	.06	.08	.08
LANGUAGE/ETHNICITY				
Francophone	-.22	-.06	.13	.23
Non-French, Non-English	-.03	-.03	-.01	.00
AGE (yrs)	.14	.14	-.03	-.04
GENDER (Female)	.02	.03	-.07	-.07
COMMUNITY SIZE (population)	-.07	-.06	-.01	.00
R^2		.15		.06

* The sign on the correlation coefficient (r) indicates whether the relationship is in a positive or negative direction. Catholics in 1979, for example, were less likely to vote Conservative than were other voters, while older persons were more likely to have done so. The strength of the relationship is indicated by the amount which the value of the statistic is above or below zero — the point at which no relationship at all exists. Interpretation of the regression coefficient (beta) is similar, except that it indicates the direction and strength of the relationship when all of the other variables have been controlled. Thus, Roman Catholics in 1979 were still less likely to vote Conservative than were other voters, even after all other factors such as region, language, and ethnicity had been taken into account.

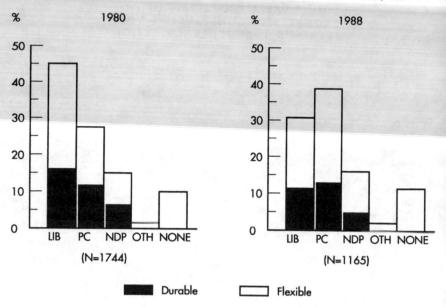

FIGURE 2. Direction of Party Identification in the Canadian Electorate. 1980, 1988

Although the fundamental characteristics of the Canadian electorate have changed relatively little over the past decade, its partisan political composition has changed quite markedly. More voters in 1988 thought of themselves as Progressive Conservatives than had been the case at the time of the 1980 federal election, and there were many fewer who identified themselves as Liberals (Figure 2). But this comparison is a potentially misleading one, because instability of partisan attachment over time has long been a characteristic of the political behaviour of many Canadians. What is somewhat more revealing is the fact that the two main parties remain close to equal in terms of the number of durable supporters associated with each of them (Figure 2). The flexible Conservative supporters of Brian Mulroney in 1984 or 1988 are potentially no more reliable in the longer term than were the flexible Liberals who abandoned Pierre Trudeau in 1972 or 1979.

I Parties and their Images I

In contrast to some European democracies, it has not been possible to explain very much of the dynamics of Canadian party politics by examining long-term forces such as social class, religion, or group alignments. Ideology has likewise been notably weak as a factor in Canadian partisanship, and the Canadian party system has long defied a simple, left-right characterization. A few long-term patterns, some of which may be fragments of past political alignments, have however continued to persist in the 1970's and 1980's. Catholics, for example, were somewhat less likely to vote Conservative in the 1979 election, just as they had been in nearly every election since such data have been available to researchers. Linguistic and regional patterns were also strong in that election, as has often been the case in national politics. But such factors, even when taken all together, were able to explain only fifteen percent of the variation in voting behaviour in the 1979 election (Table 1). This finding is similar to that reported in previous studies.[8] By 1988, such factors were capable together of explaining only six percent of the variation in Conservative support (Table 1), and the relative weight of the various forces had changed. In part because of the inroads made by the Conservatives in Quebec in the 1984 and 1988 elections, linguistic and regional patterns were quite different nine years later. Although social class related factors strengthened slightly in 1988, perhaps because of the free trade issue, the overall pattern was not very different. It would be an exercise in futility to attempt to predict with any degree of reliability the behaviour of Canadian voters on the basis of sociodemographic characteristics alone.

TABLE 2

THE STRUCTURE OF PARTY
IMAGES, 1974-1984

Percent *

	1974	1979	1984
Policy/issue	61	51	51
Style/performance	47	50	53
Leader/leadership	38	37	23
Parties/general	35	42	41
Area/group	28	27	34
Ideology	14	15	16
N =	(2445)	(2670)	(3380)

* Based on total sample. Multiple response.
Percentages do not add to 100%.

Canadian political parties cannot call upon legions of loyal supporters whose attitudes are reinforced by strong group or ideological commitments. Rather, they tend to act as "brokers" between competing interests, and attempt to harness a variety of rather unpredictable short-term forces in order to achieve their goals. Questions about the parties which have been employed in a number of the national election studies help to shed light on the way in which Canadians see political parties. Data from three of these studies are shown in Table 2. It may be seen that the largest component of the images which people hold of the various parties tends to be that of having to do with issues and public policy, followed closely by a category identified in Table 2 as "style" or "performance." The parties are most commonly viewed in terms of the dominant policies or issues of the day, and/or in terms of their performance, particularly when in government. The Liberals, for example, might have been condemned by some for their National Energy Program, and praised by others for "doing a good job" of managing the economy while in power. While some variation occurs from one election to another, depending to some extent on the specific types of issues emphasized in that election, policy and style/performance have consistently tended to be the dominant categories of images which the Canadian public holds of political parties.

Issues, however, have themselves demonstrated a high degree of volatility in federal politics.[9] Economic issues frequently dominate the political agenda in Canada, but they are not always the same economic issues. Each of the last four federal elections has seen an abrupt and dramatic shift in the particular issues which provided the main focus of the campaign and which contributed toward shaping the images which people held of the parties at the time. Not infrequently, parties have been able to manipulate issues for strategic purposes as the Conservatives did with unemployment in the 1984 election campaign or the Liberals sought to do with free trade in 1988. Sometimes, however, certain issues force themselves onto the agenda whether parties wish to emphasize them or not. But, knowing the issues which had been important in the thinking of parties and public alike in one election campaign would be of little help to the researcher in predicting the issues which are likely to arise in the next one. Parties seize upon the issues of the day, and shape their own political strategies around them.

Party leaders have also figured prominently in Canadians' perceptions of political parties. Through much of the seventies, various references to Trudeau (both positive and negative) predominated in this category. After his retirement, references to party leaders as a category declined somewhat, in part because Mulroney, Turner, and Broadbent were less well established political personalities in the public mind, and did not tend to ignite strong passions in quite the same way that Trudeau was capable of doing. This is not to suggest however that leaders have declined in importance. If anything, the pervasiveness of television and the use of televised debates between leaders in election campaigns has made them even more important. What is noteworthy is that images of political parties are shaped by current political trends, and can be subject to quite rapid change. Strong political leaders have often been able to reshape their parties around their own image. One of the quickest and surest ways for a Canadian political party to give itself a new image is to choose a new leader.

The party image data show that Canadians do not tend to think of the parties in ideological terms. References to groups or regions are also lower than the two larger categories (Table 2), and many of those that do occur are connected with current greivances. For the most part, the images which the public holds of political parties are ones which tend to be highly responsive to change over time. Images of parties connected with longer term social, historical, or ideological patterns are much less in evidence.

I The Voter Decides I

The picture of the Canadian electorate portrayed here is one with relatively weak long-term attachments to parties, low ideological commitment, and high responsiveness to short-term factors such as leaders, issues, or political events. Elections themselves however are major political events, and many of the attitudes of the voters toward parties and other political actors are shaped by things which are associated specifically with particular elections. There is often as much shifting of party preference and of voting choice between elections that have taken place at short intervals (1972-74 or 1979-80 for example) as between those that are further apart (such as 1974-79 or 1984-88).[10] Because its frame of reference is primarily short term, the public reacts mainly to events as they unfold rather than to ideological or other longer term stimuli. Only a quarter to a third of Canadian voters (primarily the durable partisans) may be said to have their minds made up with respect to voting choice well in advance of an election. A proportion of about equal size will make its decision at the time that the election is called. Sometimes, sizeable shifts in the public opinion polls will occur either directly or indirectly as a result of particular questions which may have precipitated the call of an election. Movement will also occur in response to the issues and events of the campaign itself, and in reaction to the activities of the parties and their leaders. As many as half of all voters may make their voting decisions during the course of an election campaign, with at least one in five reporting that their voting decision was made in the final

CANADIAN GOVERNMENT AND POLITICS

week (Table 3). Both the 1984 and 1988 elections saw considerable movement in the polls in the immediate period leading up to the election call. And, while the sharp movements in the polls which took place during the 1988 campaign were more extreme than normal, they are entirely consistent with the behaviour and characteristics of the Canadian electorate described in previous studies of elections.

The events leading up to the 1988 election can in fact be used to illustrate a number of the characteristics of the electorate described here. Following their massive victory in the 1984 election, the Conservatives quickly slipped in the public opinion polls, falling behind the Liberals for the first time as early as mid-1986. Like other federal governments of recent years, the Mulroney government provoked large negative public sentiment, an improving economy notwithstanding. Yet the prospects for its electoral recovery were always present, as the volatility of the polls in the pre-election period showed. However, the improvement in Conservative standing in the polls during the summer, which led to the election call, was due at least as much to the problems of the Liberals under John Turner as to better public perception of the Tories or of Brian Mulroney. In studies of the past several federal elections, reasons given by voters for switching from one party to another have often tended to be more negative than positive — an expression of discontent or disillusionment with a party previously supported rather than attraction to a party or leader.[11]

Thus, in the 1988 pre-campaign period, the perceptions of the party leaders, the state of the economy, and the ongoing debate on the free trade issue, among other factors, all accounted to some degree for the shifts in party popularity documented by the polls. But, as the campaign took hold, the activities of the leaders and the respective strategies of the parties began to affect the attitudes of the public. In particular, the televised leader debates and the rise of the free trade issue to a dominant position in the campaign were the types of events capable of producing sudden short-term swings among large numbers of voters. Opinion on the free trade issue itself began to shift, first in response to the events of the period following the signing of the agreement in January, and subsequently in response to the leader debates and the decision of the Liberals to make free trade the central element of their campaign strategy. The extremely sharp movement in the Gallup poll (Figure 3) which was taken immediately after the debates is indicative of the effect of these events. However, the recovery of the Conservatives through the last three weeks of the campaign, together with the volatility of the NDP vote, also shows that the 1988 election outcome was in some doubt almost until the very end. There were two different types of volatility at work here

| 312 |

— the shift of the attention of the electorate to a new issue, and the revision of opinions on the issue itself. The Globe-Environics poll, which tracked public opinion on the free trade issue closely throughout the 1988 campaign, showed 44% of their sample in favour of the agreement in the first week of October, and only 31% a few weeks later.[12] On free trade as on other political questions in Canada, only a minority of voters approached the issue from an ideological or strongly partisan perspective. The events of the 1988 election were perhaps unusual in their intensity and dramatic impact, but they were in many ways typical of the type of volatility which has been a feature of Canadian politics for the past three decades.

TABLE 3

REPORTED TIME OF VOTE DECISION
IN FIVE FEDERAL ELECTIONS, 1974-88

	1974 %	1979 %	1980 %	1984 %	1988 %
Before the election, "long time ago," etc.	25	38	28	32	33
When election was called [a]	30	13	37	27	24
Early-mid campaign period [b]	26	29	19	18	20
Final week, election day	19	20	16	23	23
N =	(932)	(999)	(635)	(2830)	(1047)

[a] Includes mentions of significant pre-election events, e.g. Trudeau's retirement or the conventions in 1984, events associated with the Crosbie budget or the defeat of the Clark government in 1980.
[b] Includes specific mentions of campaign events, such as the leader debates in 1979, 1984 or 1988.

Even an election which produces a seemingly high degree of parliamentary stability may frequently be shown to have exhibited much greater volatility at the level of the individual voter. In 1974, for example, the Conservative share of the total vote was virtually identical to that which they had received in the previous (1972) election (35%), and the party suffered a net decline of only eight parliamentary seats. Yet, beneath the surface of that result, studies found that there was considerable movement of Conservative voters between these two elections, and of supporters of the other parties as well.[13] Such a pattern in federal elections is a fairly commonplace one. In virtually every Canadian federal election for which adequate survey data exists, it can be shown that there was quite substantial movement among individual

| 313 |

voters, regardless of the outcome of that election. In some instances, gains and losses by each party among the same groups of voters might produce a pattern of relative aggregate stability. In others, the gains by one party in a particular region of the country, or among a specific group of voters, may be offset by losses among other groups or in other regions. Only in a few instances has the large degree of movement which appears common to nearly all recent federal elections in Canada been channeled in the same direction throughout the country and consistently worked to the benefit of one party at the expense of the others. When this happens, the electoral system will then produce large turnovers of seats and seeming electoral "landslides" like those of 1958 or 1984.

FIGURE 3. Party standings in the Gallup Poll, 1988

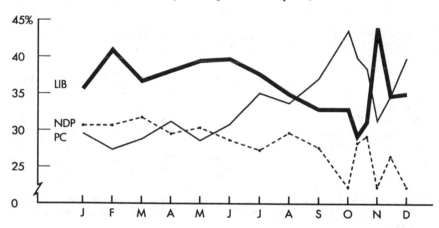

Some evidence of these patterns of voting change in Canada may be found In Table 4, which compares data on individual vote switching in three recent federal elections (Table 4, panel B). In the 1979 federal election for example, which replaced the Liberals with the short-lived minority Progressive Con-servative government of Joe Clark, slightly over one voter in four (27%) was found to have switched his/her vote from the previous (1974) election.[14] In 1984, the year of the Mulroney landslide, the comparable figure is slightly under one in three (31%). In the 1988 election, which saw wide swings in the polls both before and during the campaign, the percent of switchers was higher still (33%). Each of these figures is of course different, but it is not very different. This is especially true when it is considered that these three elections represent quite different outcomes, even though the Conservatives won all three. The percentage of voters switching is fairly high in each of

THE CANADIAN VOTER

them, but one (1988) produced a comfortable majority for the Conservatives, another (1984) a landslide victory, and the third (1979) a precarious
minority government.

TABLE 4

VOTING CHANGE IN THREE
FEDERAL ELECTIONS: 1979-88

	A. As % of total electorate			B. As % of voters in two elections only		
	1979	1984	1988	1979	1984	1988
	%	%	%	%	%	%
Voting for the same party as in previous election	55	52	53	73	69	67
Voting for different parties in two elections	20	23	27	27	31	33
Moving to or from non-voting	13	13	12			
New voters entering electorate	12	12	8			
N =	(2276)	(2693)	(1057)	(1691)	(1997)	(890)

The impact of change in elections is not of course limited to the switching
of votes from one election to the next, because the electorate itself is a
continually changing entity. In addition to the conversion of voters from the
support of one party to another, some voters are "replaced" in each election
both in the short term as a result of abstentions and in the longer term due
to the enfranchisement of new voters. Such effects are not trivial, but they
are relative constants in the equation of electoral change. New voters enter
the electorate in every election, varying only slightly in total numbers
depending upon the interval between elections and long-term population
trends. Voting turnout has tended to fluctuate only modestly in Canada from
one election to another, and has not thus far exhibited the downward trend
found in some other countries, notably the United States. On the other
hand, the approximate average of 75% of eligible Canadians who vote in
federal elections should not be taken to imply that it always is the same 75%.
There is a considerable degree of recirculation of non-voters in federal
elections over time, and the proportion of Canadians who are found not to
have voted in at least one of several elections over a period of time is quite
low.[15] There are therefore in each election a number of previous non-voters
who return to the electorate, and a number of previous voters who leave it.

CANADIAN GOVERNMENT AND POLITICS

Both of these effects have a somewhat moderating influence on change, since one would not expect all new voters or all previous non-voters to behave the same way in any given election. In fact, when these additional sources of change are taken into account, the three elections used as examples above begin to look even somewhat more alike in terms of patterns of individual behaviour (Table 4, panel A). The percentage of new voters entering the electorate in 1984 was about the same as in 1979, and turnout rates in these two elections were similar (76% in 1979, 75% in 1984), the proportion of former voters re-entering or leaving the electorate basically offsetting each other. Considered as a proportion of the total electorate however, rather than in terms of voters only, our estimate of the percentages of the Canadian electorate who might be said to represent stability in voting trends in each of these three elections ranges from a high of 55% in 1979 to a low of 52% in 1984, a range of only 3% across three very different elections. What differs in each of these three cases is the direction and impact of each of type of change, much more than its magnitude. But the differences are ones of degree only, since these basic types of change might be expected to be present in all elections.

I Into the Nineties I

It is important to examine some of these larger scale changes in the Canadian electorate, as well as those which take place at the level of the individual voter. As noted earlier, what we call "the electorate" is a constantly (but gradually) changing entity. Population growth is potentially an important catalyst of change, even though younger voters have for the most part not shown characteristics of partisanship or behaviour that would distinguish them from older cohorts.[16] The lowering of the voting age to 18 in 1970, coupled with higher post-war birth rates, had the effect of adding over two million new voters to the electorate at each four or five year interval since 1968. Immigration has been a smaller, although also important, source of population change. At the time of the 1984 election, one-third of the eligible electorate was under the age of thirty, and a majority had come of voting age during what might be called "the Trudeau years." This is already beginning to change. Although lower birth rates have now slowed down the growth of the electorate, nearly one and one-half million new voters were added to the enumeration lists in 1988. Combined with the larger number (about 2.3 million) who became eligible in 1984, more than one Canadian voter in five first voted in an election since Trudeau's retirement from public

THE CANADIAN VOTER

office. In 1988, about 38% of the electorate were "Trudeau era" voters, while the remaining 62% came from generations both older and younger (Figure 4). The mixture of old and new represented by the approximately seventeen and a half million Canadians who were eligible to participate in the 1988 election reflects both the demographic and the political trends of recent years.

FIGURE 4 : Age/Cohort Composition of the Canadian Electorate, 1988

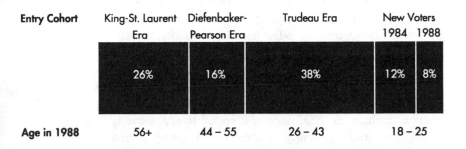

Entry Cohort	King-St. Laurent Era	Diefenbaker- Pearson Era	Trudeau Era	New Voters 1984	1988
	26%	16%	38%	12%	8%
Age in 1988	56+	44 – 55	26 – 43	18 – 25	

The combination of substantial generational change in the electorate and back-to-back Conservative election victories in 1984 and 1988 leads naturally to speculation regarding the potential for long-term realignment of the Canadian party system. Continued Conservative strength in the West, the solid (and subsequently sustained) 1984 breakthrough in Quebec, the departure of Trudeau, the growth of NDP support, all might be factors contributing to permanent changes in the relative strength of Canadian parties. Such a conclusion however is at best premature and more than likely wrong. There is little indication in Canada to date of party realignment, and considerable evidence of the persistence of what is often called "dealignment" in the electorate. Although the Conservatives have pulled ahead of the Liberals in terms of the total number of identifiers with the party (Figure 1), party identification in Canada has tended to display nearly as much volatility over time as the vote itself.[16] Over the twenty years for which national survey data have been available, there has emerged little evidence of lasting long-term change in the electorate. Volatility in the electorate of the nineties is very likely to continue to be as high as that of the seventies and eighties.

| 317 |

In part, this is because the generational changes noted above, although substantial in size, have done little to change the fundamental characteristics of the electorate. Younger voters are not greatly different from older cohorts in terms of direction, strength, or stability or partisanship. Indeed, those differences which do emerge between various generational groupings would not tend to suggest any substantial realignment of the Canadian party system in the wake of the 1984 and 1988 election results. While the Liberals have lost party adherents (as well as voters) since 1974, particularly among those voters who entered the electorate during the Trudeau years, many of these could easily return to the party in future. The Conservatives have generally not done as well among younger cohorts of voters as with older groups, although they closed this gap somewhat in 1988. Nevertheless, there is nothing in recent studies to suggest the emergence of a new Conservative generation of voters. The NDP has likewise failed to make any significant breakthrough among the younger age groups, although its position in this regard likewise improved somewhat at the expense of the Liberals in 1988. But the NDP's overall support in elections still continues to be about 10 to 15 percent more unstable than does that of the other two parties.[17] For many Canadians, an NDP vote has tended to represent a "protest" motivated by current grievances, rather than a lasting partisan commitment. Like the Liberals and Conservatives, the NDP has its "durable" supporters but must also compete anew in each election for the votes of those whose decision is determined by the politics of the moment. While it is too soon to evaluate the prospects of newer parties such as the Reform Party, past voting patterns as well as the tendency of the electoral system to discriminate against "third" parties would not suggest a bright future. Parties such as Social Credit have sometimes managed to hold a regional or provincial base of support for more than one election in the past, but have not succeeded in transforming the Canadian party system.

It is likely that the Canadian party system of the near future will continue to reflect the trends of the recent past, and to be subject to influences from new problems, policies, or leaders. The proportion of flexible partisans in the electorate continues to be high, and it is high in virtually every age cohort, every region of the country, and every significant voting group. The Canadian electorate of the nineties and beyond will almost certainly be one in which the responsiveness to short term factors such as issues, party performance and style, the personalities of leaders, or the intrusion of new political events is much greater than its responsiveness to ideology, group loyalty, or other longer term forces.

NOTES

[1] The discussion and analyses in this chapter are based on surveys of the Canadian public which have been conducted following every national election since 1965, with the exception of 1972. All of these studies were funded by the Social Sciences and Humanities Research Council of Canada. The 1965 study was conducted by John Meisel, Philip Converse, Maurice Pinard, Peter Regenstreif, and Mildred Schwartz, and the 1968 study was conducted by John Meisel. Some of the work based on these two studies is reported in John Meisel, *Working Papers In Canadian Politics* (Montreal, McGill-Queen's Press, 1975). The 1974, 1979, and 1980 studies were conducted by Harold Clarke, Jane Jenson, Lawrence LeDuc and Jon Pammett. Analyses based on these studies may be found in Clarke, et al., *Political Choice in Canada* (Toronto, McGraw-Hill Ryerson, 1979, 1980) and *Absent Mandate* (Toronto, Gage, 1984). The 1984 national election study was conducted by Ronald Lambert, Steven Brown, James Curtis, Barry Kay and John Wilson. A preliminary report of findings from this study may be found in Kay, et al., "The Character of Electoral Change," paper presented to the annual meeting of the Canadian Political Science Association, University of Montreal, 1984. A short reinterview of respondents from the 1984 study was conducted following the 1988 election by Ronald Lambert, Steven Brown, James Curtis, Barry Kay, Lawrence LeDuc and Jon Pammett. Some of the preliminary results of this study may be found in Jon Pammett, "The 1988 Vote" in Alan Frizzell, Jon Pammett and Anthony Westell, *The Canadian General Election of 1988* (Ottawa, Carleton University Press, 1989). A larger 1988 study was conducted by Richard Johnston, Andre Blais, and Jean Crete. Some preliminary findings of their study may be found in Johnston, et al., "Free Trade and the Dynamics of the 1988 Canadian Election" paper presented to the annual meeting of the American Political Science Association, Atlanta, 1989. Field work for the 1965-1984 studies was carried out by Canadian Facts, Ltd. under the direction of Mary Auvinen. Field work for the 1988 reinterview was done by the Carleton University School of Journalism Survey Centre under the direction of Alan Frizzell, and for the 1988 Johnston-Blais-Crete study by the Institute for Social Research, York University. Neither the principal investigators of any of these studies, the SSHRC, nor the survey units are responsible for the analyses or interpretations of the data presented here.

[2] *The Gallup Report*, monthly surveys. A summary of these for the period 1974-1983 may be found in Clarke, et al., *Absent Mandate*, p. 186 and for the period 1984-1988 in Alan Frizzell, "The Perils of Polling," in Frizzell, et al., *The Canadian General Election of 1988*, p. 92.

[3] *The Gallup Report*, January-March, 1988.

[4] *Absent Mandate*, Chapter 2.

[5] *Political Choice in Canada*, Chapter 5, 10. See also *Absent Mandate*, Chapter 3.

[6] Lawrence LeDuc, Harold Clarke, Jane Jenson and Jon Pammett, "Partisan Instability in Canada: Evidence From a New Panel Study," *American Political*

Science Review 78 (1984) pp. 471-83.

[7] Political Choice in Canada, Chapter 5. Absent Mandate, pp. 56-58.

[8] Political Choice in Canada, Chapter 4. See also Richard Rose, Electoral Behavior: a Comparative Handbook (Glencoe: Free Press, 1974), and William Irvine and Howard Gold, "Do Frozen Cleavages Ever Go Stale?" British Journal of Political Science, 10 (1980) pp. 213-25.

[9] See Harold Clarke, Kal Hildebrandt, Lawrence LeDuc and Jon Pammett, "Issue Volatility and Partisan Linkages in Canada, Great Britain, the United States and West Germany," European Journal of Political Research, 13 (1985) pp. 237-63. A discussion of the volatility of issues in the 1974-1980 period may also be found in Absent Mandate, ch. 4.

[10] Absent Mandate, pp. 152-58.

[11] Ibid. pp. 142-45.

[12] The Globe and Mail, November 12, 1988.

[13] Political Choice in Canada, pp. 238-42.

[14] Absent Mandate, pp. 252-58.

[15] Political Choice in Canada, pp. 66-68 and 204-05.

[16] See Lawrence LeDuc, "Canada: the Politics of Stable Dealignment," in Russell Dalton, Scott Flanagan and Paul Allen Beck (eds.), Electoral Change in Advanced Industrial Democracies (Princeton University Press, 1984).

[17] Ibid. See also LeDuc, et al., "Partisan Instability in Canada..." and LeDuc, "The Dynamic Properties of Party Identification: a Four Nation Comparison," European Journal of Political Research, 9 (1981), pp. 257-68.

[18] Political Choice in Canada, p. 240 and Absent Mandate, pp. 156-58.

ANNOTATED READINGS

Clarke, Harold D., Jane Jenson, Lawrence LeDuc, and Jon H. Pammett. *Political Choice in Canada*. Toronto, McGraw-Hill Ryerson, 1979, 1980. A study of the attitudes and behaviour of the 1974 Canadian electorate investigating topics such as regional identity, political efficacy and participation, partisanship and voting.

Clarke, Harold D., Jane Jenson, Lawrence LeDuc, and Jon H. Pammett. *Absent Mandate: the Politics of Discontent in Canada*. Toronto, Gage, 1984. Examines the forces of stability and change in Canadian politics during the 1974-80 period, and considers the effects of elections on public policy.

Dalton, Russell, Scott Flanagan, and Paul Allen Beck. *Electoral Change in Advanced Industrial Democracies*. Princeton University Press, 1984. Analyzes changing patterns of electoral politics in 12 countries including Canada and the potential for realignment or dealignment of established party systems.

Frizzell, Allan, Jon H. Pammett and Anthony Westell. *The Canadian General Election of 1988*. Ottawa, Carleton University Press, 1989. An examination of the 1988 federal election campaign, including chapters on the parties, the media, public opinion polls, and an analysis of the vote. A similar volume was compiled by Frizzell and Westell for the 1984 election. Carleton University Press, 1985.

Harrop, Martin and William L. Miller. *Elections and Voters*. London, Macmillan, 1987. A comparative introduction to the study of elections and voting behaviour drawing on a wide variety of studies in North America and Western Europe.

Penniman, Howard, ed. *Canada at the Polls: 1984*. Duke University Press, 1988. A collection of articles on the 1984 election, dealing with the campaigns waged by the parties, the role of the media, and other topics. Similar volumes were compiled by the same editor on the 1979-80 and 1974 elections, and published by the American Enterprise Institute, Washington D.C. These books are part of the "At the Polls" series of studies of national elections throughout the world.

| CHAPTER 17 |

THE ADMINISTRATION
OF JUSTICE

IAN GREENE

When I was in graduate school and trying to choose a thesis topic, I asked Professor Peter Russell for advice. Russell — undoubtedly the father of the study of law and politics in Canada — suggested the administration of justice. My heart sank because it struck me as one of the driest topics imaginable. (No doubt some readers had the same reaction when encountering the title of this chapter — except, of course, for the budding lawyers among you.) After an initial investigation of the topic, however, I changed my mind. I was surprised to learn that reality in the justice system is rather different from my original expectations. This is because the system has taken on a life somewhat independent from its original goal, which was to provide a state-sponsored means for settling disputes so that social order could be maintained. My primary objective in this chapter is to impart to the readers some of my fascination with the justice system.

The judicial process is only one means of dispute resolution — the other peaceful means being negotiation, mediation and arbitration. In negotiation, two disputing parties attempt to resolve their dispute without the aid of a neutral third party; as well, they do not necessarily look to objective standards, and there is often no enforcement mechanism. In mediation, the parties turn to a third party for help, but that person simply assists the two parties to negotiate. In arbitration, the neutral third party may impose a settlement, but the arbitrator is not usually bound by the same strict set of objective standards — the whole body of law — as a judge. The chapter will begin by considering the unique features of adjudication. The spotlight will then shift to the court structure, judges (selection and role), and the judicial decision-making process. In the concluding section, I will challenge readers to consider whether the justice system is functioning as well as it could in the context of the Canadian version of liberal democratic government.[1]

I Adjudication I

The process of decision-making in a court is known as "adjudication." Adjudication is a process by which the two parties in a dispute (the litigants) put their case before a neutral third party (the judge). The judge makes a decision based on an objective set of standards (the law). The judge's decision can be enforced by the coercive powers of the state. Usually one party wins, and the other loses. Unlike mediation or even arbitration, decisions which result in compromises are rare. The judge must decide by (1) determining the facts of the case, and then (2) applying the law to the facts.

Most countries in the world have created courts to adjudicate disputes as a way of preserving social order and promoting fairness, factors which are essential to facilitate both business activities and interpersonal relations. There are two kinds of disputes which may be adjudicated: public law disputes (disputes in which the government is a party, such as criminal law, administrative law, and constitutional law cases) and private law disputes (disputes between two private persons, such as disputes involving real estate transactions, contracts, family law, and suits for negligence).

In private law cases, adjudication is ideally the dispute resolution method of last resort to be used only when negotiation, mediation or arbitration are impossible or fail. The adjudicative service is provided by the state so that a method of last resort will be available, so that private disputes can be settled without the disruption of public order.

In public law cases involving disputes between the state and private citizens, countries adhering to the principle of the "rule of law" submit these disputes to adjudication to promote the perception that the government is fair. The rule of law means that government officials may act only as authorized by legitimate laws — which means laws enacted by elected legislatures in democracies like Canada — and that the law must be applied

CANADIAN GOVERNMENT AND POLITICS

equally to everyone. The use of adjudication to resolve disputes between, for example, the law enforcement authorities and the persons they accuse of crimes is intended to ensure that the rule of law is adhered to.

Two great adjudicative systems have developed in the world: the common law system and the civil law system.

THE COMMON LAW SYSTEM

The common law system is based on the judicial system of England and Wales, the origins of which can be traced to the time of King Henry II in the twelfth century. Henry inherited a justice system based primarily on local, traditional courts, so that the rules of commerce and the criminal law varied from one locality to another. Such a system not only discouraged inter-regional trade in England, but it also promoted disunity. Henry and his advisory council created legislation to standardize some of the criminal and trade laws across England, and the council itself heard disputes arising out of these laws.

The new legal system became a victim of its own success. Before long, more disputes were brought to the Council than it could handle, and the King's council experienced a "caseload crisis" not unlike backlog problems in today's courts. Travelling justices were appointed to relieve the pressure on the Council and to provide a more convenient dispute-resolution service to the King's subjects. As caseload pressures continued, central courts separate from the King's council were created. The travelling judges together with the judges of the central courts had jurisdiction to settle certain disputes even in the absence of decrees from the King's council. Records were kept of their decisions, and judges began to refer to these records of old cases when deciding new cases. As much as possible, the precedents set by the old cases were followed in the new cases according to the principle of *stare decisis*. This judge-made law became known as the "common law," because it was judge-made law which the judges applied to everyone.

According to the rules of *stare decisis*, as they have developed over the centuries, every court must follow the precedents established by a higher court in the same court system, and the precedents of the highest court "trump" those of any lower courts. In the absence of conflicting precedents established by a higher court, a court usually follows its own precedents. The precedents of higher or equal status courts in another common law jurisdiction are influential, but not binding. (Therefore, American Bill of Rights precedents are often cited in Canadian Charter of Rights cases, but they are only sometimes followed.) Precedents must be followed only when the facts in the current case and the precedent case are substantially the same. If a judge considers the facts in a current case to be significantly different, the judge may "distinguish" the precedent, and decide the case differently. All courts in Canada must follow precedents established by the Supreme Court. The Supreme Court itself almost always follows its own precedents. In the mid-1970s, the Court announced that it might occasionally overrule its own precedents (or those established by the Judicial Committee of the Privy Council in London, England, which was Canada's highest court of appeal until 1949) if it considered those precedents to be clearly wrong or inappropriate. Since that time, the Supreme Court has overruled fewer than ten precedents.[2] Such overruling will not occur frequently because it would destroy the predictability of the adjudicative system. However, because judges can distinguish appropriate precedents, *stare decisis* is not quite as rigid as it might first appear.

In addition to *stare decisis*, a second essential characteristic of the common law world is the adversary system. According to the adversarial approach, it is the responsibility of the litigants to present the judge or judges with all the facts and theory that they need to make a decision. Judges may not carry out an independent investigation of the facts. Although they may research legal theory and precedents on their own, they are not usually provided with many resources to do this, and they are expected to rely primarily on the information presented by counsel representing the litigants.

It has only been in recent years that Supreme Court of Canada judges and provincial appeal court judges have been assigned law clerks to assist the judges with their legal research. Lower court judges rarely have such assistance. As a result, judicial decisions about the constitution often seem to take into account only a limited range of possibilities. This is usually because the lawyers presenting the case have narrowed the possibilities in advance, often through a lack of familiarity with the policy issues associated with constitutional questions.

In the U.S. Supreme Court, law clerks often play a major role in formulating judicial decisions. Some Supreme Court justices do little more than proofread the decisions written by their fresh-out-of-college clerks.[3] Law clerks do not play nearly as influential a role in appeal court decision-making in Canada, however.

A third characteristic of the common law system is that judges do not receive specialized training in judging, but are appointed from among the ranks of lawyers. This tradition dates from thirteenth-century England. Earlier in that century, the quality of the king's judges began to deteriorate, perhaps because the kings were too busy with crusades and disputes with nobles to give the courts the attention they needed. The judges and court officials were poorly paid, and even though all the judges were clergymen, they almost inevitably resorted to accepting bribes. At the end of the twelfth century, there was a public outcry about corruption in the judicial system. In response King Edward I appointed a Royal Commission to investigate in 1289, thus setting a precedent to be followed by governments for centuries thereafter when confronted with public dissatisfaction with the administration of justice. The commission found that about half of the judges in the common law courts were corrupt, and Edward fired them. He decided to look outside the clergy for replacement judges. Since the time of Henry II, a group of legal specialists had been developing who specialized in advising litigants about how to proceed in the increasingly complex judicial system. Edward appointed some of these "lawyers" to fill the vacancies in the judiciary. Edward's solution to the crisis soon became a tradition. By early in the fourteenth century, lawyers had completely displaced clerics as judges in all but one of the royal courts.

The common law world includes most commonwealth countries and the United States; the rest of the world has adopted the civil law system.

THE CIVIL LAW SYSTEM

The civil law system began to develop in continental Europe during the past several centuries. University scholars had become fascinated with Roman law, and they urged governments to adopt uniform codes of law based on the old Roman codes. For example, Napoleon I supervised the codification of French private and criminal law into a unified French **Code Civil**. The civil codes are organized in a logical sequence, from general principles to specific rules of law.

Judges in civil law countries generally receive specialized training as judges; it is not assumed that the training and experience of a lawyer by itself is adequate for judicial duties. In France, for example, those who want to become judges attend basic law school for a year; then they may attend the National School for Jurists if their score is high enough on an admissions exam. After a year at the School and a year and a half as an apprentice, they are appointed as a judge in one of the lower courts.

A characteristic of civil law systems is that civilian judges place much less emphasis on precedent than common law judges. According to the civil law approach, whenever the Code Civil is unclear judges should look for guidance to the general principles in the Code, the reports of the framers of the Code, and scholarly writings before researching precedents. Another difference between the two systems is that Civilian judges may often conduct their own investigations of the facts of a case; this is known as the "inquisitorial approach." They need not rely entirely on evidence presented by counsel for the opposing sides.

Canada's legal system incorporates elements of both the common law and civil law approaches, although the former definitely overshadows the latter. After conquering Quebec in 1759, the British authorities attempted to obtain the support of Quebeckers by allowing the colony to maintain its civil legal system in the private law field. Today, Quebec's legal system still adheres to the civil law approach for private law matters, although the inquisitorial style of adjudication is not nearly as evident as in other civil law countries, and precedent plays a larger role because of the influence of the common law approach. With regard to public law, Quebec is a common law jurisdiction. The other provinces and the federal government are all common law jurisdictions. The Supreme Court of Canada, which is required by law to have three judges from Quebec, acts as a civil law court when it hears private law appeals from Quebec and as a common law court the rest of the time.

THE CANADIAN COURT STRUCTURE

The architects of the Canadian federation faced a dilemma when it came to designing the court system. They could have established one system of courts for disputes arising out of federal laws and another for those arising from provincial laws. The United States provides an example of such a "dual" court system. The dual system seems to cater to the logic of federalism, but establishing two court systems creates additional expenses and is confusing to litigants who may end up taking their disputes to the wrong court. The Fathers of Confederation rejected the dual court model in favour of what Peter Russell calls an "integrated" court structure. The goal of the integrated approach is to allow for most cases arising out of both federal and provincial laws to be heard in the same court system, a system for which both the federal and provincial governments have some responsibilities.

The 1867 constitution granted the federal Parliament the power to establish a Supreme Court of Canada (which it did in 1875), as well as other courts to hear non-criminal cases arising out of federal laws. Besides the Supreme Court with its nine judges, there are two other courts established by Parliament — the Federal Court (with 27 judges) and the Tax Court (with 15). Most Federal Court cases deal with federal administrative law issues. Ottawa is responsible for providing the administrative support services for the Supreme Court of Canada, the Federal Court and the Tax

Court, as well as for appointing and paying all the judges to these courts. The Supreme Court sits only in Ottawa, while the Federal and Tax courts travel between Ottawa and the provincial capitals. As of April 1, 1990, Supreme Court of Canada judges earned $166,800 per year, and Federal Court judges earned $140,400.

FIGURE 1 : Canada's Court Structure

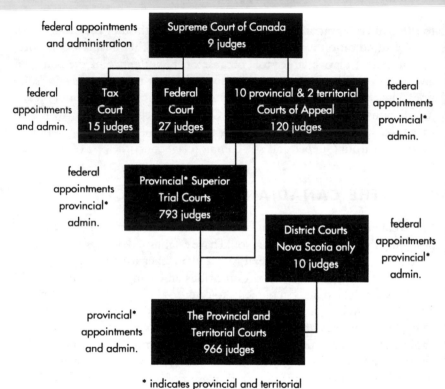

* indicates provincial and territorial

All of the other courts in Canada are established by provincial or territorial legislatures and their administrative support is provided by these governments. These provincial and territorial courts, which among them employ nearly 1,900 judges, conduct all trials for cases arising out of federal, provincial or territorial laws (except for the relatively few cases which are heard by the Federal Court or the Tax Court). There are two basic types of courts which the provincial and territorial legislatures have created:

THE ADMINISTRATION OF JUSTICE

"superior" courts and "inferior" courts. The superior courts have jurisdiction over the most serious criminal cases including jury trials, civil or private law cases except for small claims cases (which are cases involving from $500 to $15,000, depending on the province or territory) and appeals from the inferior courts. Superior court judges are distinguished by their titles. They are usually referred to as "Madame Justice" or "Mr. Justice" rather than "Judge," and are personally addressed in court as "My Lady" or "My Lord" instead of "Your Honour," a title reserved for inferior court judges. (Superior court judges are not *bona fide* "lords" as are British superior court judges, but most persons address them as in the British example out of deference to tradition.)

Even though the superior courts are established and administered by provincial and territorial authorities, their judges are appointed and paid by the federal government. This federal involvement in the provincial court system was Canada's way of avoiding the creation of a dual court system while providing both the federal and provincial authorities with roles in the administration of justice. (This model has been copied, with modifications, in Australia and India.) The superior courts have trial and appeal divisions. The trial divisions are known by such names as "Queen's Bench," "Supreme Court," or "High Court." The appeal divisions are usually known as "The Court of Appeal" of the province or territory.

Because Canada's courts are modeled on those of England and Wales, we inherited a system in which some judges travel on circuit. Many superior court judges in England and Wales were travelling judges who held "assizes," or hearings in the major county centres at least twice a year. If litigants did not wish to wait for an assize, they could travel to London where the superior courts sat more frequently. Prior to Confederation, the colonial governments in what were to become Canada's provinces established superior courts on the English model, with travelling judges holding assizes in county towns twice a year. Because travel to provincial capitals was difficult in the early years, citizens demanded that judges be appointed permanently to sit in major centres outside the capitals. In 1794, Lieutenant Governor Simcoe established a number of "district" courts in the major centres in Upper Canada. The judges in these courts had an "inferior" status, but were empowered to hear many of the kinds of cases which superior court judges would otherwise hear. Litigants could often choose between having a case settled before a district court judge, or waiting for a superior court judge's assize.

At one time, all provinces except Quebec had District Courts (sometimes known as County Courts). Since 1975, all of these provinces except for Nova

Scotia have merged their county and district courts with their superior courts. County and District court judges are appointed by the federal government.

There are approximately 800 provincial superior, county and district trial court judges in Canada. The superior court judges earn $140,400 per year, while the county and district court judges earn $135,400.

Every province and territory has at one time had an inferior court known as the "Provincial Court" or "Territorial Court." It should be kept in mind that there are three kinds of courts established by the provinces. From "lowest" to "highest," these are the "Provincial," "county and district," and "superior" courts. The fact that the provinces have chosen to name one kind of court "*the* Provincial Court" is confusing to many. The Provincial and Territorial Courts are by far the busiest in the country, hearing over 90% of all cases. The Ontario and Quebec legislatures have recently renamed their provincial courts the "Ontario Court of Justice, Provincial Division," and the "Court of Quebec," respectively. Most of the cases heard in these Provincial courts are minor to moderately serious violations of the federal Criminal Code, as well as provincial offences such as highway traffic violations. The Provincial Court judges are appointed and paid by the provincial governments. There are nearly 1,000 Provincial and Territorial Court judges in Canada, and they earn between $70,000 and $115,000 per year, depending on the province in which they preside.

Federally-appointed judges must be selected from among lawyers who have been qualified to practice law by a provincial or territorial law society for at least ten years. They must retire at age 75. Prior to the 1960s, the provincial legislatures did not require magistrates to be lawyers. Since the transformation of magistrates' courts into the Provincial Courts, all provincial legislatures except in Alberta and Newfoundland have required that Provincial Court judges be selected from among the Bar. Even in these two provinces, however, very few non-lawyers are appointed.[5] The usual retirement age of Provincial Court Judges is 70.

Reform-minded political scientists and judges such as Russell, Millar, Baar and Zuber have criticized the provincial court systems for being too hierarchical, too difficult for the average citizen to understand, and too fragmented to allow efficient operation.[6] Former Ontario Attorney General Ian Scott of Ontario was the only provincial Attorney General in this century who has attempted a major restructuring of the provincial court system. In 1989, following the recommendations of the 1987 **Zuber Commission Report**, Scott announced some sweeping reforms. The first phase of the reform, presently underway, creates an Ontario Court of Justice which includes all

THE ADMINISTRATION OF JUSTICE

judges other than those in the Court of Appeal. This court has two divisions: General and Provincial. The General Division includes all superior judges (except those on the Court of Appeal) and all District Court judges. The Provincial Division is formed from the old Provincial Court.

Besides the change in name, this reform has two major aspects to it which may impact on court reform in the other provinces. First, the administrative services for all the courts have been merged and reorganized on a regional basis rather than a "level of court" basis. Although this may sound like a fairly innocuous change, it actually has far-reaching implications. Prior to this reform, each level of court in each Ontario city had its own separate staff, leading to inefficiency and unnecessary expense. (This separation of court services is still the norm in most other parts of Canada.) The merger of court administrative services was resisted in the past by many judges, lawyers and court staff because of a reluctance to disturb the traditional pecking order. Second, it was Scott's hope eventually to merge the General and Provincial Divisions into one court. The cooperation of the federal government will be required to bring about this unified court because the Provincial Division judges will need federal appointments in order to attain the same status and jurisdiction as the General Division judges. If federal cooperation is attained, Ontario will be left with just two courts: the Ontario Court of Justice which will handle all civil and criminal trials, and the Court of Appeal.

This proposal is controversial because some in the legal community consider the superior court judges to be "better" judges, so that the quality of justice will be "watered down" by a merger of courts. Others, most notably Peter Russell, point out that the lower courts hear the great majority of cases in which ordinary Canadians are involved in. From this perspective, merger is likely to improve the chances that the quality of justice services provided will be equally available to all Canadians.[7] Thus, Scott's reforms can be considered as a testing-ground for court reform in Canada. It will be worth following the successes and failures of the Ontario reforms as they unfold.

CANADIAN GOVERNMENT AND POLITICS

| Judges |

APPOINTMENTS

The Canadian constitution gives the provincial governments the power to appoint Provincial Court judges, and the "Governor General" the power to appoint provincial superior and district court judges, as well as the judges of the federal courts (Supreme Court of Canada, Federal Court and Tax Court). In practice, the Governor General's appointing power is carried out by the federal cabinet, with the Minister of Justice and Prime Minister playing the leading roles. Decisions about the Chief Justice positions in provincial superior courts and the federal courts, however, are the sole prerogative of the Prime Minister.

Until recently, political patronage was the major factor in almost all of the federal and provincial judicial appointments. For example, 54 percent of the Quebec Court of Appeal judges between 1867 and 1972 had previously been cabinet ministers or elected legislators,[8] and a third of all judges appointed by the federal government in Ontario, Quebec and Manitoba between 1905 and 1970 had previously run for elected office — most for the party that made the judicial appointment.[9] Patronage is a less important factor now than two decades ago, but only somewhat less. In 1985, the Canadian Bar Association reported that patronage remained an important factor in judicial appointments by provincial governments in the three maritime provinces, Ontario, Manitoba and Saskatchewan. As well, concerning federal judicial appointments patronage was *not* a "significant factor" only in British Columbia, Quebec and the Supreme Court of Canada.[10] Recent research has shown that the patronage factor was as strong in the first Mulroney government as it had been during the Trudeau years.[11] The fact that patronage has remained the basis for judicial appointments for so many years indicates that it did not necessarily produce bad judges. It was just that the pool of potential judges was limited to lawyers who had paid their dues by working for the party in power.

The first crack in the patronage system appeared in 1967, when Justice Minister Pierre Trudeau began to consult the Canadian Bar Association about the suitability of persons being considered for judgeships. A committee of the Bar Association would rate the persons on the list provided by Trudeau as "well qualified," "qualified" or "not qualified." The government would then use this advice as it saw fit. This consultative approach remained in effect until 1988, and there is only one report of someone rated as "not qualified" being appointed during that time. Even with this

| 332 |

approach, however, patronage remained the prime determinant of judicial appointments because the Minister of Justice decided which names to submit to the Canadian Bar Association for review. Nevertheless, the reformed system did ensure that ability would play a greater role in federal judicial appointments than previously.

Patronage in federal judicial appointments became a key factor in deciding the outcome of the 1984 federal election. During the televised debate between John Turner and Brian Mulroney, Mulroney criticized Turner for appointing five Liberal MPs to the bench not long after Turner became Prime Minister. Turner said that he had no choice. Former Prime Minister Trudeau was planning to make the appointments before leaving office, but this would have left Turner, the new Prime Minister, without a majority of seats in the House of Commons. To save the Liberal majority Trudeau agreed not to make the appointments as long as Turner agreed to appoint the judges after the election was called. Mulroney accused Turner of failing to do the "right thing," and promised that if he were elected, he would base judicial appointments on merit rather than patronage.

This promise led to the establishment of consultative committees on judicial appointments in each of the provinces in 1988. The five-person committees (composed of representatives of the provincial or territorial law society, the Canadian Bar Association, the federal judiciary, the provincial or territorial Attorney General and the federal Minister of Justice) replaced consultation with the Canadian Bar Association. The consultative committees were not empowered to search for good judicial candidates, but only to investigate the credentials of those persons who had filed an application for a judgeship with the Commissioner of Federal Judicial Affairs. During the first year of operation of the new system, the government did not publicly advertise the new appointment procedure. As a result, most of the applicants which the new consultative committees considered were those who were already on file with the Minister of Justice under the old system. The result is that patronage remains a major ingredient in federal judicial appointments. This situation is not likely to change unless the consultative committees are given the power not only to screen candidates presented by the federal executive, but also to actively recruit good candidates to apply for judicial positions.

The provincial governments in B.C., Alberta, Ontario, Quebec and Newfoundland have been the most successful in abolishing patronage in their judicial appointments procedures. Beginning in the 1970s, these provincial governments began establishing judicial selection committees (often called Judicial Councils) — usually composed of a combination of lawyers, judges and lay persons — to assist in the judicial appointment process.[12] These committees consider not only the names submitted by the Attorney General, they also actively seek well-qualified candidates. In Ontario, for example, the Judicial Appointments Advisory Committee established in 1988 under the chairmanship of Peter Russell advertises for lawyers to apply for vacant Provincial judicial positions. After interviewing the most promising candidates, the committee draws up a short list of the most qualified candidates and presents the list via the Ontario Judicial Council to the Attorney General. The committee bases its recommendations on the applicants' "professional excellence…, community involvement and social awareness. It does not, however, attach any importance to candidates' political connections."[13]

When he was Justice Minister, Ramon Hnatyshyn rejected the suggestion that the federal consultative committees should be involved in judicial recruitment, as opposed merely to the screening of candidates. He claimed that in the five provinces where the committees are involved in recruitment, the committees do not consider as wide a range of candidates as is the case under the old patronage system.[14] It is important for Canadians to consider which system is most likely to result in the best judges, and to let their MPs and MLAs know how they feel about this important issue.

An issue related to judicial selection is judicial promotion or "elevation" as judges prefer to call it. This refers to the promotion of a lower court judge to a higher court, or the appointment of a junior judge to an administrative position such as Chief Judge or Justice. In common law countries some consider it inappropriate to promote judges from lower courts to higher ones. The reasoning is that if promotions were common, judges might decide cases in order to please the authority who may grant the promotion (the federal Minister of Justice). In fact, only four percent of the federally appointed judges in the three central provinces appointed between 1905 and 1970 were elevated from the Provincial Court.[15] It is more common for judges to be elevated from a superior trial court to an appeals court. About half of the appeals court judges in the three central Canadian provinces between 1905 and 1970 had been promoted,[16] and all but one (Justice Sopinka) of the current Supreme Court of Canada judges were promoted.

Russell has noted that little is known about what factors are taken into account by the political authorities when deciding to promote judges.[17] The consultative committees on judicial appointments established in 1988 do not have a mandate to review the files of judges being considered for promotions; these decisions are made solely by the Prime Minister (for the Supreme Court and the chief justiceships) or the Minister of Justice. This

THE ADMINISTRATION OF JUSTICE

raises the question of whether it is appropriate for such important decisions to be left to the sole fancy of one or two individuals. In no other profession are promotions so discretionary.

TRAINING

For most of Canada's history, it has been assumed that judges need no training other than a legal education and several years of experience practicing law. This approach, which is usual in common law countries, contrasts with civil law jurisdictions such as France, where would-be judges must graduate from a specialized training program for judges. After successful graduation, the newly trained judicial specialists apply for a junior judgeship, and then are promoted up the judicial hierarchy by other judges according to merit.

In 1971 Parliament established the Canadian Judicial Council to "improve the quality of judicial service" in courts staffed by federally appointed judges. The Council, which is composed of all Chief and Associate Chief Judges and Justices in these courts (totalling 39 judges in 1990), has both an educational and disciplinary role. With regard to judicial education, the Council conducts several week-long seminars each year, including one on judgement writing. As well, the Canadian Institute for the Administration of Justice (an organization composed of judges, lawyers and academics established in 1974 to promote judicial research and education) runs an annual one-week seminar for new judges with the support of the Canadian Judicial Council. The provincial judicial councils or judges associations run similar seminars for Provincial Court judges.

It is clear that although judicial education has improved dramatically during the past two decades, it remains a "patchwork quilt," to use the words of Ontario's former Chief Justice of Ontario, William Howland.[18] To promote more comprehensive judicial education, the Canadian Judicial Centre was established in Ottawa in 1987. It is jointly financed by the federal and provincial governments, and has a mandate "to design and coordinate educational services for both federally and provincially appointed judges."[19] The Centre has already organized frequent "early orientation" seminars for new judges to supplement the existing training sessions.

IMPARTIALITY

In common or civil law countries which adhere to the liberal political ideology — liberalism stresses the maximization of individual freedom, the limitation of governmental powers through laws enacted by representative legislatures, and equality in the application of the law — judges are expected to be as impartial and independent as possible. Impartiality implies that judges must hear a case with an open mind, without being biased in advance toward any of the litigants. Of course, absolute impartiality is a human impossibility, but the more impartiality that can be demonstrated by judges, the more respectable will be the adjudicative process. A number of practices have developed to promote judicial impartiality, such as the presumption that judges will disqualify themselves if a litigant is a family member or associate, the prohibition against judges holding a second job, and the expectation that judges will, upon appointment, resign from associations which are likely to litigate, or which advocate particular courses in public policy (such as political parties).

The most important principle which has developed to promote judicial impartiality, however, is judicial independence. Judicial independence implies an absence of relationships between judges and others, particularly those in the executive and legislative branches of government, which could influence the decision-making process. For example, if the cabinet could decide on an individual judge's salary, or could fire a judge, judicial independence would be compromised. If anyone tries to influence a judicial decision outside of the regular adjudicative process, the result is a violation of judicial independence. Judicial independence is considered as an important constitutional principle in Canada. With regard to criminal and quasi-criminal cases, independence and impartiality are now protected by the Charter of Rights. Section 11(d) states that persons accused of offences have a right to an independent and impartial judge.

The Supreme Court of Canada has defined the "essential conditions" for the existence of judicial independence in an extraordinary case decided in 1985.[20] In 1981, Walter Valente was charged with dangerous driving after a fatal accident. The case came to the Provincial Court in Ontario not long after the Charter of Rights came into effect in 1982. As a strategy for keeping Valente out of jail, Valente's lawyer argued that the Provincial Court judge had no jurisdiction to hear the case because he was not independent, as required by the Charter. The lawyer maintained that this lack of independence was caused by the fact that Provincial Court judges do not have the same constitutional safeguards for their independence as those possessed by superior court judges, and that unlike superior court judges, Provincial Court judges do not have their own separate benefit plans.

The Supreme Court of Canada ruled against Valente. The Court held that a judge is independent if three conditions are met. First, the judge must have "security of tenure," which means that he or she cannot be fired because the government disagrees with the judge's decisions. A judge may be removed only after a judicial inquiry recommends such action. Second, a judge must have "financial security," or a legislated right to a salary so that the cabinet cannot secretly manipulate a judge by raising or lowering his or her salary. Third, judges must have "institutional independence," or the ability to make administrative decisions in the courts which could affect judicial decision-making. The Supreme Court ruled that Provincial Court Judges in Ontario met all three conditions.

To promote judicial independence, judges in Canada are given appointments which continue until the mandatory retirement age. Under extraordinary circumstances, a judge may be dismissed, but not by a cabinet minister or legislature acting alone. A judicial inquiry must look into allegations of wrongdoing against a judge, and the inquiry must recommend dismissal before the judge can be removed. A judge cannot be dismissed for making an error in law, but only for behaviour inappropriate for a judge such as taking a bribe, not fulfilling court-related duties or making disrespectful remarks to litigants. The reason why a judge may not be removed for an error in law is that vengeful litigants with adequate financial resources, disappointed with a judicial decision, might harass a judge by pressing for his or her removal. To avoid such situations, a judge might be inclined to decide in favour of well-known "trouble makers."

DISCIPLINE AND ACCOUNTABILITY

Judicial independence is essential for the promotion of impartiality, but it may be abused occasionally. The antidotes against abuse of judicial power, however, are not well known. Persons who feel that a judge has engaged in behaviour inappropriate for a judge may complain to one of the judicial councils: to a provincial judicial council for Provincial Court judges, or the Canadian Judicial Council for federally appointed judges. The composition of the provincial judicial councils varies from province to province, but it usually consists of senior judges, or a combination of judges, lawyers and lay persons. (The membership of the Canadian Judicial Council was outlined above.) In the 1987-88 fiscal year, the Canadian Judicial Council received 47 complaints, according to its Annual Report. None produced enough evidence to warrant a judicial inquiry.

There are two other important mechanisms of promoting judicial accountability. The Chief Judges and Justices exercise a certain amount of authority over the junior judges, although this authority is very limited because of judicial independence.

CANADIAN GOVERNMENT AND POLITICS

Second, law journals publish articles which analyse and criticize judicial decisions. These journals are widely read by judges. Like playwrights, judges appreciate good reviews, and it may be that the journals help to encourage high-quality judgements.

Many courts in the United States have developed a system whereby trial lawyers may evaluate the performance of judges by filling out periodic evaluation forms, much as students evaluate the performance of their professors through filling out class evaluation forms.[21] To date, Canadian judges have generally not been receptive to such procedures, just as Canadian professors resisted student appraisals twenty years ago. Whether judicial appraisals are instituted in Canada will likely depend on whether any courts are willing to experiment with the procedure.

I The Decision-Making Process I

TRIAL COURTS

The trial courts are the courts which hear cases for the first time. Trial court judges, whether federally or provincially appointed, sit alone, although they may be assisted by juries in determining the facts in more serious criminal and civil cases. (Under the Charter of Rights, persons charged with a criminal offence who are liable to at least five years in prison if convicted have a right to trial by jury.) Another important function of judges in criminal cases is the sentencing of those found guilty. Some have suggested that because judges are rarely trained in criminology, their role should be limited to adjudication and the sentencing function should be delegated to specialized sentencing boards composed of experts in corrections.

Professor Peter McCormick and I interviewed 41 federally and provincially appointed trial court judges in Alberta and asked all of them to describe the decision-making process in trials. We found that the judges adopted one of four different approaches to decision-making. We labelled these approaches "improvisation," "strict formalism," "pragmatic formalism" and "intuition." Following are typical responses associated with each of these approaches:

> **Improvisors:** "There is no single process of making a decision because cases present too much variety. Nevertheless, different judges would probably come to the same decision about the same case." (10% of the judges)

THE ADMINISTRATION OF JUSTICE

Strict formalists: "The making of judicial decisions often revolves around highly technical and objective questions requiring little in the way of a conscious formal intellectual process for their application. Going though the correct procedures always produces the correct decision." (22% of the judges)

Pragmatic formalists: "There is a conscious, understandable process that all judges should follow in reaching a judicial decision. This process can be formulated in terms of a 'check list' of items that must be answered, or a 'shifting balance' between the weight of the arguments of the two sides, or 'water rising' to a specific level. However, even if the proper procedures are followed, different judges could reach different conclusions in the hard cases." (44% of the judges)

Intuitivists: "The process of a judicial decision is best described in terms of a 'gut-feeling' about the trial as a whole, a 'key moment' in a trial around which everything revolves, or arriving at a feeling of what the most fair outcome should be, and then putting together the rationale that justifies reaching the outcome." (24% of the judges)[22]

What these responses illustrate is that there is no consensus about the thought-processes trial judges follow when deciding cases. Although adjudication is intended to be as objective as possible, there is always a subjective element which cannot be eliminated. Nor should it: judging is an art and a human process.

APPEAL COURTS

Courts which are specifically established as appeal courts hear cases in panels of three judges or more. This is because appeal courts frequently have to decide difficult questions about the meaning of the law about which reasonable judges could differ. Thus, it is considered that several heads are likely to make better decisions than a single head. Provincial appeal courts usually sit in panels of three judges, although the court itself is usually composed of many more judges than this — for example, 11 in Alberta, and 18 in Ontario. For more complex cases, a panel of five is often struck. Membership in the panels and assignment of cases to panels is determined

CANADIAN GOVERNMENT AND POLITICS

by the Chief Justice, although he or she usually takes into consideration the preferences of the regular appeal court judges.

THE SUPREME COURT OF CANADA

In a complex court structure like Canada's, there are often several levels of court above the court in which a case was originally heard so that more than one appeal is possible. For a second or third appeal the right to appeal is sometimes limited to cases in which judges grant permission to appeal, which is known as "leave to appeal." Very few litigants have a right to appeal to the Supreme Court of Canada. Litigants whose cases involve a serious criminal offence where the provincial court of appeal rendered a non-unanimous decision about a point of law, or where the appeal court had reversed the decision of the trial court, and litigants involved in reference cases have a right of appeal to the Supreme Court. In almost all other cases, litigants must apply to the Supreme Court itself for leave to appeal.

The Supreme Court usually considers the applications for leave to appeal in panels of three. They rely heavily on written submissions which explain the importance of the case, although litigants also make oral presentations. It takes the agreement of two judges out of three to grant leave to appeal. Each year, the Court receives about 500 applications for leave to appeal and grants about 15% of them. The Court decides about 100 appeals each year, including cases from appellants granted leave to appeal and cases from appellants with an automatic right to appeal. In each of 1984 and 1985, 14 decisions were Charter of Rights cases.[23]

Once a case is past the leave-to-appeal stage a hearing is scheduled. Often the hearing may be scheduled for almost a year after leave to appeal is granted, although in urgent cases — such as Chantelle Daigle's abortion case — the Court may schedule a hearing within a week. The Court sits in panels of five, seven or the full court of nine depending on how the Chief Justice views the importance of the case. The most common panel size is seven, accounting for 80 percent of the Supreme Court hearings. Nowadays, the hearings typically last no longer than half a day. Lawyers for the various parties are assigned limited times to address the court, usually from thirty minutes to an hour. Small lights on the speaker's podium modeled on the traffic light system indicate to counsel when their time is up.

As soon as possible after the litigants conclude their arguments, the judges in the panel meet privately in a "conference." Beginning with the most recently appointed judge, the judges explain in turn how they think the case should be decided; this process can take from five minutes to several hours.

After all the judges have spoken, it is usually clear whether the judges will be unanimous or whether several different opinions will be written. A judge in the majority group will often volunteer to write the majority opinion; otherwise, the Chief Justice will ask a judge in this group to write it. After writing a draft of the opinion, the judge circulates it to the other judges on the panel, and each of them may send it back with suggestions for revisions. If the writer cannot accept the revisions, then the other judges may decide to write separate opinions.[24] Opinions which agree with the outcome of the main opinion, but which disagree with the justification for it, are known as separate "concurring" opinions. Opinions which disagree with the majority result are known as "dissenting" opinions. From 1983 to 1985, 87% of the Supreme Court's decisions were unanimous.[25] The judges seem to try particularly hard to render a unanimous decision for cases involving high-profile political controversies, such as the twin decisions on the constitutionality of Quebec's French-only commercial signs provisions. Because the process of consultation among the judges is often a lengthy one, particularly in cases in which the court desires a unanimous judgment, decisions may not be rendered for several months or occasionally years after the hearing.

I Does Our Justice System I Need Reform?

The adjudicative process in courts developed over the centuries as a response to the need of governments to keep order, and in rule-of-law countries to the need of governments to be perceived as fair. Over time, court systems tend to become more and more complex as society expands and more laws are established and as new courts are created to take the pressure off existing courts. Court procedures, originally designed to promote fairness became increasingly complex as procedural rules are modified over and over again to plug loopholes or to take into account new conditions. The law itself became increasingly dense as both statute law and common law piled up. As a result, the average person often feels lost when confronted with the law and the legal system. Without a lawyer, an encounter with the justice system can seem like being exiled to an alien world with strange customs and an incomprehensible language.

This tendency for court systems to become almost unmanageably complex has given rise to a number of problems. First, some litigants and lawyers have come to view the court system more as the opportunity to play a game of "beat the system" skillfully than as a dispute resolution service of last resort.

CANADIAN GOVERNMENT AND POLITICS

For example, half of a random sample of lawyers interviewed by Professor McCormick and I in Alberta and Ontario were not opposed to using delay tactics for their clients' advantage in certain situations, and we even spoke with a few lawyers who claimed to specialize in delay. They boasted that they could keep a case out of court almost forever through various technical procedures — if they were paid enough. Some of the judges we spoke to complained about some large corporations that took cases to court that they had no hope of winning; their strategy was to force their adversary (who could not afford to litigate a case over several years) to agree to a settlement favourable to the corporation. As well, there are numerous cases which end up in court but could be settled more effectively and with less emotional damage through negotiation or mediation. These cases include some disputes between neighbours and some family disputes. Years ago, such disputes were resolved through mediating organizations such as churches or community groups, but with the increasing urbanization and secularization of society, these means are no longer as available.

Carl Baar has shown that criminal cases can take anywhere from three months to three years on average to go to trial, depending on the location of the court. According to Baar, the courts in the Peel region (west of Toronto) are among the slowest in the world, while courts in New Brunswick routinely try almost all of their criminal cases within 90 days.[26] If a criminal trial decision is appealed, it takes an average of one year in Ontario before the appeal case can be heard. An appeal to the Supreme Court of Canada will usually add at least another year onto the process. Private law cases tend to take at least 50% longer to get through the system than criminal cases. Thus, occasionally one encounters a Supreme Court of Canada decision on a private law matter concerning a factual situation which occurred ten years earlier.

Our interviews showed that judges tend to be as frustrated as anyone by the misuse of the court system and by unnecessary delays. But to take action to reduce abuses and delays is problematic given the judge's role as an impartial third party, and given the principle of judicial independence which erects a very high fence between judges and the governmental authorities responsible for court administration. As well, provincial Attorneys General are often frustrated by problems in judicial administration but are reluctant to introduce reforms because of the complexity of the problem, the fear of violating judicial independence and public apathy. Ian Scott's initiatives in Ontario represent a real exception to this tendency.

In conclusion, Courts evolved as the official dispute-settlement institutions of government, and they developed a particular method of resolving disputes

THE ADMINISTRATION OF JUSTICE

called adjudication. Over time, courts have taken on additional functions. In the eighteenth century, the French political scientist Baron de Montesquieu described England has having three branches of government: the legislature (Parliament), the executive (the cabinet and public service) and the judiciary. He saw these three branches as checking each other's power, and thus preventing the abuse of power by any one of them. With the development of written constitutions, disputes about the meaning of the constitutions began to be referred to courts because of the judges' reputations for impartiality. And because of the increasing complexity of court systems and the law, courts came to be seen by some as weapons which they could manipulate to frustrate their enemies.

Overall, we could summarize the role of courts in our society as fourfold. Judges are official dispute-resolvers, the guardians against abuse of power, the official constitutional philosophers, and sometimes pawns in other people's battles. Court hearings are open so that the public may serve as a kind of monitoring device to ensure that courts are fulfilling the first three functions to the highest possible standards, and that the fourth function is kept to a minimum. I would encourage readers to drop in on court proceedings at any level, observe the process and consider sending their comments — both positive and critical — to the relevant authority: the federal Minister of Justice or the provincial Attorney General with regard to administrative issues not related to adjudication; the Canadian Judicial Council or the provincial judicial council regarding judicial accountability; or the appropriate Chief Justice of Chief Judge regarding administrative matters connected with adjudication.

NOTES

[1] Some of the material which follows was adapted from Peter McCormick and Ian Greene, *Judges and Judging: Inside the Canadian Judicial System* (Toronto: Lorimer, 1990), with permission of the publisher.

[2] Peter Hogg, *Constitutional Law of Canada* 2nd Ed. (Toronto: Carswell, 1985) p. 183.

[3] See Bob Woodward and Scott Armstrong, *The Brethren* (New York: Avon, 1981).

[4] Peter H. Russell, *The Judicial in Canada: The Third Branch of Government* (Toronto: McGraw-Hill Ryerson, 1987), Chapter 3.

[5] Russell, *The Judiciary in Canada* p. 110.

[6] Russell, *op. cit.*, Perry S. Millar and Carl Baar, *Judicial Administration in Canada* (Kingston and Montreal: McGill-Queen's, 1981), and Thomas Zuber, *Report of the Ontario Courts Inquiry* (Toronto: Queen's Printer for Ontario, 1987).

[7] Russell, *Ibid.*

[8] Guy Bouthillier, "Matériaux pour une analyse politique des juges de la Cour d'appel," *La Revue Juridique Thémis* (1971) p. 563.

[9] William J. Klein, "Judicial Recruitment in Manitoba, Ontario and Quebec" (Ph.D. thesis, Department of Sociology, University of Toronto, 1975).

[10] *Report of the Canadian Bar Association Committee on the Appointment of Judges,* Chapter 6.

[11] Peter H. Russell and Jacob S. Zeigel, "Federal Judicial Appointments: An Appraisal of the First Mulroney Government's Appointments," paper presented to the Canadian Political Science Association and Canadian Law and Society Association, May 29, 1989.

[12] See Peter McCormick, "Judicial Councils for Provincial Judges in Canada," *Windsor Yearbook of Access to Justice* 6 (1986) p. 160.

[13] Russell and Zeigel, "Federal Judicial Appointments," p. 28.

[14] *Ibid.* p. 29.

[15] William Klein, "Judicial Recruitment," p. 312.

[16] *Ibid.*

[17] Russell, *The Judiciary in Canada*, pp. 140-141.

[18] Canadian Judicial Council, *Annual Report 1987-1988* (Ottawa: Canadian Judicial Council, 1988) p. 6.

[19] *Ibid.*

[20] *Valente v. The Queen et al.* [1985] 2 Supreme Court Reports, 673. For more detailed commentaries on this case, see Ian Greene, *The Charter of Rights* (Toronto: Lorimer, 1981) pp. 148-150, and Ian Greene, "The Doctrine of Judicial Independence Developed by the Supreme Court of Canada," *Osgoode Hall Law Journal* 26 (1988) p. 177.

[21] Russell, *The Judiciary in Canada*, p. 189.

[22] Professor McCormick and I elaborate on these decision-making models in *Judges and Judging.*

[23] Russell, *The Judiciary in Canada*, p. 347.
[24] Madame Justice Bertha Wilson, "Decision-Making in the Supreme Court," *University of Toronto Law Journal* 36 (1986) p. 227.
[25] *Ibid.*
[26] Carl Baar, "Notes for an Address to the MacLaughlin College Public Lecture Series," York University, November 16, 1989.

CANADIAN GOVERNMENT AND POLITICS

ANNOTATED READINGS

Gall, Gerald. *The Canadian Legal System*, Second edition. Toronto: Carswell, 1983. A lay guide to the Canadian legal-judicial system written by a lawyer. Topics include the sources of law, a comparison of the common law and civil law approaches, the role of lawyers and judges in court, and some of the basic concepts of administrative law.

McCormick, Peter and Ian Greene. *Judges and Judging*. Toronto: Lorimer, 1991. An analysis of the backgrounds and decision-making strategies of judges at all levels of court in Canada. With the aid of interviews with judges in Alberta and Ontario, and retired Supreme Court of Canada judges, the authors attempt to demythologize the judicial system by considering who judges are and how they make their decisions.

Millar, Perry S. and Carl Baar. *Judicial Administration in Canada*. Kingston and Montreal: McGill-Queen's, 1981. The standard text on judicial administration in Canada. This book is not only a useful guide to court administrators, but also an important source for all who desire a better understanding of important court-related issues such the constitutional constraints on court unification or strategies for improving the efficiency of the flow of cases through the courts.

Morton, F.L. *Law, Politics and the Judicial Process in Canada*. Calgary: University of Calgary Press, 1984. A book of readings covering all the benchmarks concerning the relation between law and politics in Canada. Topics covered include the rule of law, *stare decisis*, judicial review, interest group litigation, judicial policy-making, judicial independence and judicial selection.

Russell, Peter H. *The Judiciary in Canada: The Third Branch of Government*. Toronto: McGraw-Hill Ryerson, 1987. The most comprehensive analysis of the Canadian judiciary available. The book is written from a political science perspective so that the implications of judicial organization for the Canadian political system receive careful treatment. After considering alternatives, Russell promotes the concept of a unified trial court in each province, as well as the use of non-partisan selection committees for judicial recruitment.

THE ADMINISTRATION OF JUSTICE

| CHAPTER 18 |

ISSUES IN MUNICIPAL GOVERNMENT

R.H. WAGENBERG

The metropolitan governing structures of Toronto and Montreal each have responsibility for more people than any province except Ontario and Quebec. Metropolitan Vancouver encompasses more people than six of Canada's ten provinces. Yet when students are introduced to the government and politics of Canada scant attention is usually paid to the municipalities and their role in governing. Citizens seem to confirm this implied lack of importance by voting in much smaller numbers in municipal elections than they do at the federal or provincial level. Nonetheless municipal governments have a crucial impact on the lives of their residents and the elected and administrative officials of the cities, towns, counties and districts of Canada have the responsibility for determining policies and delivering vital services to their residents.

Political scientists study power, and since municipalities do not share constitutional power as do the federal and provincial governments of Canada they have been considered minor players. The only mention of municipalities in the **Constitution Act, 1867** is in section 92(8) which mandates the exclusive powers of the provinces over "Municipal Institutions in the Province." Thus, the very existence, let alone the responsibilities, of municipalities is a question for provincial determination. Provinces retain tight control over the functions and the finances of local governments. When constitutional questions are debated municipal governments are not invited to take part as much as some of them might wish to. Major economic policies are not discussed with the leaders of the cities where a majority of Canadians live. The same is true of social policy or environmental concerns. Students of government and average citizens might be excused for not spending too much time thinking about government and politics in the cities and towns of Canada when it is Ottawa and the provincial capitals that make the major decisions and attract the heavyweight politicians. But if one reflects not on the constitutional subservience of municipalities but rather on the question of their role in the quality of life of most Canadians, then some very good reasons emerge to be concerned with municipal government.

Having their garbage collected and disposed of in an environmentally safe manner on a regular basis is of considerably greater immediate importance to most Canadians than is the question of the purchase of nuclear or conventional submarines as part of federal defence policy. Effective snow removal to allow traffic movement is more on people's minds in winter than the propriety of the "notwithstanding" clause in the *Canadian Charter of Rights and Freedoms*. The installation of sewer systems to prevent basement flooding concerns more Canadians across the country than does the issue of Senate reform. More Canadians turn out for council meetings in cities and towns to speak on planning matters that affect their neighbourhoods than would dream of attending the meetings of parliamentary task forces that occasionally travel the land looking for citizen input. None of these examples is meant to demean the importance of the national issues; but, as important as those issue are, they are somewhat abstract and lack the immediacy of the local problems that impact continually on people's daily lives. Yet, despite the importance of municipal governments, our attention is directed away from their day to day business by the concentration of the news media on international, national and to some lesser degree provincial events.

Another set of factors which may discourage interest in local government is its greater complexity and variety of forms. It is somewhat ironic that the parliamentary system with its responsible prime minister and cabinet, a feature of the federal and provincial governments that is considered to be fundamental to our political heritage, is not considered to be appropriate for our local governments. Since our understanding of politics is so involved with the parliamentary tradition we might be forgiven for thinking that local institutions that do not use these traditions are not "real" governments. Political parties have not been part of the municipal scene at all in most places in Canada and where they are they still do not operate in the same way as is the case on the federal and provincial levels. Even more fundamental however is the degree to which the feeling exists that political parties have no legitimate place in local politics. This point of view is implicitly founded on the view that the business of local government is not really political. Such a view of course can mask the decidedly political colour of civic stances, decisions and priorities. A business model of local government, for instance, merely fails to address this aspect of its operation.

I Municipal Organization I

Because the parliamentary system has not been the model, a number of alternate approaches have been allowed to develop. There are five alternative systems and two or more of them may exist in a small geographical area. Thus a person may live in a town which has one system of local government and commute to work in a city which has another system. Confusion about how municipal government works surely must be encouraged by this variety. The five systems are Council-Committee, Council-Chief Administrative Officer, Council-Commission, Council-Board of Control and Council-Executive Committee.[1] The Council-Committee system is widely used in smaller towns. In this system each of several committees of council exercise administrative control over specific departments e.g. the parks and recreation committee oversees the parks and recreation department. In larger population centres this system has lost its appeal because councils feel they should be involved in policy making rather than administration. The Council-Chief Administrative Officer (or Council-Manager) system places all administrative responsibility in the hands of the appointed Chief Administrative Officer (C.A.O.) who is in turn answerable to council. The model is very much based on business practices with the C.A.O. being the general manager and the elected council being the board of directors. This system fits the view that municipal government is largely about technical matters that should be decided without political interference. The Council-Commission system used in some places on the prairies has the same philosophy as the Council-C.A.O. system but rather than one administrator there are a few, each with responsibility over a range of departments. The Council-Board of Control system used to be required in all Ontario cities with a population of over 100,000. Now it exists at the option of the community. In this set-up usually four persons are elected at large in a city and together with the mayor they compose a Board which has responsibility for the budget and can exercise

CANADIAN GOVERNMENT AND POLITICS

wide influence over other policies as well. They also sit on and vote with the elected council. Finally the Council-Executive Committee system has gained favour in large municipalities. It has the closest resemblance to Cabinet government although it falls far short of that system in that it does not create a political executive responsible to a legislature nor does it involve a government and opposition. The members of the executive committee include the mayor and three to five councillors selected by the elected council from among their members. Each of the councillors has some responsibility for one or more departments.

It is possible that a community may choose to have elements from more than one system, for instance, a Board of Control and a chief administrative officer. The result of this variety is confusion about the nature of authority and responsibility in the municipal system. For instance, local governments have mayors who are popularly elected by the voters at large, that is by all the voters of the community. This gives that person a degree of political influence which may allow for considerable power to affect policy. Nonetheless the mayor is not like a prime minister or premier who is the head of a political party which controls a legislature and who can choose from that party colleagues to form a cabinet to govern under his or her general direction. Instead the mayor may well be faced with a majority of council who harbour views other than his or her own and may often be on the losing side of important issues. While a politically astute mayor may be able to use the advantages of having a wider popular mandate, receiving greater media attention, having continuous contact with the senior bureaucrats, chairing council meetings and having some opportunities to help or hinder members of council, nonetheless in the final analysis there is no capacity in the position to force colleagues to adopt similar views. Citizens of communities however, with their understanding of how federal and provincial governments work, are prone to blame the head of government and thus a mayor will often have to take the blame for policies that he or she has not supported. The municipal electorate may in all likelihood have no idea how individual members of council have voted on particular issues and there are rarely party labels to help citizens assess credit or blame for policies or situations. It seems clear that this lack of ability to simply judge responsibility in local government has something to do with the lack of interest and poor voter turnout in municipal elections.

The problems do not end there however. A variety of structures which divide responsibility among different local government mechanisms complicates things even further. There are county, regional and metropolitan governments which divide the responsibilities for delivering municipal

ISSUES IN MUNICIPAL GOVERNMENT

services to Canadians. A number of communities may be gathered under one government to deliver services like policing, planning, major sewer systems and sewage treatment facilities, social assistance and others while the various localities continue to provide other services such as fire protection, parks and recreation and garbage collection to name a few. These arrangements are normally referred to as two-tier local governments. Typically the council of the upper tier is drawn from members of the lower tier rather than there being separate elections for each level. More recently some regional governments in Ontario, including metropolitan Toronto, have adopted direct elections for the upper tier but that remains the exception rather than the rule. Direct election may make citizens more aware of their upper tier local governments and the councillors elected to them will be primarily interested in the wider issues of the region rather than the more narrow ones of localities. Again, however, there is a degree of complexity which makes it hard to determine responsibility for local government decisions.

The growth of urban populations has resulted in the filling up of core cities and as they have spilled over their boundaries there has been an integration of the countryside into the life of the city. While farmland may still be extensive beyond the city boundaries (although the loss of prime farmland is a growing concern) the people living beyond the city are mostly tied to the urban economy. Over recent decades various provincial governments have sought to reorganize municipal government so that the costs and benefits and municipal services are fairly distributed among municipal taxpayers. In doing so a concern is to deal with the concept of *externalities*, that is, the enjoyment of benefits by people who do not pay for them and the imposition of costs on people who do not get all the benefits. A variety of reorganization schemes have been adopted across the country to try to address both the problems of growth and equity. In New Brunswick, for instance, it led in the 1960's to a reorganization that shifted most education, health and welfare functions to the province. This allowed the creation of greater uniformity in the services available to municipalities regardless of the wealth of their citizens. In Ontario, on the other hand, reorganization first of Toronto and then in other regions, was more concerned with managing growth on the basis of planning for larger areas. The result was controversial as many people resented the loss of traditional municipal boundaries to which they had some loyalties. By the mid 1970's the backlash was sufficient to halt the trend towards full regionalization which had been envisioned. In 1989 a proposal to eliminate separate local governments for communities with populations less than 4,000 also met resistance.

From the point of view of municipal electors, however, the rather continuous debate in various provinces about the appropriate boundaries and powers for municipalities can do little to help them understand the system. Provinces can act unilaterally to take powers away from local governments or on the other hand to saddle them with responsibilities they might rather not have. Whereas federal and provincial politicians are reasonably sure of the arena in which they play and the rules of the games they play, the same cannot be said as confidently for municipal politicians.

There is one more major complicating factor at the municipal level and this is the existence of a variety of so-called *special purpose bodies*. Of these the most important are boards of education. Special purpose bodies are elected or appointed groups which have responsibilities for an aspect of local government and are not subservient to the municipal government. These vary from province to province as does their relationship to the municipal government. For instance the municipal government may or may not have representation on the special purpose body. In most provinces the municipal council has no authority over boards of education. These bodies are separately elected and their expenditures can consume as much as half of the local property tax revenue. Thus municipal governments which collect the property taxes for educational as well as other municipal purposes are often the targets of citizen anger for taxation over which they have no control. Concerned local residents therefore who wish to follow local government have in effect two or more governments to monitor. In provinces where there are both public and denominational school boards the problems are further magnified.

School boards, police commissions, utilities commissions, library boards and the like have long historical roots and were most often based on the desire to remove their subject matter from politics. This is but another reflection of the attitude that local politics is not like politics elsewhere and that local matters should be decided in a non-political manner. Yet few people have suggested that provincial education ministries be separated from provincial governments and that Canadians elect separate provincial educational legislatures. Even where at the provincial or federal levels appointed commissions are given important responsibilities, they are made to report to a minister who is in turn responsible to the legislative body. At the local level, however, elected municipal governments are often maligned because of the activities of a variety of other local bodies, elected and appointed, over whose activities they have little or no control. Where these special purpose bodies have some function that includes several communities, for instance a regional conservation authority, one may make some argument for their existence. When however the functions of such institutions are within the boundaries of a municipality for which there is an elected municipal government to serve the citizens, it is more difficult to provide a rationale that conforms to the democratic ideals we apply to other levels of Canadian government.

Canadians have allowed their municipal institutions to develop in a way that has discouraged interest and participation in government at the local level. To summarize the reasons for this development: (1) constitutional subservience; (2) the absence of the parliamentary form of government; (3) a lack of media attention; (4) the complexity and variety of municipal organization; (5) the multiplicity of local governments within a geographical area; and (6) the existence of many special purpose bodies. See figure 1 for the outline of a typical municipal government.

I Supplying and Paying for I Municipal Services

The foregoing discussion has attempted to indicate some of the reasons why municipal government has been accorded limited importance in the public mind. The provision, however, of a variety of crucial public services by local governments is an obvious reality. Sometimes these services are mandated by provincial legislation and local governments act as administrators of policies over which they have little influence. In other areas local governments have considerable scope for independent action albeit there is almost always some provision for provincial review, or just as crucially, dependence on provincial financing. These restrictions will be addressed later. Now, however, it is necessary to look at some of the issues in which local government plays a significant role.

Planning and development is the area on which much of the literature on local government concentrates. Here municipal governments, under the umbrella of provincial planning legislation, can exercise considerable scope in adopting their official plans, passing zoning bylaws governing land use and granting rezoning applications for particular properties. There is a certain irony in the fixation on planning and development by students of municipal government who seek to elevate interest and knowledge in the subject yet in so doing discount the importance of other major municipal activities. There is absolutely no doubt that planning is a crucial municipal policy field and it has an impact on other issue areas. Nevertheless, if one were to look at the agendas of municipal councils, and their committees where they exist, and to investigate the activities of municipal councillors

I 353 I

one would find that planning and development issues occupy only a portion of the municipal policy agendas. Thus before getting into further discussion of the planning and development policy field it may be useful to look at some other municipal questions.

What probably concerns municipal electors most is the level of property taxation that they will be expected to pay to support municipal services. In this regard they are not much different at the local level than they are as provincial or federal citizens. The annual setting of the mill rate like the adoption of the budgets of the senior governments creates more interest than all but the most extraordinary of other events. The budget process at the municipal level is a much more public one. It is not just handed down by the equivalent of a finance minister and adopted by a pliant majority

FIGURE 1 : Municipal Government City of Windsor, Ontario

THE ELECTORATE – Divided into 5 Wards

ELECTED BODIES

CITY COUNCIL	PUBLIC SCHOOL BOARD	SEPARATE SCHOOL BOARD	UTILITIES COMMISSION
Mayor - Elected at - large 10 Councillors - 2 elected per ward	(15 members - 3 elected per ward)	(15 – 12 elected in wards – plus 3 representatives of francophone rate payers)	Mayor + 4 elected at - large

CITY ADMINISTRATOR	SPECIAL PURPOSE BODIES
Municipal Department • Building • Clerk • Convention and Visitors Bureau • Development Commission • Finance • Fire • Huron Lodge (Home for Seniors) • Legal • Parks and Recreation • Personnel • Planning • Property and Housing • Public Works • Social Services • Traffic Engineering	Police Commission Board of Health Children's Aid Society Library Board Committee of Adjustment Transit Windsor

without debate. Rather it is prepared by municipal administrators with the degree of input by elected councillors dependent on the type of municipal system of the city or town. When it is submitted to the council there is normally a lengthy debate over the course of several special budget meetings. Media coverage usually concentrates on the percentage increase proposed and perhaps on some items sure to generate public debate such as councillors adopting a pay raise for themselves. The public is often involved, usually to lobby councils to provide expenditures for their favourite causes. This may especially be the case where councils provide grants for local artistic groups, marching bands and other private interests in need of public funding. There is a tremendous amount of variety in this process around the country and the financial situation of any particular community may fluctuate year to year. Property owners are more interested in this process than renters because they are the ones who will receive a tax notice. Renters of course will be paying property taxes as part of their rent. In earlier times in most of Canada only property owners could vote in municipal elections, it being thought that others had no stake in municipal government. While that is no longer the situation it is the case that property taxes are buried in the rent people pay rather than noted separately, and thus may generate less concern for renters. Where rent control exists, however, and a process of rent review determines increases, landlords will certainly use a property tax increase to justify rent increases and this will no doubt sensitize more people to the importance of the annual municipal budget.

While local taxpayers are concerned with their own property tax bill, they are less aware of the fact that approximately half of the revenue available to municipalities across Canada is supplied by their provincial government. The federal government's subsidies to local governments are minimal. Of the provincial grants most are conditional, that is, they are provided to subsidize a specific service, rather than unconditional which allows the municipality to spend the money as they see fit. Thus, local governments are obviously constrained in their budget decisions by the availability of provincial grants. Local priorities are not necessarily uppermost in the minds of provincial authorities when they construct their budgets and this can create difficult decisions for local politicians about which services and projects can be undertaken. The amount of unconditional grant money available will likely have an impact on whether and by how much the local property tax burden will have to increase.

Taxes on residential, commercial and industrial property supply the bulk of self-generated revenue for local governments along with taxes on businesses themselves in addition to that on the property they occupy. The other major source of revenue comes from water and utility charges and smaller sums derive from fines, licenses and investments. Property taxes are based on the assessed value of the property and thus the assessment process is a key factor in the tax system of local governments. The provinces are equally divided between those who leave the process to municipalities and those who make it a provincial function. While all provinces have legislation to guide the assessment process the ones with provincial administration seek greater uniformity in the application of assessment between municipalities as well as within them. The amount of property tax that is levied on the taxpayer is determined by applying the mill rate to the assessed value of the property. A mill is one-tenth of a cent and thus $1,000 of assessment taxed at a rate of 1 mill would yield $1. If a property were assessed at $10,000 and the mill rate was 100 then the property tax payable would be $1,000. Thus municipal taxpayers have two concerns: (1) the assessed value of their property and any changes that might be made to that assessment and (2) the percentage by which the mill rate may rise in a year. It should be kept in mind that the mill rate in most of Canada is determined by the decision of a board of education as well as by a municipal government.

This system of municipal finance has raised a number of concerns. For one thing its complexity, especially the assessment process, is daunting for most citizens. Once understood, however, there are two major issues: its adequacy to provide the necessary finance for local services and its fairness. If a community is growing in terms of the development of new homes, offices, stores and factories then the additional assessment can provide additional revenue with little or no increase in the mill rate. If, however, there is little growth then either services must be curtailed or the property tax rate must be raised, perhaps significantly. This situation can create a vicious circle since high property taxation may discourage the new development which might mitigate further tax increases and allow better services. Uneven local taxation and uneven local services are common problems across the country.

The question of fairness arises because the property tax can be regressive, that is, not based on the ability to pay. While one might argue that people who are better off live in larger homes, in better neighbourhoods and thus pay higher property taxes, that is not universally the case. Other situations are common such as retired people on reduced income having to continue to pay the same (or higher) property taxes as they did when earning more. People who are unemployed or who lose income for whatever reason get no break in property taxes. Businesses continue to pay property taxes regardless of their profitability in any particular year. When property taxes were raised for services that applied mainly to property the concept of the user paying might have been appropriate. Now, however, the property tax pays for a share of a variety of services like education, public health, social assistance, culture and recreation that do not apply directly to one's property.

Abandonment of the property tax system because of its unfairness is not imminent. Nonetheless, local governments would like to curtail the increasing burden of property tax by getting alternative sources of income. The best of these would be a percentage of the income tax and corporate tax paid to the province. Manitoba made a start at this in 1976. Other provinces have allowed municipalities to levy a variety of taxes such as amusement taxes. Still the essential problem remains that municipalities are dependent on regressive property taxes which must be raised yearly unless the community grows substantially.

To some considerable degree, concern for minimizing the growing tax burden is the impetus for what Andrew Sancton calls "boosterism."[2] This term refers to attempts to foster the image of the city as a good place to live, in which to invest and to visit as a tourist or conventioneer. Boosterism finds its institutional expression in municipal agencies dedicated to economic development and to the development of tourism. In the past these functions may have been the responsibility of the local Board of Trade or Chamber of Commerce and in smaller communities it may remain so with the financial support of the municipal government. In the medium and larger cities of Canada it has emerged as a major responsibility of local governments. It is no longer acceptable to leave the prospects of economic growth, and with it, increased assessment bases, as well as jobs, to the senior governments and the private economy.

In terms of municipal policies the quest for economic development has a variety of manifestations. In the area of planning it may mean a willingness to grant favourable rezoning decisions that allow major projects to go forward. These decisions can be controversial and may change the face of a city. I will return to this question in the discussion of planning. Municipalities may acquire tracts of land for industrial parks and service these lands with water, electricity, roads and sewers to make them available for industrial development. The aim is not to make money on property development but rather to sell as cheaply as possible to people who can be enticed to one's municipality. Decisions on the provision of other major services such as roads or sewers can often be affected by whether those services will attract new industries and possibly induce present ones to stay or expand. The competition between communities for growth in their assessment bases makes the provision of adequate services an issue of prime importance and may at times create conflict between those needs and the demands of local citizens for a

| 357 |

variety of other amenities in their own neighbourhoods.

Boosterism can also be seen in the push for a variety of public buildings like civic centres, convention halls, arenas, art galleries, museums and concert halls. As often as not the reason for these facilities is based on the contribution they will make to attracting tourists and conventions. They, of course, are also responses to local groups who want the facilities to enhance the local quality of life or at least that part of life in which they have a greater interest. In communities that are growing and prosperous these public buildings are monuments to civic pride and the visions of politicians. In our largest cities these facilities are literally "olympian" in stature. Public opinion will usually be divided on the need for or at least the scope of many of these public undertakings. The selling of these projects to the public is based considerably on the boosterism syndrome which holds that one's municipality must compete with others for a place in the sun.

The issues of municipal taxation and the quest for economic development are directly related to the taxpayer's pocketbook. There is, however, a wide variety of issues, which, although they have financial implications, are of concern to municipal governments because of their substance. The importance of various problems varies from province to province and even community to community within provinces. The size of the municipality for instance will likely have a major impact on whether traffic problems, municipal public transit or policing are important problems. On the other hand educational and environmental questions may be relevant regardless of size. The next section of this essay will discuss some of those issues.

I Education — The Other I Municipal Government

The literature on local government tends to say little about school boards and problems in education. Yet the cost to local taxpayers of education in most provinces is significant and in some municipalities in Ontario may account for as much as half of all local expenditures. It is true that in all provinces the provincial department of education plays a dominant role in setting educational policy. Nonetheless, locally elected school boards almost everywhere play a crucial role in administering these policies and have the capacity to make important decisions for their communities. The building of new schools and their location for instance are matters of great concern to local citizens and decisions on these matters are essentially local ones. In

Ontario the existence of a public school system and a Roman Catholic school system has occasioned a degree of competition for students especially at the high school level that is played out locally. The extension of full funding to Roman Catholic high schools in the late 1980's created in some municipalities the need for the public and Roman Catholic school boards to bargain over facilities. For some communities this became perhaps the dominant local political issue. In Quebec the school boards became the focus for the provincial government's language policies. The English-speaking school boards especially were expected by their local supporters to preserve traditional rights. In British Columbia in 1983 the introduction of a financially stringent budget by the provincial government placed several school boards in a politically contentious position with the province over the question of local control. The foregoing examples are only a few of the instances in which local school boards have become the focus of real political controversy.

School boards can become the focus of public concern over a variety of public issue areas which have an educational aspect. The question of race relations within schools can create the need for school boards to develop policies which may arouse considerable public debate. To the degree the school boards have some flexibility in curriculum the introduction of course segments on the native peoples of Canada and on the place of non-European immigrants beginning with black United Empire Loyalists has become a feature of education in some localities in Canada. The efficacy of integrating students with physical or mental disabilities into the educational mainstream is another question which places school board members on the front lines of policy on a developing social concern. Advocates on both sides of this question can create a politically sensitive situation. The AIDS epidemic has created the need for local policy debate about curriculum to educate students to the dangers of the disease. The availability of condoms in schools, mandated by one B.C. school board in 1989, can be expected to raise controversy in many localities across Canada. A furor over a teacher with AIDS in Nova Scotia presented a local school board with a difficult political situation in 1988 and this is not likely to be the only such case in Canada until the public educates itself about the disease and becomes less terrified of its victims.

The examples cited above are some of the more widespread problems that Canadian local educational governments have faced but in communities across Canada there may be specific questions which school boards face. These are political problems involving disputes about contending views on policy and they involve questions of expenditure of locally raised taxes. It has become more, rather than less, important for Canadians to have an understanding of and concern for the behaviour of the locally elected officials who are responsible for this aspect of local government.

I Policing I

Policing is another area which has occupied a great deal of public attention but is rarely considered as a local government problem in the traditional sense. There has been a widespread attitude that policing should be isolated from politics rather than being a subject of political direction. Nonetheless, local special purpose bodies known as police commissions or some similar designation have budgetary and other policy control over local police forces. Like school boards these commissions are independent of the municipal council but unlike school boards in most provinces they may have some members from the councils who can bring the perspective of their council to the deliberation on police matters.

In the medium and larger cities of Canada there has been a growing concern for public safety and the problem of crime. The availability and efficiency of policing services in many communities raises questions of budget and operational procedures just as does the delivery of any other municipal service. However, the power invested in police forces and their relations with the public make the service they deliver a much more sensitive question than other municipal functions. A major concern regards the method of dealing with complaints , especially alleging racism, about police behaviour. Traditionally, this has been done internally with police investigating complaints within their own departments and the police commissions making the determination on cases. In Toronto that procedure has been replaced with a civilian complaints board separate from the commission and police there and elsewhere are not happy with the innovation. The answer to the ancient question "Who is to guard the guardians?" is far from satisfactorily resolved in Canada.

As immigration has changed the composition of the Canadian population, especially in its largest cities, the relations between almost completely white police forces and citizens who are not white has become at times an explosive question. Native Canadians have also registered their concerns with the treatment accorded to members of their community in cities across Canada. Thus, the late 1980's saw a number of incidents and subsequent commissions which revealed serious problems in this area. The Donald Marshall inquiry into the false conviction and imprisonment of that Mic Mac in Sydney, Nova Scotia raised questions not only about the police procedures

ISSUES IN MUNICIPAL GOVERNMENT

in that case but also into the entire administration of justice in the province. Representatives of both native and black citizen groups used the opportunity to air their longstanding grievances over discriminatory treatment. In 1988 Metropolitan Toronto and Montreal each witnessed the fatal shooting of black youths by police during apprehension and arrest. Further shootings of black persons in Toronto by police have intensified feelings in the black community. The police on their side argue that racial considerations have no place in their actions. Investigations and inquiries which follow can only begin to seek a resolution to a festering problem that will not disappear in a short period. Canadian cities have witnessed a degree of racial tension from which the majority population thought they were free.

The police shooting of a native person in Winnipeg gave rise to an inquiry into the Manitoba justice system and relations between the police force and members of the native community in the late 1980's. In Alberta, Indian bands raised questions regarding the investigations by police of deaths among their members. These instances are only the most publicized examples of a problem which is of crucial interest to minority groups in municipalities across Canada. It is a local government problem to the degree that the staffing, discipline and general direction of police forces are matters directed by an appointed local body funded mainly by the municipal government. While police commissions were set up because of a desire to keep police functions out of politics, the concerns that members of communities have about police in fact raise highly political issues and the solutions that they seek will have to be the result of local (and provincial) political activity.

I Environmental Issues I

Environmental issues have achieved a higher prominence in municipal affairs in the last third of the twentieth century. A main cause of the pollution in Canadian rivers and lakes has been the flow of untreated sewage into bodies of water adjacent to the population centres. As late as 1989, eighty percent of Quebec municipalities did not have sewage treatment facilities.

Major efforts to deal with this despoiling of the environment began in Ontario and elsewhere in the 1960's. Large scale expenditures were involved in building the facilities necessary to treat the water before it returned to the rivers and lakes. Provincial financial support was necessary for this effort and some federal subsidies were available as well. Nonetheless, once built, municipalities were responsible for the operation of plants which required personnel and large quantities of chemicals for the treatment of the waste. Growth both of housing and industry necessitated the building of sewer systems and sometimes the expansion of treatment plants. In built-up areas the use of septic tanks for new development was often forbidden and the extension of sewer systems into areas serviced by septic tanks to replace them often became an expensive responsibility for municipal governments. This question could often be a major issue as municipalities expanded into their own previously undeveloped areas or took over neighbouring smaller, previously rural communities. Not unsurprisingly the building of major sewer systems and sewage treatment plants was often thought to be an argument for the establishment of regional governments.

Solid waste presents another environmental challenge to local governments. For the average person garbage was something put out once a week and collected by a municipal employee (or contractor) who then made it disappear. However, it reappeared in landfills somewhere out in the countryside and the people living near those sites were never happy about it. As these landfills have filled up their neighbours have sought to have them closed rather than accepting that they be expanded. People in other areas where sites have been identified as suitable for landfilling have almost always rebelled against the idea. This predictable reaction has become known as the N.I.M.B.Y. syndrome, that is, "Not in my backyard." It represents a classic case of externalities in that a rural community has to accept the costs, a landfill, of a problem, tonnes of garbage, created in an urban municipality. The balancing of costs and benefits in these circumstances is a very difficult problem. Nonetheless, the garbage must be dealt with somehow.

Recycling represents the best solution because it not only reduces the amount of garbage to be landfilled but it also saves resources by reusing materials. The co-operation of the public is vital for recycling because separating the reusable materials before collection, that is at home, is crucial to a feasible system. In the best of all environmentally sound worlds, people would create less waste to start with and recycle their food wastes in a compost heap for their garden. However, in the congested urban world of many Canadians, the most that can be reasonably hoped for is that people will separate their newspapers, glass and metal products for collection. Optimists believe that as much as half of all garbage can be recycled thus reducing the need for landfilling.

Another alternative to landfilling involves the incineration of garbage. Some of the methods proposed for burning wastes would create commercially valuable quantities of power that could be used by municipalities and industry. The technology for this approach is already in use, more in Europe

ISSUES IN MUNICIPAL GOVERNMENT

and the United States than in Canada, and it is simple and cheap. From an environmental point of view however there is concern that the burning of waste materials can create toxic emissions that would harm air quality. People in urban areas are not usually enthusiastic about having large incinerators in their community. As with many municipal policy questions one person's solution is another person's problem.

The disposal of industrial waste products, many of them highly toxic, presents a particularly difficult problem to municipalities. On the one hand, industries provide the employment that may be the basis for a community's existence. On the other hand, they pose a serious threat to the environment in which the community's citizens live. No easily agreeable solution to this question has yet emerged. Industrial waste as well as household waste are municipal problems whose resolution is both expensive and politically contentious.

I Development and I
Municipal Politics

The foregoing discussions of taxation, economic development policies, education, policing and the environment have been presented to demonstrate that municipal governments have important policy agendas that include much more than land use planning. It is true that various aspects of municipal policy may be very closely tied to land use planning questions but nevertheless much of municipal government involves political debate having little reference to the development of property. That is why the literature which reduces municipal government to little more than the relationship between large property developers and compliant municipal politicians and administrators is really a caricature of city politics. To say that is not to dismiss the importance of the property development industry or to deny that, depending on time and place, it can be the major question of municipal politics. The huge developments in the downtowns of large Canadian cities have a major impact on the faces of those cities, their life style, their traffic, even their climate. Private developers seek intensive use of property to maximize their profits while the goal of municipal planners is to create a cityscape more conducive to the enjoyment of a better quality of life for urban dwellers. It seems apparent that in too many instances the goals of the developer have trampled over those of the planner.

The large economic power of huge development companies obviously gives them major influence within municipal governments. Among other things it means those firms can employ architects, planners, traffic consultants and other professionals who offer their own version of proper planning to oppose that of municipal planning departments if there are differences of opinion. The development industry provides campaign contributions to municipal candidates who will likely support development proposals. These factors seem to confirm the view that the development industry has inordinate influence over the land use planning process and that the views of others such as citizen groups are shut out.

There is another side to this question however which is just as serious and it has to do with the attitude of mayors and councils across the country. Simply put, they tend to favour large scale development and do not need much convincing by developers. The boosterism spoken of before leads them to seek out development. The relationship between assessment and their ability to provide services without large tax increases makes large buildings an attractive proposition. Certainly the seeking out of industrial development, and the bigger the factory the better, is a top priority of municipal politicians. In their quest for development, councils have the approval by and large of their electors and the local media acts as a cheering section.

Where individual homeowners who are organized in their communities do have some influence is with changes to their neighbourhood. Usually this revolves around the rejection of any variation from the norm of a single family dwelling. While citizen groups may have little impact on the land use planning of the downtown cores of their cities they may achieve considerable influence over planning issues closer to their own concerns. The introduction of housing that is more affordable for lower income groups which usually means more intensive land use in the form of apartments, townhouses, duplexes, or single family dwelling on small lots is typically opposed by neighbourhoods (sometimes even entire municipalities) on the grounds that it will alter the nature of their community, depress property values, increase traffic, over-crowd schools and have various other negative effects. In these instances attempts by developers to use land intensively are often thwarted by middle class homeowners, who oppose the development.

Unfortunately for those seeking affordable housing, their interests are represented by developers and builders who can easily be attacked as greedy business people who are trying to undermine the character of someone's neighbourhood. When the developer is a government agency or a sponsor of co-operative housing the opposition can be even more shrill because of the prospect that the proposed housing will be inhabited by subsidized tenants.

The land use planning process in Canadian communities is complex and

ISSUES IN MUNICIPAL GOVERNMENT

often leads to political confrontation. The relationship between land use decisions and the financial health of the community, the boosterism of elected officials and civic organizations, the economic power of large development firms and the devotion of single family homeowners to maintaining the standard of housing in their neighbourhood, may all conspire to thwart what some might think is proper land use planning. It should not be surprising that various groups will not abandon what they perceive to be their interests to satisfy concepts which municipal planners and social activists prescribe for a better community. Planning decisions however have long-term ramifications and it is crucial that municipal politicians do not allow any short-run interests to dictate policies which may drastically affect the future of their community.

Only a few of the many issues that confront local governments have been touched on. Beyond these and other concerns that municipal councils and other local bodies must confront, there is a growing tendency to use these governments as sounding boards for questions which are outside of municipal jurisdiction. The relative ease with which one may appear before a council and the potential for media coverage (many councils have their meetings televised on local cable stations) attracts many groups to use the opportunity to foster their cause. Thus requests to have councils proclaim "Right to Life Week" or "Gay Pride Day" or to declare a municipality a "Nuclear Free Zone" are attempts to have municipal legislators take a stand on and help to legitimize various points of view on essentially non-municipal matters. It is questionable how useful it is for municipal councillors to expend considerable emotional energy on matters over which they have no jurisdiction especially when one considers the degree of provincial control they must confront even in their own municipal concerns.

I Municipal Politicians I
and Elections

Throughout the foregoing discussion of local government problems reference has been made to the necessity of local politicians to make policy decisions. What will follow is a brief discussion of who these people are and the processes by which they get into office. To generalize about the backgrounds of local elected officials can be a problem because of the variety of communities and of positions available. Well over half of Canadians live in 25 cities with populations of over 100,000 yet the elected representatives

CANADIAN GOVERNMENT AND POLITICS

in these cities do not make up even 10 percent of the total number of elected local politicians. Beyond that the substantial number of elected school board trustees even in the cities would not necessarily have the same kinds of backgrounds as members of municipal councils. Thus the picture one might encounter of the typical urban councillor may be considerably different than that of the large majority of elected local representatives.

As is the case with M.P.s and provincial legislators, municipal councillors are disproportionately business and professional people. Lawyers might constitute 10 percent to 15 percent of councillors, a significant percentage but considerably less than the typical 25 percent or more in the House of Commons. Self-employed business people, managers and other professionals comprise the bulk of council members. This situation fuels the view that municipal government is run in the interests of the local business community and that the non-political service to property and pro-development characteristics of most local governments derives from this circumstance. The reform era of the 1960's and 1970's may have brought to councils other people to challenge the prevailing views but these also were professionals such as teachers, professors and social workers. Urban councillors do not mirror the population of their communities in terms of occupations, incomes, education, ethnicity (where there is ethnic diversity) or sex. With regard to the last, local councils may have a somewhat higher percentage of women than the House of Commons or provincial legislatures but it is certainly nowhere near fifty percent.[3]

Widespread social attitudes and entrenched inequalities give rise to this situation. For women and visible minorities historical impediments to entry into political life has been fundamental. The prominence of the business and professional class reflects its still-preserved place near the top of the social hierarchy. Economic success, for instance, means having the financial resources and contacts which makes political success more likely than it is for those who do not have these resources at hand. A majority of councillors do not have to be convinced, let alone bought off, to agree that the ethic of business, growth, development and private enterprise will lead to the best outcomes for their community.

Elections to municipal councils differ from federal and provincial elections in a variety of ways. First of all there are fixed terms and the election dates are established by law. The three-year term is now most common although shorter terms used to be the norm. Secondly, the major political figure, the mayor, is elected directly by the entire electorate rather than taking office by virtue of leadership of a victorious political party. This is the case even where local party organizations have developed or the national parties are

ISSUES IN MUNICIPAL GOVERNMENT

involved in the contest. Of the national parties however only the NDP is a regular and open participant in municipal elections and even that party contests in only a few large cities. For the most part the national parties are content to provide some financial support and campaign workers for selected party members who run as independents like the other candidates. Financial support from the state (in its local guise) is not available to local candidates as is the case with their federal and provincial counterparts, nor can contributors claim their donations as a tax credit. Limits on expenditures and disclosure of sources of campaign contributions are not imposed consistently across Canada and even where they are imposed, they are recent innovations which are not widely enforced.

The absence of political parties at the local level has a variety of effects. Candidates are self-selected rather than chosen by political parties in a nomination process. Municipal candidates are usually on their own in terms of getting campaign funds and this raises the question of donations from particular sources, especially those interested in land use planning and development. Competition is less intense and acclamations,[4] especially in smaller communities are common, whereas at the federal and provincial levels uncontested elections are almost non-existent. Accountability is difficult to establish because each candidate runs on his/her own name and record and thus the municipal electorate does not have a party position to use as a standard for decision. Voting turnouts are lower in municipal elections because the party mechanisms which organize voters to participate are not present for the most part.

That political parties have not developed a local presence is testament to the widespread attitude that municipal government is somehow non-political. "There is no Progressive Conservative, Liberal or New Democratic Party way to fill a pothole" goes the old cliché which ignores the reality that not all potholes in all parts of a city may be filled at the same time. Whose will get priority? Beyond that, limited resources mean that devoting funds to fix potholes may reduce spending on other services which are demanded by other interests. While the technical question of how best to fill a pothole may be non-political, other aspects of the pothole issue may be highly political and can evoke different attitudes which may be best represented by political parties. In Europe political parties at the local level are a well-established democratic practice.

Another example of thinking that exists at the municipal level but is absent elsewhere is the preference for at-large elections[5] rather than ward (that is smaller geographical districts) representation. Except for Vancouver, the tendency for wards has won out in larger and medium sized Canadian cities but many municipal voters still do not like the idea and smaller towns and townships elections are still on an at-large basis. The argument most cited to support the at large system is that it encourages an appreciation of the general interests of the community rather than more parochial neighbourhood concerns. Those who make that argument do not follow up its logic by insisting, for instance, that all their provincial legislators be elected at large to pursue provincial-wide interests rather than narrow constituency concerns. And would not national unity be best served by electing to the House of Commons 295 representatives committed to national interests rather than the petty concerns of their localities? Advocates of at-large elections would counter that the limited geography and feeling of community in municipalities creates common interests rather than conflict. Such arguments of course would not get very far, yet they do at the local level. It is but another example of the prevalence of attitudes which seek to de-politicize municipal government.

More could be said about the processes of local politics, elections, candidates and the behaviour of elected and appointed officials. Appointed officials, the bureaucracy, have great influence on municipal government as they do at the other levels. The point of this chapter has not been, however, to describe local government in any complete way but rather to argue that local governments play an important role in the lives of Canadians. Moreover, local governments deal with political problems and the tendency to try to de-politicize the local government process is inconsistent with a concern for democratic processes and participation.

ISSUES IN MUNICIPAL GOVERNMENT

NOTES

[1] D.J.H. Higgins, *Local and Urban Politics in Canada* (Toronto: Gage 1989) pp. 148-164.

[2] Andrew Sancton, "Canadian City Politics in Comparative Perspective," in Magnusson, Warren and Sancton, Andrew, (eds.) *City Politics in Canada* (Toronto: University of Toronto Press, 1983) p. 293.

[3] See Higgins, *op. cit.* pp. 361-365 for reference to some studies on representation.

[4] Acclamations result when only one person seeks an office and is thus "acclaimed" without the necessity of holding an election.

[5] At-large elections for municipal councils are those in which the entire council is elected for the entire community. If there is a ten member council, each voter gets to vote for ten candidates and the top ten vote getters are elected.

ANNOTATED READINGS

Cameron, David M. "Provincial Responsibilites for Municipal Government," *Canadian Public Administration*, Volume 23, No. 2, 1980, pp. 222-235. A thoughtful article discussing the purposes of municipal government.

Feldman, Lionel, ed. *Politics and Government of Urban Canada*, Fourth edition. Toronto: Methuen, 1981. A collection of readings covering various aspects of local politics and government.

Higgins, D.J.H. *Local and Urban Politics in Canada*. Toronto: Gage, 1986. An excellent text offering a comprehensive description and analysis of urban government and politics.

Magnusson, Warren, and Andrew Sancton, eds. *City Politics in Canada*. Toronto: University of Toronto Press, 1983. Essays on the politics of Montreal, Toronto, Ottawa, Hull, Halifax, Vancouver, Winnipeg and Edmonton provide the basis for comparative analysis.

| CHAPTER 19 |

CANADA AND THE WORLD

T . A . K E E N L E Y S I D E

In the introduction of students to the study of Canadian government and politics, Canada's role in world affairs is usually accorded little attention. In fact, however, foreign policy is an extremely important aspect of the study of public policy in Canada with its own expanding and varied literature. This chapter has three main purposes. First, it sets out four of the central reasons for global affairs being important to Canada: preoccupations with 1) peace and security; 2) economic growth and independence; 3) the environment; and 4) social justice. Second, it discusses briefly the broad character of Canadian policy related to each of these themes as it has evolved over the years. And, third it comments on the contemporary challenges confronting Canada in each of the above areas.

| Peace and Security |

THE PROBLEM

For all countries, effectively managing their relations with other states is important, in that ensuring their security vis-à-vis potential aggressors is necessary for the successful attainment of their domestic goals. Conflict requires the diversion of scarce resources from economic, social, environmental and other programs that enhance the quality of life of one's citizens to generally unproductive but costly military purposes. Further, defeat at the hands of other powers risks the complete collapse of a state's capacity to realize its goals, the destruction of its culture and values and perhaps the loss of sovereignty itself. All states, then, inevitably concern themselves with international relations to maximize their security in an uncertain world.

For a country like Canada, however, there are arguably particular security reasons for becoming involved in global politics. First, it is a neighbour of the two super powers, situated on the shortest air route between them. It would be part of the battlefield should war ever erupt between the United States and the Soviet Union and it thus has a particular, vested interest in seeing them manage their relationship peaceably. At the same time, sharing a close partnership with the United States based on geography, related histories, similar cultures and shared values, Canada has an opportunity bilaterally and through its international institutional involvement to influence modestly the shaping of United State policy on a wide range of itnernational issues and thereby to affect to a greater degree than might otherwise be the case the prospects for enhanced global stability. Finally, Canada is dependent on international commerce for its well-being to a far higher degree than most countries. Almost one-third of its gross national product is derived from foreign trade. Tension and conflict in world politics tend to be accompanied by tariff wars and other disruptions to the normal flow of goods and services, jeopardizing the stable economic order so central to Canada's welfare. This economic concern thus furnishes an additional reason for active internationalism on Canada's part in the interests of attaining global conditions of peace and security.

THE RESPONSE

Since World War II, Canada has pursued this first and paramount goal of foreign policy by essentially two broad means, military alliance commitments, and support, via the United Nations in particular, for international mediation of disputes, peacekeeping, arms control and disarmament. Regarding alliances, commencing with the Ogdensburg Agreement of 1940 and the creation of the Permanent Joint Defence Board to plan the defence of North America during World War II, Canada has been bound militarily with the United States. This cooperation climaxed in 1958 with the creation of the North American Air Defence Command (NORAD), now known as the North American Aerospace Command, a bilateral pact that principally protects the continent against a manned bomber attack by the Soviet Union.

Under NORAD, Canada and the United States devised an integrated command structure for continental air defence, built and manned radar stations in the Canadian north in order to detect a conventional air strike and developed the capacity to intercept and shoot down attacking bombers.

In addition to bilateral security arrangements, Canada has been a participant in the North Atlantic Treaty Organization since its inception in 1949. This is a multilateral pact that joins Canada and the United States together with a number of Western European countries in mutual obligations to assist each other in the event any member is a victim of external aggression. Under NATO, Canada has had forces stationed in Europe since 1951. Until the sudden collapse in 1989 of the ideological divide between Eastern and Western Europe, these forces were intended to help protect the Western European countries against advances by the Soviet bloc — encroachments which, it was feared, could in the end also endanger the security of Canada and the United States.

With respect to the United Nations, Canada was a strong supporter immediately after the war of the idea of using this organization to guarantee the security of members through the collective application of economic and military sanctions against would-be aggressors. When deadlock between the United States and the Soviet Union ended the prospects of the organization's functioning effectively in this fashion, not only did Canada turn to the alliances mentioned earlier, but it also became involved in new, secondary UN roles related to fostering international peace and stability — United Nations observer and peacekeeping forces. These operations have been designed, inter alia, to monitor ceasefire agreements in regional conflicts in the third world, oversee the withdrawal of combatants and ensure the preservation of peace and order thereafter. Since one of the purposes of such missions has been to prevent limited regional conflicts from escalating to larger wars into which the United States and the Soviet Union might be drawn at the risk of nuclear holocaust, by their very nature the great powers have had to be excluded from participation. Canada, however, possessing well-trained and highly disciplined forces with a variety of specialized skills necessary for the success of peacekeeping, has been well suited for this activity. As a consequence, performing UN observer and peacekeeping duties has long been one of Canada's central contributions to fostering global security. Canada has been involved at some stage in virtually every UN peacekeeping operation, a unique record among member states. Nearly 80,000 Canadians have served abroad in peacekeeping functions, again more soldiers than those of any other country.

Similarly, from the creation of the original ten-nation UN Committee on

CANADIAN GOVERNMENT AND POLITICS

Disarmament to its current participation in the 40-nation Conference on Disarmament, Canada has been actively involved since World War II in fostering global security through its support for arms control measures. As a state with modest military capabilities which voluntarily chose after the war to eschew the development of its own independent nuclear arsenal, Canada necessarily plays a secondary role in such deliberations and the attendant agreements. Nevertheless, it has made a contribution of some significance, especially in the technical area of solving the problem of verifying states' adherence to the terms of agreements in such fields as nuclear non-proliferation, the abolition of chemical weapons and the partial banning of underground nuclear tests.

THE CONTEMPORARY CHALLENGES

The major reshaping of Soviet defence and foreign policy since 1985 under the leadership of Mikhail Gorbachev combined with the sudden demise in 1989 of the Soviet system of satellite states in Eastern Europe has raised exciting new opportunities and challenges for the shaping of future Canadian security policy.

At the time of writing, the United States and the Soviet Union were close to concluding agreements entailing significant reductions in both nuclear and conventional weapons that had important implications for the future of NATO and NORAD. Canada has had a vested interest in the achievement by the super powers of simultaneous reductions in strategic nuclear weapons, conventional forces and cruise missiles. If intercontinental ballistic missiles alone were significantly reduced, the effect might be to induce a build-up of other types of weapons on both sides to replace the lost strategic arsenals. That could entail in particular an increase in the number of Soviet supersonic bombers and long-range air and sea-launched cruise missiles potentially directed at North America, requiring of Canada costly new commitments to improve the detection and interception capabilities of NORAD. Success in Soviet-American negotiations on all classes of armaments has thus been important to Canada, and it must continue to press for further arms control measures in the future in order to ensure that its NORAD obligations remain relatively modest.

With respect to NATO, U.S.-Soviet progress in reducing conventional as well as nuclear armaments is a welcome development because it brings closer the time when Canada will be in a position to withdraw entirely its NATO forces from Europe. However, at this historic time in the building of a new Europe, it is arguably more important than ever that Canada continue to be an active participant in NATO. Until the evolution of new, post–Cold War institutional structures, NATO remains the principal organization through which Canada can attempt in a limited way to influence American and alliance policy and thereby affect the course of events in Europe.

Maintaining its alliance commitments and pressing the super powers through bilateral diplomacy and international institutional linkages to forge ahead with disarmament are not, however, in and of themselves a sufficient security policy for Canada today. It must as well seek out creative ways to cement the new, emerging European order with its promise of greater security for the entire international system. In this respect, the cold war rhetoric of the Mulroney government's 1987 defence white paper and the government's hesitancy, at least until 1989, in forging strong bilateral relations with the Gorbachev government after the latter's proclamation of *perestroika* and *glasnost* was disappointing. At one time, Canada was in the forefront in looking for openings to pierce the iron curtain and, through the development of trade and cooperative agreements, to build an atmosphere of trust and mutual dependence. For instance, in the early 1970's the government of Pierre Trudeau was instrumental in negotiating Industrial and General Exchange Agreements with the U.S.S.R. as well as a Protocol on Consultations. A major increase in bilateral trade paralleled these initiatives.

This progress was largely shattered by the Soviet intervention in Afghanistan starting in December, 1979 and by subsequent developments that set back the process of detente. By the end of the 1980's, there had been some restoration of the earlier linkages, but they were not yet at the level of the early 1970's despite the much more promising environment for fashioning ties that would build confidence on each side and thus enhance mutual security. Further, unlike in the past, Canada was lagging behind other of the allies in rebuilding its bilateral relations with Eastern Europe now that the proverbial curtain had been lifted. More attention needs to be given by the Canadian government to opportunities for forging trade, investment and other economic ties as well as people-to-people linkages in the areas of industry, education, science, the arts, sports and even the military. It is also important that Ottawa look seriously at the Soviet proposal advanced in 1987 to make the Arctic a nuclear free zone, step down military activities in the north and encourage scientific cooperation among the Arctic countries. In short, Canada must in its own small way look for opportunities to encourage the current process of change in Eastern Europe and not wait for others, especially the United States, to take the lead.

Regarding contributions to international security via United Nations peacekeeping, the circumstances are in many respects right for Canada to play a major role in the future. In light of the much more forthcoming attitude of the Soviet Union towards the United Nations today and its apparent interest in resolving regional conflicts so that it can reduce its own military outlays and its obligations to assist client states, the prospects are good that new operations can obtain the approval of the UN Security Council. Further, they are likely to be needed because there remain a number of trouble spots where it is difficult to envisage effective transitions to peaceful and stable conditions without some form of international presence.

Rather than the traditional peacekeeping function, however, Canada's latest external military involvement has been in the realm of enforcement — as a participant in the U.S. led coalition of forces fighting to overturn Iraq's August 1990 occupation of Kuwait. While authorized by the U.N. Security Council, this operation is under U.S. rather than U.N. supervision, and, whatever the rights or wrongs of participation, Canada's involvement is likely to preclude it from playing a U.N. peacekeeping role in the Persian Gulf region at the conclusion of the conflict.

Given the professional, bilingual character of Canada's armed forces, the restraint they have traditionally shown under circumstances of extreme provocation and given their capabilities in such specialized areas as signals, transport, reconnaissance and administration, Canada is eminently suited for the peacekeeping function. It thus deserves a greater emphasis in Canadian security policy than it received in the foreign policy and defence reviews of either the Trudeau or Mulroney governments. The organization, training and equipping of the Canadian armed forces should be undertaken today with peacekeeping very much in mind, and Canada should be exploring opportunities for strengthening the UN's capacity to undertake this function. Canada could, for instance, consider establishing an international training centre for peacekeeping operations where forces from other countries frequently chosen for such missions would train with Canadians in simulated peacekeeping exercises. Leadership also needs to be shown in seeking solutions to the perennial problems related to authorization, control, financing, logistics and the status of peacekeeping forces in the host countries.

In sum, the contribution that Canada can make to global stability through the roles it plays in military alliances, conferences on arms control and disarmament and via its bilateral diplomacy is likely always to be limited. However, in the theatre of peacekeeping, it has been a star at centre stage.

The old actor has willingly accepted the accolades showered on it by a grateful international audience for its past performances, but Canada must not rest on its laurels. The peacekeeping part must still be played and plumbed to new depths to meet the challenges of the future in the quest for international peace and security.

I Economic Growth and Independence I

THE PROBLEM

Maximizing domestic economic growth is another goal of states, leading them into international activity. Like security, the attainment of wealth is central to a country's capacity to provide at an advanced level the variety of services demanded by its citizens. Some states, endowed with natural resources and possessing large populations with sophisticated skills, are capable of generating economic growth essentially by internal means. However, almost all states rely to a certain degree on trade with other countries and on inward and outward flows of capital and technical knowledge to maximize their economic potential. The search for economic growth thus inevitably leads countries to interact with each other.

As previously indicated, Canada is one of those states particularly reliant on international economic relations for its well-being. It ranks second after West Germany in its dependence on international trade for the creation of national wealth and the jobs of roughly one-third of Canadians are linked in some way to trade. This reliance is principally a product of Canada's small population base. The domestic market has a limited absorptive capacity for the natural resources and manufactured products that Canada produces. They must, therefore, be sold abroad in order for Canada to earn the foreign exchange required to purchase the variety of goods and services it does not itself produce, but which are important to a high standard of living. Possessing a small and scattered population of traditionally cautious investors, Canada has also not always been able to generate (or effectively organize) the large amounts of capital required for the high-cost projects related to exploiting its natural resources and developing a sophisticated manufacturing sector. It thus has also looked outside Canada for its capital needs. These have generally been readily met by foreign investors who have been anxious to gain access to Canadian resources, have seen Canada as a politically and economically stable country in which to do business, and have used the building of branch plants as a means of circumventing the tariff barriers that Canada erected after Confederation to protect the development of domestic industries.

I 377 I

While economic considerations have served to push Canada into international affairs, at the same time a variety of circumstances have led to a situation where the majority of Canadian economic activity takes place with just one country, the United States. Geographic isolation with the American giant on the North American continent is the principal explanation. Canada's distance from other markets and the presence elsewhere of trading blocs from which, as a North American country, Canada has been excluded have rendered it more often than not uncompetitive outside North America. These problems of geography have been compounded by Canada's small domestic market which has frequently denied its producers the economies of scale that would enable them to price their goods low enough to appeal to buyers in distant countries. At the same time, Canadian suppliers are situated close to the enormous U.S. market. Transportation costs and extended delivery times are not major obstacles. As well, the United States is hungry for Canadian resources and other products and has an almost boundless absorptive capacity. Further, the two countries share the same language and similar cultures and tastes. Naturally they have been drawn to each other economically and as a result they share the largest trading relationship between any two countries in the world. However, Canada is much more dependent upon this trade than is the United States. At the end of the 1980's, roughly 75 percent of Canada's combined exports and imports were with the United States, while the latter's trade with Canada accounted for only roughly 20 percent of its world trade. Further, Canada's greater dependence is compounded by the fact that almost one-third of its gross national product is derived from foreign trade while in the case of the United States the figure is less than 10 percent. Similarly, for the reasons already indicated, Canada has relied heavily on inflows of American capital to finance its economic growth. At the end of the 1980's roughly 23 percent of Canadian industry was foreign-controlled (a figure substantially lower than at the beginning of the decade) and close to 80 percent of that was American.

Ironically, then, in the case of Canada, international commerce is of vital importance to its economic growth and capacity to meet the needs and demands of its citizens, but at the same time, in the view of many, Canada's over-reliance economically on the United States poses threats to its independence. The trade and investment ties with the United States mean that Canada is highly vulnerable to fluctuations in American economic performance and to decisions taken by American boards of directors often in response to American governmental policies rather than Canadian. Historically, it has also meant that Canada could potentially be coerced into pursuing policies compatible with U.S. rather than Canadian interests by threats to the disruption of the free flow of goods, services and capital. Finally, in the view of many, the gradual process toward closer economic integration with the United States poses the ultimate danger of the loss of Canadian sovereignty itself as new forms of collaboration are introduced to help resolve problems arising from the immediately preceding stages of cooperation until the point of political union itself is finally reached. In short, Canada faces the paradox of necessarily being drawn into international relations to achieve the economic growth its citizens expect, while creating in the process challenges to its independence.

THE RESPONSE

Recognizing the importance of foreign trade to its economic prosperity, Canada has long made efforts to enlarge its market opportunities abroad. It has, for example, engaged in vigorous bilateral and multilateral diplomatic efforts to reduce the tariff and non-tariff barriers to international commerce. Early on, it developed a strong trade commissioners service to support the efforts of Canadian business in securing foreign markets. In 1982, this service was integrated into the Department of External Affairs and in 1989 the department changed its name to External Affairs and International Trade Canada, moves which manifested the importance Ottawa attaches to commerce in its foreign policy. The government has also adopted a variety of incentive schemes to help Canadian businesses expand their activities abroad, underwriting certain of the costs and risks associated with attempting to penetrate distant markets.

Canada has also long recognized the potentially serious implications of its heavy economic (as well as cultural and military) reliance upon the United States. It was not until the early 1970's, however, that the government of Pierre Trudeau officially adopted the strategy of attempting to reduce Canadian dependence upon the United States by the diversification of economic and other relations and the implementation domestically of policies designed to achieve a higher level of Canadian ownership of the economy. The Trudeau years saw intensive efforts to cultivate expanded relations with a number of countries that seemed to offer sound prospects as countervailing economic partners. These included, inter alia, the Chinese People's Republic, Japan, the member states of the Association of Southeast Asian Nations, the Soviet Union, Saudi Arabia and Brazil.

A variety of domestic economic (and cultural) measures were also taken in response to the perceived American challenge to Canadian sovereignty. Two are particularly important to note. In 1973, the Trudeau government

CANADIAN GOVERNMENT AND POLITICS

created the Foreign Investment Review Agency to screen foreign takeovers of Canadian firms, the establishment of wholly new enterprises in Canada by foreign investors and the expansion of existing subsidiaries to ensure that in all instances investments were of significant benefit to Canada. In 1980, the Liberals adopted a National Energy Program designed to achieve two broad goals: 51 percent Canadian ownership in the oil and gas industry and self-sufficiency of supply by 1990. These and other interventionist measures of the Trudeau years were intensely disliked in the United States where they were perceived as artificial impediments to free market forces, and they sparked considerable friction in Canadian-American relations.

By the 1980's it was clear the policy of attempting to diversify Canada's trade relations was not working effectively. While substantial absolute increases in Canadian trade with other markets occurred over the Trudeau period, in fact, in relative terms, Canada was considerably more dependent upon trade with the United States at the end than at the outset of this era. The traditional impediments to extra-continental trade referred to above had conspired to undermine the efforts of the government. Moreover, by the 1980's there was considerable anxiety in Ottawa over a growing climate of protectionism in the United States that was seen as jeopardizing future growth in Canadian exports to that market, especially if the Canadian dollar significantly appreciated in value. Securing assured access to the United States market by some form of bilateral agreement became the new solution to assuring Canada's future prosperity. Thus, by the time the Mulroney government came to power in 1984 a comprehensive free trade deal was being touted not only as central to sustaining Canadian economic growth, but as an instrument for enhancing Canadian independence, in that expanding wealth was necessary for Canada to sustain the social, cultural and other programs that gave it an identity distinct from that of the United States. Further, it was argued that the increased productivity of Canadian industry, streamlined by the demands of free trade and now benefiting from economies of scale, would be better able to penetrate distant markets, bringing about the diversification of trade long sought as a means of preserving Canadian sovereignty.

In so far as reliance upon foreign investment is concerned, the Trudeau years did see a decrease of more than 10 percent in the percentage of foreign ownership of Canadian industry. However, after 1984, the Mulroney government took a different view of foreign capital, arguing that Canada needed more not less of it to sustain its economic growth. The real risk was seen in capital moving offshore to resource-rich countries where production costs were lower. A free trade deal with the United States was thus favoured in part because it was anticipated that it would lead to new capital inflows by investors, confident about opening plants in Canada if they would have ready access for their production in the entire North American market.

Starting in 1984, then, the Mulroney government undertook a major reversal of Canadian policies related to economic growth and independence. The Conservatives have dismantled the Foreign Investment Review Agency and replaced it by Investment Canada, a body that actually seeks out new foreign capital, largely disbanded the National Energy Program, and, most importantly, successfully negotiated a free trade deal with the United States that went into effect on January 1, 1989. In short, a strikingly new approach to Canada's traditional, interrelated goals of achieving economic growth and preserving independence was launched.

THE CONTEMPORARY CHALLENGES

There are legitimate differences of opinion within Canada regarding the appropriateness of the policy reorientation described above and especially the wisdom of the Free Trade Agreement. Almost all would agree, however, that the new environment confronts Canada with stimulating challenges. The principal one is perhaps the imperative of the private sector moving swiftly and creatively in adapting to the terms of the Free Trade Agreement in order to take advantage of the opportunities to reorganize operations and increase productivity so as to penetrate effectively the American and other markets. This section, however, focuses on the foreign policy challenges posed by the agreement.

One of the benefits of the pact for Canada is the partial removal of a means by which the United States had the potential capacity to influence Canadian decision-making in a manner that would ensure it was compatible with American interests. The United States has lost its freedom to impose arbitrarily tariff surcharges, as it did in 1971 for example, in an effort to induce Canada and other trading partners to alter their economic policies so as to buy more from the United States, thus helping it to correct its balance of payments deficit. For the moment, however, Canada's protection from this sort of coercive measure is not complete. During negotiation of the FTA, agreement was not reached on what constitute fair and unfair trade practices between the two countries — in effect what are and what are not subsidies that affect the competitive edge of producers in one or other country. These rules of bilateral trade are currently being negotiated, but in the interim the United States (like Canada) is free to resort to countervailing duties in response to any Canadian practices which, under American law, are

| 381 |

deemed to be unfair and discriminatory. Already numerous disputes related to trade practices have arisen and vigilant diplomatic efforts are required on Canada's part to ensure that the majority of these are resolved without U.S. resort to measures damaging to Canada's critically important access to the U.S. market.

From the standpoint of many Canadians concerned about Canada's future capacity to pursue its own economic, social and other programs, the current negotiations over trade practices are also a matter of some anxiety. It is anticipated that certain Canadian programs — for instance those that induce industry to locate in economically disadvantaged regions — may be forced onto the bargaining table by the United States which sees them as trade-distorting. Once again, it is going to require tough-minded bargaining on Canada's part to preserve in tact programs that give Canada a distinct identity vis-à-vis the United States. Moreover, Canada is in the weaker bargaining position in these negotiations. The impact of the FTA on Canada is much greater than on the United States and accordingly Canada is having to make much more substantial economic adjustments to cope with the new trading environment. As a result, an unraveling of the agreement would be much more disruptive to Canada than the United States. The U.S. is thus in a position to use the threat of tearing up the agreement to nudge Canada into making the concessions it wishes. Nor will potential American use of this weapon necessarily end with the current negotiations on trade practices. The threat of abrogating the agreement will hereafter be a tool in Washington's hands, replacing the former threat of tariff surcharges, as a plausible means of coercing Canada into doing the United States' bidding. Canada is going to have to display some mettle to deal effectively with this new cudgel.

The FTA also has the potential to influence Canadian foreign policy on matters that go beyond bilateral Canadian-American relations, for it could create United States expectations that, parallel with the forging of closer economic linkages, a consensus will be reached on wider international matters. Canada could thus find itself under increased United States pressure to "tow the line" on issues where heretofore there has not been full agreement. If such a development occurs, it will take considerable resolve on Ottawa's part not to bend under U.S. pressure, for the effect of not doing so could be to create new stresses and strains in Canadian-American relations.

With respect to the rest of the world, if all works out well under the FTA and Canada's international competitiveness increases, then the country may be able to sustain or even increase the existing level of business it conducts outside of North America. On the other hand, however, if in relative terms Canada's commercial dependence upon the United States increases still further, the country may find that it is no longer treated seriously by extra-continental countries as a separate sovereign entity from the United States. Increasingly, international economic negotiations and even political discussions among the major industrial powers may take place trilaterally among the United States, Japan and the member countries of the European Community with Canada treated as a mere appendage of the American diplomatic team. This risk has always been there for Canada, but it is magnified as a result of the new pact with the United States.

This potential problem points to the principal foreign policy challenge for Canada resulting from its new economic circumstances. Every effort must be made to sustain and expand Canada's relations with countries other than the United States. The FTA must not be treated as an economic panacea for Canada. The government and corporate community must not be lulled into focussing almost exclusively on the United States at the expense of attempting to enlarge Canada's relations, especially economic ones, with countries outside North America, some of which represent more dynamic markets for the future than the United States itself. Multilateral trade negotiations under the auspices of the General Agreement on Tariffs and Trade must continue to be a major focus of Canadian foreign policy. Slow and frustrating though they may be, these negotiations are critical to the removal of tariff and non-tariff barriers to trade in goods and services that must be accomplished for a diversification of Canadian economic relations to be possible. Bilaterally, Canada must show new vigour in forging commercial and other relations with countries on all continents, but especially in Asia which seems to offer the greatest potential.

New initiatives are, however, necessary on Canada's part to take advantage of the opportunities in this and other regions. Efforts need to be made to develop Canadian trading companies, along the lines of those in Japan, to help smaller Canadian firms overcome the costs and other impediments associated with attempting, in distant and exotic areas, to market, ship and store their goods. Incentive schemes for exporters could be usefully expanded and more trading conferences organized to persuade business leaders to explore new market outlets and to approach them as long-term propositions, not short-term means of disposing of surplus products developed specifically for North American consumers. Measures should be taken to graduate from Canadian universities more people conversant in foreign languages and knowledgeable about the customs of other cultures in order for Canada to be able to respond sensitively and effectively to the opportunities to develop new economic and other ties. Nowhere is this more important than in dealing with Japan, Canada's second most important

CANADIAN GOVERNMENT AND POLITICS

commercial partner. Finally, a shift seems called for in Canadian diplomatic resources from Europe, where Canadian exports have been in continual, relative decline over recent decades, to Asia whose share of Canada's worldwide export market has increased over the same period.

In short, Canada's situation today cries out for global involvement and a new focus on the traditional foreign policy goal of forging extra-continental links as one of the surest means of achieving economic growth and preserving Canadian independence.

I The Environment I

THE PROBLEM

For decades the international community largely ignored the warning signs of humankind's degradation of the global environment in the rush towards industrial development. Now suddenly the signals of the incompatibility of our modern way of life with the very survival of the planet have become too obvious and grave to be ignored. Depletion of the ozone layer threatens humankind with a major increase in the incidence of cancer. Emissions from coal and oil-burning plants, automobiles and other sources and the destruction of the tropical rain forests are increasing the carbon dioxide in the atmosphere and setting in train a global warming trend that may turn vast tracts of cultivatable land into arid deserts. The world's variety of flora and fauna are also jeopardized by these developments. Acid rain is ravaging the lakes and forests of North America and Europe. Effluent from industrial plants and the run-off of pesticides from farmers' fields is poisoning the world's supply of fresh water. Oil spillages and the dumping of sewage and garbage are polluting the oceans and over-fishing is robbing future generations of a vital and traditional source of protein in the diets of millions. The threats to the environment are numerous and suddenly the world's leaders, prodded by their concerned publics, are starting to pay attention to them. Sustainable development is the new buzz word and the environment now appears likely to be a dominant issue on the international agenda for the remainder of this century and well into the next. Pollution recognizes no state boundaries and environmental issues must as a result be confronted jointly in the mutual interests of all. These concerns thus propel all states towards collaborative, international involvement.

For Canada there are particular reasons to be concerned. Possessing the longest coastlines of any country in the world, including ecologically fragile

Arctic waters, and being one of the world's leading fishing nations, it is inevitably concerned with the pollution of the oceans and the depletion of fish stocks. The Great Lakes, which Canada shares with the United States, supply 40 percent of the world's fresh water and are the principal source of drinking water for nearly 40 million people. Yet, this vital resource is seriously threatened by chemical and other pollutants. Finally, before the initiation of recent abatement programs, smokestacks and exhaust pipes in North America were spewing some 50 million tonnes a year of sulphur and nitrogen into the air which was then falling as acid rain. Roughly half the damage caused to Canada's forests and lakes has come from emissions originating in the United States. Faced with these and other problems, it is not surprising that Canada was one of the first countries to give serious attention to environmental issues in its foreign policy.

THE RESPONSE

In a major review of foreign policy in 1970, the Liberal government of Pierre Trudeau set a harmonious natural environment as one of the basic goals of Canadian foreign policy and since that time a number of important initiatives related to this end have been undertaken. In 1969, a giant U.S. tanker, the *Manhattan*, traversed the Northwest Passage, thereby demonstrating the feasibility of transporting oil and gas from the southern slopes of Alaska through the Canadian Arctic to supply eastern American consumers. The voyage was not only a challenge to Canada's control over the Northwest Passage, but it also raised the risk of future oil spills in Arctic waters — spills that, under permafrost conditions, could do irreparable ecological damage. In response, Canada passed the *Arctic Waters Pollution Prevention Act*, asserting its jurisdiction for purposes of controlling pollution 160 kilometres out to sea from the islands of the Arctic archipelago. Under the act, Canada claimed the right, inter alia, to set standards regarding the hulls of vessels plying Arctic waters and to board and inspect such ships. In 1977, Canada declared a 200 nautical mile fisheries zone off its coasts, assuming responsibility for regulating stocks within such waters. Nevertheless, it continues to have disagreements with a number of countries regarding the size of the annual catch, inside and outside this zone, that is compatible with the long-term health of the ocean fisheries. In sum, controversies related to protecting the oceans and their resources for future generations have formed an important dimension of Canadian foreign policy in recent years.

With respect to the degradation of its lakes and forests, Canada has been active bilaterally on the diplomatic front with the United States. In 1972 and 1978, the two countries entered into Great Lakes Water Quality Agreements, setting agreed standards, in the latter instance, on effluent emissions into the lakes. A new agreement in 1987 extended the scope of the clean-up beyond obvious sources of toxic waste to include secondary contaminants. This pact also committed both governments to move toward zero discharge of waste. Throughout the 1970's and early 1980's, Canada also engaged in protracted diplomatic efforts to curb North Dakota's Garrison Diversion project because of its concerns that if the full project went ahead, it would seriously pollute rivers and lakes in Manitoba, cause springtime flooding, and damage the valuable Lake Winnipeg fishery. In the end, under pressure from Canada and more especially the anti-Garrison environmental lobby in the United States, the project was halted.

The thorniest bilateral environmental issue has, however, been that of acid rain. In August of 1980, at the end of the Carter administration, a Canada-United States memorandum of intent was signed, committing both countries to start negotiating an air quality agreement. However, throughout the ensuing Reagan presidency, the United States resisted making any progress on this issue, stubbornly insisting that there was insufficient research evidence regarding the environmental damage caused by acid rain. Thus, while the administration agreed to spend additional funds on research, it refused to consider new air pollution controls and to commit itself to emission standards. The Bush administration has, however, adopted a more forthcoming attitude and at the time of writing a clean air bill had been introduced to Congress, committing the United States to a 10 million ton reduction in sulphur dioxide emissions by early in the twenty-first century. Washington has agreed, following passage of the bill, to enter into an accord with Canada setting limits on cross-border emissions.

Some environmental issues of concern to Canada, of course, go well beyond the continent and its adjacent waters. Thus, Canada was an active participant in the 1987 Montreal conference on the ozone layer and a strong supporter of the protocol agreed to at that conference aimed at curtailing the emission of substances that deplete the ozone layer. The 1989 Paris summit of the Group of Seven major industrial powers also devoted a good deal of attention to global environmental issues, providing a political impetus for the negotiation of an international treaty on the environment. Given its varied environmental concerns, Canada can be expected to play an active diplomatic role in dealing with these broader issues in the future.

CANADA AND THE WORLD

THE CONTEMPORARY CHALLENGES

The principal challenge of the 1990's posed by the environmental problems plaguing the Earth is to transform the words of states' leaders into deeds. The rhetorical emphasis of late has to some degree been a calculated response of politicians, sensitive to public opinion polls, to the perceived concerns of their electorates. This has been as true in Canada as elsewhere. There is thus no assurance that without sustained societal pressure the necessary concrete action will be taken.

The circumstances are, however, right for meaningful international action. The scientific evidence of the threats is overwhelming and the public is increasingly informed about environmental issues. Further, the Eastern European countries have for the first time begun to take environmental concerns seriously. Even many of the developing countries, long suspicious that the effect of international environmental regulation would be to condemn them forever to the poverty of pre-industrial societies, have started to recognize the urgency of cooperative action. However, it will take the leadership of countries like Canada to ensure that an adequate regime of international regulation is put in place. Devising agreed international standards is also only the first step. It must be followed by the establishment of effective means of monitoring and enforcement.

On the environmental issues of specific concern to Canada, intensive diplomatic activity is necessary to protect its interests, but at the same time Canada must match its demands on others by redoubled efforts of its own. For instance, Canada has legitimate grievances against other countries which have been over-fishing the Atlantic continental shelf, but former catches by Canadian fishermen beyond what the stocks could support and misrepresentations of the sizes of catches have also contributed to the problem and to past errors by authorities in calculating acceptable annual harvests. With respect to the Great Lakes Water Quality Agreements, while the Reagan years saw more foot-dragging by the United States than Canada in getting on with the clean-up, both countries and their respective provinces and states have been dilatory in moving towards the goal of zero discharge. No timetable has been set for achieving this goal and no specific commitments have been made regarding the expenditure of funds. Canada and the U.S. have also lagged behind countries like West Germany, France and Japan in adopting the sophisticated technology necessary to safeguard the cleanliness of the lakes and rivers of North America. Bolder initiatives are thus required if the bilateral agreements to improve the quality of shared bodies of water are to have real meaning.

At the time of writing, President Bush's proposed clean air legislation held out promise of significant progress in reducing sulphur dioxide emissions. However, this is only one of many substances polluting the environment and commitments by Canada, the United States and other countries are needed covering other contaminants. It is noteworthy that at the June 1988 economic summit in Toronto, the Mulroney government placed the issue of the environment on the agenda, prompting scientists to call for a 20 percent reduction in carbon dioxide emissions by 2005, yet, at the time of writing, Canada itself had not adopted this target and on a per capita basis was the worst emitter of carbon among the industrialized countries. Much thus remains to be accomplished in the field of air quality.

One of the most important contributions that Canada can make globally to the environment is through its assistance to developing countries, helping them thereby to resolve their own problems. This entails not only targeting aid directly at combating pollution, but selecting for support developmental projects that are compatible with long-term environmental integrity. Finally, it must not be forgotten that the presence and testing of nuclear and chemical weapons pose potentially cataclysmic threats to the Earth's environment. This third theme of foreign policy thus intersects with that of peace and security on the critical issue of arms control and disarmament.

I Social Justice I

THE PROBLEM

The foreign policy theme of social justice has, in effect, two interrelated dimensions to it — improving the economic well-being of the disadvantaged peoples of the world and enhancing the degree of respect shown by governments for the basic rights of their citizens. Like the environment, the attention of countries to this theme is partly a result of societal pressure.

To a certain degree, the peoples of Western, developed countries have recognized that the obligation they have shown to improve the lot of the less affluent within their own societies (as reflected in their support of progressive tax systems and social programs that redistribute wealth) extends to the poor of the third world. Hence, they have supported modest levels of economic aid to developing countries. Similarly, their lives enhanced by the respect generally shown by their governments for a range of fundamental rights of the individual, citizens of Western countries have cried out against the gross and persistent repression of others and turned to their governments for a response. To some degree, too, the focus on social justice internationally has stemmed from a sense that it is related to the attainment of justice within the Western democracies themselves. This lofty motive was reflected on Canada's part in 1970 when, in its review of Canadian foreign policy, the Trudeau government asserted that a truly just society could not be created within Canada unless the country was prepared to play its part in building a more just society globally.

Arguably, however, the theme of social justice has found a place in the foreign policy of states largely for reasons related to national interests more narrowly defined. Greater prosperity in the third world provides new trade and investment opportunities for developed states. For a country like Canada, highly dependent on international trade, but often uncompetitive in distant markets, an aid program, heavily tied to the provision of Canadian goods and services, offers Canadian firms new outlets abroad out of which long-term commercial relationships may develop. Politically, aid to third world countries has been perceived as a means of buttressing friendly countries against the blandishments of communism, promoting military alliances and buying support in general for the goals of one's own state. In the case of Canada, for instance, in the late 1960's and 1970's, a sizable aid program was launched in francophone Africa to discourage these countries from supporting Quebec's aspirations of developing an international status of its own.

Enhancing respect for basic human rights around the world arguably also serves the political and economic interests of Western countries, including Canada. The end result of harsh repression is often civil unrest and revolution and the creation of unstable conditions that may tempt foreign states to intervene, leading to local wars that damage global peace and security. The strategic interests of Canada and other Western states may also be threatened if the outcome of repression is that an authoritarian but politically friendly regime is overthrown and replaced by one hostile to the interests of Western countries. Likewise, states that respect basic rights make better long-term trade and investment partners than countries where persisting and gross violations of human rights serve to perpetuate underdevelopment, inequality and a concomitant climate of uncertainty, inimical to the secure conduct of business activity.

A variety of selfish as well as altruistic considerations have, then, led Western states, including Canada, into international involvement in the purported pursuit of social justice, whether or not that is really their goal.

THE RESPONSE

With regard to third world development, Canada has steadily increased the absolute level of its aid disbursements since the launching of its aid program in 1950. From a very modest technical assistance program at the outset, Canada has now reached the point where its annual aid disbursements amount to more than $3 billion for a wide range of purposes. The period since 1968 in particular has witnessed a rapid rise in Canadian aid, and since this has occurred over years in which there has been a lagging of effort on the part of other donors, including the United States and Britain, Canada has become an increasingly important development partner for third world countries, especially those of the Commonwealth and francophone Africa. In relative terms as well, Canadian aid has increased over the years. In 1961, Canadian assistance amounted to only .19 percent of Canada's gross national product, but by the 1975-76 fiscal year, the figure had reached an all-time high of .56. Since that time, however, Canada's performance has slipped somewhat and in the 1989-90 fiscal year its disbursements totalled only .43 percent of GNP.

The terms of Canadian aid have also been generous. Loans to third world countries were formerly offered at zero or 3 percent interest with repayments over 30 or 50 years, but in 1986 Canada shifted to an all-grant program. Canada has shown less largess in terms of untying its aid to enable recipient states to use Canadian funds to purchase goods and services wherever desired based on price and/or quality. However, a reasonable proportion of Canadian aid is now provided on an untied basis through multilateral channels and in 1987 Canada reduced the tying provisions for its bilateral aid (exclusive of food aid) to 50 percent for the countries designated as least developed by the United Nations and for all African recipients south of the Sahara. Elsewhere, two-thirds of bilateral aid must be spent on goods and services from Canada.

Canada has also initiated some creative ventures related to development. For instance, it operates a program of matching grants to non-governmental organizations which, in turn, through private agencies in third world countries, support developmental projects targeted at the most disadvantaged. Further, in 1970, it created the International Development Research Centre which, operating with an international board of governors, has directed funds at research in the third world itself on grassroots developmental problems. Outside the field of foreign aid, Canada's contributions to third world development have been less significant. However, in 1973 it did establish a relatively modest tariff preference scheme for developing countries to facilitate their exports to Canada.

With respect to human rights observance, Canada has long been active at the multilateral level in efforts to define the meaning of human rights, establish conventions setting out agreed norms of behaviour, and to put in place machinery for monitoring violations. Canada was an active participant in the drafting of the UN's *Universal Declaration of Human Rights*, the conventions and declarations on genocide, torture and disappearance, the elimination of discrimination based on race, religion and sex, and the UN covenants on economic, social and cultural rights and civil and political rights. Further, it has been heavily involved in the various UN commissions, committees and working groups concerned with the implementation of these multilateral accords. Finally, Canada has used meetings of the Commonwealth and la francophonie and the follow-up conferences to the 1975 Helsinki Conference on European Security and Cooperation to press for improved human rights observance in developing countries, South Africa and Eastern Europe in particular.

Bilaterally, Canada has used quiet diplomacy to encourage improved human rights observance and in some instances it has applied modest economic and other strictures against states guilty of serious and protracted human rights abuses. A creative undertaking at the end of the 1980's that holds promise of being a constructive contribution to human rights observance was the establishment in Montreal of a Centre for Human Rights and Democratic Development. In cooperation with various agencies of the Canadian government, it will be responsible for initiating abroad projects in such areas as the strengthening of judicial institutions, legal and police training, the establishment of human rights offices and ombudsmen and the development of democratic election procedures.

THE CONTEMPORARY CHALLENGES

International social justice is still only a hope, not a reality. The initiatives of Canada and other countries related to this theme have been of some help to the oppressed and disadvantaged, but they are not nearly enough, and the efficacy of the action taken has often been undermined by the mix of motives driving foreign policy in this area.

After some forty years of developmental endeavours, large segments of the world's population still lack the basic requisites of a decent life: adequate nutrition, health care, shelter and education. Some 13 to 18 million people are dying each year from hunger-related causes, three-quarters of them children under five; 800 million don't receive health care of any kind; 1.4 billion lack clean water to drink; and almost half of the Earth's population

| 391 |

is still illiterate. Moreover, by the end of the 1980's, the developing countries had accumulated an external debt of $1.3 trillion (U.S.). As a result, revenues for development are drained away in repayments to the developed countries while budget cuts and other structural adjustments further reduce their capacity to meet the basic needs of their citizens.

The situation with respect to human rights is just as bleak.

Amnesty International annually documents a variety of serious human rights abuses in well over 100 countries, including such practices as arbitrary arrest and protracted detention without trial of political dissidents, torture, extra-judicial killings and disappearances. A large proportion of the world's population clearly lives in a climate of perpetual terror where intimidation and violence, perpetrated by those in authority, or agents acting on their behalf, are regular features of daily life. In sum, the challenges facing any country serious about international social justice are, indeed, daunting.

There is cause to be concerned about the nature of Canada's developmental effort over the decade of the 1990's. In its deficit-fighting budget in the spring of 1989, Ottawa announced a slash of $1.8 billion in aid expenditures over five years. The aid program was thus asked to bear by far the largest share of the government's cuts in spending. In the past, Canada had committed itself on a number of occasions to meeting relatively modest targets of aid-giving, ranging from .6 to one percent of GNP in the form of aid. While these goals were never reached, they, nevertheless, served as an indication of intent as well as a benchmark against which to measure Canadian performance. Following the cut in aid spending in 1989, however, projections indicated that it was unlikely that Canada would again reach even the figure of .5 percent until the turn of the century. Reversing the current downward trend in Canada's developmental effort is one of the principal tasks that must be pursued to preserve the legitimacy of Canada's purported commitment to social justice.

The government's new aid strategy, unveiled in 1988, included announcements that held some promise regarding Canada's focussing its developmental efforts in the future on the world's most disadvantaged. These included the decision to concentrate on "human resource" development (i.e. people rather than capital projects), to decentralize CIDA administration to the field, improving thereby the agency's capacity to identify and respond to small-scale projects targeted at the neediest, and to emphasize Ottawa's "partnership programs," which, inter alia, channel resources to grassroots development through non-governmental organizations. In addition, as previously indicated, a modest increase in aid untying was announced, providing Canada with somewhat greater flexibility in the selection of projects in the most impoverished countries that will directly address the fundamental problems of the poorest in their societies. It remains to be seen, however, whether or not a significant reorientation of Canadian aid towards human development — and of the world's most disadvantaged — will actually occur, for there are pressures at work pushing Canada in a different direction. In particular, these arise from the temptation in an intensely competitive international trading environment to use Canadian aid to advance the country's immediate commercial interests. Careful monitoring and societal pressure are thus required to ensure that the hopeful direction of the 1988 strategy is seriously pursued and that existing programs that deflect aid away from the poorest in the poorest countries towards projects and states of commercial promise to Canada are effectively curbed.

The impact of selfish interests on the extent to which Canada makes a meaningful contribution to social justice is even more starkly apparent with respect to Canada's non-aid contributions to development. The tariff preference scheme for developing countries that Canada put into effect in 1973 offered only modest cuts and it excluded from its purview many of the products of particular interest to developing countries in exporting to Canada, including textiles and footwear. It also has other built-in safeguards against injury to Canadian producers. In addition, Canada has long applied quantitative restrictions against the import of commodities like textiles and clothing, and the number of products and developing countries subject to such restraints on exporting to Canada has increased.

Canada has also exhibited little generosity in the negotiation of commodity price stabilization agreements that would provide developing countries with better and more stable prices for the staple exports on which they often depend. To a significant degree, then, the meaningfulness of Canada's commitment to social justice over the decade of the 1990's will be measurable by the degree to which it pursues more generous policies outside the area of traditional aid, including seeking solutions to the debt crisis of the third world.

The complex area of human rights requires of Canada a careful blend of persuasion and subtle pressure, for there are clear limits to its capacity to influence the internal affairs of other countries and inappropriate actions could do more harm than good. What seems particularly called for is an end to the inconsistency and symbolism that has often characterized Canadian policy in the past. Canada has been far more inclined to take punitive action against states with which it has limited economic and political relations than those where its commercial, developmental and political-strategic interests are substantial. Policy has thus been based not on careful, objective assess-

| 393 |

ments of the relative severity of human rights violations in different countries, but on calculations of the impact of initiatives on Canada's own interests. Canadian actions, therefore, often appear not only inconsistent, but hypocritical. Moreover, when Canada has applied strictures against gross violators of human rights, it has not always been explicit that its actions were in response to human rights abuses and frequently the sanctions applied have been so insubstantial as to be of little consequence. Greater consistency, transparency and effectiveness are all required in the future. At the same time, there must be a readiness on Canada's part to commit the resources necessary for effective human rights monitoring and the identification and implementation of projects that can make a positive contribution to improved human rights observance.

The challenges to the attainment of social justice are numerous and complex, and the commitment of Canada, based as it is on a mixture of altruistic and selfish motives, is unclear. Under the circumstances, its accomplishments are likely to be limited without sustained pressure from an informed public that believes in the right of all inhabitants of the Earth to lives of dignity and worth.

I Conclusion I

These four themes only partly explain the factors that impel Canada towards a role in world affairs, and make the study of Canadian foreign policy an important dimension of Canadian politics. There are many others. They include, for instance, the need for a middle power like Canada to reach out to the world to sustain at home a vigorous culture and standards of excellence in such fields as education, science and industrial technology. The desire of Canada's different ethnic groups to maintain ties with their homelands and the particular interest of Quebec in links with la francophonie in order to help nurture the French language and culture in North America are other important factors pressing Canada into international relationships. There is also the positive effect on a sense of national identity to be derived from Canada's making a large and constructive contribution to global affairs. The four dimensions discussed above provide, however, the principal explanations for Canada's international involvement, and the actions pursued by Canada pertinent to each indicate the variety and complexity of Canadian foreign policy. The four themes also illustrate that there are imposing international problems that Canada must contend with in the years ahead. They ensure that foreign policy will remain an important aspect of the study of Canadian government and politics, offering exciting challenges to students concerned not only about the future of Canada, but the wider international community.

ANNOTATED READINGS

A Bibliography of Works on Canadian Foreign Relations. Toronto: Canadian Institute of International Affairs, 1973– . A comprehensive, well indexed listing of virtually all material pertaining to Canadian foreign policy, including a number of unpublished works. The first volume is for 1945 to 1970 and thereafter supplements cover five-year periods.

Cohen, Andrew. "Canada's Foreign Policy: The Outlook for the Second Mulroney Mandate" in *Behind the Headlines*, Volume 46, No. 4 (Summer, 1989). A useful, brief survey of the key issues on Canada's international agenda for the decade of the 1990's.

Holmes, John and John Kirton, eds. *Canada and the New Internationalism.* Toronto: Centre for International Studies, University of Toronto and Canadian Institute of International Affairs, 1988. An interesting collection of short articles on Canada's contemporary role in world affairs via its participation in various international institutions. Written by both academics and leading practitioners of Canadian foreign policy, the articles focus on the challenges facing Canada as of 1986.

Molot, Maureen Appel and Brian W. Tomlin, eds. *Canada Among Nations.* Toronto: Lorimer, 1985– . An annual volume of essays surveying, since 1984, the latest issues in Canadian foreign policy in such areas as security, international commerce, Third World development and Canada-U.S. relations. It also contains a useful chronology of events and comparative statistics for 10 major Western countries, including Canada.

Nossal, Kim Richard. *The Politics of Canadian Foreign Policy.* Scarborough: Prentice-Hall, 1989. The most useful and up-to-date introductory text for the study of Canadian foreign policy. This work focusses on the domestic and international context in which Canadian foreign policy takes place and on the institutions involved in the policy-making process rather than on the substance of Canadian policy.

|I N D E X|*

* Unless noted, entries refer to Canada.

CANADIAN GOVERNMENT AND POLITICS

at Meech Lake 60–66, 149, 159; see
  Meech Lake Accord
and regionalism 12, 77
conservatism 6, 7, 10, 30–34, 58, 72,
  77–81; see also political parties
  (Progressive Conservative), third
  parties
constitution
  amending formulas: see amendment
  American Bill of Rights 26, 52, 139, 324
  British 52, 139
  BNA Act: see Constitution Act, 1867
  Canadian documents: see Bill of Rights
    (Canadian), Charter, Constitution
    Act 1867, Constitution Act 1982
  changes to: see amendment, Meech
    Lake Accord
  Declaration of the Rights of Man and
    the Citizen (France) 26
  and Quebec: see Quebec, Meech Lake
    Accord
  unwritten 42–43, 45–46, 50, 139
Constitution Act, 1867
  amendment of: see amendment, Meech
    Lake Accord
  as BNA Act 42, 43–44, 45, 50, 53, 56,
    87–88, 136–137, 140–142, 143,
    327, 347
  preamble 139
  ss. 91–95 (fed-prov jurisdiction)
    43–44, 48, 50, 136, 141, 347
  s. 109 (resource ownership) 120,
    124–126, 140, 141
  s. 133 (official languages) 44, 141–142,
    223
Constitution Act, 1982 42, 44, 59, 60,
  61, 241, 261 see also Charter
courts: see judiciary, Supreme Court of
  Canada
criminal law 43–44, 58, 323, 336–337, 338
crown corporations: see also media,
  resources ownership
  federal 31, 154, 158, 185–189, 239
  provincial 31, 37, 90–91, 98–99, 132

culture
  languages: see language issues
  and media: see media
  political: see political cutlure
  religion: see religious influences

demographic issues: see also class,
  education, elites,municipal institutions,
  native peoples, rural factors, social
  assistance, urban factors
  birthrate 10, 93, 316
  in cabinet representation 160–171
  immigration 7, 13, 19, 37, 62,
    104–105, 119, 120, 124,
    126–127, 316, 359, 360–361
  migration (interprovincial) 72, 127–128
  population patterns 4, 14, 72, 87,
    121–122 123–128, 206–207,
    216, 316, 347, 377
  rural-urban shift 72, 76, 86, 88, 351
  socioeconomic representation 107,
    108–109, 161, 191–193, 366
  voting patterns 18, 306, 308–309, 316
Detroit Free Press, The 274
Deutsch Report, The (on maritime union)
  76
Diefenbaker, John (PC PM) 37, 53, 131,
  171, 259, 303, 305
Dominion Lands' Policy 123
Donald Marshall Royal Commission
  Report, The (1989) 81; see also native
  peoples
Duplessis, Maurice (Q. UN premier) 10,
  89, 147

economy: see also business community,
  taxation, trade, provinces, regions, and
  territories by name
  debt/deficit 32, 150, 170, 393
  depression/recession 30, 48, 96, 124,
    125, 127, 144
  in elections 309
  federal-provincial jurisdiction 50, 59,
    62, 140, 145–150, 241

CANADIAN GOVERNMENT AND POLITICS

CANADIAN GOVERNMENT AND POLITICS

Lévesque, René (Q. Lib. premier) 11–12, 44, 59, 94–95
liberal democracy/liberalism 26–30, 51–52, 191–193, 225, 249–250, 335–336
Liberal Party: *see* political parties, Liberal premiers and prime ministers by name
lobbying: *see* interest groups

Manitoba: *see also* Prairie region
  and Confederation 119, 120, 140
  justice system inquiry 361
  and language rights 53, 129, 141, 142
  and native peoples 7, 120, 122, 129, 361
  political orientation 14
  population patterns 127
  resources 140–141
  Winnipeg 127, 361
Marxist ideology 24, 25, 35, 36, 232–234
Mass Media, Report of the Special Senate Committee on (Davey Committee Report, 1970) 275, 280
Macdonald, Sir John A. (PC PM) 49, 73, 78, 123, 129, 159, 163
McKenna, Frank (NB Lib. premier) 71, 77
media 268–283; *see also* openness, public opinion, newspapers by name
  centred in Ontario 103
  constituency 215
  CRTC 17, 184; *see also* regulation of
  and cultural independence from USA 16–17, 277–279
  and elections 272, 276, 279, 294, 311, 312, 333
  elitism in 270, 276, 280
  ethics/bias 270, 273, 276
  foreign 16–17, 277–282
  freedom on 26, 269–270, 272–274, 276
  and interest groups 226, 255, 257
  leadership conventions 293

and municipal politics 348, 350, 355, 364, 365
ownership of 185, 240, 274, 275–277, 280
and party leaders 157, 176, 279
polls reported by 80, 281; *see* opinion polls
press 92–93, 215, 268, 272, 274, 280–281
and regionalism 47
regulation of 17, 184, 185, 240, 274, 277
reporting by 110, 210, 272, 274, 279–282, 348
roles of 271–272
types of (ideological) 269–270
used by government 149, 213, 226–227, 227, 260, 264, 277–278
Meech Lake Accord 50–51, 60–66, 72, 75, 99, 130, 150, 158, 224, 291
  distinct societies 62, 224
  by executive federalism 60, 61, 63, 150
  and fishery 75
  and immigration control 62
  opposition to 60–63, 72
  opting out (cost-share programs) 59, 62
  Quebec's constitutional veto 44, 50, 62
  Quebec and Constitution Act, 1982 60, 61
  Supreme Court appointments 49, 63
mining: *see* resources
Ministries and Ministers of State Act (1970) 160
monarchy (Crown) 6, 45, 78, 154, 155, 158
Moores, Frank (Nfld. PC premier) 187
Morgentaler case: see abortion issue
Mulroney, Brian (Pc PM) 15, 58, 60, 61, 98, 99, 127, 128, 150, 160, 162, 163, 164, 165, 166, 167, 168, 172–173, 175, 187, 188, 189, 211, 214, 252, 261, 303, 305, 308, 310, 312, 314, 332, 333, 375, 376, 380, 388

public sector in 107–108
-Quebec relations 114
urbanization 104, (Toronto) 89, 104,
    160, 347, 351, 360
openness 29
of budget 259, 274, 354
of cabinet 15, 156, 171, 175, 251, 273
of caucus 214
of courts 343
of interest groups 250, 259, 264
of intergovernmental meetings 149
of lobby-government consultation 251
of media 269–270, 272–274
of municipal government 354, 365
of policy-making discourse 226–228
opinion polls 80, 157, 201, 213, 278,
    279, 288, 295–299, 211–313; *see also*
    elections, media, public opinion
organized interest: *see* interest groups

parliament (British) 43, 44, 50, 52, 139;
    see also Privy Council (British)
parliament (fed): *see also* cabinet, House
    of Commons, prime minister, public
    service, Senate
    constitutional conventions of 45–46
    dissolution of 157, 158
    provincial representation 10, 14,
        46–47, 103, 130–131; *see also*
        regionalism
    supremacy of 27, 45, 53, 54–56, 139,
        154; *see also* judiciary (legislative
        review by)
Parliamentary Government 198
Parti Québecois (PQ): *see* Quebec
patronage 74, 79–80, 94, 158, 161, 165,
    166, 187, 189–191, 293, 332–334
Pearson, Lester (Lib. PM) 127, 131, 147,
    161, 171, 191, 260, 298
Peckford, Brian (Nfld. PC premier) 71,
    75, 77, 79
pension issues (fed jurisdiction) 36, 90,
    91, 146, 261

policing 122, 352, 360–361
policy-making 225–243; *see also* economy,
    education, environmental issues,
    foreign policy, health care, housing,
    pension issues, resources, social
    assistance, taxation, trade,
    transportaion
    in budget 353–355
    and business 229–231 *see* Quebec-based
        business
    by cabinet 155, 156, 173–176
    for election 296–299
    economic planning councils for 75, 90,
        171–175
    by executive federalism 51; *see*
        conferences
    by Finance Department 170
    foreign 371–394
    and interest groups 28–29, 33, 56–58,
        171, 229–230, 252–257
    and media 226–227
    municipal 353–365
    and public servants 107–108,
        170–171, 174–175, 184–185,
        187–189, 222, 234–236, 255,
        352, 367
    public 222–224, 237, 238, 326
    in Speech from the Throne 155, 163,
        175
    and taxation 239, 241; *see* taxation
    theories of power for 229–236
Political Choice in Canada 306
political culture(s) 1–20
    American influences 5–6, 15–17, 36,
        277–279, 382
    compared 7, 13–14, 47–81
    linguistic characteristics 5, 10–12; *see*
        language
    and national identity 5, 17, 37, 64–66;
        see national identity, Quebec
    nature of 1–8
    orientation 4, 14–15, 18–19, 25,
        78–79

CANADIAN GOVERNMENT AND POLITICS

CANADIAN GOVERNMENT AND POLITICS

774019